P9-CJJ-451

The World Treasury of Children's Literature

BOOK THREE

SELECTED AND WITH COMMENTARY BY

CLIFTON FADIMAN

WITH ILLUSTRATIONS BY

LESLIE MORRILL

LITTLE, BROWN AND COMPANY

BOSTON TORONTO

Library of Congress Cataloging in Publication Data
(Revised for vol 3)

Main entry under title:

The World treasury of children's literature.

(Vols. 1 and 2 continuously paged [xxii, 629 p.])
Includes indexes.
A three-volume anthology of classical and contemporary children's stories, poems, myths, and legends from many countries.
1. Children's literature. 2. Literature—Collections.
I. Fadiman, Clifton, 1904– . II. Morrill, Leslie H., ill.
PZ5.W832 1984 [Fic] 84–14343
ISBN 0–316–27302–3 (v. 1, 2)
ISBN 0–316–27303–1 (v. 3)

The editor gratefully acknowledges the following publishers and individuals for permission to reprint the selections indicated:

Excerpt from BORN FREE by Joy Adamson. Copyright © 1960 by Joy Adamson. Reprinted by permission of Pantheon Books, a division of Random House, Inc., and Collins Publishers.

Chapter 1, "The Assistant Pig-Keeper," from THE BOOK OF THREE by Lloyd Alexander. Copyright © 1964 by Lloyd Alexander. Reprinted by permission of Holt, Rinehart & Winston, Publishers.

(*Continued on facing page*)

RRD

Published simultaneously in Canada
by Little, Brown & Company (Canada) Limited

PRINTED IN THE UNITED STATES OF AMERICA

"As I Was Laying on the Green" ("As I Was Laying"), "In the Family Drinking Well" ("Little Willie"), and "Willie Poisoned Auntie's Tea" ("Willie the Poisoner"), anonymous verses, appear in William Cole, HUMOROUS POETRY FOR CHILDREN, published by Philomel Books.

"How Spider Got a Thin Waist" from THE ADVENTURES OF SPIDER: WEST AFRICAN FOLK TALES by Joyce Cooper Arkhurst. Copyright © 1964 by Joyce Cooper Arkhurst. Reprinted by permission of Little, Brown and Company.

"The Feeling of Power" from NINE TOMORROWS by Isaac Asimov. Copyright © 1957 by Quinn Publishing Co. Reprinted by permission of Doubleday & Company, Inc.

"Nuts" from THE DEVIL'S STORYBOOK by Natalie Babbitt. Copyright © 1974 by Natalie Babbitt. Reprinted by permission of Farrar, Straus & Giroux, Inc.

"What Does the Clock Say?" and "The Cheetah, My Dearest, Is Known Not to Cheat," from RUNES AND RHYMES by George Barker. Reprinted by permission of Faber & Faber, Ltd.

"Explanations" from A REAL TIN FLOWER by Aliki Barnstone. Copyright © 1968 by Aliki Barnstone. Reprinted by permission of Macmillan Publishing Co., Inc.

Haiku from A HAIKU JOURNEY: BASHŌ'S NARROW ROAD TO A FAR PROVINCE (Copyright © 1974) by Matsuo Bashō, translated by Dorothy Britton, are reprinted by permission of Kodansha International, Ltd.

"Nancy Hanks" and "Abigail Adams" from A BOOK OF AMERICANS by Rosemary and Stephen Vincent Benét. Copyright 1933 by Rosemary & Stephen Vincent Benét; Copyright renewed © 1961 by Rosemary Carr Benét. Reprinted by permission of Brandt & Brandt Literary Agents, Inc. "Daniel Boone" by Stephen Vincent Benét from A BOOK OF AMERICANS by Rosemary and Stephen Vincent Benét. Copyright 1933 by Rosemary & Stephen Vincent Benét; Copyright renewed © 1961 by Rosemary Carr Benét. Reprinted by permission of Brandt & Brandt Literary Agents, Inc.

"The Woman Who Always Argued" by Leila Berg reprinted by permission of Hodder & Stoughton Children's Books.

"The Birthday Bash" from TALES OF A FOURTH GRADE NOTHING by Judy Blume, illustrated by Roy Doty. Text Copyright © 1972 by Judy Blume. Reprinted by permission of E. P. Dutton, Inc.

"Nothing" from THE WILY WITCH by Godfried Bomans reprinted by permission of Stemmer House and Elsevier Boekerij.

"The Pedestrian" by Ray Bradbury. Copyright 1951 by The Fortnightly Publishing Co. Copyright renewed © 1979 by Ray Bradbury. Reprinted by permission of The Harold Matson Company, Inc.

"Bruno and the Mirror" from BRUNO by Achim Broger. Translated from the German by Hilda van Stockum. English translation Copyright © 1975 by William Morrow and Company, Inc. By permission of the publisher.

Excerpt from FLAT STANLEY by Jeff Brown (as it originally appeared in *Cricket* magazine, 1974, under the title "Some Adventures of Flat Stanley"). Copyright © 1964 by Jeff Brown. Reprinted by permission of Harper & Row, Publishers, Inc.

"Giddy Liddy Gandaway" and "Today I Found a Secret" from THE SILVER NUTMEG; story and pictures by Palmer Brown. Copyright © 1956 by Palmer Brown. By permission of Harper & Row, Publishers, Inc.

Excerpt from HIGH WATER AT CATFISH BEND by Ben Lucien Burman. Copyright 1979 by Ben Lucien Burman. Reprinted by permission of George Wieser of Wieser & Wieser, Inc.

An episode from THE INCREDIBLE JOURNEY by Sheila Burnford. Copyright © 1960 by Sheila Burnford. Reprinted by permission of Little, Brown and Company in association with The Atlantic Monthly Press.

"The Blanket" by Francelia Butler. Reprinted by permission of the author.

"Colonel Fazackerley" from FIGGIE HOBBIN by Charles Causley. Copyright © 1973 by Charles Causley. Reprinted by permission of Walker and Company and David Higham Associates Limited.

"Doctor Concocter" by Kornei Chukovsky reprinted by permission of Oxford University Press.

Text of "All about Boys and Girls" from YOU READ TO ME, I'LL READ TO YOU by John Ciardi. Copyright © 1962 by John Ciardi. By permission of J. B. Lippincott, Publishers. Text of "Warning" from THE MAN WHO SANG THE SILLIES by John Ciardi. Copyright © 1961 by John Ciardi. By permission of J. B. Lippincott, Publishers.

"The Nine Billion Names of God" by Arthur C. Clarke. Reprinted by permission of the author and the author's agent, Scott Meredith Literary Agency, Inc., 845 Third Avenue, New York, NY 10022.

"Shame" from EVERY MAN WILL SHOUT by Malcolm Cragg. Reprinted by permission of Oxford University Press.

"In Just-" reprinted from TULIPS & CHIMNEYS by E. E. Cummings with permission of Liveright Publishing Corporation. Copyright 1923, 1925 and renewed 1951, 1953 by E. E. Cummings. Copyright © 1973, 1976 by Nancy T. Andrews. Copyright © 1973, 1976 by George James Firmage.

"Augustus Gloop Goes up the Pipe" from CHARLIE AND THE CHOCOLATE FACTORY by Roald Dahl. Copyright © 1964 by Roald Dahl. Reprinted by permission of Alfred A. Knopf, Inc.

"The Dog and the Rooster" from ALONG CAME A DOG by Meindert DeJong. Copyright © 1958 by Meindert DeJong. By permission of Harper & Row, Publishers, Inc.

"Silver," "Jim Jay," "Bones" by Walter de la Mare reprinted by permission of The Literary Trustees of Walter de la Mare and the Society of Authors as their representative.

The poem entitled "Song of an Unlucky Man" from A CROCODILE HAS ME BY THE LEG by Leonard W. Doob. Copyright © 1966, 1967 by Leonard W. Doob. Used with permission from the publisher, Walker and Company.

"The Song of the Jellicles" from OLD POSSUM'S BOOK OF PRACTICAL CATS by T. S. Eliot. Reprinted by permission of Harcourt Brace Jovanovich, Inc., and Faber and Faber, Publishers.

Chapter entitled "The Storm" from THE BLACK STALLION by Walter Farley. Copyright 1941 by Walter Farley. Reprinted by permission of Random House, Inc.

Text excerpt from pages 142–155 of HARRIET THE SPY by Louise Fitzhugh. Copyright © 1964 by Louise Fitzhugh. By permission of Harper & Row, Publishers, Inc.

MCBROOM TELLS A LIE by Sid Fleischman. Copyright © 1976 by Albert S. Fleischman. Reprinted by permission of Little, Brown and Company in association with The Atlantic Monthly Press.

"Easy Diver" from STREET POEMS by Robert Froman. Copyright © 1971 by Robert Froman. Reprinted by permission of Robert Froman.

"The Pasture" and "Stopping by Woods on a Snowy Evening" from THE POETRY OF ROBERT FROST edited by Edward Connery Latham. Copyright 1923, 1939, © 1967, 1969 by Holt, Rinehart and Winston. Copyright 1951 by Robert Frost. Reprinted by permission of Holt, Rinehart & Winston, Publishers.

Text excerpt from JULIE OF THE WOLVES by Jean Craighead George. A Newbery Medal winner. Text copyright © 1972 by Jean Craighead George. By permission of Harper & Row, Publishers, Inc.

"The Song of Mr. Toad" from THE WIND IN THE WILLOWS by Kenneth Grahame. (New York: Charles Scribner's Sons, 1908.)

"'Foul Shot'" by Edwin A. Hoey reprinted by permission of Xerox Education Publications.

"Supermarket" from AT THE TOP OF MY VOICE, AND OTHER POEMS by Felice Holman. Copyright © 1970 by Felice Holman (New York: Charles Scribner's Sons, 1976). Reprinted by permission of Charles Scribner's Sons.

"Mother to Son" from SELECTED POEMS OF LANGSTON HUGHES by Langston Hughes. Copyright 1926 by Alfred A. Knopf, Inc., and renewed 1954 by Langston Hughes. By permission of Alfred A. Knopf, Inc.

"My Uncle Dan" from MEET MY FOLKS by Ted Hughes. Copyright © 1961, 1973 by Ted Hughes. Reprinted by permission of Faber & Faber Ltd. and Bobbs-Merrill Company, Inc.

"The Too-Many Professors" from THE INCREDIBLE ADVENTURES OF PROFESSOR BRANESTAWM by Norman Hunter reprinted by permission of The Bodley Head.

"Bats" from THE BAT-POET by Randall Jarrell. Copyright © Macmillan Publishing Co., Inc., 1963, 1964. Reprinted by permission of Macmillan Publishing Co., Inc.

Chapter 7, "The Royal Banquet," from THE PHANTOM TOLLBOOTH by Norton Juster. Copyright © 1961 by Norton Juster. Reprinted by permission of Random House, Inc.

"How Many Donkeys?" from ONCE THE HODJA by Alice Geer Kelsey. Reprinted by permission of David McKay, Publishers.

Chapter One from DINKY HOCKER SHOOTS SMACK! by M. E. Kerr. Copyright © 1972 by M. E. Kerr. By permission of Harper & Row, Publishers, Inc.

"There's This That I Like about Hockey, My Lad" by John Kieran from THE AMERICAN SPORTING SCENE by John Kieran and J. W. Golinkin. Copyright 1941 by John Kieran and J. W. Golinkin; Copyright renewed © 1969. Reprinted by permission of Macmillan Publishing Co., Inc.

Chapter 3 from THE MIXED-UP FILES OF MRS. BASIL E. FRANKWEILER by E. L. Konigsburg. Copyright © 1967 by E. L. Konigsburg (New York: Atheneum, 1967). Reprinted by permission of Atheneum Publishers.

"Snail" from NO ONE WRITES A LETTER TO A SNAIL by Maxine Kumin. Text copyright © 1962 by Maxine Kumin. Reprinted by permission of Curtis Brown, Ltd.

The text of "Rules" from DOGS & DRAGONS TREES & DREAMS by Karla Kuskin. Copyright © 1962 by Karla Kuskin. By permission of Harper & Row, Publishers, Inc.

"Eleanor Rigby" by John Lennon and Paul McCartney excerpted from the book THE BEATLES ILLUSTRATED LYRICS I edited by Alan Aldridge. Lyrics Copyright © 1963, 1964, 1965, 1966, 1967, 1968, 1969 by Northern Songs Limited (London). Reprinted by permission of Delacorte Press/Seymour Lawrence.

"A Hike in New York City" from IN ONE ERA AND OUT THE OTHER by Sam Levenson. Copyright © 1973 by Sam Levenson. Reprinted by permission of Simon & Schuster, Inc.

Text only of "Lucy Looks into a Wardrobe" and "What Lucy Found There" in THE LION, THE WITCH AND THE WARDROBE. Copyright 1950 by The Trustees of the Estate of C. S. Lewis, © renewed 1978 by Arthur Owens Barfield. Reprinted by permission of Macmillan Publishing Company.

"Cat" by Sinclair Lewis. Copyright © 1959 by Western Publishing Company, Inc. Reprinted by permission of the Estate of Sinclair Lewis.

"Pippi Moves into Villa Villekulla" from PIPPI LONGSTOCKING by Astrid Lindgren. Copyright 1950 by The Viking Press, Inc., © renewed 1978 by Viking Penguin Inc. Reprinted by permission of Viking Penguin Inc.

"Order" from THE WAY THINGS ARE, AND OTHER POEMS by Myra Cohn Livingston. Copyright © 1974 by Myra Cohn Livingston. A Margaret K. McElderry Book (New York: Atheneum, 1974). Reprinted with permission of Atheneum Publishers.

"Smells," "The Rock," from THE STORY OF DOCTOR DOLITTLE by Hugh Lofting. Reprinted by permission of Christopher Lofting.

"The Doughnuts" from HOMER PRICE written and illustrated by Robert McCloskey. Copyright 1943, renewed © 1971 by Robert McCloskey. Reprinted by permission of Viking Penguin Inc.

"This Is My Rock" from ONE AT A TIME by David McCord. Copyright © 1974 by David McCord. Reprinted by permission of Little, Brown and Company.

"Sea Fever" and "Cargoes" from POEMS by John Masefield. Copyright 1912 by Macmillan Publishing Co., copyright renewed 1940 by John Masefield. Reprinted by permission of Macmillan Publishing Co., Inc.

Text of "The Acrobats," "The Land of Happy," "The Battle," and "A Poem on the Neck of a Running Giraffe," from WHERE THE SIDEWALK ENDS: THE POEMS AND DRAWINGS OF SHEL SILVERSTEIN. Copyright © 1974 by Shel Silverstein. By permission of Harper & Row, Publishers, Inc.

"Shrewd Todie and Lyzer the Miser" from WHEN SCHLEMIEL WENT TO WARSAW AND OTHER STORIES by Isaac Bashevis Singer. Pictures by Margot Zemach. Text copyright © 1968 by Isaac Bashevis Singer. Reprinted by permission of Farrar, Straus & Giroux, Inc.

"Eat-It-All Elaine" from DON'T EVER CROSS A CROCODILE by Kaye Starbird. Copyright © 1963 by Kaye Starbird. Reprinted by permission of Paul R. Reynolds, Inc., 12 East 41st Street, New York, NY 10017.

"The Fugitives" by Rosemary Sutcliff reprinted by permission of Oxford University Press.

"Of Ships and Trees" from LE TRÉSOR DE L'HOMME by Beatrice Tanaka. Copyright © 1971 by Beatrice Tanaka. Published in *Cricket* magazine. Reprinted by permission of La Farandole.

MANY MOONS by James Thurber. Copyright 1943 by James Thurber. Copyright © 1971 by Helen W. Thurber and Rosemary T. Sauers. Originally published by Harcourt Brace Jovanovich, Inc. Reprinted by permission of Mrs. James Thurber.

"Riddles in the Dark," an adaptation of Chapter V from THE HOBBIT by J. R. R. Tolkien. Copyright © 1966 by J. R. R. Tolkien. "Cat" from ADVENTURES OF TOM BOMBADIL by J. R. R. Tolkien. Reprinted by permission of Houghton Mifflin Company and George Allen & Unwin.

Slightly abridged version of "Laughing Gas" from MARY POPPINS by P. L. Travers. Copyright 1934, 1962 by P. L. Travers. Reprinted by permission of Harcourt Brace Jovanovich, Inc.

"January" and "September" from A CHILD'S CALENDAR by John Updike. Copyright © 1965 by John Updike and Nancy Burkert. Reprinted by permission of Alfred A. Knopf, Inc.

"The Giant Crab" from THE TRUANTS by John Walsh. Reprinted by permission of Mrs. A. M. Walsh.

The text of Chapter V, "Charlotte," from CHARLOTTE'S WEB, written by E. B. White, illustrated by Garth Williams. Copyright 1952 by E. B. White. Text copyright renewed 1980 by E. B. White. By permission of Harper & Row, Publishers, Inc.

#6, #12, #18, #39 from OPPOSITES by Richard Wilbur. Copyright © 1973 by Richard Wilbur. Reprinted by permission of Harcourt Brace Jovanovich, Inc.

Text of "Little House in the Big Woods," from LITTLE HOUSE IN THE BIG WOODS written by Laura Ingalls Wilder, illustrated by Garth Williams. Copyright 1932, as to text, by Laura Ingalls Wilder. Renewed 1959 by Roger L. MacBride. By permission of Harper & Row, Publishers, Inc.

"Bartek the Doctor" from WINTER TALES FROM POLAND by Maia Wojciechowska. Copyright © 1973 by Maia Wojciechowska. Reprinted by permission of Doubleday & Company, Inc.

"Lies" from SELECTED POEMS by Yevgeny Yevtushenko, translated by Robin Milner-Gulland and Peter Levi (Penguin Modern European Poets, 1962). Copyright © Robin Milner-Gulland and Peter Levi, 1962. Reprinted by permission of Viking Penguin Ltd.

To the Reader

In your hands is Book Three of *The World Treasury of Children's Literature*. This final volume is aimed more or less at older readers—from ages nine through thirteen or fourteen, and on up. Books One and Two of the *Treasury* are intended for younger children, ranging perhaps from ages four through eight.

At the very beginning of Book One you will find an introduction to the whole set, entitled "Let's Talk." As I suggested in that introduction, there's really no such thing as an eight-year-old reader or a twelve-year-old reader. What we like to read depends on our age as well as our taste, personality, intelligence, background, the kind of parents or homes we have, and a lot of other things. You can grade a high-jumper by the height of the bar he clears. Readers, however, can't be precisely graded by the arithmetic of age levels. For example, everything I chose to include in the *Treasury*'s three books had first of all to give pleasure to a reader who, as he writes these words, is eighty-one.

Nevertheless, it's true that this volume contains stories, poems, memories, and extracts from novels that are a bit more complicated than those in the first two books. They demand the kind of attention we can give to reading only as we get a little older. Indeed, at least three stories (they're by Ray Bradbury, Arthur C. Clarke, and Isaac Asimov) were originally written for grown-ups. However, I have found that often younger persons get more out of them than do their elders.

The contents of this book are arranged roughly in order of difficulty, so that the selections in the first half may appeal to somewhat younger readers, and those in the second half to somewhat older ones. But if I were you I wouldn't pay too much attention to the arrangement. You'll find your own way around.

At the end of this volume is a pretty long essay labeled "For Grown-ups Only." In it I've set down some thoughts on children's literature. I've tried to explain my interest in the subject, a lifelong interest that has resulted in this *Treasury*. The essay is meant mainly for parents, teachers, or any adult who thinks children's literature is important and would like to learn more about it. The title, "For Grown-ups Only," needn't, however, be taken literally. You yourself may find parts of it interesting.

But for all readers, whatever their age, it's the rest of the book that really counts.

Contents

BOOK III

The World Treasury of Children's Literature

ANON.

Anon. (which stands for Anonymous) is a varied and productive writer who's been working at his or her craft for thousands of years. Here are a few samples of his or her work. My favorite is the first one, about Carlyle's *Essay on Burns*. In high school I had to fight my way though that essay, and Carlyle won. Whoever wrote this verse is a literary critic of high order, with a fine independent notion of grammar.

As I Was Laying on the Green

As I was laying on the green,
A small English book I seen.
Carlyle's *Essay on Burns* was the edition,
So I left it laying in the same position.

Little Willie

Little Willie from his mirror,
  Licked the mercury right off,
Thinking, in his childish error,
  It would cure the whooping cough.
At the funeral his mother
  Smartly said to Mrs. Brown:
  " 'Twas a chilly day for Willie
When the mercury went down."

Willie the Poisoner

Willie poisoned Auntie's tea,
Auntie died in agony.
Uncle came and looked quite vexed,
"Really, Will," said he, "what next?"

Sister Nell

In the family drinking well
Willie pushed his sister Nell.
She's there yet, because it kilt her —
Now we have to buy a filter.

I Raised a Great Hullabaloo

I raised a great hullabaloo
When I found a large mouse in my stew,
  Said the waiter, "Don't shout
  And wave it about,
Or the rest will be wanting one, too!"

The Donkey

I saw a donkey
One day old,
His head was too big
For his neck to hold;
His legs were shaky
And long and loose,
They rocked and staggered
And weren't much use.

He tried to gambol
And frisk a bit,
But he wasn't quite sure
Of the trick of it.
His queer little coat
Was soft and gray,
And curled at his neck
In a lovely way.

 ANON.

His face was wistful
And left no doubt
That he felt life needed
Some thinking about.
So he blundered round
In venturesome quest,
And then lay flat
On the ground to rest.

He looked so little
And weak and slim,
I prayed the world
Might be good to him.

LAURA INGALLS WILDER

A librarian, reordering a supply of Mrs. Wilder's *Little House* books, once said, "These books don't get damaged or lost. They are simply read to death." About ten million copies of this famous series have been sold. They've also been made into a popular television program.

Mrs. Wilder was in her sixties when she began to set down her recollections of her pioneer childhood and youth. Almost everything she wrote about seems strange and wonderful to us now, and I think that's why we love her books. When she was quite a small girl she lived, with her parents and two sisters, in a lonely log cabin in Wisconsin. Later on the family moved to Minnesota, then Iowa, Missouri, Kansas, into Indian Territory, back to Minnesota, then into the wild Dakota Territory.

How did our tremendous, almost empty country get settled? One way of finding out is to read these eight *Little House* books. Here are their titles:

Little House in the Big Woods
Little House on the Prairie
Farmer Boy
On the Banks of Plum Creek
By the Shores of Silver Lake
The Long Winter
Little Town on the Prairie
These Happy Golden Years

When we've read them we know exactly how Laura and her family built a log cabin, or made a button lamp, or encountered bears, or spent their Sundays, or used wood chips for smoking venison. No fake Hollywood West, no television sweetening—but the way it actually was.

Little House in the Big Woods, the first book in the series, starts this way.

Little House in the Big Woods

CHAPTER ONE

ONCE upon a time, sixty years ago, a little girl lived in the Big Woods of Wisconsin, in a little gray house made of logs.

The great, dark trees of the Big Woods stood all around the house, and beyond them were other trees and beyond them were more trees. As far as a man could go to the north in a day, or a week, or a whole month, there was nothing but woods. There were no houses. There were no roads. There were no people. There were only trees and the wild animals who had their homes among them.

Wolves lived in the Big Woods, and bears, and huge wildcats. Muskrats and mink and otter lived by the streams. Foxes had dens in the hills and deer roamed everywhere.

To the east of the little log house, and to the west, there were miles upon miles of trees, and only a few little log houses scattered far apart in the edge of the Big Woods.

So far as the little girl could see, there was only the one little house where she lived with her Father and Mother, her sister Mary and baby sister Carrie. A wagon track ran before the house, turning and twisting out of sight in the woods where the wild animals lived, but the little girl did not know where it went, nor what might be at the end of it.

The little girl was named Laura and she called her father, Pa, and her mother, Ma. In those days and in that place, children did not say Father and Mother, nor Mamma and Papa, as they do now.

At night, when Laura lay awake in the trundle bed, she listened and could not hear anything at all but the sound of the trees whispering together. Sometimes, far away in the night, a wolf howled. Then he came nearer, and howled again.

It was a scary sound. Laura knew that wolves would eat little girls. But she was safe inside the solid log walls. Her father's gun hung over the door and good old Jack, the brindle bulldog, lay on guard before it. Her father would say, "Go to sleep, Laura. Jack won't let the wolves in." So Laura snuggled under the covers of the trundle bed, close beside Mary, and went to sleep.

One night her father picked her up out of bed and carried her to the window so that she might see the wolves. There were two of them sitting in front of the house. They looked like shaggy dogs. They pointed their noses at the big, bright moon, and howled.

Jack paced up and down before the door, growling. The hair stood up along his back and he showed his sharp, fierce teeth to the wolves. They howled, but they could not get in.

The house was a comfortable house. Upstairs there was a large attic, pleasant to play in when the rain drummed on the roof. Downstairs was the small bedroom, and the big room. The bedroom had a window that closed with a wooden shutter. The big room had two windows with glass in the panes, and it had two doors, a front door and a back door.

All around the house was a crooked rail fence, to keep the bears and the deer away.

In the yard in front of the house were two beautiful big oak trees. Every morning as soon as she was awake Laura ran to look out of the window, and one morning she saw in each of the big trees a dead deer hanging from a branch.

Pa had shot the deer the day before and Laura had been asleep when he brought them home at night and hung them high in the trees so the wolves could not get the meat.

That day Pa and Ma and Laura and Mary had fresh venison for dinner. It was so good that Laura wished they could eat it all. But most of the meat must be salted and smoked and packed away to be eaten in the winter.

For winter was coming. The days were shorter, and frost crawled up the windowpanes at night. Soon the snow would come. Then the log house would be almost buried in snowdrifts, and the lake and the streams would freeze. In the bitter cold weather Pa could not be sure of finding any wild game to shoot for meat.

The bears would be hidden away in their dens where they slept soundly all winter long. The squirrels would be curled in their nests in hollow trees, with their furry tails wrapped snugly around their noses. The deer and the rabbits would be shy and swift. Even if Pa could get a deer, it would be poor and thin, not fat and plump as deer are in the fall.

Pa might hunt alone all day in the bitter cold, in the Big Woods covered with snow, and come home at night with nothing for Ma and Mary and Laura to eat.

So as much food as possible must be stored away in the little house before winter came.

Pa skinned the deer carefully and salted and stretched the hides, for he would make soft leather of them. Then he cut up the meat, and sprinkled salt over the pieces as he laid them on a board.

Standing on end in the yard was a tall length cut from the trunk of a big hollow tree. Pa had driven nails inside as far as he could reach from each end. Then he stood it up, put a little roof over the top, and cut a little door on one side near the bottom. On the piece that he cut out he fastened leather hinges; then he fitted it into place, and that was the little door, with the bark still on it.

After the deer meat had been salted several days, Pa cut a hole near the end of each piece and put a string through it. Laura watched him do this, and then she watched him hang the meat on the nails in the hollow log.

He reached up through the little door and hung meat on the nails, as far up as he could reach. Then he put a ladder against the log, climbed up to the top, moved the roof to one side, and reached down inside to hang meat on those nails.

Then Pa put the roof back again, climbed down the ladder, and said to Laura:

"Run over to the chopping block and fetch me some of those green hickory chips—new, clean, white ones."

So Laura ran to the block where Pa chopped wood, and filled her apron with the fresh, sweetsmelling chips.

Just inside the little door in the hollow log Pa built a fire of tiny bits of bark and moss, and he laid some of the chips on it very carefully.

Instead of burning quickly, the green chips smoldered and filled the hollow log with thick, choking smoke. Pa shut the door, and a little smoke squeezed through the crack around it and a little smoke came out through the roof, but most of it was shut in with the meat.

"There's nothing better than good hickory smoke," Pa said. "That will make good venison that will keep anywhere, in any weather."

Then he took his gun, and slinging his ax on his shoulder he went away to the clearing to cut down some more trees.

Laura and Ma watched the fire for several days. When smoke stopped coming through the cracks, Laura would bring more hickory chips and Ma would put them on the fire under the meat. All the time there was a little smell of smoke in the yard, and when the door was opened a thick, smoky, meaty smell came out.

At last Pa said the venison had smoked long enough. Then they let the fire go out, and Pa took all the strips and pieces of meat out of the hollow tree. Ma wrapped each piece neatly in paper and hung them in the attic where they would keep safe and dry.

One morning Pa went away before daylight with the horses and wagon, and that night he came home with a wagonload of fish. The big wagon box was piled full, and some of the fish were as big as Laura. Pa had gone to Lake Pepin and caught them all with a net.

Ma cut large slices of flaky white fish, without one bone, for Laura and Mary. They all feasted on the good, fresh fish. All they did not eat fresh was salted down in barrels for the winter.

Pa owned a pig. It ran wild in the Big Woods, living on acorns and nuts and roots. Now he caught it and put it in a pen made of logs, to fatten. He would butcher it as soon as the weather was cold enough to keep the pork frozen.

Once in the middle of the night Laura woke up and heard the pig squealing. Pa jumped out of bed, snatched his gun from the wall, and ran outdoors. Then Laura heard the gun go off, once, twice.

When Pa came back, he told what had happened. He had seen a big black bear standing beside the pigpen. The bear was reaching into the pen to grab the pig, and the pig was running and squealing. Pa saw this in the starlight and he fired quickly. But the light was dim and in his haste he missed the bear. The bear ran away into the woods, not hurt at all.

Laura was sorry Pa did not get the bear. She liked bear meat so much. Pa was sorry, too, but he said, "Anyway, I saved the bacon."

The garden behind the little house had been growing all summer. It was so near the house that the deer did not jump the fence and eat the vegetables in the daytime, and at night Jack kept them away. Sometimes in the morning there were little hoofprints among the carrots and the cabbages. But Jack's tracks were there, too, and the deer had jumped right out again.

Now the potatoes and carrots, the beets and turnips and cabbages were gathered and stored in the cellar, for freezing nights had come.

Onions were made into long ropes, braided together by their tops, and then were hung in the attic beside wreaths of red peppers strung on threads. The pumpkins and the squashes were piled in orange and yellow and green heaps in the attic's corners.

The barrels of salted fish were in the pantry, and the yellow cheeses were stacked on the pantry shelves.

Then one day Uncle Henry came riding out of the Big Woods. He had come to help Pa butcher. Ma's big butcher knife was already sharpened, and Uncle Henry had brought Aunt Polly's butcher knife.

Near the pigpen Pa and Uncle Henry built a bonfire, and heated a great kettle of water over it. When the water was boiling they went to kill the hog. Then Laura ran and hid her head on the bed and stopped her ears with her fingers so she could not hear the hog squeal.

"It doesn't hurt him, Laura," Pa said. "We do it so quickly." But she did not want to hear him squeal.

In a minute she took one finger cautiously out of an ear, and listened. The hog had stopped squealing. After that, Butchering Time was great fun.

It was such a busy day, with so much to see and do. Uncle Henry and Pa were jolly, and there would be spareribs for dinner, and Pa had promised Laura and Mary the bladder and the pig's tail.

As soon as the hog was dead Pa and Uncle Henry lifted it up and down in the boiling water till it was well scalded. Then they laid it on a board and scraped it with their knives, and all the bristles came off. After that they hung the hog in a tree, took out the insides, and left it hanging to cool.

When it was cool they took it down and cut it up. There were hams and shoulders, side meat and spareribs and belly. There was the heart and the liver and the tongue, and the head to be made into headcheese, and the dishpan full of bits to be made into sausage.

The meat was laid on a board in the back-door shed, and every piece was sprinkled with salt. The hams and the shoulders were put to pickle in brine, for they would be smoked, like the venison, in the hollow log.

"You can't beat hickory-cured ham," Pa said.

He was blowing up the bladder. It made a little white balloon, and he tied the end tight with a string and gave it to Mary and Laura to play with. They could throw it into the air and spat it back and forth with their hands. Or it would bounce along the ground and they could kick it. But even better fun than a balloon was the pig's tail.

Pa skinned it for them carefully, and into the large end he thrust a sharpened stick. Ma opened the front of the cookstove and raked hot coals out into the iron hearth. Then Laura and Mary took turns holding the pig's tail over the coals.

It sizzled and fried, and drops of fat dripped off it and blazed on the coals. Ma sprinkled it with salt. Their hands and their faces got very hot, and Laura burned her finger, but she was so excited she did not care. Roasting the pig's tail was such fun that it was hard to play fair, taking turns.

At last it was done. It was nicely browned all over, and how good it smelled! They carried it into the yard to cool it, and even before it was cool enough they began tasting it and burned their tongues.

The ate every little bit of meat off the bones, and then they gave the bones to Jack. And that was the end of the pig's tail. There would not be another one till next year.

Uncle Henry went home after dinner, and Pa went away to his work in the Big Woods. But for Laura and Mary and Ma, Butchering Time had only begun. There was a great deal for Ma to do, and Laura and Mary helped her.

All that day and the next, Ma was trying out the lard in big iron pots on the cookstove. Laura and Mary carried wood and watched the fire. It must be hot, but not too hot, or the lard would burn. The big pots simmered and boiled, but they must not smoke. From time to time Ma skimmed out the brown cracklings. She put them in a cloth and squeezed out every bit of the lard, and then she put the cracklings away. She would use them to flavor johnny-cake later.

Cracklings were very good to eat, but Laura and Mary could have only a taste. They were too rich for little girls, Ma said.

Ma scraped and cleaned the head carefully, and then she boiled it till all the meat fell off the bones. She chopped the meat fine with her chopping knife in the wooden bowl, she seasoned it with pepper and salt and spices. Then she mixed the pot-liquor with it, and set it away in a pan to cool. When it was cool it would cut in slices, and that was headcheese.

The little pieces of meat, lean and fat, that had been cut off the large pieces, Ma chopped and chopped until it was all chopped fine. She seasoned it with salt and pepper and with dried sage leaves from the garden. Then with her hands she tossed and turned it until it was well mixed, and she molded it into balls. She put the balls in a pan out in the shed, where they would freeze and be good to eat all winter. That was the sausage.

When Butchering Time was over, there were the sausages and the headcheese, the big jars of lard and the keg of white salt-pork out in the shed, and in the attic hung the smoked hams and shoulders.

The little house was fairly bursting with good food stored away for the long winter. The pantry and the shed and the cellar were full, and so was the attic.

Laura and Mary must play in the house now, for it was cold outdoors and the brown leaves were all falling from the trees. The fire in the cookstove never went out. At night Pa banked it with ashes to keep the coals alive till morning.

The attic was a lovely place to play. The large, round, colored pumpkins made beautiful chairs and tables. The red peppers and the onions dangled overhead. The hams and the venison hung in their paper wrappings, and all the bunches of dried herbs, the spicy herbs for cooking and the bitter herbs for medicine, gave the place a dusty-spicy smell.

Often the wind howled outside with a cold and lonesome sound. But in the attic Laura and Mary played house with the squashes and the pumpkins, and everything was snug and cozy.

Mary was bigger than Laura, and she had a rag doll named Nettie. Laura had only a corncob wrapped in a handkerchief, but it was a good doll. It was named Susan. It wasn't Susan's fault that she was only a corncob. Sometimes Mary let Laura hold Nettie, but she did it only when Susan couldn't see.

The best times of all were at night. After supper Pa brought his traps in from the shed to grease them by the fire. He rubbed them bright and greased the hinges of the jaws and the springs of the pans with a feather dipped in bear's grease.

There were small traps and middle-sized traps and great bear traps with teeth in their jaws that Pa said would break a man's leg if they shut on to it.

While he greased the traps, Pa told Laura and Mary little jokes and stories, and afterward he would play his fiddle.

The doors and windows were tightly shut, and the cracks of the window frames stuffed with cloth, to keep out the cold. But Black Susan, the cat, came and went as she pleased, day and night, through the swinging door of the cat-hole in the bottom of the front door. She always went very quickly, so the door would not catch her tail when it fell shut behind her.

One night when Pa was greasing the traps he watched Black Susan come in, and he said:

"There was once a man who had two cats, a big cat and a little cat."

Laura and Mary ran to lean on his knees and hear the rest.

"He had two cats," Pa repeated, "a big cat and a little cat. So he made a big cat-hole in his door for the big cat. And then he made a little cat-hole for the little cat."

There Pa stopped.

"But why couldn't the little cat—" Mary began.

"Because the big cat wouldn't let it," Laura interrupted.

"Laura, that is very rude. You must never interrupt," said Pa.

"But I see," he said, "that either one of you has more sense than the man who cut the two cat-holes in his door."

The he laid away the traps, and he took his fiddle out of its box and began to play. That was the best time of all.

JONATHAN SWIFT

AEIOU

We are very little creatures,
All of different voice and features;
One of us in glass is set,
One of us you'll find in jet.
T'other you may see in tin,
And the fourth a box within.
If the fifth you should pursue,
It can never fly from you.

MAIA WOJCIECHOWSKA

Bartek the Doctor

THERE ONCE lived a woman in a Polish village who had the misfortune of having given birth to a son who was a good-for-nothing. Some people called him Bartek the Idler. Others called him Bartek the Fool. Still others called him names that had better be forgotten. But all agreed that he was the laziest, the stupidest boy in all of Poland.

And they were quite right.

Until he was twenty, there was only one thing that Bartek could do, and he did it better than anyone else in the world. And that one thing was *nothing*.

When he did do *something*, he did it very badly and not for long.

Bartek actually did only four things each year. In the spring he would stretch himself. And each and every spring as he stretched, he would pull a muscle. In the summer he would count the flies on his mother's cow. But since he could only count to two, the counting did nobody any good. In the fall he would roast potatoes in the ashes. They always came out raw because he was too lazy to put them into the ashes while they were still hot. In the winter he would lie by the stove. He would lie down at the end of November and would not get up, except to eat and go to the outhouse, until the first of May.

His poor widowed mother had to work from morning till night, and sometimes from night till morning as well, just to feed her big, lazy, stupid son. And Bartek ate almost as well as he did nothing, except that his food would dribble down his shirtfront and sometimes, in his haste, he'd bite his tongue.

When Bartek was twenty and his mother could no longer bear things as they were, she spoke to him:

"I cannot put up with you any longer," she said. "From now on you must work for your keep."

Bartek, who was dozing, yawned. He would have stretched himself, but he was afraid he'd do himself some harm. And besides, it was not yet spring.

"You're twenty," his mother was saying, the tears came to her tired eyes. "You must make your own way in the world."

"But I can't," Bartek said slowly.

"And why not?" his mother asked.

"Because." Bartek stopped to think for a while. "Because," he finally decided to tell her as much as he knew about himself, "because I am a good-for-nothing, stupid and lazy."

His mother couldn't very well disagree with that. She had often told him exactly this herself.

"That's true," his mother said and began to cry. She cried for a long time while Bartek went back to dozing. Finally when she could cry no more, she woke him up. "I am sending you into the world," she said. "More for your own sake than mine. Take the cow. Sell her in the marketplace in town. You will have some money to start you on your way."

Bartek was moved enough by her tears to get off the stove.

"All right," he said. "I'll go."

His mother tied Bartek to the cow. She didn't trust him as much as she trusted the cow to find the town's marketplace. Then she kissed him, waved good-bye, and cried some more as she saw him go off.

Dusk was falling when Bartek arrived at the town's gate. As the cow led him toward the marketplace, he passed by a most splendid-looking house. It was larger and taller than anything he had ever seen.

Bartek stood for a long time in front of the house. For the first time in his life he wanted something that he didn't have. He wanted to live in that house.

The owner of the house, the town pharmacist, was in need of an assistant, and when he saw Bartek standing in front of his house, he called to him.

"Nothing will come of you standing idle. Come inside. I have room and food for you. And you can work for me."

At the sound of the word *work* Bartek reeled back as if struck.

"If one day," the pharmacist was saying, "you expect to have a house of your own, you had better start working for it now. You'll never amount to anything and you won't ever have anything being led by a cow. Come, I will teach you my trade."

"How long would it take me to learn?" Bartek asked.

"A few years if you're bright," the pharmacist said. "Nothing happens overnight."

But he was wrong. Something did happen overnight. Bartek went to live at the pharmacist's house, and that very night his master received word that he was needed in a town some miles away. When Bartek woke up the next morning, he found himself the only occupant of the splendid house.

He found the larder stocked with sausages, cream and fresh bread, and after he had breakfasted to his heart's content he was about to lie down for a nap, but someone knocked on the front door.

"Go away, whoever you are," Bartek called.

"Please open the door," a voice from the outside begged.

Bartek opened the door. An old peasant, a cap in his hands, was standing in front of him.

"What do you want?" Bartek asked.

"You must help me," the old peasant said. And before Bartek could tell him that he was not the pharmacist, the old man began to cry. "My wife's got a terrible fever. She will surely die unless you give me some medicine for her."

Bartek looked behind. There were vials and boxes and containers of all sorts on the shelves. He reached for the smallest and prettiest of the bottles and handed it to the old man.

"Make your wife drink this," he said.

"Thank you," the old peasant said, kissed his hand and was gone.

Bartek closed the door and then went to sleep. He had slept only a few hours when he was awakened by someone knocking on the door.

"This is hard work," Bartek said to himself. "I don't know if I can stand it for very long."

The same old peasant was standing on the steps of the house.

"You've saved my wife," he cried. "No sooner did she drink the medicine than she got better."

Having said this the peasant handed Bartek a sackful of money.

"This is all I have," the old man said, "and it's yours for saving my wife's life."

Bartek stood for a while without moving after the peasant left. Then he smiled to himself, looked at the money, and although he could not really count, he knew it was a lot. At this rate, he thought, I will be rich in no time.

When the pharmacist got back that evening, Bartek told him what had happened.

"That was nothing but luck," the man said. "You must learn the trade properly; only then you know what you are doing. And once you know that, you won't need luck and you will become as rich as I."

Bartek stayed on for two years with the pharmacist. At first he chopped wood, lighted the stove, arranged the vials, boxes and bottles, sorted herbs, cleaned the house. But after a few months he was allowed to prepare the different medicines. He learned fast and was surprised at that because he did not know that he had a good brain. He did not know this because he had never made use of it before.

It got so that Bartek, instead of minding work, began to enjoy it. He grew cheerful and would wake up each morning smiling at the thought of learning more. He slept well at night, but then, he never had any trouble falling asleep.

At twenty-two, when he thought he had made enough progress and that there was very little else that the pharmacist could teach him, Bartek decided to leave.

"I want to see my mother," he told his master. "I will go back to my village, and I will become a doctor."

"It takes years of studying to become a doctor," the pharmacist said." But if you wish to go back to see your mother, I certainly won't stop you."

He gave Bartek his wages and made him a present of an old book where all possible and impossible sicknesses and remedies were mentioned.

"If you learn to read," the pharmacist said, "and if you read this book from cover to cover a few dozen times, you will have made a start toward becoming a doctor."

Bartek thanked him, shook hands and went on his way. He was taking the cow back to his mother. And now it was he who was leading her.

After walking for some time Bartek came across an old woman. She seemed so very old and so very tired, wrinkled, shriveled up and yellow with age, that he took pity on her and stopped to talk to her.

"Can I help you?" he asked.

Her black eyes looked at him. In her hand she held a little bell, but although her hand trembled, the bell did not ring. No sound at all came from it, not even the faintest tinkle.

"My boy," the old woman said, "I thank you for offering to help. I'd like to get across this swamp. I have much to do on the other side."

"Much to do? At your age?" Bartek laughed. "What work could you possibly do?"

"Don't you see? I ring this bell."

Bartek laughed again.

"Much good that does! It doesn't make a sound."

"So much the better for you, my boy. So much the better for you. Carry me on your back."

"Climb up, old woman."

Bartek carried the old woman across the swamp, and she seemed as light as air.

"You were kind to me," the old woman said. "I'd like to repay you for that."

Once again Bartek laughed.

"If only you could," he said.

"I can do anything you want me to do," the old woman said.

Bartek didn't believe her at all. All she was, he thought, was a beggar woman with a mind that had gone weak with age.

"What would you have me do?" she asked.

"There is only one thing I wish for," Bartek said.

"And what is that?"

"I'd like to become a doctor. But I must first learn to read and to write. And then I must read this book a dozen times or more. And that would only be a start."

This time the woman laughed.

"You won't need to go to all that trouble," she said. Her piercing black eyes looked sharply at the young man. "Look at me well. Do you know who I am?"

"No," Bartek said, "although you do resemble my dead grandmother." He crossed himself and drew back. For a moment he thought that perhaps the old woman was actually his grandmother's ghost.

"No," the old woman said. "I am no ghost. I am Death."

Bartek swallowed hard and was about to run away, but she spoke again.

"Don't be frightened. I am going to help you, just as I said. I am going to teach you the one secret without which you cannot become a doctor. Whenever you attend someone who is sick, watch for me. Watch where

I stand. If I am at the patient's head, he will die and you won't be able to do a thing to help. But if I am at the patient's feet, do all you can for him, or nothing at all, for the patient will live, even without your help."

Bartek wanted to thank her, but she wouldn't let him.

"One good turn deserves another," she said. "Now we must part. Farewell, Bartek."

"Farewell, Death," Bartek said and watched her disappear in the evening mist.

When Bartek arrived at his village, people who saw him laughed at the sight of him.

"Bartek the Fool is back!"

"Just look at that! Bartek the Idiot is carrying a book!"

"Bartek the Idler is here. Now we can all watch him loaf."

"He looks as stupid as ever."

"How could he change? Good-for-nothings never do."

Bartek heard them, but he did not feel offended. He smiled at the villagers, and then when they encircled him to have a better look at him, he spoke to them:

"I left this village a fool and an idler, but I've come back a famous doctor."

They laughed so hard that some of them fell down and all had tears in their eyes. He smiled at them and then continued on toward his house. His mother, who had given up hope of ever seeing him, was very happy that he was back. And she was happy to see that he had brought back with him her only cow.

"I've changed," Bartek told her after he embraced her. "I'm sorry about the way I used to be. I have not wasted those two years. I've come back to be a doctor."

His mother, hearing this, thought that Bartek had lost his mind. A doctor indeed! But she said nothing, not wishing to spoil his good mood.

The next day Bartek had the sign maker make a big sign. When it was ready, he hung it over the door of his hut. It said:

HERE LIVES BARTEK
THE FAMOUS DOCTOR

At first the villagers just laughed. They would stand for hours looking at the sign and laugh very hard. But during that first week after Bartek came back a young girl took sick, and her mother, at night when she could not be seen, came to Bartek's hut.

"You must help my daughter," she begged.

Bartek followed her to her house. As soon as he came into the sick girl's room, he saw Death. She was standing at the girl's feet. Bartek did all he could to cheer up the family.

"You have nothing to fear," he told them. "She will be fine."

But they didn't believe him.

"Can't you give her some medicine?" they asked. "What kind of a doctor are you?"

"There is no need for medicine," he said, "but if it would make you feel better, I will mix some herbs and bring them to you.

And he did just that. But even before he came back with the herbs, the girl was out of bed and playing with her doll.

That was the beginning of his fame.

He cured all those who had Death standing at their feet. Those with Death standing at their heads he refused to attend.

"It's no use," he would say. "No one can do anything against Death."

And he was always right.

His fame spread fast all over Poland. People came to him from near and far and sometimes had him fetched. And whatever he predicted always came to pass.

One day when he was coming back from one of his trips, a neighbor met him halfway to his house.

"Your mother suddenly took sick," the neighbor said.

Bartek's heart leaped with fear. He raced to her side. She was lying in bed, her face white, and Bartek was so worried, so frightened, that he did not notice Death or where she stood. He bent over his mother.

"You will be all right," he said.

She smiled weakly at him.

"You are always right but not this time. I've grown too old," she said.

He looked up then. And saw her. Death was standing at his mother's head.

"No!" he shouted. "Pass on to the foot of the bed."

"I won't," Death said.

Bartek grew pale and begged her again.

"You have only to take a few steps."

"Impossible," said Death.

"Please," Bartek cried. "She's my mother. She's the only family I have. She worked so hard all her life. I gave her no joy."

"Stop asking me for that which I cannot do," said Death.

"I begged you," Bartek cried. "Now I order you to stand at her feet."

"No," Death said.

"But what can it matter to you?" Bartek cried. "It would be just as easy for you to stand at her feet."

"Today I must stand at the head."

"Listen, Death." Bartek grabbed her thin arm. "The very next patient I have, I shall give him to you. But spare my mother. Let her live."

"No," said Death.

Bartek grew very angry.

"Is that your last word?" he shouted.

"It is my last word."

Bartek bent down and lifted his mother in his arms. In a twinkling of an eye he turned her around so that her feet now rested on the pillows, while her head was at the end of the bed. Death was no longer at her head. She stood at his mother's feet.

And Death, for the first time, was cheated of her due.

A few days later Bartek's mother was back at the oven, making fresh bread for her son, whom she loved more than ever before. And Bartek was very pleased with himself.

Ding! Ding! Dong!

Bartek turned around at the sound of the bell. Death was seated by the side of the road.

"Follow me," she said.

Bartek fell into step behind Death. He was surprised that for once the old woman's bell worked. It kept ringing as they walked. And they walked for several days. They crossed rivers and mountains and valleys. And then they reached a ravine and plunged into an underground passageway. From then on they walked in complete darkness. Bartek would have lost his way had he not had the bell to guide him. It kept ringing without a pause.

Ding! Ding! Dong!

Suddenly they were inside a grotto illuminated by a thousand flickering lights. They were all over, in the hollows of the rocks, on every ledge, on the ground, in every nook and cranny. And the flickering, Bartek now saw, came from candles. Some of them burned with a high flame, some were sputtering, on the point of going out, and some had just gone out and were still smoking or were quite dead.

"This is my kingdom," Death said. "Do you see all those flames? They are human souls. When a man or a woman or a child is about to die, the candle goes out and I leave my kingdom to go to them. No one dies without my being there. And no one dies without hearing my bell. When they hear the bell they can make peace with God. It's their warning that they will die."

Bartek looked down at the little bell in the old woman's hand. It still kept ringing and he shuddered.

"Look here," Death was saying. "Here is your mother's candle. It is burning bright, and yet, a few days ago, it had gone out. And look here." She pointed to a candle that had just gone out. "This is yours."

Bartek looked at the smoke from the dead candle and then at Death.

"You saved your mother," Death said. "But in exchange you must give me your life."

"It is only fair," Bartek said. "She lived her life for me. I should die for her."

Ding! Ding! Dong! went the bell once more, and then he could hear it no longer.

He was dead.

RICHARD WILBUR

Opposites

What is the opposite of *string?*
It's *gnirts*, which doesn't mean a thing.
What is the opposite of *two?*
A lonely me, a lonely you.
The opposite of *doughnut?* Wait
A minute while I meditate.
This isn't easy. Ah, I've found it!
A cookie with a hole around it.
The opposite of *opposite?*
That's much too difficult. I quit.

P. L. TRAVERS

When P. L. Travers's first book about Mary Poppins came out she received a letter from her sister. In it her sister said that when they were both small children Pamela (that's Ms. Travers's first name) had told her some of these same stories. But Ms. Travers doesn't remember that at all. She says she began to write the Mary Poppins stories to amuse herself while recovering from an illness.

There are five books in the series: *Mary Poppins; Mary Poppins Comes Back; Mary Poppins Opens the Door; Mary Poppins in the Park; Mary Poppins in Cherry Tree Lane.* The selection below is taken from the first of the series.

Probably some of you know about Mary Poppins from the Julie Andrews film. Miss Andrews is lovely, but in my opinion Mary Poppins isn't. She looks "rather like a wooden Dutch doll." Also Mary Poppins is not a lady, not the way Julie Andrews is.

In the book the setting is London at a time when some people employed not only a children's nurse but a cook, maid, and boy-of-all-work. To the Bankses and their two older children, Jane and Michael, comes the new Nannie, Mary Poppins, blown in by the wind, with her umbrella and a bag of magic tricks. She starts her job by sliding *up* the banister. Mary Poppins is strict, no-nonsense, a kind of good witch. The children feel at once that she is "frightening and at the same time most exciting."

I like especially the story called "Laughing Gas," and here it is.

Laughing Gas

"ARE YOU quite sure he will be at home?" said Jane, as they got off the Bus, she and Michael and Mary Poppins.

"Would my Uncle ask me to bring you to tea if he intended to go out, I'd like to know?" said Mary Poppins, who was evidently very offended by the question. She was wearing her blue coat with the silver buttons and the blue hat to match, and on the days when she wore these it was the easiest thing in the world to offend her.

All three of them were on the way to pay a visit to Mary Poppins's uncle, Mr. Wigg, and Jane and Michael had looked forward to the trip for so long that they were more than half afraid that Mr. Wigg might not be in, after all.

"Why is he called Mr. Wigg—does he wear one?" asked Michael, hurrying along beside Mary Poppins.

"He is called Mr. Wigg because Mr. Wigg is his name. And he doesn't wear one. He is bald," said Mary Poppins. "And if I have any more questions, we will just go Back Home." And she sniffed her usual sniff of displeasure.

Jane and Michael looked at each other and frowned. And the frown meant: "Don't let's ask her anything else or we'll never get there."

Mary Poppins put her hat straight at the Tobacconist's Shop at the corner. It had one of those curious windows where there seem to be three of you instead of one, so that if you look long enough at them you begin to feel you are not yourself but a whole crowd of somebody else. Mary Poppins sighed with pleasure, however, when she saw three of herself, each wearing a blue coat with silver buttons and a blue hat to match. She thought it was such a lovely sight that she wished there had been a dozen of her or even thirty. The more Mary Poppins the better.

"Come along," she said sternly, as though they had kept *her* waiting. Then they turned the corner and pulled the bell of Number Three, Robertson Road. Jane and Michael could hear it faintly echoing from a long way away and they knew that in one minute, or two at the most, they would be having tea with Mary Poppins's uncle, Mr. Wigg, for the first time ever.

"If he's in, of course," Jane said to Michael in a whisper.

At that moment the door flew open and a thin, watery-looking lady appeared.

"Is he in?" said Michael quickly.

"I'll thank you," said Mary Poppins, giving him a terrible glance, "to let *me* do the talking."

"How do you do, Mrs. Wigg," said Jane politely.

"Mrs. Wigg!" said the thin lady, in a voice even thinner than herself. "How dare you call me Mrs. Wigg? No, thank you! I'm plain Miss Persimmon *and* proud of it. Mrs. Wigg indeed!" She seemed to be quite upset, and they thought Mr. Wigg must be a very odd person if Miss Persimmon was so glad not to be Mrs. Wigg.

"Straight up and first door on the landing," said Miss Persimmon, and she went hurrying away down the passage saying "Mrs. Wigg indeed!" to herself in a high, thin, outraged voice.

Jane and Michael followed Mary Poppins upstairs. Mary Poppins knocked at the door.

"Come in! Come in! And welcome!" called a loud, cheery voice from inside. Jane's heart was pitter-pattering with excitement.

"He *is* in!" she signaled to Michael with a look.

Mary Poppins opened the door and pushed them in front of her. A large cheerful room lay before them. At one end of it a fire was burning brightly and in the center stood an enormous table laid for tea—four cups and saucers, piles of bread and butter, crumpets, coconut cakes and a large plum cake with pink icing.

"Well, this is indeed a Pleasure," a huge voice greeted them, and Jane and Michael looked round for its owner. He was nowhere to be seen. The room appeared to be quite empty. Then they heard Mary Poppins saying crossly:

"Oh, Uncle Albert—not *again?* It's not your birthday, is it?"

And as she spoke she looked up at the ceiling. Jane and Michael looked up too and to their surprise saw a round, fat, bald man who was hanging in the air without holding on to anything. Indeed, he appeared to be *sitting* on the air, for his legs were crossed and he had just put down the newspaper which he had been reading when they came in.

"My dear," said Mr. Wigg, smiling down at the children, and looking apologetically at Mary Poppins, "I'm very sorry, but I'm afraid it *is* my birthday."

"Tch, tch, tch!" said Mary Poppins.

"I only remembered last night and there was no time then to send you a postcard asking you to come another day. Very distressing, isn't it?" he said, looking down at Jane and Michael.

"I can see you're rather surprised," said Mr. Wigg. And, indeed, their mouths were so wide open with astonishment that Mr. Wigg, if he had been a little smaller, might almost have fallen into one of them.

"I'd better explain, I think," Mr. Wigg went on calmly. "You see, it's this way. I'm a cheerful sort of man and very disposed to laughter. You wouldn't believe, either of you, the number of things that strike me as being funny. I can laugh at pretty nearly everything, I can."

And with that Mr. Wigg began to bob up and down, shaking with laughter at the thought of his own cheerfulness.

"Uncle Albert!" said Mary Poppins, and Mr. Wigg stopped laughing with a jerk.

"Oh, beg pardon, my dear. Where was I? Oh, yes. Well, the funny thing about me is—all right, Mary, I won't laugh if I can help it!—that whenever my birthday falls on a Friday, well, it's all up with me. Absolutely U.P.," said Mr. Wigg.

"But why—?" began Jane.

"But how—?" began Michael.

"Well, you see, if I laugh on that particular day I become so filled with Laughing Gas that I simply can't keep on the ground. Even if I smile it happens. The first funny thought, and I'm up like a balloon. And until I can think of something serious I can't get down again." Mr. Wigg began to chuckle at that, but he caught sight of Mary Poppins's face and stopped the chuckle, and continued:

"It's awkward, of course, but not unpleasant. Never happens to either of you, I suppose?"

Jane and Michael shook their heads.

"No, I thought not. It seems to be my own special habit. Once, after I'd been to the Circus the night before, I laughed so much that—would you believe it?—I was up here for a whole twelve hours, and couldn't get down till the last stroke of midnight. Then, of course, I came down with a flop because it was Saturday and not my birthday anymore. It's rather odd, isn't it? Not to say funny?

"And now here it is Friday again and my birthday, and you two and Mary P. to visit me. Oh, Lordy, Lordy, don't make me laugh, I beg of you—" But although Jane and Michael had done nothing very amusing, except to stare at him in astonishment, Mr. Wigg began to laugh again loudly, and as he laughed he went bouncing and bobbing about in the air, with the newspaper rattling in his hand and his spectacles half on and half off his nose.

He looked so comic, floundering in the air like a great human bubble, clutching at the ceiling sometimes and sometimes at the gas bracket as he passed it, that Jane and Michael, though they were trying hard to be polite, just couldn't help doing what they did. They laughed. *And* they laughed. They shut their mouths tight to prevent the laughter escaping, but that didn't do any good. And presently they were rolling over and over on the floor, squealing and shrieking with laughter.

"Really!" said Mary Poppins. "Really, *such* behavior!"

"I can't help it, I can't help it!" shrieked Michael as he rolled into the fender. "It's so terribly funny. Oh, Jane, *isn't* it funny?"

Jane did not reply, for a curious thing was happening to her. As she laughed she felt herself growing lighter and lighter, just as though she were being pumped full of air. It was a curious and delicious feeling and it made her want to laugh all the more. And then suddenly, with a bouncing bound, she felt herself jumping through the air. Michael, to his astonishment, saw her go soaring up through the room. With a little bump her head touched the ceiling and then she went bouncing along it till she reached Mr. Wigg.

"*Well!*" said Mr. Wigg, looking very surprised indeed. "Don't tell me it's *your* birthday, too?" Jane shook her head.

"It's not? Then this Laughing Gas must be catching! Hi—whoa there, look out for the mantelpiece!" This was to Michael, who had suddenly risen from the floor and was swooping through the air, roaring with laughter, and just grazing the china ornaments on the mantelpiece as he passed. He landed with a bounce right on Mr. Wigg's knee.

"How do you do," said Mr. Wigg, heartily shaking Michael by the hand. "I call this really friendly of you—bless my soul, I do! To come up to me since I couldn't come down to you—eh?" And then he and Michael looked at each other and flung back their heads and simply howled with laughter.

"I say," said Mr. Wigg to Jane, as he wiped his eyes. "You'll be thinking I have the worst manners in the world. You're standing and you ought to be sitting—a nice young lady like you. I'm afraid I can't offer you a chair up here, but I think you'll find the air quite comfortable to sit on. I do."

Jane tried it and found she could sit down quite comfortably on the air. She took off her hat and laid it down beside her and it hung there in space without any support at all.

"That's right," said Mr. Wigg. Then he turned and looked down at Mary Poppins.

"Well, Mary, we're fixed. And now I can inquire about *you*, my dear. I must say, I am very glad to welcome you and my two young friends here today—why, Mary, you're frowning. I'm afraid you don't approve of—er—all this."

He waved his hand at Jane and Michael, and said hurriedly:

"I apologize, Mary, my dear. But you know how it is with me. Still, I must say I never thought my two young friends here would catch it, really I didn't, Mary! I suppose I should have asked them for another day or tried to think of something sad or something—"

"Well, I must say," said Mary Poppins primly, "that I have never in my life seen such a sight. And at your age, Uncle—"

"Mary Poppins, Mary Poppins, do come up!" interrupted Michael. "Think of something funny and you'll find it's quite easy."

"Ah, now do, Mary!" said Mr. Wigg persuasively.

"We're lonely up here without you!" said Jane, and held out her arms towards Mary Poppins. "*Do* think of something funny!"

"Ah, *she* doesn't need to," said Mr. Wigg sighing. "She can come up if she wants to, even without laughing—and she knows it." And he looked mysteriously and secretly at Mary Poppins as she stood down there on the hearth rug.

"Well," said Mary Poppins, "it's all very silly and undignified, but, since you're all up there and don't seem able to get down, I suppose I'd better come up, too."

With that, to the surprise of Jane and Michael, she put her hands down at her sides and without a laugh, without even the faintest glimmer of a smile, she shot up through the air and sat down beside Jane.

"How many times, I should like to know," she said snappily, "have I told you to take off your coat when you come into a hot room?" And she unbuttoned Jane's coat and laid it neatly on the air beside the hat.

"That's right, Mary, that's right," said Mr. Wigg contentedly, as he leant down and put his spectacles on the mantelpiece. "Now we're all comfortable—"

"There's comfort *and* comfort," sniffed Mary Poppins.

"And we can have tea," Mr. Wigg went on, apparently not noticing her remark. And then a startled look came over his face.

"My goodness!" he said. "How dreadful! I've just realized—that table's down there and we're up here. What *are* we going to do? We're here and it's there. It's an awful tragedy—awful! But oh, it's terribly comic!" And he hid his face in his handkerchief and laughed loudly into it. Jane and Michael, though they did not want to miss the crumpets and the cakes, couldn't help laughing too, because Mr. Wigg's mirth was so infectious.

Mr. Wigg dried his eyes.

"There's only one thing for it," he said. "We must think of something serious. Something sad, very sad. And then we shall be able to get down. Now—one, two, three! Something *very* sad, mind you!"

They thought and thought, with their chins on their hands.

Michael thought of school, and that one day he would have to go there. But even that seemed funny today and he had to laugh.

Jane thought: "I shall be grown up in another fourteen years!" But that didn't sound sad at all but quite nice and rather funny. She could not help smiling at the thought of herself grown up, with long skirts and a handbag.

"There was my poor old Aunt Emily," thought Mr. Wigg out loud. "She was run over by an omnibus. Sad. Very sad. Unbearably sad. Poor Aunt Emily. But they saved her umbrella. That was funny, wasn't it?" And before he knew where he was, he was heaving and trembling and bursting with laughter at the thought of Aunt Emily's umbrella.

"It's no good," he said, blowing his nose. "I give it up. And my young friends here seem to be no better at sadness than I am. Mary, can't *you* do something? We want our tea."

To this day Jane and Michael cannot be sure of what happened then. All they know for certain is that, as soon as Mr. Wigg had appealed to Mary Poppins, the table below began to wriggle on its legs. Presently it was swaying dangerously, and then with a rattle of china and with cakes lurching off their plates onto the cloth, the table came soaring through the room, gave one graceful turn, and landed beside them so that Mr. Wigg was at its head.

"Good girl!" said Mr. Wigg, smiling proudly upon her. "I knew you'd fix something. Now, will you take the foot of the table and pour out, Mary? And the guests on either side of me. That's the idea," he said, as Michael ran bobbing through the air and sat down on Mr. Wigg's right. Jane was at his left hand. There they were, all together, up in the air and the table between them. Not a single piece of bread-and-butter or a lump of sugar had been left behind.

Mr. Wigg smiled contentedly.

"It is usual, I think, to begin with bread-and-butter," he said to Jane and Michael, "but as it's my birthday we will begin the wrong way—which I always think is the *right* way—with the Cake!"

And he cut a large slice for everybody.

"More tea?" he said to Jane. But before she had time to reply there was a quick, sharp knock at the door.

"Come in!" called Mr. Wigg.

The door opened, and there stood Miss Persimmon with a jug of hot water on a tray.

"I thought, Mr. Wigg," she began, looking searchingly round the room, "you'd be wanting some more hot—Well, I never! I simply *never!"* she said, as she caught sight of them all seated on the air round the table. "Such goings-on I never did see. In all my born days I never saw such. I'm sure, Mr. Wigg, I always knew *you* were a bit odd. But I've closed my eyes to it—being as how you paid your rent regular. But such behavior as this—having tea in the air with your guests—Mr. Wigg, sir, I'm astonished at you! It's that undignified, and for a gentleman of your age—I never did—"

"But perhaps you will, Miss Persimmon!" said Michael.

"Will what?" said Miss Persimmon haughtily.

"Catch the Laughing Gas, as we did," said Michael.

Miss Persimmon flung back her head scornfully.

"I hope, young man," she retorted, "I have more respect for myself than to go bouncing about in the air like a rubber ball on the end of a bat. I'll stay on my own feet, thank you, or my name's not Amy Persimmon, and—oh dear, oh *dear*, my goodness, oh *DEAR*—what *is* the matter? I can't walk, I'm going, I—oh, help, *HELP!*"

For Miss Persimmon, quite against her will, was off the ground and was stumbling through the air, rolling from side to side like a very thin barrel, balancing the tray in her hand. She was almost weeping with distress as she arrived at the table and put down her jug of hot water.

"Thank you," said Mary Poppins in a calm, very polite voice.

Then Miss Persimmon turned and went wafting down again, murmuring as she went: "So undignified—and me a well-behaved, steady-going woman. I must see a doctor—"

When she touched the floor she ran hurriedly out of the room, wringing her hands, and not giving a single glance backwards.

"So undignified!" they heard her moaning as she shut the door behind her.

"Her name can't be Amy Persimmon, because she *didn't* stay on her own feet!" whispered Jane to Michael.

But Mr. Wigg was looking at Mary Poppins—a curious look, half amused, half accusing.

"Mary, Mary, you shouldn't—bless my soul, you shouldn't, Mary. The poor old body will never get over it. But, oh, my Goodness, didn't she look funny waddling through the air—my Gracious Goodness, but didn't she?"

And he and Jane and Michael were off again, rolling about the air, clutching their sides and gasping with laughter at the thought of how funny Miss Persimmon had looked.

"Oh dear!" said Michael. "Don't make me laugh any more. I can't stand it! I shall break!"

"Oh, oh, oh!" cried Jane, as she gasped for breath, with her hand over her heart.

"Oh, my Gracious, Glorious, Galumphing Goodness!" roared Mr. Wigg, dabbing his eyes with the tail of his coat because he couldn't find his handkerchief.

"IT IS TIME TO GO HOME." Mary Poppins's voice sounded above the roars of laughter like a trumpet.

And suddenly, with a rush, Jane and Michael and Mr. Wigg came down. They landed on the floor with a huge bump, all together. The thought that they would have to go home was the first sad thought of the afternoon, and the moment it was in their minds the Laughing Gas went out of them.

Jane and Michael sighed as they watched Mary Poppins come slowly down the air, carrying Jane's coat and hat.

Mr. Wigg sighed, too. A great, long, heavy sigh.

"Well, isn't that a pity?" he said soberly. "It's very sad that you've got to go home. I never enjoyed an afternoon so much—did you?"

"Never," said Michael sadly, feeling how dull it was to be down on the earth again with no Laughing Gas inside him.

"Never, never," said Jane, as she stood on tiptoe and kissed Mr. Wigg's withered-apple cheeks. "Never, never, never, never . . . !"

KAYE STARBIRD

Eat-It-All Elaine

I went away last August
To summer camp in Maine,
And there I met a camper
Called Eat-it-all Elaine.
Although Elaine was quiet,
She liked to cause a stir
By acting out the nickname
Her campmates gave to her.

The day of our arrival
At Cabin Number Three
When girls kept coming over
To greet Elaine and me,
She took a piece of Kleenex
And calmly chewed it up,
Then strolled outside the cabin
And ate a buttercup.

Elaine, from that day forward,
Was always in command.
On hikes, she'd eat some birch bark
On swims, she'd eat some sand.
At meals, she'd swallow prune pits
And never have a pain,
While everyone around her
Would giggle, "Oh, Elaine!"

One morning, berry picking,
A bug was in her pail,
And though we thought for certain
Her appetite would fail,
Elaine said, "Hmm, a stinkbug."
And while we murmured, "Ooh,"
She ate her pail of berries
And ate the stinkbug, too.

The night of Final Banquet
When counselors were handing
Awards to different children
Whom they believed outstanding,
To every *thinking* person
At summer camp in Maine
The Most Outstanding Camper
Was Eat-it-all Elaine.

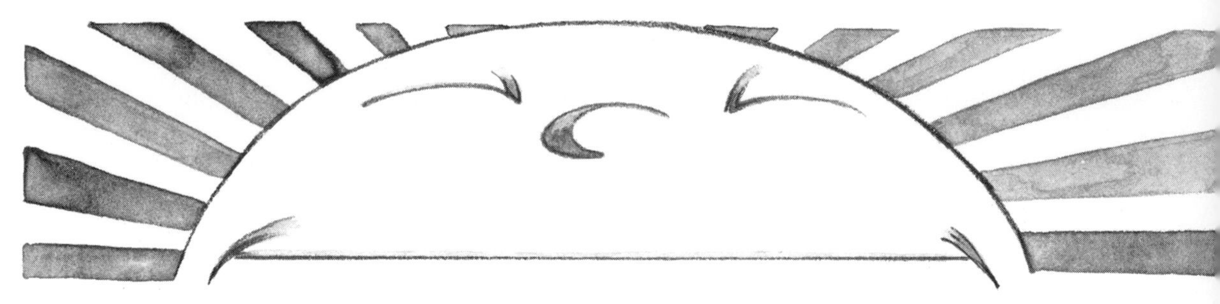

JAMES THURBER

Many Moons

ONCE UPON A TIME, in a kingdom by the sea, there lived a little princess named Lenore. She was ten years old, going on eleven. One day Lenore fell ill of a surfeit of raspberry tarts and took to her bed.

The royal physician came to see her and took her temperature and felt her pulse and made her stick out her tongue. The royal physician was worried. He sent for the king, Lenore's father, and the king came to see her.

"I will get you anything your heart desires," the king said. "Is there anything your heart desires?"

"Yes," said the princess. "I want the moon. If I can have the moon, I will be well again."

Now the king had a great many wise men who always got for him anything he wanted, so he told his daughter that she could have the moon. Then he went to the throne room and pulled a bell cord, three long pulls and a short pull, and presently the lord high chamberlain came into the room.

The lord high chamberlain was a large, fat man who wore thick glasses which made his eyes seem twice as big as they really were. This made the lord high chamberlain seem twice as wise as he really was.

"I want you to get the moon," said the king. "The Princess Lenore wants the moon. If she can have the moon, she will get well again."

"The moon?" exclaimed the lord high chamberlain, his eyes widening. This made him look four times as wise as he really was.

"Yes, the moon," said the king. "M-o-o-n, moon. Get it tonight, tomorrow at the latest."

The lord high chamberlain wiped his forehead with a handkerchief and then blew his nose loudly. "I have got a great many things for you in my time, Your Majesty," he said. "It just happens that I have with me a list of the things I have got for you in my time." He pulled a long scroll of parchment out of his pocket. "Let me see, now." He glanced at the list, frowning. "I have got ivory, apes, and peacocks, rubies, opals, and emeralds, black orchids, pink elephants, and blue poodles, gold bugs, scarabs, and flies in amber, humming-birds' tongues, angels' feathers, and unicorns' horns, giants, midgets, and mermaids, frankincense, ambergris, and myrrh, troubadours, minstrels, and dancing women, a pound of butter, two dozen eggs, and a sack of sugar—sorry, my wife wrote that in there."

"I don't remember any blue poodles," said the king.

"It says blue poodles right here on the list, and they are checked off with a little check mark," said the lord high chamberlain. "So there must have been blue poodles. You just forget."

"Never mind the blue poodles," said the king. "What I want now is the moon."

"I have sent as far as Samarkand and Araby and Zanzibar to get things for you, Your Majesty," said the lord high chamberlain. "But the moon is out of the question. It is thirty-five thousand miles away and it is bigger than the room the princess lies in. Furthermore, it is made of molten copper. I cannot get the moon for you. Blue poodles, yes; the moon, no."

The king flew into a rage and told the lord high chamberlain to leave the room and to send the royal wizard to the throne room.

The royal wizard was a little, thin man with a long face. He wore a high red peaked hat covered with silver stars, and a long blue robe covered with golden owls. His face grew very pale when the king told him that he wanted the moon for his little daughter, and that he expected the royal wizard to get it.

"I have worked a great deal of magic for you in my time, Your Majesty," said the royal wizard. "As a matter of fact, I just happen to have in my pocket a list of wizardries I have performed for you." He drew a paper from a deep pocket of his robe. "It begins: 'Dear Royal Wizard: I am returning herewith the so-called philosopher's stone which you claimed'—no, that isn't it." The royal wizard brought a long scroll of parchment from another pocket of his robe. "Here it is," he said. "Now, let's see. I have squeezed blood out of turnips for you, and turnips out of blood. I have produced rabbits out of silk hats, and silk hats out of rabbits. I have conjured up flowers, tambourines, and doves out of nowhere, and nowhere out of flowers, tambourines, and doves. I have brought you divining rods, magic wands, and crystal spheres in which to behold the future. I have compounded philters, unguents, and potions, to cure heartbreak, surfeit, and ringing in the ears. I have made you my own special mixture of wolfbane, nightshade, and eagles' tears, to ward off witches, demons, and things that go bump in the night. I have given you seven-league boots, the golden touch, and a cloak of invisibility—"

"It didn't work," said the king. "The cloak of invisibility didn't work."

"Yes, it did," said the royal wizard.

"No, it didn't," said the king. "I kept bumping into things, the same as ever."

"The cloak is supposed to make you invisible," said the royal wizard. "It is not supposed to keep you from bumping into things."

"All I know is, I kept bumping into things," said the king.

The royal wizard looked at his list again. "I got you," he said, "horns from Elfland, sand from the Sandman, and gold from the rainbow. Also a spool of thread, a paper of needles, and a lump of beeswax—sorry, those are things my wife wrote down for me to get her."

"What I want you to do now," said the king, "is to get me the moon. The Princess Lenore wants the moon, and when she gets it, she will be well again."

"Nobody can get the moon," said the royal wizard. "It is a hundred and fifty thousand miles away, and it is made of green cheese, and it is twice as big as this palace."

The king flew into another rage and sent the royal wizard back to his cave. Then he rang a gong and summoned the royal mathematician.

The royal mathematician was a bald-headed, nearsighted man, with a skullcap on his head and a pencil behind each ear. He wore a black suit with white numbers on it.

"I don't want to hear a long list of all the things you have figured out for me since 1907," the king said to him. "I want you to figure out right now how to get the moon for the Princess Lenore. When she gets the moon, she will be well again."

"I am glad you mentioned all the things I have figured out for you since 1907," said the royal mathematician. "It so happens that I have a list of them with me."

He pulled a long scroll of parchment out of a pocket and looked at it. "Now let me see. I have figured out for you the distance between the horns of a dilemma, night and day, and A and Z. I have computed how far is Up, how long it takes to get to Away, and what becomes of Gone. I have discovered the length of the sea serpent, the price of the priceless, and the square of the hippopotamus. I know where you are when you are at Sixes and Sevens, how much Is you have to have to make an Are, and how many birds you can catch with the salt in the ocean—187,796,132, if it would interest you to know."

"There aren't that many birds," said the king.

"I didn't say there were," said the royal mathematician. "I said if there were."

"I don't want to hear about seven hundred million imaginary birds," said the king. "I want you to get the moon for the Princess Lenore."

"The moon is three hundred thousand miles away," said the royal mathematician. "It is round and flat like a coin, only it is made of asbestos, and it is half the size of this kingdom. Furthermore, it is pasted on the sky. Nobody can get the moon."

The king flew into still another rage and sent the royal mathematician away. Then he rang for the court jester. The jester came bounding into the throne room in his motley and his cap and bells, and sat at the foot of the throne.

"What can I do for you, Your Majesty?" asked the court jester.

"Nobody can do anything for me," said the king mournfully. "The Princess Lenore wants the moon, and she cannot be well till she gets it, but nobody can get it for her. Every time I ask anybody for the moon, it gets larger and farther away. There is nothing you can do for me except play on your lute. Something sad."

"How big do they say the moon is," asked the court jester, "and how far away?"

"The lord high chamberlain says it is thirty-five thousand miles away, and bigger than the Princess Lenore's room," said the king. "The royal wizard says it is a hundred and fifty thousand miles away, and twice as big as this palace. The royal mathematician says it is three hundred thousand miles away, and half the size of this kingdom."

The court jester strummed on his lute for a little while. "They are all wise men," he said, "and so they must all be right. If they are all right, then the moon must be just as large and as far away as each person thinks it is. The thing to do is find out how big the Princess Lenore thinks it is, and how far away."

"I never thought of that," said the king.

"I will go and ask her, Your Majesty," said the court jester. And he crept softly into the little girl's room.

The Princess Lenore was awake, and she was glad to see the court jester, but her face was very pale and her voice very weak.

"Have you brought the moon to me?" she asked.

"Not yet," said the court jester, "but I will get it for you right away. How big do you think it is?"

"It is just a little smaller than my thumbnail," she said, "for when I hold my thumbnail up at the moon, it just covers it."

"And how far away is it?" asked the court jester.

"It is not as high as the big tree outside my window," said the princess, "for sometimes it gets caught in the top branches."

"It will be very easy to get the moon for you," said the court jester. "I will climb the tree tonight when it gets caught in the top branches and bring it to you."

Then he thought of something else. "What is the moon made of, princess?" he asked.

"Oh," she said, "it's made of gold, of course, silly."

The court jester left the Princess Lenore's room and went to see the royal goldsmith. He had the royal goldsmith make a tiny round golden moon just a little smaller than the thumbnail of the Princess Lenore. Then he had him string it on a golden chain so the princess could wear it around her neck.

"What is this thing I have made?" asked the royal goldsmith when he had finished it.

"You have made the moon," said the court jester. "That is the moon."

"But the moon," said the royal goldsmith, "is five hundred thousand miles away and is made of bronze and is round like a marble."

"That's what you think," said the court jester as he went away with the moon.

The court jester took the moon to the Princess Lenore, and she was overjoyed. The next day she was well again and could get up and go out in the gardens to play.

But the king's worries were not yet over. He knew that the moon would shine in the sky again that night, and he did not want the Princess Lenore to see it. If she did, she would know that the moon she wore on a chain around her neck was not the real moon.

So the king sent for the lord high chamberlain and said: "We must keep the Princess Lenore from seeing the moon when it shines in the sky tonight. Think of something."

The lord high chamberlain tapped his forehead with his fingers thoughtfully and said: "I know just the thing. We can make some dark glasses for the Princess Lenore. We can make them so dark that she will not be able to see anything at all through them. Then she will not be able to see the moon when it shines in the sky."

This made the king very angry, and he shook his head from side to side. "If she wore dark glasses, she would bump into things," he said, "and then she would be ill again." So he sent the lord high chamberlain away and called the royal wizard.

"We must hide the moon," said the king, "so that the Princess Lenore will not see it when it shines in the sky tonight. How are we going to do that?"

The royal wizard stood on his hands and then he stood on his head and then he stood on his feet again. "I know what we can do," he said. "We can stretch some black velvet curtains on poles. The curtains will cover all the palace gardens like a circus tent, and the Princess Lenore will not be able to see through them, so she will not see the moon in the sky."

The king was so angry at this that he waved his arms around. "Black velvet curtains would keep out the air," he said. "The Princess Lenore would not be able to breathe, and she would be ill again." So he sent the royal wizard away and summoned the royal mathematician.

"We must do something," said the king, "so that the Princess Lenore will not see the moon when it shines in the sky tonight. If you know so much, figure out a way to do that."

The royal mathematician walked around in a circle, and then he walked around in a square, and then he stood still. "I have it!" he said. "We can set off fireworks in the gardens every night. We will make a lot of silver fountains and golden cascades, and when they go off, they will fill the sky with so many sparks that it will be as light as day and the Princess Lenore will not be able to see the moon."

The king flew into such a rage that he began jumping up and down. "Fireworks would keep the Princess Lenore awake," he said. "She would not get any sleep at all and she would be ill again." So the king sent the royal mathematician away.

When he looked up again, it was dark outside and he saw the bright rim of the moon just peeping over the horizon. He jumped up in a great fright and rang for the court jester. The court jester came bounding into the room and sat down at the foot of the throne.

"What can I do for you, Your Majesty?" he asked.

"Nobody can do anything for me," said the king, mournfully. "The moon is coming up again. It will shine into the Princess Lenore's bedroom, and she will know it is still in the sky and that she does not wear it on a golden chain around her neck. Play me something on your lute, something very sad, for when the princess sees the moon, she will be ill again."

The court jester strummed on his lute. "What do your wise men say?" he asked.

"They can think of no way to hide the moon that will not make the Princess Lenore ill," said the king.

The court jester played another song, very softly. "Your wise men know everything," he said, "and if they cannot hide the moon, then it cannot be hidden."

The king put his head in his hands again and sighed. Suddenly he jumped up from his throne and pointed to the windows. "Look!" he cried. "The moon is already shining into the Princess Lenore's bedroom. Who can explain how the moon can be shining in the sky when it is hanging on a golden chain around her neck?"

The court jester stopped playing on his lute. "Who could explain how to get the moon when your wise men said it was too large and too far away? It was the Princess Lenore. Therefore, the Princess Lenore is wiser than your wise men and knows more about the moon than they do. So I will ask *her*." And before the king could stop him, the court jester slipped quietly out of the throne room and up the wide marble staircase to the Princess Lenore's bedroom.

The princess was lying in bed but she was wide awake and she was looking out the window at the moon shining in the sky. Shining in her hand was the moon the court jester had got for her. He looked very sad, and there seemed to be tears in his eyes.

"Tell me, Princess Lenore," he said mournfully, "how can the moon be shining in the sky when it is hanging on a golden chain around your neck?"

The princess looked at him and laughed. "That is easy, silly," she said. "When I lose a tooth, a new one grows in its place, doesn't it?"

"Of course," said the court jester. "And when the unicorn loses his horn in the forest, a new one grows in the middle of his forehead."

"That is right," said the princess. "And when the royal gardener cuts the flowers in the garden, other flowers come to take their place."

"I should have thought of that," said the court jester, "for it is the same way with the daylight."

"And it is the same way with the moon," said the Princess Lenore. "I guess it is the same way with everything." Her voice became very low and faded away, and the court jester saw that she was asleep. Gently he tucked the covers in around the sleeping princess.

But before he left the room, he went over to the window and winked at the moon, for it seemed to the court jester that the moon had winked at him.

SHEL SILVERSTEIN

The Acrobats

I'll swing
By my ankles,
She'll cling
To your knees
As you hang
By your nose
From a high-up
Trapeze.
But just one thing, please,
As we float through the breeze—
Don't sneeze.

The Battle

Would you like to hear
Of the terrible night
When I bravely fought the—
No?
All right.

The Land of Happy

Have you been to the Land of Happy,
Where everyone's happy all day,
Where they joke and they sing
Of the happiest things,
And everything's jolly and gay?
There's no one unhappy in Happy,
There's laughter and smiles galore.
I have been to the Land of Happy—
What a bore!

A Poem on the Neck of a Running Giraffe

PLEASE
DONOT
MAKE F
UN OF
ME AN
D PLEAS
EDON'T
LAUGH
IT ISN'T
EASY T
O WRIT
E A PO
EM ON
THE NE
CK OF
A RUN
NING
GIRA
FFE.

BEATRICE TANAKA

Of Ships and Trees
A Folktale from Vietnam

WHEN SOMEONE comes home after a long trip, the villagers who have never traveled farther than the neighboring market always listen wide-eyed to the traveler's tales. It is an invitation to brag, and some returning travelers just can't resist the temptation.

One young man, back from a long journey, once told his admiring audience a new story every evening—each story stranger and more wonderful than the last.

"I once saw a ship in a foreign port," he said one evening, "and it was sooooo enormous you couldn't even imagine its size if you tried! Why, a young boy who set out from the prow would arrive at the stern an old, white-haired man."

"Oooooooh!" gasped the audience.

"What is so wonderful about that?" asked a woodcutter, who was getting annoyed with these nightly bragging sessions. "In the forest not far from here, I once saw some trees so huge, sooo old, sooooo tall, that a bird that had been flying for ten years hadn't even reached halfway to the top."

"Liar!" cried the traveler. "Trees like that don't exist."

The woodcutter smiled. "Then where do you suppose the carpenters found the wood for your ship's mast?" he asked.

CHRISTINA ROSSETTI

Who Has Seen the Wind?

Who has seen the wind?
  Neither I nor you:
But when the leaves hang trembling
  The wind is passing thro'.

Who has seen the wind?
  Neither you nor I:
But when the trees bow down their heads
  The wind is passing by.

GEORGE SELDEN

George Selden's *Cricket in Times Square* starts with Tucker the mouse who lives in an abandoned drainpipe in the Times Square subway station in New York City. He's a 100 percent city mouse, a bit of a wisecracker, tough, street-wise. In the station is a not very prosperous newsstand tended by Mama and Papa Bellini and their son Mario. One evening, while Mario is in charge of the stand, both he and Tucker hear a very unsubwayish sound—"like a harp that had been plucked suddenly." It's a cricket. Mario puts him in a matchbox to keep as a pet.

The episode following introduces us to Tucker, Chester Cricket, and Tucker's best friend, Harry Cat. The adventures of Harry, Tucker, Chester—and of the Bellinis, whom they want so badly to help—make up a story well worth reading in full. There are a couple of sequels, too, that you can find in the library.

Chester

TUCKER MOUSE had been watching the Bellinis and listening to what they said. Next to scrounging, eavesdropping on human beings was what he enjoyed most. That was one of the reasons he lived in the Times Square subway station. As soon as the family disappeared, he darted out across the floor and scooted up to the newsstand. At one side the boards had separated and there was a wide space he could jump through. He'd been in a few times before—just exploring. For a moment he stood under the three-legged stool, letting his eyes get used to the darkness. Then he jumped up on it.

"Psst!" he whispered. "Hey you up there—are you awake?"

There was no answer.

"Psst! Psst! Hey!" Tucker whispered again, louder this time.

From the shelf above came a scuffling, like little feet feeling their way to the edge. "Who is that going 'psst'?" said a voice.

"It's me," said Tucker. "Down here on the stool."

A black head, with two shiny black eyes, peered down at him. "Who are you?"

"A mouse," said Tucker. "Who are *you?*"

"I'm Chester Cricket," said the cricket. He had a high, musical voice. Everything he said seemed to be spoken to an unheard melody.

"My name's Tucker," said Tucker Mouse. "Can I come up?"

"I guess so," said Chester Cricket. "This isn't my house anyway."

Tucker jumped up beside the cricket and looked him all over. "A cricket," he said admiringly. "So you're a cricket. I never saw one before."

"I've seen mice before," the cricket said. "I knew quite a few back in Connecticut."

"Is that where you're from?" asked Tucker.

"Yes," said Chester. "I guess I'll never see it again," he added wistfully.

"How did you get to New York?" asked Tucker Mouse.

"It's a long story," sighed the cricket.

"Tell me," said Tucker, settling back on his haunches. He loved to hear stories. It was almost as much fun as eavesdropping—if the story was true.

"Well, it must have been two—no, three days ago," Chester Cricket began. "I was sitting on top of my stump, just enjoying the weather and thinking how nice it was that summer had started. I live inside an old tree stump, next to a willow tree, and I often go up to the roof to look around. And I'd been practicing jumping that day too. On the other side of the stump from the willow tree there's a brook that runs past, and I'd been jumping back and forth across it to get my legs in condition for the summer. I do a lot of jumping, you know."

"Me too," said Tucker Mouse. "Especially around the rush hour."

"And I had just finished jumping when I smelled something," Chester went on, "liverwurst, which I love."

"You like liverwurst?" Tucker broke in. "Wait! Wait! Just wait!"

In one leap, he sprang down all the way from the shelf to the floor and dashed over to his drainpipe. Chester shook his head as he watched him go. He thought Tucker was a very excitable person—even for a mouse.

Inside the drainpipe, Tucker's nest was a jumble of papers, scraps of cloth, buttons, lost jewelry, small change, and everything else that can be picked up in a subway station. Tucker tossed things left and right in a wild search. Neatness was not one of the things he aimed at in life. At last he discovered what he was looking for: a big piece of liverwurst he had found earlier that evening. It was meant to be for breakfast tomorrow, but he decided that meeting his first cricket was a special occasion. Holding the liverwurst between his teeth, he whisked back to the newsstand.

"Look!" he said proudly, dropping the meat in front of Chester Cricket. "Liverwurst! You continue the story—we'll enjoy a snack too."

"That's very nice of you," said Chester. He was touched that a mouse he had known only a few minutes would share his food with him. "I had a little chocolate before, but besides that, nothing for three days."

"Eat! Eat!" said Tucker. He bit the liverwurst into two pieces and gave Chester the bigger one. "So you smelled the liverwurst—then what happened?"

"I hopped down from the stump and went off toward the smell," said Chester.

"Very logical," said Tucker Mouse, munching with his cheeks full. "Exactly what I would have done."

"It was coming from a picnic basket," said Chester. "A couple of tuffets away from my stump the meadow begins, and there was a whole bunch of people having a picnic. They had hard boiled eggs, and cold roast chicken, and roast beef, and a whole lot of other things besides the liverwurst sandwiches, which I smelled."

Tucker Mouse moaned with pleasure at the thought of all that food.

"They were having such a good time laughing and singing songs that they didn't notice me when I jumped into the picnic basket," continued Chester. "I was sure they wouldn't mind if I had just a taste."

"Naturally not," said Tucker Mouse sympathetically. "Why mind? Plenty for all. Who could blame you?"

"Now I have to admit," Chester went on, "I had more than a taste. As a matter of fact, I ate so much that I couldn't keep my eyes open—what with being tired from the jumping and everything. And I fell asleep right there in the picnic basket. The first thing I knew, somebody had put a bag on top of me that had the last of the roast beef sandwiches in it. I couldn't move!"

"Imagine!" Tucker exclaimed. "Trapped under roast beef sandwiches! Well, there are worse fates."

"At first I wasn't too frightened," said Chester. "After all, I thought, they probably come from New Canaan or some other nearby town. They'll have to unpack the basket sooner or later. Little did I know!" He shook his head and sighed. "I could feel the basket being carried into a car and riding somewhere and then being lifted down. That must have been the railroad station. Then I went up again and there was a rattling and roaring sound, the way a train makes. By this time I was pretty scared. I knew every minute was taking me further away from my stump, but there wasn't anything I could do. I was getting awfully cramped too, under those roast beef sandwiches."

"Didn't you try to eat your way out?" asked Tucker.

"I didn't have any room," said Chester. "But every now and then the train would give a lurch and I managed to free myself a little. We traveled on and on, and then the train stopped. I didn't have any idea where we were, but as soon as the basket was carried off, I could tell from the noise it must be New York."

"You never were here before?" Tucker asked.

"Goodness no!" said Chester. "But I've heard about it. There was a swallow I used to know who told about flying over New York every spring and fall on her way to the North and back. But what would I be doing here?" He shifted uneasily from one set of legs to another. "I'm a country cricket."

"Don't worry," said Tucker Mouse. "I'll feed you liverwurst. You'll be all right. Go on with the story."

"It's almost over," said Chester. "The people got off one train and walked a ways and got on another—even noisier than the first."

"Must have been the subway," said Tucker.

"I guess so," Chester Cricket said. "You can imagine how scared I was. I didn't know *where* I was going! For all I knew they could have been heading for Texas, although I don't guess many people from Texas come all the way to Connecticut for a picnic."

"It could happen," said Tucker, nodding his head.

"Anyway I worked furiously to get loose. And finally I made it. When they got off the second train, I took a flying leap and landed in a pile of dirt over in the corner of this place where we are."

"Such an introduction to New York," said Tucker, "to land in a pile of dirt in the Times Square subway station. Tsk, tsk, tsk."

"And here I am," Chester concluded forlornly. "I've been lying over there for three days not knowing what to do. At last I got so nervous I began to chirp."

"That was the sound!" interrupted Tucker Mouse. "I heard it, but I didn't know what it was."

"Yes, that was me," said Chester. "Usually I don't chirp until later on in the summer—but my goodness, I had to do *something!*"

The cricket had been sitting next to the edge of the shelf. For some reason—perhaps it was a faint noise, like padded feet tiptoeing across the floor—he happened to look down. A shadowy form that had been crouching silently below in the darkness made a spring and landed right next to Tucker and Chester.

"Watch out!" Chester shouted, "A cat!" He dove headfirst into the matchbox.

Harry Cat

CHESTER BURIED HIS HEAD in the Kleenex. He didn't want to see his new friend, Tucker Mouse, get killed. Back in Connecticut he had sometimes watched the one-sided fights of cats and mice in the meadow, and unless the mice were near their holes, the fights always ended in the same way. But this cat had been upon them too quickly: Tucker couldn't have escaped.

There wasn't a sound. Chester lifted his head and very cautiously looked behind him. The cat—a huge tiger cat with gray-green and black stripes along his body—was sitting on his hind legs, switching his tail around his forepaws. And directly between those forepaws, in the very jaws of his enemy, sat Tucker Mouse. He was watching Chester curiously. The cricket began to make frantic signs that the mouse should look up and see what was looming over him.

Very casually Tucker raised his head. The cat looked straight down on him. "Oh him," said Tucker, chucking the cat under the chin with his right front paw, "he's my best friend. Come out from the matchbox."

Chester crept out, looking first at one, then the other.

"Chester, meet Harry Cat," said Tucker. "Harry, this is Chester. He's a cricket."

"I'm very pleased to make your acquaintance," said Harry Cat in a silky voice.

"Hello," said Chester. He was sort of ashamed because of all the fuss he'd made. "I wasn't scared for myself. But I thought cats and mice were enemies."

"In the country, maybe," said Tucker. "But in New York we gave up those old habits long ago. Harry is my oldest friend. He lives with me over in the drainpipe. So how was scrounging tonight, Harry?"

"Not so good," said Harry Cat. "I was over in the ash cans on the East Side, but those rich people don't throw out as much garbage as they should."

"Chester, make that noise again for Harry," said Tucker Mouse.

Chester lifted the black wings that were carefully folded across his back and with a quick, expert stroke drew the top one over the bottom. A *thrumm* echoed through the station.

"Lovely—very lovely," said the cat. "This cricket has talent."

"I thought it was singing," said Tucker. "But you do it like playing a violin, with one wing on the other?"

"Yes," said Chester. "These wings aren't much good for flying, but I prefer music anyhow." He made three rapid chirps.

Tucker Mouse and Harry Cat smiled at each other.

"It makes me want to purr to hear it," said Harry.

"Some people say a cricket goes 'chee chee chee,' " explained Chester. "And others say, 'treet treet treet,' but we crickets don't think it sounds like either one of those."

"It sounds to me as if you were going 'crik crik crik,' " said Harry.

"Maybe that's why they call him a 'cricket,' " said Tucker.

They all laughed. Tucker had a squeaky laugh that sounded as if he were hiccuping. Chester was feeling much happier now. The future did not seem nearly as gloomy as it had over in the pile of dirt in the corner.

ELIZABETH MADOX ROBERTS

Firefly: A Song

A little light is going by,
Is going up to see the sky,
A little light with wings.

I never could have thought of it,
To have a little bug all lit
And made to go on wings.

GIANNI RODARI

I think Gianni Rodari is the best Italian writer of children's books in our time. He's well-known in Europe, less so elsewhere. The two stories printed below are taken from his *Telephone Tales*.

It seems that a certain Mr. Bianchi, who lived in the north of Italy, had a little daughter who was fond of bedtime stories. But her father, a traveling salesman, was home only on Sunday nights. So every other night at exactly seven o'clock Mr. Bianchi, no matter where he happened to be, phoned his daughter and told her a story on the telephone. Since long distance is expensive, the stories had to be short. It was no use for other people to try to phone Mr. Bianchi's town at seven because all the telephone operators were busy listening in on his stories. Here are two of them.

Telling Stories Wrong

Translated by Patrick Creagh

ONCE UPON A TIME there was a little girl called Little Yellow Riding Hood."

"No! *Red* Riding Hood!"

"Oh yes, of course: Red Riding Hood. Well, one day her mother called and said, 'Little Green Riding Hood . . .' "

"Red!"

"Sorry! Red. 'Now, my child, go to Aunt Mary and take her these potatoes.' "

"No! It doesn't go like that! 'Go to Grandma and take her these cakes.' "

"All right. So the little girl went off and in the wood she met a giraffe."

"What a mess you're making of it! It was a wolf!"

"And the wolf said: 'What's six times eight?' "

"No! No! The wolf asked her where she was going."

"So he did. And Little Black Riding Hood replied . . ."

"Red! Red!! Red!!!"

"She replied: 'I'm going to the market to buy some tomatoes.' "

"No, she didn't. She said: 'I'm going to my grandma who is sick, but I've lost my way.' "

"Of course! And the horse said . . ."

"What horse? It was a wolf."

"So it was. And this is what it said: 'Take the 75 bus, get out at the main square, turn right, and at the first doorway you'll find three steps.

Leave the steps where they are, but pick up the sixpence you'll find lying on them, and buy yourself a packet of chewing gum.' "

"Grandpa, you're terribly bad at telling stories. You get them all wrong. But all the same, I wouldn't mind some chewing gum."

"All right. Here's sixpence."

And the old man turned back to his newspaper.

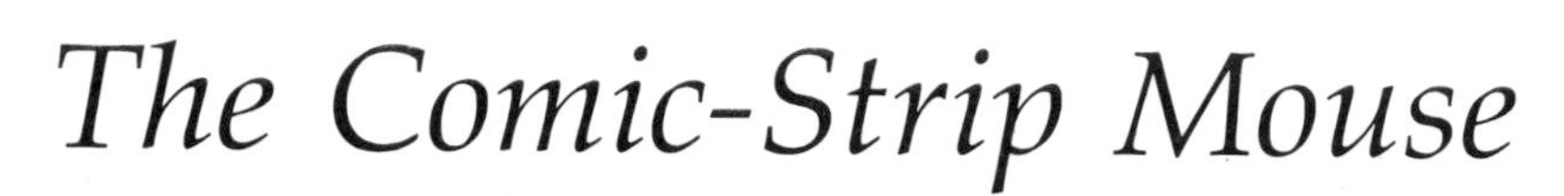

The Comic-Strip Mouse

Translated by Patrick Creagh

A COMIC-STRIP MOUSE, tired of living between the pages of a children's comic, and wanting to exchange the smell of paper for the smell of cheese, gave a great jump and found himself in the real world—the world of real mice.

"*Yeow! Erk!*" he exclaimed at once, as he smelled the smell of cat.

"What did you say?" squeaked the other mice, puzzled by such an odd sort of word.

"*Sploom, bang, gulp!*" said the comic-strip mouse, who only knew the language of comics.

"He must be a Turk," said an old veteran mouse who had sailed over the Mediterranean. So he said good morning to the comic-strip mouse in Turkish. The comic-strip mouse gazed at him in amazement and replied:

"*Zipp, flash, bronk.*"

"He's not a Turk," announced the veteran mouse.

"Then what is he?"

"How do I know?"

So they called him How-do-I-know, and treated him like the village idiot.

"How-do-I-know," they asked him, "do you prefer plain cheese, or Gorgonzola?"

"*Awlk! Whoosh! Splat! Groogh!*" replied the comic-strip mouse.

All the other mice burst out laughing, and the tiniest weeniest mice would tweak his tail just to be able to hear him complain: "*Zoong, splash, whizz!*"

One fine day they all went off hunting together in a windmill, where there were hundreds of sacks of flour. The mice ripped open the bags and tucked in, and as they chewed away their jaw went *cric cric cric*, as a mouse's jaws always do when he chews. Not so the comic-strip mouse. The sound he made was *crek crek sckerereksch.*

"You really must learn to eat properly," said the old veteran mouse. "Your table manners are abominable. Don't you realize that you're making a most disgusting noise?"

"*Agh-h!*" said the comic-strip mouse, and started on a fresh sack of flour.

Then the old veteran mouse gave a wink, and very quietly all the real mice scampered away and left the poor comic-strip mouse with his head buried in a sack of flour. They were sure he'd never be able to find his way home.

The comic-strip mouse went on guzzling, and when at last he realized that he was alone it was too dark to set out for home. He decided to spend the night at the windmill. He was just dropping off to sleep when he heard a soft padding of feet and saw two yellow lights in the darkness like the lights of a car. Heavens! A cat!

"*Oof! Squash!*" exclaimed the comic-strip mouse with a shudder.

"*Gragrragow!*" replied the cat. Thank goodness! It was a comic-strip cat! The real cats had all chased him away because he couldn't say *meeow* properly.

The two castaways threw themselves into each other's arms and swore eternal friendship. They spent the whole night chatting away in the strange language of comics:

"*Gnowgrraghowgh!*"

"*Glonk, tweek, slam!*"

JACK PRELUTSKY

Toucans Two

Whatever one toucan can do
is sooner done by toucans two,
and three toucans (it's very true)
can do much more than two can do.

And toucans numbering two plus two can
manage more than all the zoo can.
In short, there is no toucan who can
do what four or three or two can.

The Zebra

The zebra is undoubtedly
a source of some confusion,
his alternating stripes present
an optical illusion.

Observing them is difficult,
one quickly loses track
of whether they are black on white
or rather, white on black.

FELIX SALTEN

Felix Salten, who was an Austrian journalist and novelist, is famous for only one book. *Bambi* is the life story of a forest deer, but perhaps it is also about just growing up. The episode following tells us about Bambi's first encounter with man.

In his foreword to the book the eminent English novelist John Galsworthy wrote, "I particularly recommend it to sportsmen." Read "He" and you will see why.

He

Translated by Whittaker Chambers

BAMBI WALKED under the great oak on the meadow. It sparkled with dew. It smelled of grass and flowers and moist earth, and whispered of a thousand living things. Friend Hare was there and seemed to be thinking over something important. A haughty pheasant strutted slowly by, nibbling at the grass seeds and peering cautiously in all directions. The dark, metallic blue on his neck gleamed in the sun.

One of the Princes was standing close to Bambi. Bambi had never seen any of the fathers so close before. The stag was standing right in front of him next to the hazel bush and was somewhat hidden by the branches. Bambi did not move. He wanted the Prince to come out completely, and was wondering whether he dared speak to him. He wanted to ask his mother and looked around for her. But his mother had already gone away and was standing some distance off, beside Aunt Ena. At the same time Gobo and Faline came running out of the woods. Bambi was still thinking it over without stirring. If he went up to his mother and the others now he would have to pass by the Prince. He felt as if he couldn't do it.

"Oh well," he thought, "I don't have to ask my mother first. The old Prince spoke to me and I didn't tell Mother anything about it. I'll say, 'Good morning, Prince.' He can't be offended at that. But if he does get angry, I'll run away fast." Bambi struggled with his resolve, which began to waver again.

Presently the Prince walked out from behind the hazel bush onto the meadow.

"Now," thought Bambi.

Then there was a crash like thunder.

Bambi shrank together and didn't know what had happened. He saw the Prince leap into the air under his very nose and watched him rush past him into the forest with one great bound.

Bambi looked around in a daze. The thunder still vibrated. He saw how his mother and Aunt Ena, Gobo and Faline fled into the woods. He saw how Friend Hare scurried away like mad. He saw the pheasant running with his neck outstretched. He noticed that the forest grew suddenly still. He started and sprang into the thicket. He had made only a few bounds when he saw the Prince lying on the ground in front of him, motionless. Bambi stopped horrified, not understanding what it meant. The Prince lay bleeding from a great wound in his shoulder. He was dead.

"Don't stop!" a voice beside him commanded. It was his mother, who rushed past him at full gallop. "Run," she cried. "Run as fast as you can!" She did not slow up, but raced ahead, and her command brought Bambi after her. He ran with all his might.

"What is it, Mother?" he asked. "What is it, Mother?"

His mother answered between gasps, "It—was—He!"

Bambi shuddered and they ran on. At last they stopped for lack of breath.

"What did you say? Tell me what it was you said," a soft voice called down from overhead. Bambi looked up. The squirrel came chattering through the branches.

"I ran the whole way with you," he cried. "It was dreadful."

"Were you there?" asked the mother.

"Of course I was there," the squirrel replied. "I am still trembling in every limb." He sat erect, balancing with his splendid tail, displaying his small white chest, and holding his forepaws protectively against his body. "I'm beside myself with excitement," he said.

"I'm quite weak from fright myself," said the mother. "I don't understand it. Not one of us saw a thing."

"Is that so?" the squirrel said pettishly. "I saw Him long before."

"So did I," another voice cried. It was the magpie. She flew past and settled on a branch.

"So did I," came a croak from above. It was the jay, who was sitting on an ash.

A couple of crows in the treetops cawed harshly, "We saw Him, too."

They all sat around talking importantly. They were unusually excited and seemed to be full of anger and fear.

"Whom?" Bambi thought. "Whom did they see?"

"I tried my best," the squirrel was saying, pressing his forepaws against his heart. "I tried my best to warn the poor Prince."

"And I," the jay rasped. "How often did I scream? But he didn't care to hear me."

"He didn't hear me either," the magpie croaked. "I called him at least ten times. I wanted to fly right past him, for, thought I, he hasn't heard me yet; I'll fly to the hazel bush where he's standing. He can't help hearing me there. But at that minute it happened."

"My voice is probably louder than yours, and I warned him as well as I could," the crow said in an impudent tone. "But gentlemen of that stamp pay little attention to the likes of us."

"Much too little, really," the squirrel agreed.

"Well, we did what we could," said the magpie. "We're certainly not to blame when an accident happens."

"Such a handsome Prince," the squirrel lamented. "And in the very prime of life."

"Akh!" croaked the jay. "It would have been better for him if he hadn't been so proud and had paid more attention to us."

"He certainly wasn't proud."

"No more so than the other Princes of his family," the magpie put in.

"Just plain stupid," sneered the jay.

"You're stupid yourself," the crow cried down from overhead. "Don't you talk about stupidity. The whole forest knows how stupid you are."

"I!" replied the jay, stiff with astonishment. "Nobody can accuse me of being stupid. I may be forgetful but I'm certainly not stupid."

"Oh just as you please," said the crow solemnly. "Forget what I said to you, but remember that the Prince did not die because he was proud or stupid, but because no one can escape Him."

"Akh!" croaked the jay. "I don't like that kind of talk." He flew away.

The crow went on, "He has already outwitted many of my family. He kills what He wants. Nothing can help us."

"You have to be on your guard against Him," the magpie broke in.

"You certainly do," said the crow sadly. "Goodbye." He flew off, his family accompanying him.

Bambi looked around. His mother was no longer there.

"What are they talking about now?" thought Bambi. "I can't understand what they are talking about. Who is this 'He' they talk about? That was He, too, that I saw in the bushes, but He didn't kill me."

Bambi thought of the Prince lying in front of him with his bloody, mangled shoulder. He was dead now. Bambi walked along. The forest sang again with a thousand voices, the sun pierced the treetops with its broad rays. There was light everywhere. The leaves began to smell. Far above the falcons called, close at hand a woodpecker hammered as if nothing had happened. Bambi was not happy. He felt himself threatened by something dark. He did not understand how the others could be so carefree and happy while life was so difficult and dangerous. Then the desire seized him to go deeper and deeper into the woods. They lured him into their depths. He wanted to find some hiding place where, shielded on all sides by impenetrable thickets, he could never be seen. He never wanted to go to the meadow again.

Something moved very softly in the bushes. Bambi drew back violently. The old stag was standing in front of him.

Bambi trembled. He wanted to run away, but he controlled himself and remained. The old stag looked at him with his great deep eyes and asked, "Were you out there before?"

"Yes," Bambi said softly. His heart was pounding in his throat.

"Where is your mother?" asked the stag.

Bambi answered, still very softly, "I don't know."

The old stag kept gazing at him. "And still you're not calling for her?" he said.

Bambi looked into the noble, iron-gray face, looked at the stag's antlers and suddenly felt full of courage. "I can stay by myself, too," he said.

The old stag considered him for a while; then he asked gently, "Aren't you the little one that was crying for his mother not long ago?"

Bambi was somewhat embarrassed, but his courage held. "Yes, I am," he confessed.

The old stag looked at him in silence and it seemed to Bambi as if those deep eyes gazed still more mildly. "You scolded me then, Prince," he cried excitedly, "because I was afraid of being left alone. Since then I haven't been."

The stag looked at Bambi appraisingly and smiled a very slight, hardly noticeable smile. Bambi noticed it, however. "Noble Prince," he asked confidently, "what has happened? I don't understand it. Who is this 'He' they are all talking about?" He stopped, terrified by the dark glance that bade him be silent.

Another pause ensued. The old stag was gazing past Bambi into the distance. Then he said slowly, "Listen, smell, and see for yourself. Find out for yourself." He lifted his antlered head still higher. "Farewell," he said, nothing else. Then he vanished.

Bambi stood transfixed and wanted to cry. But that farewell still rang in his ears and sustained him. Farewell, the old stag had said, so he couldn't have been angry.

Bambi felt himself thrill with pride, felt inspired with a deep earnestness. Yes, life was difficult and full of danger. But come what might he would learn to bear it all.

He walked slowly deeper into the forest.

RON PADGETT

The Giraffe

The 2 f's
in giraffe
are like
2 giraffes
running through
the word giraffe

The 2 f's
run through giraffe
like 2 giraffes

MARILYN SACHS

Marilyn Sachs writes about American kids here and now, and does it very well. *Veronica Ganz* is one of her best novels.

Veronica Ganz, thirteen, is the biggest girl in her class. She's a bully, frequently beating up on other kids, boys as well as girls. Her extra-special enemy is Peter Wedemeyer. He's much smaller but a better poet, always making up rhymes like

Veronica Ganz
Doesn't wear pants,

or

Veronica Ganz
Has ants in her pants.

The story is all about how Veronica learned it wasn't worthwhile being a bully. The selection following, however, shows her being nice to her five-year-old half brother Stanley. What I like most about this bit is the way she tells the Bluebeard story to little Stanley. It makes me laugh every time, even though—or maybe just because—the Bluebeard story is really so horrible!

Veronica Ganz

FROM CHAPTER THREE

AFTER SUPPER, Mama and Ralph went into the kitchen and shut the door. But first, Mama said, "You can put Stanley to bed tonight."

Mary Rose immediately got up and walked off.

"Who, me?" Veronica said.

"Yes, you."

"Why me?" Veronica grumbled. "Why do I have to always be the one?"

"You aren't always the one." Mama began talking, her voice rising higher and higher as she spoke. "You hardly ever do it, but tonight you have to do it because I SAID SO." She slammed the kitchen door.

Stanley was sitting on the floor in his parents' bedroom when Veronica stamped into the room. He had two decks of cards spread out around him and was trying to match all the same ones together. He was holding the jack of hearts in his hand and looking around for its mate.

"Pick those cards up off the floor," Veronica said, "and get into your pajamas."

Stanley looked happy. "You putting me to bed, Veronica?"

Veronica began pulling Stanley's trundle bed out from under the big bed. "Get a move on," she said. "I've got things to do."

"Sure, Veronica, sure." Stanley quickly began gathering all his cards together. "I'm glad you're putting me to bed. I like when you put me to bed."

Veronica took the blanket and pillow out of the closet. "Come on, hurry," she said, "and go to the bathroom first."

When Stanley came back, he pulled all his clothes off and dropped them on the floor.

"What's that?" Veronica said, pointing to a red circle on his shoulder.

"Where? Oh, that. That's where Jimmy Reilly bit me."

"Bit you? Why'd he bite you?"

"He always bites me," Stanley said in a melancholy voice.

"And what do you do when he bites you?"

"I tell him, 'Stop it!' But he won't."

Veronica exploded. "You're such a spineless little coward," she screamed at him. "That's why they're always hitting you, and pushing you, and biting you. You're the biggest kid in your class, and everybody picks on you, and you never lift a finger. Why didn't you hit him back?"

Stanley's big eyes blinked and blinked. "Maybe tomorrow," he said softly. "Maybe tomorrow I'll hit him back."

"Sure, sure," Veronica sneered, "tomorrow you'll hit him back! Baloney! If it wasn't for me, they'd tear you to pieces, and you'd let them." She put her face up close to his. "I've always got to be pulling some kid or other off you, and I don't like smacking little kids."

"So why do you do it?" Stanley said, moving his head back a little.

"Because you don't do it for yourself. But after this, I'm finished. Whatever happens to you, I'm not going to lift a finger to help you. Do you hear me?"

"O.K., Veronica," Stanley said meekly. He touched the bite on his shoulder. "It doesn't really hurt so much, any more." He drew his pajamas on, crept into his bed, and pulled the covers up to his chin.

"Good night!" Veronica said, putting out the light.

"Veronica!"

"What?"

"Tell me a story."

"Not tonight," said Veronica. "I'm busy." She began walking out the door, and a gentle hiccup followed her. Oh, that rotten kid! He'll start hiccuping again, and Mama'll chew my head off.

"All right, all right," Veronica snapped, coming back into the room. "Just stop hiccuping."

"I'll try." Stanley hicced again.

Veronica sat down on the big bed.

"Tell me the one about Bluebeard," Stanley pleaded.

"Oh, all right. Just don't hiccup."

"I won't," Stanley said in a strangled voice between his teeth.

"Once upon a time," said Veronica quickly, "there was a man named Bluebeard because he had a beard that was so black it looked blue. And he came to a country where nobody knew him. And he married a beautiful girl named . . . named . . ."

"Veronica," Stanley offered.

"No, Loretta. So he took her home to his house. It was a great big house, kind of dark, and smelly, and gloomy."

"Like school?"

"No, bigger, and gloomier, and smellier. And he gave her a bunch of keys and said she could look in every room in the house except the one up in the attic. But one day, when he wasn't home—"

"Veronica," Stanley said, "come and sit on my bed."

Veronica bent down and sat on the edge of Stanley's bed, and Stanley turned over on his side with his face against her leg, and one arm in her lap.

"Well, so he wasn't home, and she opened the door to the room in the attic, and she saw—"

"Bodies," Stanley said contentedly, "lots of bodies."

"All over the place," Veronica continued. "And some had their heads off, and some had their arms and legs off, and pieces of ladies were hanging up all over the walls."

Veronica began describing all the horrors the room contained, and

Stanley nestled closer and closer to her. Her voice grew low as she told how Loretta sent a message to her brothers, big, strong men—

"Like Papa?" Stanley suggested.

Veronica let that pass without comment, and went on to tell how Bluebeard discovered that Loretta had been in the room. How he told her to prepare to die. How she stalled for time. How her brothers arrived just as Bluebeard was chasing her around the kitchen table, and proceeded to hack him into many pieces.

"How many?" Stanley asked.

"Oh, lots and lots."

"Maybe a thousand," Stanley murmured happily, without a single hiccup.

"Maybe," Veronica said agreeably. Stanley's hand was in hers by this time, and his head was in her lap. She couldn't see his face in the darkness, and maybe that was why she forgot to be sore at him. Gently, she put his hand down, stood up, and walked quietly to the door.

"Veronica!"

"Now what?"

"I'm scared."

"What of?"

"That window shade," Stanley murmured. "It keeps flapping."

Veronica pulled the window shade down below the level of the window and started out once more.

"Veronica!"

"What?"

"That was a nice story, Veronica," Stanley said sleepily.

"Good night," said Veronica, closing the door. She made a mental note to catch Jimmy Reilly tomorrow and gave him a few slaps for biting Stanley.

OGDEN NASH

The Eel

I don't mind eels
Except as meals
And the way they feels.

The Adventures of Isabel

Isabel met an enormous bear,
Isabel, Isabel, didn't care.
The bear was hungry, the bear was ravenous,
The bear's big mouth was cruel and cavernous.
The bear said, Isabel, glad to meet you,
How do, Isabel, now I'll eat you!
Isabel, Isabel, didn't worry;
Isabel didn't scream or scurry.
She washed her hands and she straightened her hair up,
Then Isabel quietly ate the bear up.

The Parent

Children aren't happy with nothing to ignore,
And that's what parents were created for.

The Panther

The panther is like a leopard,
Except it hasn't been peppered.
Should you behold a panther crouch,
Prepare to say Ouch.
Better yet, if called by a panther,
Don't anther.

The Lama

The one-l lama,
He's a priest,
The two-l llama,
He's a beast.
And I will bet
A silk pyjama
There isn't any
Three-l lllama.

ARTHUR RANSOME

Arthur Ransome's best-known books are about a family of English children and their adventures sailing around the lakes of England's beautiful Lake District. If you like sailing (and wonderful writing) read the first of the series, *Swallows and Amazons.* I guarantee you'll want to read the others. But the episodes in them are so long they just wouldn't fit into this book. I thought instead you might like to read a story (I like it just as well) from Ransome's first book for children, *Old Peter's Russian Tales.*

A long time ago, before the Russian revolution, Old Peter lived in a little hut in the deep Russian forest with his two grandchildren, Vanya and Maroosia. There being no television in those days, they entertained themselves with stories. Here is one of them.

Salt

ONE EVENING, when they were sitting round the table after their supper, old Peter asked the children what story they would like to hear. Vanya asked whether there were any stories left which they had not already heard.

"Why," said old Peter, "you have heard scarcely any of the stories, for there is a story to be told about everything in the world."

"About everything, Grandfather?" asked Vanya.

"About everything," said old Peter.

"About the sky, and the thunder, and the dogs, and the flies, and the birds, and the trees and the milk?"

"There is a story about every one of those things."

"I know something there isn't a story about," said Vanya.

"And what's that?" asked old Peter, smiling in his beard.

"Salt," said Vanya. "There can't be a story about salt." He put the tip of his finger into the little box of salt on the table, and then he touched his tongue with his finger to taste.

"But of course there is a story about salt," said old Peter.

"Tell it to us," said Maroosia; and presently, when his pipe had been lit twice and gone out, old Peter began.

Once upon a time there were three brothers, and their father was a great merchant who sent his ships far over the sea, and traded here and there in countries the names of which I, being an old man, can never rightly call to mind. Well, the names of the two elder brothers do not matter, but the youngest was called Ivan the Ninny, because he was always playing and never working; and if there was a silly thing to do, why, off he went and did it. And so, when the brothers grew up, the father sent the two elder ones off, each in a fine ship laden with gold and jewels, and rings and bracelets, and laces and silks, and sticks with little bits of silver hammered into their handles, and spoons with patterns of blue and red, and everything else you can think of that costs too much to buy. But he made Ivan the Ninny stay at home, and did not give him a ship at all. Ivan saw his brothers go sailing off over the sea on a summer morning, to make their fortunes and come back rich men; and then, for the first time in his life, he wanted to work and do something useful. He went to his father and kissed his hand, and he kissed the hand of his little old mother, and he begged his father to give him a ship so that he could try his fortune like his brothers.

"But you have never done a wise thing in your life, and no one could count all the silly things you've done if he spent a hundred days in counting," said his father.

"True," said Ivan; "but now I am going to be wise, and sail the sea and come back with something in my pockets to show that I am not a ninny any longer. Give me just a little ship, father mine—just a little ship for myself."

"Give him a little ship," said the mother. "He may not be a ninny after all."

"Very well," said his father. "I will give him a little ship; but I am not going to waste good rubles by giving him a rich cargo."

"Give me any cargo you like," said Ivan.

So his father gave him a little ship, a little old ship, and a cargo of rags and scraps and things that were not fit for anything but to be thrown away. And he gave him a crew of ancient old sailormen who were past work; and Ivan went on board and sailed away at sunset, like the ninny he was. And the feeble, ancient old sailormen pulled up the ragged, dirty sails, and away they went over the sea to learn what fortune, good or bad, God had in mind for a crew of old men with a ninny for a master.

The fourth day after they set sail there came a great wind over the sea. The feeble old men did the best they could with the ship; but the old, torn sails tore from the masts, and the wind did what it pleased, and threw the little ship on an unknown island away in the middle of the sea. Then the wind dropped, and left the little ship on the beach, and Ivan the Ninny and his ancient old men, like good Russians, praising God that they were still alive.

"Well, children," said Ivan, for he knew how to talk to sailors, "do you stay here and mend the sails, and make new ones out of the rags we carry as cargo, while I go inland and see if there is anything that could be of use to us."

So the ancient old sailormen sat on deck with their legs crossed, and made sails out of rags, of torn scraps of old brocades, of soiled embroidered shawls, of all the rubbish that they had with them for a cargo. You never saw such sails. The tide came up and floated the ship, and they threw out anchors at bow and stern, and sat there in the sunlight, making sails and patching them and talking of the days when they were young. All this while Ivan the Ninny went walking off into the island.

Now in the middle of that island was a high mountain, a high mountain it was, and so white that when he came near it Ivan the Ninny began thinking of sheepskin coats, although it was midsummer and the sun was hot in the sky. The trees were green round about, but there was nothing growing on the mountain at all. It was just a great white mountain piled up into the sky in the middle of a green island. Ivan walked a little way up the white slopes of the mountain, and then, because he felt thirsty, he thought he would let a little snow melt in his mouth. He took some in his fingers and stuffed it in. Quickly enough it came out again, I can tell you, for the mountain was not made of snow but of good Russian salt. And if you want to try what a mouthful of salt is like, you may.

"No, thank you, Grandfather," the children said hurriedly together.

Old Peter went on with his tale.

Ivan the Ninny did not stop to think twice. The salt was so clean and shone so brightly in the sunlight. He just turned round and ran back to shore, and called out to his ancient old sailormen and told them to empty everything they had on board over into the sea. Over it all went, rags and tags and rotten timbers, till the little ship was as empty as a soup bowl after supper. And then those ancient old men were set to work carrying salt from the mountain and taking it on board the little ship, and stowing it away below deck till there was not room for another grain. Ivan the Ninny would have liked to take the whole mountain, but there was not room in the little ship. And for that the ancient old sailormen thanked God, because their backs ached and their old legs were weak, and they said they would have died if they had had to carry any more.

Then they hoisted up the new sails they had patched together out of the rags and scraps of shawls and old brocades, and they sailed away once more over the blue sea. And the wind stood fair, and they sailed before it, and the ancient old sailors rested their backs, and told old tales, and took turn and turn about at the rudder.

And after many days' sailing they came to a town, with towers and churches and painted roofs, all set on the side of a hill that sloped down into the sea. At the foot of the hill was a quiet harbor, and they sailed in there and moored the ship and hauled down their patchwork sails.

Ivan the Ninny went ashore, and took with him a little bag of clean white salt to show what kind of goods he had for sale, and he asked his way to the palace of the Tsar of that town. He came to the palace, and went in and bowed to the ground before the Tsar.

"Who are you?" says the Tsar.

"I, great lord, am a Russian merchant, and here in a bag is some of my merchandise, and I beg your leave to trade with your subjects in this town."

"Let me see what is in the bag," says the Tsar.

Ivan the Ninny took a handful from the bag and showed it to the Tsar.

"Good Russian salt, says Ivan the Ninny.

Now in the country they had never heard of salt, and the Tsar looked at the salt, and he looked at Ivan and he laughed.

"Why, this," says he, "is nothing but white dust, and that we can pick up for nothing. The men of my town have no need to trade with you. You must be a ninny."

Ivan grew very red, for he knew what his father used to call him. He was ashamed to say anything. So he bowed to the ground, and went away out of the palace.

But when he was outside he thought to himself, "I wonder what sort of salt they use in these parts if they do not know good Russian salt when they see it. I will go to the kitchen."

So he went round to thc back door of the palace, and put his head into the kitchen, and said, "I am very tired. May I sit down here and rest a little while?"

"Come in," says one of the cooks. "But you must sit just there, and not put even your little finger in the way of us; for we are the Tsar's cooks and we are in the middle of making ready his dinner." And the cook put a stool in a corner out of the way, and Ivan slipped in round the door, and sat down in the corner and looked about him. There were seven cooks at least, boiling and baking, and stewing and toasting, and roasting and frying. And as for scullions, they were as thick as cockroaches, dozens of them, running to and fro, tumbling over each other, and helping the cooks.

Ivan the Ninny sat on his stool, with his legs tucked under him and the bag of salt on his knees. He watched the cooks and the scullions, but he did not see them put anything in the dishes which he thought could take the place of salt. No; the meat was without salt, the kasha was without salt, and there was no salt in the potatoes. Ivan nearly turned sick at the thought of the tastelessness of all that food.

There came the moment when all the cooks and scullions ran out of the kitchen to fetch the silver platters on which to lay the dishes. Ivan slipped down from his stool, and running from stove to stove, from saucepan to frying pan, he dropped a pinch of salt, just what was wanted, no more no less, in every one of the dishes. Then he ran back to the stool in the corner, and sat there, and watched the dishes being put on the silver platters and carried off in gold-embroidered napkins to be the dinner of the Tsar.

The Tsar sat at table and took his first spoonful of soup.

"The soup is very good today," says he, and he finishes the soup to the last drop.

"I've never known the soup so good," says the Tsaritza, and she finishes hers.

"This is the best soup I ever tasted," says the Princess, and down goes hers, and she, you know, was the prettiest princess who ever had dinner in this world.

It was the same with the kasha and the same with the meat. The Tsar and the Tsaritza and the Princess wondered why they had never had so good a dinner in all their lives before.

"Call the cooks," says the Tsar. And they called the cooks, and the cooks all came in, and bowed to the ground, and stood in a row before the Tsar.

"What did you put in the dishes today that you never put before?" says the Tsar.

"We put nothing unusual, your greatnesss," say the cooks, and bowed to the ground again.

"Then why do the dishes taste better?"

"We do not know, your greatness," say the cooks.

"Call the scullions," says the Tsar. And the scullions were called, and they too bowed to the ground, and stood in a row before the Tsar.

"What was done in the kitchen today that has not been done there before?" says the Tsar.

"Nothing, your greatness," say all the scullions except one.

And that one scullion bowed again, and kept on bowing, and then he said, "Please, your greatness, please, great lord, there is usually none in the kitchen but ourselves; but today there was a young Russian merchant, who sat on a stool in the corner and said he was tired."

"Call the merchant," says the Tsar.

So they brought in Ivan the Ninny, and he bowed before the Tsar, and stood there with his little bag of salt in his hand.

"Did you do anything to my dinner?" says the Tsar.

"I did, your greatness," says Ivan.

"What did you do?"

"I put a pinch of Russian salt in every dish."

"That white dust?" says the Tsar.

"Nothing but that."

"Have you got any more of it?"

"I have a little ship in the harbor laden with nothing else," says Ivan.

"It is the most wonderful dust in the world," says the Tsar, "and I will buy every grain of it you have. What do you want for it?"

Ivan the Ninny scratched his head and thought. He thought that if the Tsar liked it as much as all that it must be worth a fair price, so he said, "We will put the salt into bags, and for every bag of salt you must give me three bags of the same weight—one of gold, one of silver and one of precious stones. Cheaper than that, your greatness, I could not possibly sell."

"Agreed," says the Tsar. "And a cheap price, too, for a dust so full of magic that it makes dull dishes tasty, and tasty dishes so good that there is no looking away from them."

So all the day long, and far into the night, the ancient old sailormen bent their backs under sacks of salt, and bent them again under sacks of gold and silver and precious stones. When all the salt had been put in the Tsar's treasury—yes, with twenty soldiers guarding it with great swords shining in the moonlight—and when the little ship was loaded with riches, so that even the deck was piled high with precious stones, the ancient old men lay down among the jewels and slept till morning, when Ivan the Ninny went to bid good-bye to the Tsar.

"And whither shall you sail now?" asked the Tsar.

"I shall sail away to Russia in my little ship," says Ivan.

And the Princess, who was very beautiful, said, "A little Russian ship?"

"Yes," says Ivan.

"I have never seen a Russian ship," says the Princess, and she begs her father to let her go to the harbor with her nurses and maids, to see the little Russian ship before Ivan set sail.

She came with Ivan to the harbor, and the ancient old sailormen took them on board.

She ran all over the ship, looking now at this and now at that, and Ivan told her the names of everything—deck, mast and rudder.

"May I see the sails?" she asked. And the ancient old men hoisted the ragged old sails, and the wind filled the sails and tugged.

"Why doesn't the ship move when the sails are up?" asked the Princess.

"The anchor holds her," said Ivan.

"Please let me see the anchor," says the Princess.

"Haul up the anchor, my children, and show it to the Princess," says Ivan to the ancient old sailormen.

And the old men hauled up the anchor, and showed it to the Princess; and she said it was a very good little anchor. But, of course, as soon as the anchor was up the ship began to move. One of the ancient old men bent over the tiller, and with a fair wind behind her, the little ship slipped out of the harbor and away to the blue sea. When the Princess looked round, thinking it was time to go home, the little ship was far from land, and away in the distance she could only see the gold towers of her father's palace, glittering like pinpoints in the sunlight. Her nurses and maids wrung their hands and made an outcry, and the Princess sat down on a heap of jewels, and put a handkerchief to her eyes, and cried and cried and cried.

Ivan the Ninny took her hands and comforted her, and told her of the wonders of the sea that he would show her, and the wonders of the land.

And she looked up at him while he talked, and his eyes were kind and hers were sweet; and the end of it was that they were both very well content, and agreed to have a marriage feast as soon as the little ship should bring them to the home of Ivan's father. Merry was that voyage. All day long Ivan and the Princess sat on deck and said sweet things to each other, and at twilight they sang songs, and drank tea, and told stories. As for the nurses and maids, the Princess told them to be glad; and so they danced and clapped their hands, and ran about the ship, and teased the ancient old sailormen.

When they had been sailing many days, the Princess was looking out over the sea, and she cried out to Ivan, "See, over there, far away, are two big ships with white sails, not like our sails of brocade and bits of silk."

Ivan looked, shading his eyes with his hands.

"Why, those are the ships of my elder brothers," said he. "We shall all sail home together."

And he made the ancient old sailormen give a hail in their cracked old voices. And the brothers heard them, and came on board to greet Ivan and his bride. And when they saw that she was a Tsar's daughter, and that the very decks were heaped with precious stones, because there was no room below, they said one thing to Ivan and something else to each other.

To Ivan they said, "Thanks be to God, he has given you good trading?"

But to each other, "How can this be?" says one. "Ivan the Ninny bringing back such a cargo, while we in our fine ships have only a bag or two of gold."

"And what is Ivan the Ninny doing with a princess?" says the other.

And they ground their teeth, and waited their time, and came up suddenly, when Ivan was alone in the twilight, and picked him up by his head and his heels, and hove him overboard into the dark blue sea.

Not one of the old men had seen them, and the Princess was not on deck. In the morning they said that Ivan the Ninny must have walked overboard in his sleep. And they drew lots. The eldest brother took the Princess, and the second brother took the little ship laden with gold and silver and precious stones. And so the brothers sailed home very well content. But the Princess sat and wept all day long, looking down into the blue water. The elder brother could not comfort her, and the second brother did not try. And the ancient old sailormen muttered in their beards, and were sorry, and prayed to God to give rest to Ivan's soul; for although he had been a ninny, and although he had made them carry a lot of salt and other things, yet they loved him, because he knew how to talk to ancient old sailormen.

But Ivan was not dead. As soon as he splashed into the water, he crammed his fur hat a little tighter on his head, and began swimming in the sea. He swam about until the sun rose, and then, not far away, he saw a floating timber log, and he swam to the log, and got astride of it, and thanked God. And he sat there on the log in the middle of the sea, twiddling his thumbs for want of something to do.

There was a strong current in the sea that carried him along, and at last, after floating for many days without ever a bite for his teeth or a drop for his gullet, his feet touched land. Now that was at night, and he left the log and walked up out of the sea, and lay down on the shore and waited for morning.

When the sun rose he stood up, and saw that he was on a bare island, and he saw nothing at all on the island except a huge house as big as a mountain; and as he was looking at the house the great door creaked with a noise like that of a hurricane among the pine forests, and opened; and a giant came walking out, and came to the shore, and stood looking down at Ivan.

"What are you doing here, little one?" says the giant.

Ivan told him the whole story, just as I have told it to you.

The giant listened to the very end, pulling at his monstrous whiskers. Then he said, "Listen, little one. I know more of the story than you, for I can tell you that tomorrow morning your eldest brother is going to marry your Princess. But there is no need for you to take on about it. If you want to be there, I will carry you and set you down before the house in time for the wedding. And a fine wedding it is like to be, for your father thinks well of those brothers of your bringing back all those precious stones, and silver and gold enough to buy a kingdom."

And with that he picked up Ivan the Ninny and set him on his great shoulders, and set off striding through the sea.

He went so fast that the wind of his going blew off Ivan's hat.

"Stop a moment," shouts Ivan, "my hat has blown off."

"We can't turn back for that," says the giant, "we have already left your hat five hundred versts behind us."* And he rushed on, splashing through the sea. The sea was up to his armpits. He rushed on, and the sea was up to his waist. He rushed on, and before the sun had climbed to the top of the blue sky he was splashing up out of the sea with the water about his ankles. He lifted Ivan from his shoulders and set him on the ground.

"Now," says he, "little man, off you run, and you'll be in time for the feast. But don't you dare to boast about your riding on my shoulders. If you open your mouth about that you'll smart for it, if I have to come ten thousand thousand versts."

Ivan the Ninny thanked the giant for carrying him through the sea, promised that he would not boast, and then ran off to his father's house. Long before he got there he heard the musicians in the courtyard playing as if they wanted to wear out their instruments before night. The wedding feast had begun, and when Ivan ran in, there, at the high board, was sitting the Princess, and beside her his eldest brother. And there were his father and mother, his second brother, and all the guests. And every one of them was as merry as could be, except the Princess, and she was as white as the salt he had sold to her father.

Suddenly the blood flushed into her cheeks. She saw Ivan in the doorway. Up she jumped at the high board, and cried out, "There, there is my true love, and not this man who sits beside me at the table."

*A verst is a Russian unit of distance equal to about two-thirds of a mile.

"What is this?" says Ivan's father, and in a few minutes knew the whole story.

He turned the two elder brothers out of doors, gave their ships to Ivan, married him to the Princess, and made him his heir. And the wedding feast began again, and they sent for the ancient old sailormen to take part in it. And the ancient old sailormen wept with joy when they saw Ivan and the Princess, like two sweet pigeons, sitting side by side; yes, and they lifted their flagons with their old shaking hands, and cheered with their old cracked voices, and poured the wine down their dry old throats.

There was wine enough and to spare, beer too, and mead—enough to drown a herd of cattle. And as the guests drank and grew merry and proud they set to boasting. This one bragged of his riches, that one of his wife. Another boasted of his cunning, another of his new house, another of his strength, and this one was angry because they would not let him show how he could lift the table on one hand. They all drank Ivan's health, and he drank theirs, and in the end he could not bear to listen to their proud boasts.

"That's all very well," says he, "but I am the only man in the world who rode on the shoulders of a giant to come to his wedding feast."

The words were scarcely out of his mouth before there were a tremendous trampling and a roar of a great wind. The house shook with the footsteps of the giant as he strode up. The giant bent down over the courtyard and looked in at the feast.

"Little man, little man," says he, "you promised not to boast of me. I told you what would come if you did, and here you are and have boasted already."

"Forgive me," says Ivan; "it was the drink that boasted, not I."

"What sort of drink is it that knows how to boast?" says the giant.

"You shall taste it," says Ivan.

And he made his ancient old sailormen roll a great barrel of wine into the yard, more than enough for a hundred men, and after that a barrel of beer that was as big, and then a barrel of mead that was no smaller.

"Try the taste of that," says Ivan the Ninny.

Well, the giant did not wait to be asked twice. He lifted the barrel of wine as if it had been a little glass, and emptied it down his throat. He lifted the barrel of beer as if it had been an acorn, and emptied it after the wine. Then he lifted the barrel of mead as if it had been a very small pea, and swallowed every drop of mead that was in it. And after that he began stamping about and breaking things. Houses fell to pieces this way and that, and trees were swept flat like grass. Every step the giant took was followed by the crash of breaking timbers. Then suddenly he fell flat on his back and slept. For three days and nights he slept without waking. At last he opened his eyes.

"Just look about you," says Ivan, "and see the damage that you've done."

"And did that little drop of drink make me do all that?" says the giant. "Well, well, I can well understand that a drink like that can do a bit of bragging. And after that," says he, looking at the wrecks of houses, and all the broken things scattered about—"after that," says he, "you can boast of me for a thousand years, and I'll have nothing against you."

And he tugged at his great whiskers, and wrinkled his eyes, and went striding off into the sea.

That is the story about salt, and how it made a rich man of Ivan the Ninny, and besides, gave him the prettiest wife in the world, and she a Tsar's daughter.

LILIAN MOORE

I Left My Head

I left my head
somewhere
today.
Put it down for
just
a minute.
Under the
table?
On a chair?
Wish I were
able
to say
where.
Everything I need
is
in it!

MANUS PINKWATER

Blue Moose

MR. BRETON had a little restaurant on the edge of the big woods. When winter came, the north wind blew through the trees and froze everything solid. Then it snowed. Mr. Breton didn't like it.

Mr. Breton was a very good cook. Every day people from the town came to his restaurant. They ate gallons of his special clam chowder. They ate plates of his special beef stew. They ate fish stew and special homemade bread. The people from the town never talked much, and they never said anything about Mr. Breton's cooking.

"Did you like your clam chowder?" Mr. Breton would ask.

"Yup," the people from the town would say.

Mr. Breton wished they would say, "Delicious!" or "Good chowder, Breton!" All they ever said was, "Yup." In winter they came on skis and snowshoes.

Every morning Mr. Breton went out behind his house to get firewood. He wore three sweaters, a scarf, galoshes, a woolen hat, a big checkered coat, and mittens. He still felt cold. Sometimes raccoons and rabbits came out of the woods to watch Mr. Breton. The cold didn't bother them. It bothered Mr. Breton even more when they watched him.

One morning there was a moose in Mr. Breton's yard. It was a blue moose. When Mr. Breton went out his back door, the moose was there, looking at him. After a while Mr. Breton went back in and made a pot of coffee while he waited for the moose to go away. It didn't go away; it just stood in Mr. Breton's yard, looking at his back door. Mr. Breton drank a cup of coffee. The moose stood in the yard. Mr. Breton opened the door again. "Shoo! Go away!" he said to the moose.

"Do you mind if I come in and get warm?" said the moose. "I'm just about frozen." He brushed past Mr. Breton and walked into the kitchen. His antlers almost touched the ceiling.

The moose sat down on the floor next to Mr. Breton's stove. He closed his eyes and sat leaning toward the stove for a long time. Wisps of steam began to rise from his blue fur. After a long time the moose sighed. It sounded like a foghorn.

"Can I get you a cup of coffee?" Mr. Breton asked the moose. "Or some clam chowder?"

"Clam chowder," said the moose.

Mr. Breton filled a bowl with creamy clam chowder and set it on the floor. The moose dipped his big nose into the bowl and snuffled up the chowder. He made a sort of slurping, whistling noise.

"Sir," the moose said, "this is wonderful clam chowder."

Mr. Breton blushed a very deep red. "Do you really mean that?"

"Sir," the moose said, "I have eaten some very good chowder in my time, but yours is the very best."

"Oh my," said Mr. Breton, blushing even redder. "Oh my. Would you like some more?"

"Yes, with crackers," said the moose.

The moose ate seventeen bowls of chowder with crackers. Then he had twelve pieces of hot gingerbread and forty-eight cups of coffee. While the moose slurped and whistled, Mr. Breton sat in a chair. Every now and then he said to himself, "Oh my. The best he's ever eaten. Oh my."

Later, when some people from the town came to Mr. Breton's house, the moose met them at the door. "How many in your party, please?" the moose asked. "I have a table for you; please follow me."

The people from the town were surprised to see the moose. They felt like running away, but they were too surprised. The moose led them to a table, brought them menus, looked at each person, snorted, and clumped into the kitchen. "There are some people outside; I'll take care of them," he told Mr. Breton.

The people were whispering to one another about the moose when he clumped back to the table. "Are you ready to order?" he asked.

"Yup," said the people from the town. They waited for the moose to ask them if they would like some chowder, the way Mr. Breton always did. But the moose just stared at them as though they were very foolish. The people felt uncomfortable. "We'll have the clam chowder."

"Chaudière de clam; very good," the moose said. "Do you desire crackers or homemade bread?"

"We will have crackers," said the people from the town.

"I suggest you have the bread; it is hot," said the moose.

"We will have bread," said the people from the town.

"And for dessert," said the moose, "will you have fresh gingerbread or apple jacquette?"

"What do you recommend?" asked the people from the town.

"After the chaudière de clam, the gingerbread is best."

"Thank you," said the people from the town.

"It is my pleasure to serve you," said the moose. He brought bowls of chowder balanced on his antlers.

At the end of the meal, the moose clumped to the table. "Has everything been to your satisfaction?"

"Yup," said the people from the town, their mouths full of gingerbread.

"I beg your pardon?" said the moose. "What did you say?"

"It was very good," said the people from the town. "It was the best we've ever eaten."

"I will tell the chef," said the moose.

The moose clumped into the kitchen and told Mr. Breton what the people from the town had said. Mr. Breton rushed out of the kitchen and out of the house. The people from the town were sitting on the porch, putting on their snowshoes.

"Did you tell the moose that my clam chowder was the best you've ever eaten?" Mr. Breton asked.

"Yup," said the people from the town. "We said that. We think that you are the best cook in the world; we have always thought so."

"Always?" asked Mr. Breton.

"Of course," the people from the town said. "Why do you think we walk seven miles on snowshoes just to eat here?"

The people from the town walked away on their snowshoes. Mr. Breton sat on the edge of the porch and thought it over. When the moose came out to see why Mr. Breton was sitting outside without his coat on, Mr. Breton said, "Do you know, those people think I am the best cook in the whole world?"

"Of course they do," the moose said. "By the way, aren't you cold out here?"

"No, I'm not the least bit cold," Mr. Breton said. "This is turning out to be a very mild winter."

When spring finally came, the moose became moody. He spent a lot of time staring out the back door. Flocks of geese flew overhead, returning to lakes in the north, and the moose always stirred when he heard their honking.

"Chef," said the moose one morning, "I will be going tomorrow. I wonder if you would pack some gingerbread for me to take along."

Mr. Breton baked a special batch of gingerbread, packed it in parcels, and tied the parcels with string so the moose could hang them from his antlers. When the moose came downstairs, Mr. Breton was sitting in the kitchen, drinking coffee. The parcels of gingerbread were on the kitchen table.

"Do you want a bowl of coffee before you go?" Mr. Breton asked.

"Thank you," said the moose.

"I shall certainly miss you," Mr. Breton said.

"Thank you," said the moose.

"You are the best friend I have," said Mr. Breton.

"Thank you," said the moose.

"Do you suppose you'll ever come back?" asked Mr. Breton.

"Not before Thursday or Friday," said the moose. "It would be impolite to visit my uncle for less than a week." The moose hooked his antlers into the loops of string on the parcels of gingerbread. "My uncle will like this." He stood up and turned toward the door.

"Wait!" Mr. Breton shouted. "Do you mean that you are not leaving forever? I thought you were lonely for the life of a wild moose. I thought you wanted to go back to the wild free places."

"Chef, do you have any idea how cold it gets in the wild free places?" the moose said. "And the food! Terrible!"

"Have a nice time at your uncle's," said Mr. Breton.

"I'll send you a postcard," said the moose.

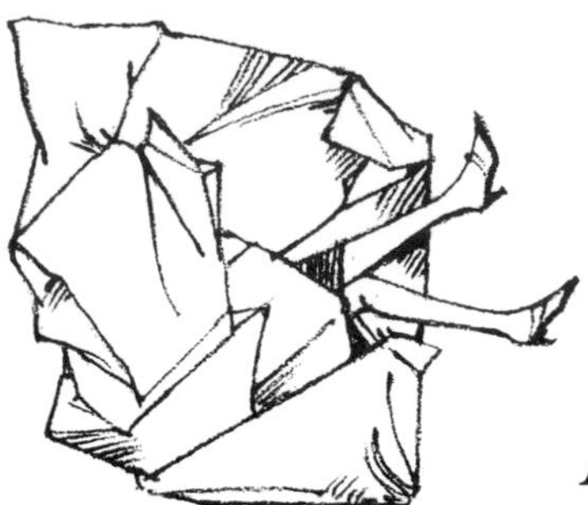

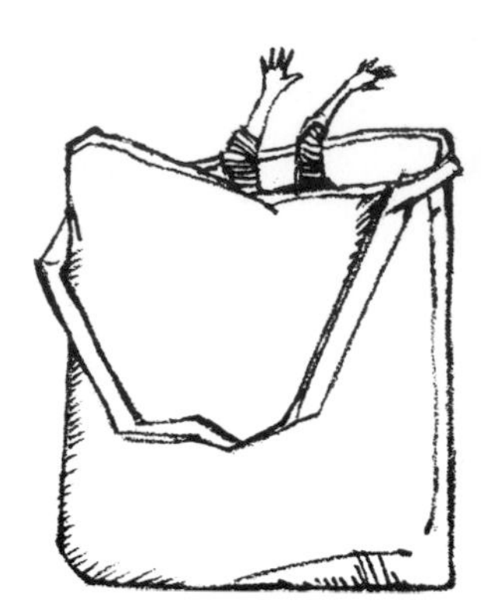

ALF PRØYSEN

Mrs. Pepperpot to the Rescue

ON THE LAST DAY of school, when the summer vacation is about to begin, all the children of the village bring flowers to decorate the classroom. They pick them in their own gardens, or they get them from their uncles and aunts, and then they carry their big bunches along the road, while they sing and shout because it is the end of the term. Their mothers and fathers wave to them and wish them a happy last day of school.

But in one window stands a little old woman who just watches the children go by. That is Mrs. Pepperpot.

She has no one now to wish a happy vacation, for all her own children are long since grown up and gone away, and none of the young ones think of asking her for flowers.

Well, that's not quite true! I do know of one little girl who picked flowers in Mrs. Pepperpot's garden. But that was several years ago, not long after the little old woman first started shrinking to the size of a pepperpot at the most inconvenient moments.

That particular summer Mrs. Pepperpot's garden was fairly bursting with flowers: there were white lilac with boughs almost laden to the ground, blue and red anemones on strong, straight stalks, poppies with graceful nodding yellow heads, and many other lovely flowers. But no one had asked Mrs. Pepperport for any of them, so she just stood in her window and watched as the children went by, singing and shouting, on their way to the day-before-vacation party.

The very last to cross the yard in front of her house was a little girl, and she was walking, oh, so slowly, and carried nothing in her hands. Mrs. Pepperpot's cat was lying on the doorstep and greeted her with a *Meow!* But the little girl only made a face and said, "Stupid animal!" And when Mrs. Pepperpot's dog, which was chained to the wall, started barking and wagging his tail the little girl snapped, "Hold your tongue!"

Then Mrs. Pepperpot opened the window to throw a bone out to the dog and the little girl whirled around and shouted angrily, "Don't you throw that dirty bone on my dress!"

That was enough. Mrs. Pepperpot put her hands on her hips and told the little girl that no one had any right to cross the yard in front of her house and throw insulting words at her or her cat and dog, which were doing no harm to anybody.

The little girl began to cry. "I want to go home," she sobbed. "I've an awful pain in my tummy and I don't want to go to the school party! Why should I go when I have a pain in my tummy?"

"Where's your mother, child?" asked Mrs. Pepperpot.

"None of your business!" snapped the girl.

"Well, where's your father, then?" asked Mrs. Pepperpot.

"Never you mind!" said the girl, still more rudely. "But if you want to know why I don't want to go to school today, it's because I haven't any flowers. We haven't a garden, anyway, as we've only been here since Christmas. But Dad's going to build us a house now that he's working at the steel mills, and then we'll have a garden. My mother makes paper flowers and puts the paper around them, see? Anything more you'd like to know? Oh well, I might as well go to school, I suppose. Teacher can say what she likes—I don't care! If *she'd* been going from school to school for three years she wouldn't know much either! So pooh to her and her flowers!" And the little girl stared defiantly at Mrs. Pepperpot.

Mrs. Pepperpot stared back at the little girl and then she said, "That's the spirit! But I think I can help you with the flowers. Just you go out in the garden and pick some lilac and anemones and poppies and anything else you like. I'll go and find some paper for you to wrap them in."

So the girl went into the garden and started picking flowers while Mrs. Pepperpot went indoors for some paper. But just as she was coming back to the door she shrank!

Roly poly! And there she was, tucked up in the paper like jam in a pudding, when the little girl came running back with her arms full of flowers.

"Here we are!" shouted the little girl.

"And here *we* are!" said Mrs. Pepperpot as she disentangled herself from the paper. "Don't be scared; this is something that happens to me from time to time, and I never know when I'm going to shrink. But now I've got an idea; I want you to put me in your schoolbag and take me along with you to school. We're going to have a game with them all! What's your name, by the way?"

"It's Rita," said the little girl, who was staring at Mrs. Pepperpot with open mouth.

"Well, Rita, don't just stand there. Hurry up and put the paper around those flowers. There's no time to lose!"

When they got to the school the party was well under way, and the teacher didn't look particularly pleased even when Rita handed her the lovely bunch of flowers. She just nodded and said, "Thanks."

"Take no notice," said Mrs. Pepperpot from Rita's schoolbag.

"Go to your desk," said the teacher. Rita sat down with her schoolbag on her knee.

"We'll start with a little arithmetic," said the teacher. "What are seven times seven?"

"Forty-nine!" whispered Mrs. Pepperpot from the schoolbag.

"Forty-nine!" said Rita.

This made the whole class turn around and stare at Rita, for up to now Rita had hardly been able to count to thirty! But Rita stared back at them and smiled. Then she stole a quick look at her schoolbag.

"What's that on your lap?" asked the teacher. "Nobody is allowed to use a crib. Give me your schoolbag at once!"

So Rita had to carry it up to the teacher's desk, where it was hung on a peg.

The teacher went on to the next question: "If we take fifteen from eighteen what do we get?"

All the children started counting on their fingers, but Rita saw that Mrs. Pepperpot was sticking both her arms and one leg out of the schoolbag.

"Three!" said Rita before the others had had time to answer.

This time nobody suspected her of cheating and Rita beamed all over while Mrs. Pepperpot waved to her from between the pages of her exercise books.

"Very strange, I must say," said the teacher. "Now we'll have a little history and geography. Which country is it that has a long wall running around it and has the oldest culture in the world?"

Rita was watching the schoolbag the whole time, and now she saw Mrs. Pepperpot's head pop up again. The little old woman had smeared her face with yellow chalk and now she put her fingers in the corners of her eyes and pulled them into narrow slits.

"China!" shouted Rita.

The teacher was quite amazed at this answer, but she had to admit that Rita was right. Then she made an announcement.

"Children," she said, "I have decided to award a treat to the one of you who gave the most right answers. Rita gave me all the right answers, so she is the winner, and she will be allowed to serve coffee to the teachers in the staff room afterwards."

Rita felt very pleased and proud; she was so used to getting meals ready when she was alone at home that she was sure she could manage this all right. So, when the other children went home, she took her schoolbag from the teacher's desk and went out into the kitchen. But, oh dear, it wasn't a bit like home! The coffeepot was far too big and the huge cake with icing on it was very different from the plate of bread-and-butter she usually got ready for her parents at home. Luckily the cups and saucers and plates and spoons had all been laid out on the table beforehand. All the same, it seemed too much to Rita, and she just sat down and cried. In a moment she heard the sound of scratching from the schoolbag, and out stepped Mrs. Pepperpot.

"If you're the girl I take you for," said the little old woman, putting her hands on her hips, "you won't give up halfway like this! Come on, just you lift me up on the table, we'll soon have this job done! As far as I could see from my hiding place, there are nine visiting teachers and your own Miss Snooty. That makes two cups of water and two dessertspoons of coffee per person—which makes twenty cups of water and twenty dessertspoons of coffee in all—right?"

"I think so. Oh, you're wonderful!" said Rita, drying her tears. "I'll measure out the water and coffee at once, but I don't know how I'm going to cut up that cake!"

"That'll be all right," said Mrs. Pepperpot. "As far as I can see the cake is about ninety paces—my paces—around. So if we divide it by ten that'll make each piece nine paces. But that will be too big for each slice, so we'll divide nine by three and make each piece three paces thick. Right?"

"I expect so," said Rita, who was getting a bit lost.

"But first we must mark a circle in the middle of the cake," went on Mrs. Pepperpot. "Lift me up on your hand, please."

Rita lifted her carefully onto her hand.

"Now take me by the legs and turn me upside down. Then, while you swing me around, I can mark a circle with one finger in the icing. Right; let's go!"

So Rita swung Mrs. Pepperpot around upside down and the result was a perfect little circle drawn right in the middle of the cake.

"Crumbs are better than no bread!" said Mrs. Pepperpot as she stood there, swaying giddily and licking her finger. "Now I'll walk right around the cake, and at every third step I want you to make a little notch in the icing with the knife. Here we go!

"One, two, three, notch!
One, two, three, notch!
One, two, three, notch!"

And in this way Mrs. Pepperpot marched all around the cake, and Rita notched it so that it made exactly thirty slices when it was cut.

When they had finished someone called from the staff room: "Where's that clever girl with the coffee? Hurry up and bring it in, dear, then you can fetch the cake afterwards."

Rita snatched up the big coffepot, which was boiling now, and hurried in with it, and Mrs. Pepperpot stood listening to the way the teachers praised Rita as she poured the coffee into the cups with a steady hand.

After a while she came out for the cake. Mrs. Pepperpot clapped her hands: "Well done, Rita! There's nothing to worry about now."

But she shouldn't have said that, for while she was listening to the teachers telling Rita again how clever she was, she suddenly heard that Miss Snooty raising her voice:

"I'm afraid you've forgotten two things, dear," she said.

"Oh dear!" thought Mrs. Pepperpot, "the cream pitcher and the sugar bowl! I shall have to look and see if they are both filled."

The cream pitcher was full, but when Mrs. Pepperpot leaned over the edge of the sugar bowl she toppled in! And at the same moment Rita rushed in, put the lid on the sugar bowl, and put it and the cream pitcher on a little tray. Then she turned around and went back to the staff room.

First Mrs. Pepperpot wondered if she should tell Rita where she was, but she was afraid the child might drop the tray altogether, so instead she buried herself well down in the sugar bowl and hoped for the best.

Rita started carrying the tray around. But her teacher hadn't finished with her yet. "I hope you remembered the sugar tongs," she said.

Rita didn't know what to say, but Mrs. Pepperpot heard the remark, and when the visiting school principal took the lid off, Mrs. Pepperpot popped up like a jack-in-the-box, holding a lump of sugar in her outstretched hand. She stared straight in front of her and never moved an eyelid, so the principal didn't notice anything odd. He simply took the sugar lump and waved Rita on with the tray. But his neighbor at the table looked hard at Mrs. Pepperpot and said, "What very curious sugar tongs—I suppose they're made of plastic. Whatever will they think of next?" Then he asked Rita if she had brought them with her from home, and she said yes, which was strictly true, of course.

After that everyone wanted to have a look at the curious sugar tongs, till in the end Rita's teacher called her over.

"Let me have a look at those tongs," she said. She reached out her hand to pick them up, but this was too much for Mrs. Pepperpot. In a moment she had the whole tray over and everything fell on the floor. The cream pitcher was smashed and the contents of the sugar bowl rolled under the cupboard, which was just as well for Mrs. Pepperpot!

But the teacher thought it was she who had upset the tray, and suddenly she was sorry she had been so hard on the little girl. She put her arms around Rita and gave her a hug. "It was all my fault." she said. "You've been a very good little parlormaid."

Later, when all the guests had gone, and Rita was clearing the table, the teacher pointed to the dark corner by the cupboard and said, "Who is that standing there?"

And out stepped Mrs. Pepperpot as large as life and quite unruffled. "I've been sent to lend a hand with the dishwashing," she said. "Give me that tray, Rita. You and I will go out into the kitchen."

When at last the two of them were walking home, Rita said, "Why did you help me all day when I was so horrid to you this morning?"

"Well," said Mrs. Pepperpot, "perhaps it was because you were so horrid. Next time maybe I'll help that Miss Snooty of yours. She looks pretty horrid, too, but she might be nice underneath."

MYRA COHN LIVINGSTON

Order

You mean, if I'd keep my room clean
And never stuff things under the bed
And hang up my jacket
And get straight *A's*
And be polite
And work hard
And never get into trouble
I could someday grow up to be President?

Forget it!

BEATRIX POTTER

The Tailor of Gloucester

IN THE TIME of swords and periwigs and full-skirted coats with flowered lappets—when gentlemen wore ruffles, and gold-laced waistcoats of paduasoy and taffeta—there lived a tailor in Gloucester.

He sat in the window of a little shop in Westgate Street, cross-legged on a table from morning till dark.

All day long while the light lasted he sewed and snippeted, piecing out his satin, and pompadour, and lutestring; stuffs had strange names, and were very expensive, in the days of the Tailor of Gloucester.

But although he sewed fine silk for his neighbors, he himself was very, very poor—a little old man in spectacles, with a pinched face, old crooked fingers, and a suit of threadbare clothes.

He cut his coats without waste, according to his embroidered cloth; they were very small ends and snippets that lay about upon the table—"Too narrow breadths for naught—except waistcoats for mice," said the tailor.

One bitter cold day near Christmastime the tailor began to make a coat (a coat of cherry-colored corded silk embroidered with pansies and roses) and a cream-colored satin waistcoat (trimmed with gauze and green worsted chenille) for the Mayor of Gloucester.

The tailor worked and worked, and he talked to himself. He measured the silk, and turned it round and round, and trimmed it into shape with his shears; the table was all littered with cherry-colored snippets.

"No breadth at all, and cut on the cross; it is no breadth at all; tippets for mice and ribbons for mobs! for mice!" said the Tailor of Gloucester.

When the snowflakes came down against the small leaded window-panes and shut out the light, the tailor had done his day's work; all the silk and satin lay cut out upon the table.

There were twelve pieces for the coat and four pieces for the waistcoat; and there were pocket-flaps and cuffs and buttons, all in order. For the lining of the coat there was fine yellow taffeta, and for the buttonholes of the waistcoat there was cherry-colored twist. And everything was ready to sew together in the morning, all measured and sufficient—except that there was wanting just one single skein of cherry-colored twisted silk.

The tailor came out of his shop at dark; for he did not sleep there at night; he fastened the window and locked the door, and took away the key. No one lived there at night but little brown mice, and *they* ran in and out without any keys!

For behind the wooden wainscots of all the old houses in Gloucester, there are little mouse staircases and secret trapdoors; and the mice run from house to house through those long, narrow passages; they can run all over the town without going into the streets.

But the tailor came out of his shop and shuffled home through the snow; he lived quite near by in College Court, next the doorway to College Green. And although it was not a big house, the tailor was so poor he only rented the kitchen.

He lived alone with his cat; it was called Simpkin.

Now all day long while the tailor was out at work, Simpkin kept house by himself; and he also was fond of the mice, though he gave them no satin for coats!

"Miaw?" said the cat when the tailor opened the door, "miaw?"

The tailor replied: "Simpkin, we shall make our fortune, but I am worn to a raveling. Take this groat (which is our last fourpence), and, Simpkin, take a china pipkin, buy a penn'orth of bread, a penn'orth of milk, and a penn'orth of sausages. And oh, Simpkin, with the last penny of our fourpence buy me one penn'orth of cherry-colored silk. But do not lose the last penny of the fourpence, Simpkin, or I am undone and worn to a thread-paper, for I have NO MORE TWIST."

Then Simpkin again said "Miaw!" and took the groat and the pipkin, and went out into the dark.

The tailor was very tired and beginning to be ill. He sat down by the hearth and talked to himself about that wonderful coat.

"I shall make my fortune—to be cut bias—the Mayor of Gloucester is to be married on Christmas Day in the morning, and he hath ordered a coat and an embroidered waistcoat—to be lined with yellow taffeta—and the taffeta sufficeth; there is no more left over in snippets than will serve to make tippets for mice—"

Then the tailor started; for suddenly, interrupting him, from the dresser at the other side of the kitchen came a number of little noises—

Tip tap, tip tap, tip tap tip!

"Now what can that be?" said the Tailor of Gloucester, jumping up from his chair. The dresser was covered with crockery and pipkins, willow pattern plates, and teacups and mugs.

The tailor crossed the kitchen, and stood quite still beside the dresser, listening, and peering through his spectacles. Again from under a teacup came those funny little noises—

Tip tap, tip tap, tip tap tip!

"This is very peculiar," said the Tailor of Gloucester, and he lifted up the teacup which was upside down.

Out stepped a little live lady mouse, and made a curtsy to the tailor! Then she hopped away down off the dresser, and under the wainscot.

The tailor sat down again by the fire, warming his poor cold hands, and mumbling to himself:—

"The waistcoat is cut out from peach-colored satin—tambour stitch and rosebuds in beautiful floss silk! Was I wise to entrust my last fourpence to Simpkin? One-and-twenty buttonholes of cherry-colored twist!"

But all at once, from the dresser, there came other little noises—

Tip tap, tip tap, tip tap tip!

"This is passing extraordinary!" said the Tailor of Gloucester, and turned over another teacup, which was upside down.

Out stepped a little gentleman mouse, and made a bow to the tailor!

And then from all over the dresser came a chorus of little tappings, all sounding together, and answering one another, like watchbeetles in an old worm-eaten window shutter—

Tip tap, tip tap, tip tap tip!

And out from under teacups and from under bowls and basins stepped other and more little mice, who hopped away down off the dresser and under the wainscot.

The tailor sat down, close over the fire, lamenting: "One-and-twenty buttonholes of cherry-colored silk! To be finished by noon of Saturday: and this is Tuesday evening. Was it right to let loose those mice, undoubtedly the property of Simpkin? Alack, I am undone, for I have no more twist!"

The little mice came out again and listened to the tailor; they took notice of the pattern of that wonderful coat. They whispered to one another about the taffeta lining and about little mouse tippets.

And then suddenly they all ran away together down the passage behind the wainscot, squeaking and calling to one another as they ran from house to house; and not one mouse was left in the tailor's kitchen when Simpkin came back with the pipkin of milk!

Simpkin opened the door and bounced in, with an angry "G-r-r-miaw!" like a cat that is vexed; for he hated the snow, and there was snow in his ears, and snow in his collar at the back of his neck. He put down the loaf and the sausages upon the dresser, and sniffed.

"Simpkin," said the tailor, "where is my twist?"

But Simpkin set down the pipkin of milk upon the dresser, and looked suspiciously at the teacups. He wanted his supper of little fat mouse!

"Simpkin," said the tailor, "where is my TWIST?"

But Simpkin hid a little parcel privately in the teapot, and spit and growled at the tailor; and if Simpkin had been able to talk, he would have asked: "Where is my MOUSE?"

"Alack, I am undone!" said the Tailor of Gloucester, and went sadly to bed.

All that night long Simpkin hunted and searched through the kitchen, peeping into cupboards and under the wainscot, and into the teapot where he had hidden that twist; but still he found never a mouse!

And whenever the tailor muttered and talked in his sleep, Simpkin said: "Miaw-ger-r-w-s-s-ch!" and made strange, horrid noises, as cats do at night.

For the poor old tailor was very ill with a fever, tossing and turning in his four-post bed; and still in his dreams he mumbled: "No more twist! No more twist!"

All that day he was ill, and the next day, and the next; and what should become of the cherry-colored coat? In the tailor's shop in Westgate Street the embroidered silk and satin lay cut out upon the table—one-and-twenty buttonholes—and who should come to sew them, when the window was barred, and the door was fast locked?

But that does not hinder the little brown mice; they run in and out without any keys through all the old houses in Gloucester!

Out-of-doors the market folks went trudging through the snow to buy their geese and turkeys, and to bake their Christmas pies; but there would be no Christmas dinner for Simpkin and the poor old tailor of Gloucester.

The tailor lay ill for three days and nights; and then it was Christmas Eve, and very late at night. The moon climbed up over the roofs and chimneys, and looked down over the gateway into College Court. There were no lights in the windows, nor any sound in the houses; all the city of Gloucester was fast asleep under the snow.

And still Simpkin wanted his mice, and mewed as he stood beside the four-post bed.

But it is in the old story that all the beasts can talk in the night between Christmas Eve and Christmas Day in the morning (though there are very few folk that can hear them, or know what it is that they say).

When the Cathedral clock struck twelve there was an answer—like an echo of the chimes—and Simpkin heard it, and came out of the tailor's door, and wandered about in the snow.

From all the roofs and gables and old wooden houses in Gloucester came a thousand merry voices singing the old Christmas rhymes—all the old songs that ever I heard of, and some that I don't know, like Whittington's bells.

First and loudest the cocks cried out: "Dame, get up, and bake your pies!"

"Oh, dilly, dilly, dilly!" sighed Simpkin.

And now in a garret there were lights and sounds of dancing, and cats came from over the way.

"Hey, diddle, diddle, the cat and the fiddle! All the cats in Gloucester—except me," said Simpkin.

Under the wooden eaves the starlings and sparrows sang of Christmas pies; the jackdaws woke up in the Cathedral tower; and although it was the middle of the night the throstles and robins sang; the air was quite full of little twittering tunes.

But it was all rather provoking to poor hungry Simpkin.

Particularly he was vexed with some little shrill voices from behind a wooden lattice. I think that they were bats, because they always have very small voices—especially in a black frost, when they talk in their sleep, like the Tailor of Gloucester.

They said something mysterious that sounded like—

"Buzz, quoth the blue fly; hum, quoth the bee;
Buzz and hum they cry, and so do we!"

and Simpkin went away shaking his ears as if he had a bee in his bonnet.

From the tailor's shop in Westgate came a glow of light; and when

Simpkin crept up to peep in at the window it was full of candles. There was a snippeting of scissors, and snappeting of thread; and little mouse voices sang loudly and gaily:

"Four-and-twenty tailors
Went to catch a snail,
The best man amongst them
Durst not touch her tail;
She put out her horns
Like a little Kyloe cow.
Run, tailors, run!
Or she'll have you all e'en now!"

Then without a pause the little mouse voices went on again:

"Sieve my lady's oatmeal,
Grind my lady's flour,
Put it in a chestnut,
Let it stand an hour—"

"Mew! Mew!" interrupted Simpkin, and he scratched at the door. But the key was under the tailor's pillow; he could not get in.

The little mice only laughed, and tried another tune—

"Three little mice sat down to spin,
Pussy passed by and she peeped in.
What are you at, my fine little men?
Making coats for gentlemen.
Shall I come in and cut off your threads?
Oh, no, Miss Pussy, you'd bite off our heads!"

"Mew! Mew!" cried Simpkin.

"Hey diddle dinkety!" answered the little mice—

"Hey diddle dinkety, poppety pet!
The merchants of London they wear scarlet;
Silk in the collar, and gold in the hem,
So merrily march the merchantmen!"

They clicked their thimbles to mark the time, but none of the songs pleased Simpkin; he sniffed and mewed at the door of the shop.

"And then I bought
A pipkin and a popkin,
A slipkin and a slopkin,
All for one farthing—

and upon the kitchen dresser!" added the rude little mice.

"Mew! scratch! scratch!" scuffled Simpkin on the windowsill; while the little mice inside sprang to their feet, and all began to shout at once in little twittering voices: "No more twist! No more twist!" And they barred up the window shutters and shut out Simpkin.

But still through the nicks in the shutters he could hear the click of thimbles, and little mouse voices singing: "No more twist! No more twist!"

Simpkin came away from the shop and went home considering in his mind. He found the poor old tailor without fever, sleeping peacefully.

Then Simpkin went on tiptoe and took a little parcel of silk out of the teapot; and looked at it in the moonlight; and he felt quite ashamed of his badness compared with those good little mice!

When the tailor awoke in the morning, the first thing which he saw, upon the patchwork quilt, was a skein of cherry-colored twisted silk, and beside his bed stood the repentant Simpkin!

"Alack, I am worn to a raveling," said the tailor of Gloucester, "but I have my twist!"

The sun was shining on the snow when the tailor got up and dressed, and came out into the street with Simpkin running before him.

The starlings whistled on the chimney stacks, and the throstles and robins sang—but they sang their own little noises, not the words they had sung in the night.

"Alack," said the tailor, "I have my twist; but no more strength—nor time—than will serve to make me one single buttonhole; for this is Christmas Day in the Morning! The Mayor of Gloucester shall be married by noon—and where is his cherry-colored coat?"

He unlocked the door of the little shop in Westgate Street, and Simpkin ran in, like a cat that expects something.

But there was no one there! Not even one little brown mouse!

The boards were swept and clean; the little ends of thread and the little silk snippets were all tidied away, and gone from off the floor.

But upon the table—oh joy! the tailor gave a shout—there, where he had left plain cuttings of silk—there lay the most beautifullest coat and embroidered satin waistcoat that ever were worn by a Mayor of Gloucester!

There were roses and pansies upon the facing of the coat; and the waistcoat was worked with poppies and cornflowers.

Everything was finished except just one single cherry-colored buttonhole, and where that buttonhole was wanting there was pinned a scrap of paper with these words—in little teeny weeny writing—

NO MORE TWIST.

And from then began the luck of the Tailor of Gloucester; he grew quite stout, and he grew quite rich.

He made the most wonderful waistcoats for all the rich merchants of Gloucester, and for all the fine gentlemen of the country round.

Never were seen such ruffles, or such embroidered cuffs and lappets! But his buttonholes were the greatest triumph of it all.

The stitches of those buttonholes were so neat—*so* neat—I wonder how they could be stitched by an old man in spectacles, with crooked old fingers, and a tailor's thimble.

The stitches of those buttonholes were so small—*so* small—they looked as if they had been made by little mice!

FELICE HOLMAN

Supermarket

I'm
lost
among a
maze of cans,
behind a pyramid
of jams, quite near
asparagus and rice,
close to the Oriental spice,
and just before sardines.
I hear my mother calling, "Joe.
Where are you, Joe? Where did you
Go?" And I reply in voice concealed among
the candied orange peel, and packs of Chocolate Dreams.

"I
hear
you, Mother
dear, I'm here—
quite near the ginger ale
and beer, and lost among a
maze
of cans
behind a
pyramid of jams,
quite near asparagus
and rice, close to the
Oriental spice, and just before sardines."

But
still
my mother
calls me, "Joe!
Where are you, Joe?
Where did you go?"

"Somewhere
around asparagus
that's in a sort of
broken glass,
beside a kind of m-
ess-
y jell
that's near a tower of cans that f
e
l
l
and squashed the Chocolate Dreams."

HUGH LOFTING

When Hugh Lofting was a boy in England he kept pets in the family linen closet—at least for a time. Years later he invented his famous character Doctor Dolittle, who kept a squirrel in *his* linen closet (as well as white mice in the piano and other assorted animals in assorted places).

Hugh Lofting fought and was wounded in World War I. He noticed that wounded men were given proper attention, but wounded horses were simply shot. And so he imagined a doctor (not a vet, but a real M.D.) who might treat all the diseases of all animals—first, of course, learning their languages. He created a tubby, kind, wise, high-hatted Doctor Dolittle—and wrote about him in letters home to his children, Colin and Elizabeth. These letters, including delightful drawings, grew into a book—*The Story of Doctor Dolittle*—and that was followed by eleven others. They are read all over the world and were once made into a not very good film.

The notion of communication between animals and humans traces back so far in literature and legend that sometimes we get the odd feeling that at one time such communication really existed. Today scientists seem to be going back to this ancient idea. Some are trying to learn the language of the brainy dolphins and whales, and others are trying, with some success, to teach chimpanzees and gorillas our own language.

Here's how Doctor Dolittle became a genius at animal talk. It was his parrot Polynesia who started him off by explaining that the animals badly needed a doctor who could talk to his patients. "Could I learn?" he asked. "I don't see why not," she replied. "You're quite intelligent." And so Doctor Dolittle, helped by his friends Jip the dog, Gub-Gub the pig, Dab-Dab the duck, Chee-Chee the chimp, Too-Too the owl, and other highly conversational beasts, achieved a great reputation in Puddleby-on-the-Marsh, a little English village.

He's just about established himself when he's called away to Africa to cure the monkeys of a dread disease. He succeeds, and on the way back he and his crew discover a little boy stowaway who's in search of his uncle who has disappeared. The selection following, from the first and best of the Dolittle books, starts at this point.

Smells

OUR UNCLE must now be *found,*" said the Doctor—"that is the next thing—now that we know he wasn't thrown into the sea."

Then Dab-Dab came up to him again and whispered, "Ask the eagles to look for the man. No living creature can see better than an eagle. When they are miles high in the air they can count the ants crawling on the ground. Ask the eagles."

So the Doctor sent one of the swallows off to get some eagles.

And in about an hour the little bird came back with six different kinds of eagles: a Black Eagle, a Bald Eagle, a Fish Eagle, a Golden Eagle, an Eagle-Vulture, and a White-tailed Sea Eagle. Twice as high as the boy they were, each one of them. And they stood on the rail of the ship, like round-shouldered soldiers all in a row, stern and still and stiff; while their great, gleaming, black eyes shot darting glances here and there and everywhere.

Gub-Gub was scared of them and got behind a barrel. He said he felt as though those terrible eyes were looking right inside of him to see what he had stolen for lunch.

And the Doctor said to the eagles, "A man has been lost—a fisherman with red hair and an anchor marked on his arm. Would you be so kind as to see if you can find him for us? This boy is the man's nephew."

Eagles do not talk very much. And all they answered in their husky voices was, "You may be sure that we will do our best—for John Dolittle."

Then they flew off—and Gub-Gub came out from behind his barrel to see them go. Up and up and up they went—higher and higher and higher still. Then, when the Doctor could only just see them, they parted company and started going off all different ways—North, East, South and West, looking like tiny grains of black sand creeping across the wide, blue sky.

"My gracious!" said Gub-Gub in a hushed voice. "What a height! I wonder they don't scorch their feathers—so near the sun!"

They were gone a long time. And when they came back it was almost night.

And the eagles said to the Doctor, "We have searched all the seas and all the countries and all the islands and all the cities and all the villages in this half of the world. But we have failed. In the main street of Gibraltar we saw three red hairs lying on a wheelbarrow before a baker's door. But they were not the hairs of a man—they were the hairs out of a fur coat. Nowhere, on land or water, could we see any sign of this boy's uncle. And if *we* could not see him, then he is not to be seen. . . . For John Dolittle—we have done our best."

Then the six great birds flapped their big wings and flew back to their homes in the mountains and the rocks.

"Well," said Dab-Dab, after they had gone, "what are we going to do now? The boy's uncle *must* be found—there's no two ways about that. The lad isn't old enough to be knocking around the world by himself. Boys aren't like ducklings—they have to be taken care of till they're quite old. . . . I wish Chee-Chee were here. He would soon find the man. Good old Chee-Chee! I wonder how he's getting on!"

"If we only had Polynesia with us," said the white mouse. "*She* would soon think of some way. My, but she was a clever one!"

"I don't think so much of those eagle fellows," said Jip. "They're just conceited. They may have very good eyesight and all that; but when you ask them to find a man for you, they can't do it—and they have the cheek to come back and say that nobody else could do it. They're just conceited—like that collie in Puddleby. And I don't think a whole lot of those gossipy old porpoises either. All they could tell us was that the man isn't in the sea. We don't want to know where he *isn't*—we want to know where he *is*."

"Oh, don't talk so much," said Gub-Gub. "It's easy to talk; but it isn't so easy to find a man when you have got the whole world to hunt him in. Maybe the fisherman's hair has turned white, worrying about the boy; and that was why the eagles didn't find him. You don't know everything. You're just talking. You are not doing anything to help. You couldn't find the boy's uncle any more than the eagles could—you couldn't do as well."

"Couldn't I?" said the dog. "That's all you know, you stupid piece of warm bacon! I haven't begun to try yet, have I? You wait and see!"

Then Jip went to the Doctor and said, "Ask the boy if he has anything in his pockets that belonged to his uncle, will you, please?"

So the Doctor asked him. And the boy showed them a gold ring which he wore on a piece of string around his neck because it was too big for his finger. He said his uncle gave it to him when they saw the pirates coming.

Jip smelled the ring and said, "That's no good. Ask him if he has anything else that belonged to his uncle."

Then the boy took from his pocket a great big red handkerchief and said, "This was my uncle's too."

As soon as the boy pulled it out, Jip shouted, "*Snuff*, by Jingo!—Black Rappee snuff. Don't you smell it? His uncle took snuff—ask him, Doctor."

The Doctor questioned the boy again; and he said, "Yes. My uncle took a lot of snuff."

"Fine!" said Jip. "The man's as good as found. 'Twill be as easy as stealing milk from a kitten. Tell the boy I'll find his uncle for him in less than a week. Let us go upstairs and see which way the wind is blowing."

"But it is dark now," said the Doctor. "You can't find him in the dark!"

"I don't need any light to look for a man who smells of Black Rappee snuff," said Jip as he climbed the stairs. "If the man had a hard smell, like string, now—or hot water, it would be different. But *snuff!*—tut, tut!"

"Does hot water have a smell?" asked the Doctor.

"Certainly it has," said Jip. "Hot water smells quite different from cold water. It is warm water—or ice—that has the really difficult smell. Why, I once followed a man for ten miles on a dark night by the smell of the hot water he had used to shave with—for the poor fellow had no soap. . . . Now then, let us see which way the wind is blowing. Wind is very important in long-distance smelling. It mustn't be too fierce a wind—and of course it must blow the right way. A nice, steady, damp breeze is the best of all. . . . Ha!—this wind is from the North."

Then Jip went up to the front of the ship and smelled the wind; and he started muttering to himself, "Tar; Spanish onions; kerosene oil; wet raincoats; crushed laurel leaves; rubber burning; lace curtains being washed—no, my mistake, lace curtains hanging out to dry; and foxes—hundreds of 'em—cubs; and—"

"Can you really smell all those different things in this one wind?" asked the Doctor.

"Why, of course!" said Jip. "And those are only a few of the easy smells—the strong ones. Any mongrel could smell those with a cold in the head. Wait now, and I'll tell you some of the harder scents that are coming on this wind—a few of the dainty ones."

Then the dog shut his eyes tight, poked his nose straight up in the air, and sniffed hard with his mouth half open.

For a long time he said nothing. He kept as still as a stone. He hardly seemed to be breathing at all. When at last he began to speak, it sounded almost as though he were singing, sadly, in a dream.

"Bricks," he whispered, very low—"old yellow bricks, crumbling with age in a garden wall; the sweet breath of young cows standing in a mountain stream; the lead roof of a dovecote—or perhaps a granary—with the midday sun on it; black kid gloves lying in a bureau drawer of walnut wood; a dusty road with a horses' drinking-trough beneath the sycamores; little mushrooms bursting through the rotting leaves; and—and—and—"

"Any parsnips?" asked Gub-Gub.

"No," said Jip. "You always think of things to eat. No parsnips whatever. And no snuff—plenty of pipes and cigarettes, and a few cigars. But no snuff. We must wait till the wind changes to the South."

"Yes, it's a poor wind, that," said Gub-Gub. "I think you're a fake, Jip. Who ever heard of finding a man in the middle of the ocean just by smell! I told you you couldn't do it."

"Look here," said Jip, getting really angry. "You're going to get a bite on the nose in a minute! You needn't think that just because the Doctor won't let us give you what you deserve, that you can be as cheeky as you like!"

"Stop quarreling!" said the Doctor. "Stop it! Life's too short. Tell me, Jip, where do you think those smells are coming from?"

"From Devon and Wales—most of them," said Jip. "The wind is coming that way."

"Well, well!" said the Doctor. "You know that's really quite remarkable—quite. I must make a note of that for my new book. I wonder if you could train me to smell as well as that. . . . But no—perhaps I'm better off the way I am. 'Enough is as good as a feast,' they say. Let's go down to supper. I'm quite hungry."

"So am I," said Gub-Gub.

The Rock

UP THEY GOT, early next morning, out of the silken beds; and they saw that the sun was shining brightly and that the wind was blowing from the South.

Jip smelled the South wind for half an hour. Then he came to the Doctor, shaking his head.

"I smell no snuff as yet," he said. "We must wait till the wind changes to the East."

But even when the East wind came, at three o'clock that afternoon, the dog could not catch the smell of snuff.

The little boy was terribly disappointed and began to cry again, saying that no one seemed to be able to find his uncle for him. But all Jip said to the Doctor was, "Tell him that when the wind changes to the West, I'll find his uncle even though he be in China—so long as he is still taking Black Rappee snuff."

Three days they had to wait before the West wind came. This was on a Friday morning, early—just as it was getting light. A fine rainy mist lay on the sea like a thin fog. And the wind was soft and warm and wet.

As soon as Jip awoke he ran upstairs and poked his nose in the air. Then he got most frightfully excited and rushed down again to wake the Doctor up.

"Doctor!" he cried. "I've got it! Doctor! Doctor! Wake up! Listen! I've got it! The wind's from the West and it smells of nothing but snuff. Come upstairs and start the ship—quick!"

So the Doctor tumbled out of bed and went to the rudder to steer the ship.

"Now I'll go up to the front," said Jip; "and you watch my nose—whichever way I point it, you turn the ship the same way. The man cannot be far off—with the smell as strong as this. And the wind's all lovely and wet. Now watch me!"

So all that morning Jip stood in the front part of the ship, sniffing the wind and pointing the way for the Doctor to steer; while all the animals and the little boy stood round with their eyes wide open, watching the dog in wonder.

About lunchtime Jip asked Dab-Dab to tell the Doctor that he was getting worried and wanted to speak to him. So Dab-Dab went and fetched the Doctor from the other end of the ship and Jip said to him, "The boy's uncle is starving. We must make the ship go as fast as we can."

"How do you know he is starving?" asked the Doctor.

"Because there is no other smell in the West wind but snuff," said Jip. "If the man were cooking or eating food of any kind, I would be bound to smell it too. But he hasn't even fresh water to drink. All he is taking is snuff—in large pinches. We are getting nearer to him all the time, because the smell grows stronger every minute. But make the ship go as fast as you can, for I am certain that the man is starving."

"All right," said the Doctor; and he sent Dab-Dab to ask the swallows to pull the ship, the same as they had done when the pirates were chasing them.

So the stout little birds came down and once more harnessed themselves to the ship.

And now the boat went bounding through the waves at a terrible speed. It went so fast that the fishes in the sea had to jump for their lives to get out of the way and not be run over.

And all the animals got tremendously excited; and they gave up looking at Jip and turned to watch the sea in front, to spy out any land or islands where the starving man might be.

But hour after hour went by and still the ship went rushing on, over the same flat, flat sea; and no land anywhere came in sight.

And now the animals gave up chattering and sat around silent, anxious and miserable. The little boy again grew sad. And on Jip's face there was a worried look.

At last, late in the afternoon, just as the sun was going down, the owl, Too-Too, who was perched on the tip of the mast, suddenly startled them all by crying out at the top of his voice, "Jip! Jip! I see a great, great rock in front of us—look—way out there where the sky and the water meet. See the sun shine on it—like gold! Is the smell coming from there?"

And Jip called back, "Yes, That's it. That is where the man is. At last, at last!"

And when they got nearer they could see that the rock was very large—as large as a big field. No trees grew on it, no grass—nothing. The great rock was as smooth and as bare as the back of a tortoise.

Then the Doctor sailed the ship right round the rock. But nowhere on it could a man be seen. All the animals screwed up their eyes and looked as hard as they could; and John Dolittle got a telescope from downstairs.

But not one living thing could they spy—not even a gull, nor a starfish, nor a shred of seaweed.

They all stood still and listened, straining their ears for any sound. But the only noise they heard was the gentle lapping of the little waves against the sides of their ship.

Then they all started calling, "Hulloa, there!—HULLOA!" till their voices were hoarse. But only the echo came back from the rock.

And the little boy burst into tears and said, "I am afraid I shall never see my uncle any more! What shall I tell them when I get home!"

But Jip called to the Doctor, "He must be there—he must—*he must!* The smell goes on no further. He must be there, I tell you! Sail the ship close to the rock and let me jump out on it."

So the Doctor brought the ship as close as he could and let down the anchor. Then he and Jip got out of the ship onto the rock.

Jip at once put his nose down close to the ground and began to run all over the place. Up and down he went, back and forth — zigzagging, twisting, doubling and turning. And everywhere he went, the Doctor ran behind him, close at his heels—till he was terribly out of breath.

At last Jip let out a great bark and sat down. And when the Doctor came running up to him, he found the dog staring into a big, deep hole in the middle of the rock.

"The boy's uncle is down there," said Jip quietly. "No wonder those silly eagles couldn't see him! It takes a dog to find a man."

So the Doctor got down into the hole, which seemed to be a kind of cave, or tunnel, running a long way under the ground. Then he struck a match and started to make his way along the dark passage with Jip following behind.

The Doctor's match soon went out; and he had to strike another and another and another.

At last the passage came to an end; and the Doctor found himself in a kind of tiny room with walls of rock.

And there, in the middle of the room, his head resting on his arms, lay a man with very red hair—fast asleep!

Jip went up and sniffed at something lying on the ground beside him. The Doctor stooped and picked it up. It was an enormous snuffbox. And it was full of Black Rappee!

ROBERT FROMAN

Easy Diver

Pigeon on the roof.
Dives.
Go-
ing
fa-
st.
G
O
I
N
G

T
O

HIT HARD!

O p e n s w i n g s .

Softly, gently,

down.

ANON.

In Turkey and the countries around it people have been telling tales for over five hundred years about a character named Nasr-ed-Din Hodja. Call him the Hodja for short. The Hodja is foolish, lovable, sometimes wise. In this story, told by Alice Geer Kelsey, he's two out of these three things.

How Many Donkeys?
A Folktale from Turkey

THERE WAS the tinkle of tiny bells, the sharp clip of small hooves, the throaty drone of a solitary singer. Nasr-ed-Din Hodja was bringing the donkeys back from the mill, their saddlebags filled with freshly ground wheat. The hot Turkish sun beat down on his turbaned head. The brown dust from the donkey's hooves puffed about him. The staccato trot of his donkey jiggled him back and forth. But Nasr-ed-Din Hodja was too pleased to be uncomfortable.

"I'll show them," he chuckled. "They gave me plenty of advice about taking care of their donkeys and their wheat. As though I did not know more about donkeys than any man in Ak Shehir."

His eyes rested lazily on the road ahead. At first it followed the brook running away from Mill Valley, the brook that turned the heavy stones to grind the wheat. Then the road disappeared over a hilltop.

"Just over that hill," he mused contentedly, "is Ak Shehir, where they are waiting for their donkeys. There is not a scratch or a bruise on one of the little creatures. No donkeys in all Turkey have had better treatment today than these nine."

Idly he began counting them.

"What?" he gasped. "Eight donkeys?"

He jumped from his donkey and ran hither and yon, looking behind rocks and over hilltops, but no stray donkey could he see. At last he stood beside the donkeys and counted again. This time there were nine. With a sigh of relief he climbed onto his own donkey and went swinging along the road. His long legs in their baggy pantaloons swung easily back and forth in time to the donkey's trot. Passing through a cluster of trees he thought it time to count the donkeys again.

"One—two—three" and up to eight he counted, but no ninth donkey was to be seen. Down from his donkey's back he came. Behind all the trees he peered. Not a hair of a donkey could he find.

Again he counted, standing beside his donkeys. There they all were—nine mild little donkeys waiting for orders to move on. Nasr-ed-Din Hodja scratched his poor head in bewilderment. Was he losing his mind or were the donkeys all bewitched? Again he counted. Yes, surely there were nine.

"Ughr-r-r-r." Nasr-ed-Din Hodja gave the low guttural which is Turkish for "Giddap." As he rode on, he looked about him for the evil spirits which must be playing tricks on him. Each donkey wore the blue beads which should drive away the evil spirits. Were there evil spirits abroad stronger even than the blue beads?

He was glad to see a friend coming toward him down the road.

"Oh, Mustapha Effendi," he cried. "Have you seen one of these donkeys? I have lost a donkey and yet I have not lost it."

"What can you mean, Hodja Effendi?" asked Mustapha.

"I left the mill with nine donkeys," explained the Hodja. "Part of the way home there have been nine and part of the way there have been eight. Oh, I am bewitched! Help me! Help me!"

Mustapha was used to the queer ways of the Hodja, but he was surprised. He counted the donkeys silently.

"Let me see you count the donkeys," he ordered the Hodja.

"One—two—three," began the Hodja, pointing at each one as he counted up to eight.

As he said the last number, he stopped and looked at his friend with a face full of helplessness and terror. His terror turned to amazement as Mustapha slapped his knee and laughed until he almost fell from his donkey.

"What is so funny?" asked the Hodja.

"Oh, Hodja Effendi!" Mustapha laughed. "When you are counting your brothers, why, oh why, do you not count the brother on whom you are riding?"

Nasr-ed-Din Hodja was silent for a moment to think through this discovery. Then he kissed the hand of his deliverer, pressed it to his forehead and thanked him a thousand times for his help. He rode, singing, on to Ak Shehir to deliver the donkeys to their owners.

ASTRID LINDGREN

Astrid Lindgren is the best-known Swedish writer of children's books and one of the most popular in all of Europe. Her character Pippi Longstocking made her famous. Since Pippi, she's written more than a score of other books, including a hilarious series featuring the detective Bill Bergson, as well as two Pippi follow-ups: *Pippi Goes on Board* and *Pippi in the South Seas*. Perhaps her funniest book is *Emil in the Soup Tureen*, and I wish I had space to reprint something from it.

Astrid Lindgren was a farmer's daughter, born in 1907. When her own daughter, Karen, was seven and was recovering from pneumonia, Mrs. Lindgren kept her happy by telling her stories about the superchild, Pippi Longstocking. Three years later Mrs. Lindgren slipped on the ice during a snowstorm, broke her ankle, had to stay in bed, and wrote down the stories to keep herself busy. That was in 1944, when Mrs. Lindgren was thirty-seven years old.

The next year *Pippi Longstocking* was published. Children liked it but some grown-ups didn't. Teachers were shocked: Pippi doesn't go to school. Parents were shocked: Pippi gets along fine with neither father nor mother, and has a horse and a monkey for company. However, it didn't take long for everyone to fall in love with Pippi, because, though she does what she pleases, she is generous, courageous, and—most of all—funny. Today in Sweden when a child does a good deed in school she's allowed to call herself "Little Pippi."

Here is the first episode of *Pippi Longstocking*. Get the book and see what happens next as Pippi visits a classroom, goes to the circus, entertains two burglars, and does any number of impossible and unpredictable things.

Pippi Moves into Villa Villekulla

Translated by Florence Lamborn

WAY OUT at the end of a tiny little town was an old overgrown garden, and in the garden was an old house, and in the house lived Pippi Longstocking. She was nine years old, and she lived there all alone. She had no mother and no father, and that was of course very nice because there was no one to tell her to go to bed just when she was having the most fun, and no one who could make her take cod-liver oil when she much preferred caramel candy.

Once upon a time Pippi had had a father of whom she was extremely fond. Naturally she had had a mother too, but that was so long ago that Pippi didn't remember her at all. Her mother had died when Pippi was just a tiny baby and lay in a cradle and howled so that nobody could go anywhere near her. Pippi was sure that her mother was now up in Heaven, watching her little girl through a peephole in the sky, and Pippi often waved up at her and called, "Don't you worry about me. I'll always come out on top."

Her father Pippi had not forgotten. He was a sea captain who sailed on the great ocean, and Pippi had sailed with him in his ship until one day her father blew overboard in a storm and disappeared. But Pippi was absolutely certain that he would come back. She would never believe that he had drowned; she was sure he had floated until he landed on an island inhabited by cannibals. And she thought he had become the king of all the cannibals and went around with a golden crown on his head all day long.

"My papa is a cannibal king; it certainly isn't every child who has such a stylish papa," Pippi used to say with satisfaction. "And as soon as my papa has built himself a boat he will come and get me, and I'll be a cannibal princess. Heigh-ho, won't that be exciting?"

Her father had bought the old house in the garden many years ago. He thought he would live there with Pippi when he grew old and couldn't sail the seas any longer. And then this annoying thing had to happen, that he blew into the ocean, and while Pippi was waiting for him to come back she went straight home to Villa Villekulla. That was the name of the house. It stood there ready and waiting for her. One lovely summer evening she had said good-bye to all the sailors on her father's boat. They were all so fond of Pippi, and she of them.

"So long, boys," she said and kissed each one on the forehead. "Don't you worry about me. I'll always come out on top."

Two things she took with her from the ship: a little monkey whose name was Mr. Nilsson—he was a present from her father—and a big suitcase full of gold pieces. The sailors stood up on the deck and watched as long as they could see her. She walked straight ahead without looking back at all, with Mr. Nilsson on her shoulder and her suitcase in her hand.

"A remarkable child," said one of the sailors as Pippi disappeared in the distance.

He was right. Pippi was indeed a remarkable child. The most remarkable thing about her was that she was so strong. She was so very strong that in the whole wide world there was not a single police officer who was as strong as she. Why, she could lift a whole horse if she wanted to! And she wanted to. She had a horse of her own that she had bought with one of her many gold pieces the day she came home to Villa Villekulla. She had always longed for a horse, and now here he was living on the porch. When Pippi wanted to drink her afternoon coffee there, she simply lifted him down into the garden.

Beside Villa Villekulla was another garden and another house. In that house lived a father and mother and two charming children, a boy and a girl. The boy's name was Tommy and the girl's Annika. They were good, well-brought-up, and obedient children. Tommy would never think of biting his nails, and he always did exactly what his mother told him to do. Annika never fussed when she didn't get her own way, and she always looked so pretty in her little well-ironed cotton dresses; she took the greatest care not to get them dirty. Tommy and Annika played nicely with each other in their garden, but they had often wished for a playmate. While Pippi was still sailing on the ocean with her father, they often used to hang over the fence and say to each other, "Isn't it silly that nobody ever moves into that house. Somebody ought to live there—somebody with children."

On that lovely summer evening when Pippi for the first time stepped over the threshold of Villa Villekulla, Tommy and Annika were not at home. They had gone to visit their grandmother for a week; and so they had no idea that anybody had moved into the house next door. On the first day after they came home again they stood by the gate, looking out onto the street, and even then they didn't know that there actually was a playmate so near. Just as they were standing there considering what they should do and wondering whether anything exciting was likely to happen or whether it was going to be one of those dull days when they couldn't think of anything to play—just then the gate of Villa Villekulla opened and a little girl stepped out. She was the most remarkable girl Tommy and Annika had ever seen. She was Miss Pippi Longstocking out for her morning promenade. This is the way she looked:

Her hair, the color of a carrot, was braided in two tight braids that stuck straight out. Her nose was the shape of a very small potato and was dotted all over with freckles. It must be admitted that the mouth under this nose was a very wide one, with strong white teeth. Her dress was rather unusual. Pippi herself had made it. She had meant it to be blue, but there wasn't quite enough blue cloth, so Pippi had sewed little red pieces on it here and there. On her long thin legs she wore a pair of long stockings, one brown and the other black; and she had on a pair of black shoes that were exactly twice as long as her feet. These shoes her father had bought for her in South America so that Pippi should have something to grow into, and she never wanted to wear any others.

But the thing that made Tommy and Annika open their eyes widest of all was the monkey sitting on the strange girl's shoulder. It was a little monkey, dressed in blue pants, yellow jacket, and a white straw hat.

Pippi walked along the street with one foot on the sidewalk and the other in the gutter. Tommy and Annika watched as long as they could see her. In a little while she came back, and now she was walking backward. That was because she didn't want to turn around to get home. When she reached Tommy's and Annika's gate she stopped.

The children looked at each other in silence. At last Tommy spoke. "Why did you walk backward?"

"Why did I walk backward?" said Pippi. "Isn't this a free country? Can't a person walk any way he wants to? For that matter, let me tell you that in Egypt everybody walks that way, and nobody thinks it's the least bit strange."

"How do you know?" asked Tommy. "You've never been in Egypt, have you?"

"I've never been in Egypt? Indeed I have. That's one thing you can be sure of. I have been all over the world and seen many things stranger than people walking backward. I wonder what you would have said if I had come along walking on my hands the way they do in Farthest India."

"Now you must be lying," said Tommy.

Pippi thought a moment. "You're right," she said sadly, "I am lying."

"It's wicked to lie," said Annika, who had at last gathered up enough courage to speak.

"Yes, it's very wicked to lie," said Pippi even more sadly. "But I forget it now and then. And how can you expect a little child whose mother is an angel and whose father is king of a cannibal island and who herself has sailed on the ocean all her life—how can you expect her to tell the truth always? And for that matter," she continued, her whole freckled face lighting up, "let me tell you that in the Belgian Congo there is not a single person who tells the truth. They lie all day long. Begin at seven in the morning and keep on until sundown. So if I should happen to lie now and then, you must try to excuse me and to remember that it is only because I stayed in the Belgian Congo a little too long. We can be friends anyway, can't we?"

"Oh, sure," said Tommy and realized suddenly that this was not going to be one of those dull days.

"By the way, why couldn't you come and have breakfast with me?" asked Pippi.

"Why not?" said Tommy. "Come on, let's go."

"Oh, yes, let's," said Annika.

"But first I must introduce you to Mr. Nilsson," said Pippi, and the little monkey took off his cap and bowed politely.

Then they all went in through Villa Villekulla's tumbledown garden gate, along the gravel path, bordered with old moss-covered trees—really good climbing trees they seemed to be—up to the house, and onto the porch. There stood the horse, munching oats out of a soup bowl.

"Why do you have a horse on the porch?" asked Tommy. All horses he knew lived in stables.

"Well," said Pippi thoughtfully, "he'd be in the way in the kitchen, and he doesn't like the parlor."

Tommy and Annika patted the horse and then went on into the house. It had a kitchen, a parlor, and a bedroom. But it certainly looked as if Pippi had forgotten to do her Friday cleaning that week. Tommy and Annika looked around cautiously just in case the King of the Cannibal Isles might be sitting in a corner somewhere. They had never seen a cannibal king in all their lives. But there was no father to be seen, nor any mother either.

Annika said anxiously, "Do you live here all alone?"

"Of course not!" said Pippi. "Mr. Nilsson and the horse live here too."

"Yes, but I mean, don't you have any mother or father here?"

"No, not the least little tiny bit of a one," said Pippi happily.

"But who tells you when to go to bed at night and things like that?" asked Annika.

"I tell myself," said Pippi. "First I tell myself in a nice friendly way; and then, if I don't mind, I tell myself again more sharply; and if I still don't mind, then I'm in for a spanking—see?"

Tommy and Annika didn't see at all, but they thought maybe it was a good way. Meanwhile they had come out into the kitchen and Pippi cried,

"Now we're going to make a pancake,
Now there's going to be a pankee,
Now we're going to fry a pankye."

Then she took three eggs and threw them up in the air. One fell down on her head and broke so that the yolk ran into her eyes, but the others she caught skillfully in a bowl, where they smashed to pieces.

"I always did hear that egg yolk was good for the hair," said Pippi, wiping her eyes. "You wait and see—mine will soon begin to grow so fast it crackles. As a matter of fact, in Brazil all the people go about with eggs in their hair. And there are no bald-headed people. Only once was there a man who was so foolish that he ate his eggs instead of rubbing them on his hair. He became completely bald-headed, and when he showed himself on the street there was such a riot that the radio police were called out."

While she was speaking Pippi had neatly picked the eggshells out of the bowl with her fingers. Now she took a bath brush that hung on the wall and began to beat the pancake batter so hard that it splashed all over the walls. At last she poured what was left onto the griddle that stood on the stove.

When the pancake was brown on one side she tossed it halfway up to the ceiling, so that it turned right around in the air, and then she caught it on the griddle again. And when it was ready she threw it straight across the kitchen right onto a plate that stood on the table.

"Eat!" she cried. "Eat before it gets cold!"

And Tommy and Annika ate and thought it a very good pancake.

Afterward Pippi invited them to step into the parlor. There was only one piece of furniture in there. It was a huge chest with many tiny drawers. Pippi opened the drawers and showed Tommy and Annika all the treasures she kept there. There were wonderful birds' eggs, strange shells and stones, pretty little boxes, lovely silver mirrors, pearl necklaces, and many other things that Pippi and her father had bought on their journeys around the world. Pippi gave each of her new playmates a little gift to remember her by. Tommy got a dagger with a shimmering mother-of-pearl handle, and Annika a little box with a cover decorated with pink shells. In the box there was a ring with a green stone.

"Suppose you go home now," said Pippi, "so that you can come back tomorrow. Because if you don't go home you can't come back, and that would be a shame."

Tommy and Annika agreed that it would indeed. So they went home—past the horse, who had now eaten up all the oats, and out through the gate of Villa Villekulla. Mr. Nilsson waved his hat at them as they left.

CHARLES CAUSLEY

Colonel Fazackerley

Colonel Fazackerley Butterworth-Toast
Bought an old castle complete with a ghost,
But someone or other forgot to declare
To Colonel Fazack that the specter was there.

On the very first evening, while waiting to dine,
The Colonel was taking a fine sherry wine,
When the ghost, with a furious flash and a flare,
Shot out of the chimney and shivered, "Beware!"

Colonel Fazackerley put down his glass
And said, "My dear fellow, that's really first class!
I just can't conceive how you do it at all.
I imagine you're going to a Fancy Dress Ball?"

At this, the dread ghost gave a withering cry.
Said the Colonel (his monocle firm in his eye),
"Now just how you do it I wish I could think.
Do sit down and tell me, and please have a drink."

The ghost in his phosphorous cloak gave a roar
And floated about between ceiling and floor.
He walked through a wall and returned through a pane
And backed up the chimney and came down again.

Said the Colonel, "With laughter I'm feeling quite weak!"
(As trickles of merriment ran down his cheek.)
"My house-warming party I hope you won't spurn.
You *must* say you'll come and you'll give us a turn!"

At this, the poor specter—quite out of his wits—
Proceeded to shake himself almost to bits.
He rattled his chains and he clattered his bones
And he filled the whole castle with mumbles and moans.

But Colonel Fazackerley, just as before,
Was simply delighted and called out, "Encore!"
At which the ghost vanished, his efforts in vain,
And never was seen at the castle again.

"Oh dear, what a pity!" said Colonel Fazack.
"I don't know his name, so I can't call him back."
And then with a smile that was hard to define,
Colonel Fazackerley went in to dine.

SID FLEISCHMAN

McBroom Tells a Lie

IT'S TRUE—I did tell a lie once.

I don't mean the summer nights we hung caged chickens in the farmhouse for lanterns. Those hens had eaten so many lightning bugs they glowed brighter'n kerosene lamps.

And I don't mean the cold snap that came along so sudden that blazing sunshine froze to the ground. We pickaxed chunks of it for the stove to cook on.

That's the genuine truth, sure and certain as my name's Josh McBroom.

When I told a lie—well, I'd best start with the time the young'uns began building a hoopdedoodle of some sort in the barn. The scamps kept it covered with a sheet. I reckoned they'd tell us when they were ready.

"Will*jill*hester*chester*peter*polly*tim*tom*mary*larry*and little*clarinda!*" my dear wife Melissa called out every evening. "Supper!"

We had hardly sat down to eat, when Jill asked, "Pa, would Mexican jumping beans grow on our farm?"

I hadn't seen anything yet that wouldn't grow on our wonderful one-acre farm. That trifling patch of earth is so amazing rich we could plant and harvest two-three crops a day—with time left over for a game of horseshoes.

"Will you let us grow a crop?" Polly asked. "We need bushels and bushels of jumping beans."

"For our invention," Tom put in.

"In that case," I smiled, "jump to it, my lambs."

They traded with a boy at school who owned a jar of the hopping beans. First thing Saturday morning the young'uns lit out the back door to plant their crop.

Well, that was a mistake. I should have known that our soil was too powerful strong for jumping beans. The seeds sprouted faster'n the twitch of a sheep's tail, and those Mexican bushes shot up lickety-bang. As they quick-dried in the prairie sun, the pods began to shake and rattle, and Chester shouted, "Pa, look!"

Merciful powers! Those buzzing, jumping, wiggle-waggling pods jerked the roots clear out of the ground. And off those bushes went, leaping and hopping every which way.

"Willjillhesterchesterpeterpollytimtommarylarryandlittleclarinda!" I called out. "After them, my lambs!"

Didn't those plants lead us a merry chase! Most of them got clean away, hopping and bucking and rattling across the countryside. We did manage to capture a few bushes, but the young'uns said it wasn't near enough for their invention. They'd have to think of something else.

At breakfast a day or two later the older young'uns started breaking fresh eggs into skillets. "Pa—there's something wrong with these eggs," said Will.

"Pa, come look," said Jill from the stove.

"Pa—come quick, but stand back!" my dear wife Melissa exclaimed.

I hopped to the stove as she broke another fresh egg into a skillet. Why, soon as it was fried on one side, that egg jumped up in the air. It flipped over and landed on the other side to fry.

"Well, don't that beat all," I said. "The hens must have been eating your Mexican jumping beans. Yup, and they're laying eggs that *flip* themselves."

"Well, our invention won't run on flip-flopping eggs," Will said gloomily.

After supper my dear wife Melissa tried to jolly everybody up. "Let's pop some corn."

Well, a strange look came over the young'uns' faces. "Popcorn," Jill whispered.

"POPCORN!" Will laughed. "Bet that'll run our invention!"

Didn't those kids light out for the barn in a hurry! In no time at all they were clanking and hammering to do over their contraption to work on popcorn instead of jumping beans.

They were still at it the next day when our neighbor, Heck Jones, came storming along. He was a skinny, rattle-boned man and mean as the law allowed. More'n once he had tried to trick us out of our wonderful one-acre farm.

"I'll have the law on you, McBroom!"

"Do tell," I said.

"You grew them jumping beans, didn't you?"

"I did."

"Look there at my blue-ribbon cow, Princess Prunella!"

My eyes near shot out of my head. There on the horizon that stupid,worthless cow of his was leaping and high-jumping and bucking.

"Kicked holes right through the barn roof!" Heck Jones snorted. "You allowed them dangerous bushes of yours to get loose, and now Princess Prunella's five stomachs are full of jumping beans!"

"Your roof already had holes in it," I said.

"That cow's ruined. Reckon I'll have to shoot her before she does any more damage," he said, beginning to dab at his eyes.

Well, all that dabbing didn't fool me. Heck Jones could peel an acre of onions without dropping a tear. But I reckoned I was responsible, letting those bushes get away from us.

"Sir," I said. "If you'll guarantee to keep off our farm, I'll pay for a barn roof. And I'll buy that ignorant cow from you. I reckon when she settles down she'll give churned butter for a month."

"Don't think you're going to slip out so light and easy," Heck Jones snapped. "I intend to see you in jail, McBroom! Unless—"

"I'm listening, sir."

He cleared his throat. "If you want to trade farms, we'll call it fair and square."

"Well, no sir and nohow," I said.

He lifted his thin nose into the wind—that man could sniff things miles off. "Neighbor, I'm a kindly man," he said. "You just grow me a crop of tomatoes to make up for my barn roof, and we'll call it square."

"I'll deliver' em before supper," I said.

"No, neighbor. Not yet." He whipped out a pencil and piece of paper. "I'll just write out the agreement. Best to do things honest and legal. You deliver the tomatoes when I say so—fresh off the vine, mind you—and I'll guarantee not to set foot on your farm again."

Glory be! We'd be rid of that petty scoundrel at last.

"But fair's fair, McBroom. I'm entitled to a guarantee, too. If you don't live up to the bargain—why, this useless, worn-out one-acre farm is mine. Sign here."

Useless? Worn-out? My pride rose up and I signed. Why, I could grow a crop of tomatoes in an hour. I had the best of the bargain for certain!

But as he ambled off, I thought I heard him snicker through his nose.

Just then the young'uns rolled their invention out of the barn and whipped off the sheet. "It's finished, Pa," Will said.

Glory be! There stood an odds-and-ends contraption on four wheels. A rain barrel with three tin funnels mounted in front and the scamps had fixed up broken chairs to seat all eleven of them.

"It's a Popcornmobile," Jill said.

"That's the exhaust pipe," Chester said, pointing to a black tin stovepipe they'd attached with baling wire underneath the floorboards.

"And look, Pa!" Larry said. "We got headlights, too!"

Indeed, they did! Two quart canning jars were fixed to the front. And the rascals had filled the jars with lightning bugs.

"Pile in, everybody," Will said, "and let's start'er up."

Mary fetched a clod of frozen sunlight out of the icehouse while Will, Jill, and Hester poured shelled corn through the funnels. Mary pitched the chunks of sunlight into the barrel. They took their seats and waited for the sunshine to thaw and pop the corn and start the machinery they'd rigged up.

It was growing dark, the prairie wind had turned a mite gritty—and suddenly there stood Heck Jones.

"Evenin,' neighbors," he said. There was a tricksy look in his eye and a piece of paper in his hand. "McBroom, you guaranteed to deliver a crop of tomatoes on demand. Well, I'm demanding 'em *now.*"

My eyebrows jumped. "Drat it, you can see the sun's down!" I declared.

"There's nothing about the sun in the contract. You read it."

"And it's going to kick up a dust storm before long."

"Nothing in the contract about a dust storm. You signed it."

"Sir, you expect me to grow you a crop of tomatoes *at night in a dust storm?*"

"*Hee-haw*, neighbor. If you don't, this farm's mine. I'll give you till sunup. Not a moment later, McBroom!"

And off he went, chuckling and snickering and *hee-hawing* through his nose.

"Oh, Pa," my dear wife Melissa cried. Even the young'uns were getting a mite onion-eyed.

Just then corn began popping like firecrackers inside the young'uns' rain barrel.

"Pa, we're moving!" Jill exclaimed.

Sure enough, the chunk of frozen sunlight had thawed out, and the corn was exploding from the stored-up heat.

I tried to raise a smile. Will grabbed the steering wheel tight and began driving the young'uns around the barn. Popcorn shot out the exhaust pipe, white as snow.

I knew we didn't have enough of that frozen sunshine left to grow a crop, worse luck! But when I saw those two headlights coming around the barn, my heart leaped back in place. The jars full of fireflies lit up the way like high noon!

"Willjillhesterchesterpeterpollytimtommarylarryandlittleclarinda!" I shouted. "Fetch canning jars. Fill'em up with lightning bugs. Quick, my lambs. Not a moment to waste."

Chester said, "The critters have got kind of scarce around here, Pa."

"The thickest place is way the other side of Heck Jones's place," Mary said.

"A powerful long walk," said Larry.

"Who said anything about walking?" I laughed. "You've got your Popcornmobile, haven't you?"

Didn't we get busy! The young'uns fetched all the canning jars in the cellar and bushels of corn for fuel. With a fresh chunk of frozen sunshine in the barrel, off they took—spraying popcorn behind them.

I set to work planting tomato seeds. It was full dark, but I could see fine. My dear wife Melissa held up a chicken by the feet—one of those lantern-glowing hens I was telling you about.

Then I began pounding stakes in the ground for the tomatoes to climb up.

"I do hope the young'uns don't get lost," my dear wife Melissa said. "It's going to blow a real dust storm by morning."

"Heck Jones had sniffed it coming," I declared. "But lost? Not our scamps. I can hear 'em now."

They were still a long way off, but that Popcornmobile sounded like the Fourth of July, loud enough to wake snakes. All the kids were waving and laughing. I reckoned that was the best ride they'd ever had.

"That's a jim-dandy machine you built." I smiled. "And I see you found a lightning bug or two."

Well, it didn't take long to hang those jars of fireflies on the tomato stakes. And glory be! They lit up the farm bright as day.

It wasn't a moment before the tomato sprouts came busting up through the earth. They broke into leaf and the vines started toward those canning jars. I do believe they preferred that homemade sunshine!

We loaded up the Popcornmobile with bushel baskets of tomatoes. We made so many trips to Heck Jones's place that the popcorn piled up along the road like a snowbank. Finally, minutes before dawn I hammered at his door.

"Wake up, Heck Jones!" I called.

"Hee-haw!" He opened the door and stood there in his nightcap, the legal paper in his hand.

"It's dawn by the clock, McBroom, and that powerful rich, git-up-and-git acre is all mine!"

"Yup, it's dawn," I said. "And there's my end of the bargain."

When he saw that crop of tomatoes he just about swallowed his teeth. His mouth puckered up tighter'n bark on a tree.

The young'uns and I all piled into the Popcornmobile to start for home. That's when I saw Princess Prunella. Only she wasn't jumping anymore.

"Merciful powers!" I declared. "Look there! That numbskull cow mistook all this popcorn for snow and has froze to death!"

We got home for a big breakfast and just in time. That prairie dust storm rolled in and stayed for weeks on end.

Now it's true—I did tell a lie once. That cow of his didn't *really* freeze to death in all the popcorn. But she did catch a terrible cold.

WILLIAM BLAKE

The Lamb

Little Lamb, who made thee?
Dost thou know who made thee?
Gave thee life, and bid thee feed,
By the stream, and o'er the mead;
Gave thee clothing of delight,
Softest clothing, woolly, bright;
Gave thee such a tender voice,
Making all the vales rejoice?
    Little Lamb, who made thee?
    Dost thou know who made thee?

    Little Lamb, I'll tell thee,
    Little Lamb, I'll tell thee:
He is called by thy name,
For He calls Himself a Lamb.
He is meek, and He is mild;
He became a little child.
I a child, and thou a lamb,
We are callèd by His name.
    Little Lamb, God bless thee!
    Little Lamb, God bless thee!

The Echoing Green

The Sun does arise,
And make happy the skies;
The merry bells ring
To welcome the Spring;
The skylark and thrush,
The birds of the bush,
Sing louder around
To the bells' cheerful sound,
While our sports shall be seen
On the Echoing Green.

Old John, with white hair,
Does laugh away care,
Sitting under the oak,
Among the old folk.
They laugh at our play,
And soon they all say:
"Such, such were the joys
When we all, girls and boys,
In our youth-time were seen
On the Echoing Green."

Till the little ones, weary,
No more can be merry;
The Sun does descend,
And our sports have an end.
Round the laps of their mothers
Many sisters and brothers,
Like birds in their nest,
Are ready for rest,
And sport no more seen
On the darkening Green.

C. S. LEWIS

They tell me that nowadays young readers don't care for fantasy or stories in which magic plays a part. It's hard to reconcile this with the popularity of science fiction (especially on the screen), which—most of it at any rate—is straight fantasy, with no "scientific" basis whatsoever.

Good writers of fantasy choose that form because they can say things in it that they couldn't say as well writing stories about the family next door. That's point number one. Point number two is this: Something in the human mind remains unsatisfied with what our five senses tell us. And so we "imagine" or "invent" small (sometimes large) worlds of the imagination that give us pleasure or consolation or merely add interest to life. Thus a small child will create out of a doll or stuffed animal a companion that for a time is quite real to him or her.

This *Treasury* contains quite a lot of fantasy, fairy tales, stories of the impossible. When we read them—if they're well written—we do not usually condemn them as "unreal." Instead, they seem to be interesting because they are telling us about human life, our own human lives, even though they may be full of creatures and happenings that in our own experience we will never encounter. Thus, the story of Cinderella is known to all of us and liked by all of us. Yet probably not one of my girl readers will ever marry a prince. A mysterious business, fantasy.

The seven volumes of Narnia stories by C. S. Lewis are a case in point. In one of them Mr. Lewis remarks, "Most of us have a secret country." Narnia, an imaginary kingdom, is his.

In Narnia you will meet not merely several children who enter it from the real world but also Fauns, Satyrs, Dwarfs, Giants, Talking Beasts, Trees that walk, Specters, Ghouls, Monopods. There's a Chief Mouse named Reepicheep and a wonderful creature called Puddleglum the Marsh-wiggle. Opposed to the evil White Witch and her fellows is the noble lion Aslan.

When our daughter Anne, aged eight, read the Narnia stories she at once decided that Aslan, representing Good, suggested also Jesus and in some ways God. She got a great pleasure out of her realization that Mr. Lewis was telling a funny and fascinating story and at the same time expressing his Christian faith. I must emphasize that this did not incline her in any way either toward or away from Christianity. I see no reason why Muslim or Buddhist children cannot enjoy the Narnia series, even though they may be ignorant of the Christian religion.

For most of his life Mr. Lewis was a professor of literature, first at Oxford, then Cambridge, in England. Also for most of his life he was a bachelor, as many great writers of children's literature have been. He doesn't seem to have known many children and may not even have cared for them much.

The Lion, the Witch and the Wardrobe, the first volume of the Narnia series, came out in 1950. But if you want to read the seven volumes chronologically—that is, according to the time of the action—you should read them in this order:

The Magician's Nephew
The Lion, the Witch and the Wardrobe
The Horse and His Boy
Prince Caspian
The Voyage of the Dawn Treader
The Silver Chair
The Last Battle

I've chosen the first two chapters of *The Lion, the Witch and the Wardrobe* because they get you right into Narnia and then you can decide whether you want to explore further.

There was an actual small boy at Oxford for whom Narnia became so real that he broke his way through the back of his wardrobe and even partly through the brick wall of his home in order to find Aslan. I have never found it necessary to do this. Narnia is real enough for me in Mr. Lewis's pages.

Lucy Looks into a Wardrobe

ONCE there were four children whose names were Peter, Susan, Edmund and Lucy. This story is about something that happened to them when they were sent away from London during the war because of the air raids. They were sent to the house of an old Professor who lived in the heart of the country, ten miles from the nearest railway station and two miles from the nearest post office. He had no wife and he lived in a very large house with a housekeeper called Mrs. Macready and three servants. (Their names were Ivy, Margaret and Betty, but they do not come into the story much.) He himself was a very old man with shaggy white hair, which grew over most of his face as well as on his head, and they liked him almost at once; but on the first evening when he came out to meet them at the front door he was so odd-looking that Lucy (who was the youngest) was a little afraid of him, and Edmund (who was the next youngest) wanted to laugh and had to keep on pretending he was blowing his nose to hide it.

As soon as they had said good night to the Professor and gone upstairs on the first night, the boys came into the girls' room and they all talked it over.

"We've fallen on our feet and no mistake," said Peter. "This is going to be perfectly splendid. That old chap will let us do anything we like."

"I think he's an old dear," said Susan.

"Oh, come off it!" said Edmund, who was tired and pretending not to be tired, which always made him bad-tempered. "Don't go on talking like that."

"Like what?" said Susan; "and anyway, it's time you were in bed."

"Trying to talk like Mother," said Edmund. "And who are you to say when I'm to go to bed? Go to bed yourself."

"Hadn't we all better go to bed?" said Lucy. "There's sure to be a row if we're heard talking here."

"No there won't," said Peter. "I tell you this is the sort of house where no one's going to mind what we do. Anyway, they won't hear us. It's about ten minutes' walk from here down to that dining room, and any amount of stairs and passages in between."

"What's that noise?" said Lucy suddenly. It was a far larger house than she had ever been in before and the thought of all those long passages and rows of doors leading into empty rooms was beginning to make her feel a little creepy.

"It's only a bird, silly," said Edmund.

"It's an owl," said Peter. "This is going to be a wonderful place for birds. I shall go to bed now. I say, let's go and explore tomorrow. You might find anything in a place like this. Did you see those mountains as we came along? And the woods? There might be eagles. There might be stags. There'll be hawks."

"Badgers!" said Lucy.

"Snakes!" said Edmund.

"Foxes!" said Susan.

But when next morning came, there was a steady rain falling, so thick that when you looked out of the window you could see neither the mountains nor the woods nor even the stream in the garden.

"Of course it *would* be raining!" said Edmund. They had just finished breakfast with the Professor and were upstairs in the room he had set apart for them—a long, low room with two windows looking out in one direction and two in another.

"Do stop grumbling, Ed," said Susan. "Ten to one it'll clear up in an hour or so. And in the meantime we're pretty well off. There's a wireless and lots of books."

"Not for me," said Peter. "I'm going to explore in the house."

Everyone agreed to this and that was how the adventures began. It was the sort of house that you never seem to come to the end of, and it was full of unexpected places. The first few doors they tried led only into spare bedrooms, as everyone had expected that they would; but soon they came to a very long room full of pictures and there they found a suit of armor; and after that was a room all hung with green, with a harp in one corner; and then came three steps down and five steps up, and then a kind of little upstairs hall and a door that led out onto a balcony, and then a whole series of rooms that led into each other and were lined with books—most of them very old books and some bigger than a Bible in a church. And shortly after that they looked into a room that was quite empty except for one big wardrobe; the sort that has a looking-glass in the door. There was nothing else in the room at all except a dead bluebottle on the windowsill.

"Nothing there!" said Peter, and they all trooped out again—all except Lucy. She stayed behind because she thought it would be worth-while trying the door of the wardrobe, even though she felt almost sure that it would be locked. To her surprise it opened quite easily, and two mothballs dropped out.

Looking into the inside, she saw several coats hanging up—mostly long fur coats. There was nothing Lucy liked so much as the smell and feel of fur. She immediately stepped into the wardrobe and got in among the coats and rubbed her face against them, leaving the door open, of course, because she knew that it is very foolish to shut oneself into any wardrobe. Soon she went further in and found that there was a second row of coats hanging up behind the first one. It was almost quite dark in there and she kept her arms stretched out in front of her so as not to bump her face into the back of the wardrobe. She took a step further in—then two or three steps—always expecting to feel woodwork against the tips of her fingers. But she could not feel it.

"This must be a simply enormous wardrobe!" thought Lucy, going still further in and pushing the soft folds of the coats aside to make room for her. Then she noticed that there was something crunching under her feet. "I wonder is that more mothballs?" she thought, stooping down to feel it with her hands. But instead of feeling the hard, smooth wood of the floor of the wardrobe, she felt something soft and powdery and extremely cold. "This is very queer," she said, and went on a step or two further.

Next moment she found that what was rubbing against her face and hands was no longer soft fur but something hard and rough and even prickly. "Why, it is just like branches of trees!" exclaimed Lucy. And then she saw that there was a light ahead of her; not a few inches away where the back of the wardrobe ought to have been, but a long way off. Something cold and soft was falling on her. A moment later she found that she was standing in the middle of a wood at nighttime with snow under her feet and snowflakes falling through the air.

Lucy felt a little frightened, but she felt very inquisitive and excited as well. She looked back over her shoulder and there, between the dark tree-trunks, she could still see the open doorway of the wardrobe and even catch a glimpse of the empty room from which she had set out. (She had, of course, left the door open, for she knew that it is a very silly thing to shut oneself into a wardrobe.) It seemed to be still daylight there. "I can always get back if anything goes wrong," thought Lucy. She began to walk forward, *crunch-crunch*, over the snow and through the wood towards the other light.

In about ten minutes she reached it and found that it was a lamppost. As she stood looking at it, wondering why there was a lamppost in the middle of a wood and wondering what to do next, she heard a pitter patter of feet coming towards her. And soon after that a very strange person stepped out from among the trees into the light of the lamppost.

He was only a little taller than Lucy herself and he carried over his head an umbrella, white with snow. From the waist upwards he was like a man, but his legs were shaped like a goat's (the hair on them was glossy black) and instead of feet he had goat's hoofs. He also had a tail, but Lucy did not notice this at first because it was neatly caught up over the arm that held the umbrella so as to keep it from trailing in the snow. He had a red woolen muffler round his neck and his skin was rather reddish too. He had a strange but pleasant little face with a short pointed beard and curly hair, and out of the hair there stuck two horns, one on each side of his forehead. One of his hands, as I have said, held the umbrella: in the other arm he carried several brown paper parcels. What with the parcels and the snow it looked just as if he had been doing his Christmas shopping. He was a Faun. And when he saw Lucy he gave such a start of surprise that he dropped all his parcels.

"Goodness gracious me!" exclaimed the Faun.

What Lucy Found There

"GOOD evening," said Lucy. But the Faun was so busy picking up his parcels that at first he did not reply. When he had finished he made her a little bow.

"Good evening, good evening," said the Faun. "Excuse me—I don't want to be inquisitive—but should I be right in thinking that you are a Daughter of Eve?"

"My name's Lucy," said she, not quite understanding him.

"But you are—forgive me—you are what they call a girl?" asked the Faun.

"Of course I'm a girl," said Lucy.

"You are in fact Human?"

"Of course I'm human," said Lucy, still a little puzzled.

"To be sure, to be sure," said the Faun. "How stupid of me! But I've never seen a Son of Adam or a Daughter of Eve before. I am delighted. That is to say—" and then he stopped as if he had been going to say something he had not intended but had remembered in time. "Delighted, delighted," he went on. "Allow me to introduce myself. My name is Tumnus."

"I am very pleased to meet you, Mr. Tumnus," said Lucy.

"And may I ask, O Lucy, Daughter of Eve," said Mr. Tumnus, "how you have come into Narnia?"

"Narnia? What's that?" said Lucy.

"This is the land of Narnia," said the Faun, "where we are now; all that lies between the lamppost and the great castle of Cair Paravel on the eastern sea. And you—you have come from the wild woods of the west?"

"I—I got in through the wardrobe in the spare room," said Lucy.

"Ah!" said Mr. Tumnus in a rather melancholy voice, "if only I had worked harder at geography when I was a little Faun, I should no doubt know all about those strange countries. It is too late now."

"But they aren't countries at all," said Lucy, almost laughing. "It's only just back there—at least—I'm not sure. It is summer there."

"Meanwhile," said Mr. Tumnus, "it is winter in Narnia, and has been for ever so long, and we shall both catch cold if we stand here talking in the snow. Daughter of Eve from the far land of Spare Oom where eternal summer reigns around the bright city of War Drobe, how would it be if you came and had tea with me?"

"Thank you very much, Mr. Tumnus," said Lucy. "But I was wondering whether I ought to be getting back."

"It's only just round the corner," said the Faun, "and there'll be a roaring fire—and toast—and sardines—and cake."

"Well, it's very kind of you," said Lucy. "But I shan't be able to stay long."

"If you will take my arm, Daughter of Eve," said Mr. Tumnus, "I shall be able to hold the umbrella over both of us. That's the way. Now—off we go."

And so Lucy found herself walking through the wood arm in arm with this strange creature as if they had known one another all their lives.

They had not gone far before they came to a place where the ground became rough and there were rocks all about and little hills up and little hills down. At the bottom of one small valley Mr. Tumnus turned suddenly aside as if he were going to walk straight into an unusually large rock, but at the last moment Lucy found he was leading her into the entrance of a cave. As soon as they were inside she found herself blinking in the light of a wood fire. Then Mr. Tumnus stooped and took a flaming piece of wood out of the fire with a neat little pair of tongs, and lit a lamp. "Now we shan't be long," he said, and immediately put a kettle on.

Lucy thought she had never been in a nicer place. It was a little, dry, clean cave of reddish stone with a carpet on the floor and two little chairs ("one for me and one for a friend," said Mr. Tumnus) and a table and a dresser and a mantelpiece over the fire and above that a picture of an old Faun with a gray beard. In one corner there was a door which Lucy thought must lead to Mr. Tumnus's bedroom, and on one wall was a shelf full of books. Lucy looked at these while he was setting out the tea things. They had titles like *The Life and Letters of Silenus* or *Nymphs and Their Ways* or *Men, Monks and Gamekeepers; a Study in Popular Legend* or *Is Man a Myth?*

"Now, Daughter of Eve!" said the Faun.

And really it was a wonderful tea. There was a nice brown egg, lightly boiled, for each of them, and then sardines on toast, and then buttered toast, and then toast with honey, and then a sugar-topped cake. And when Lucy was tired of eating the Faun began to talk. He had wonderful tales to tell of life in the forest. He told about the midnight dances and how the Nymphs who lived in the wells and the Dryads who lived in the trees came out to dance with the Fauns; about long hunting parties after the milk-white Stag who could give you wishes if you caught him; about feasting and treasure-seeking with the wild Red Dwarfs in deep mines and caverns far beneath the forest floor; and then about summer when the woods were green and old Silenus on his fat donkey would come to visit them, and sometimes Bacchus himself, and then the streams would run with wine instead of water and the whole forest would give itself up to jollification for weeks on end. "Not that it isn't always winter now," he added gloomily. Then to cheer himself up he took out from its case on the dresser a strange little flute that looked as if it were made of straw and began to play. And the tune he played made Lucy want to cry and laugh and dance and go to sleep all at the same time. It must have been hours later when she shook herself and said, "Oh, Mr. Tumnus—I'm sorry to stop you, and I do love that tune—but really, I must go home. I only meant to stay for a few minutes."

"It's no good *now*, you know," said the Faun, laying down his flute and shaking his head at her very sorrowfully.

"No good?" said Lucy, jumping up and feeling rather frightened. "What do you mean? I've got to go home at once. The others will be wondering what has happened to me." But a moment later she asked, "Mr. Tumnus! Whatever is the matter?" for the Faun's brown eyes had filled with tears and then the tears began trickling down his cheeks, and soon they were running off the end of his nose; and at last he covered his face with his hands and began to howl.

"Mr. Tumnus! Mr. Tumnus!" said Lucy in great distress. "Don't! Don't! What is the matter? Aren't you well? Dear Mr. Tumnus, do tell me what is wrong." But the Faun continued sobbing as if his heart would break. And even when Lucy went over and put her arms round him and lent him her handkerchief, he did not stop. He merely took the handkerchief and kept on using it, wringing it out with both hands whenever it got too wet to be any more use, so that presently Lucy was standing in a damp patch.

"Mr. Tumnus!" bawled Lucy in his ear, shaking him. "Do stop. Stop it at once! You ought to be ashamed of yourself, a great big Faun like you. What on earth are you crying about?"

"Oh—oh—oh!" sobbed Mr. Tumnus, "I'm crying because I'm such a bad Faun."

"I don't think you're a bad Faun at all," said Lucy. "I think you are a very good Faun. You are the nicest Faun I've ever met."

"Oh—oh—you wouldn't say that if you knew," replied Mr. Tumnus between his sobs. "No, I'm a bad Faun. I don't suppose there ever was a worse Faun since the beginning of the world."

"But what have you done?" asked Lucy.

"My old father, now," said Mr. Tumnus, "that's his picture over the mantelpiece. He would never have done a thing like this."

"A thing like what?" said Lucy.

"Like what I've done," said the Faun. "Taken service under the White Witch. That's what I am. I'm in the pay of the White Witch."

"The White Witch? Who is she?"

"Why, it is she that has got all Narnia under her thumb. It's she that makes it always winter. Always winter and never Christmas; think of that!"

"How awful!" said Lucy. "But what does she pay *you* for?"

"That's the worst of it," said Mr. Tumnus with a deep groan. "I'm a kidnapper for her, that's what I am. Look at me, Daughter of Eve. Would you believe that I'm the sort of Faun to meet a poor innocent child in the wood, one that had never done me any harm, and pretend to be friendly with it, and invite it home to my cave, all for the sake of lulling it asleep and then handing it over to the White Witch?"

"No," said Lucy. "I'm sure you wouldn't do anything of the sort."

"But I have," said the Faun.

"Well," said Lucy rather slowly (for she wanted to be truthful and yet not to be too hard on him), "well, that was pretty bad. But you're so sorry for it that I'm sure you will never do it again."

"Daughter of Eve, don't you understand?" said the Faun. "It isn't something I *have* done. I'm doing it now, this very moment."

"What do you mean?" cried Lucy, turning very white.

"You are the child," said Mr. Tumnus. "I had orders from the White Witch that if ever I saw a Son of Adam or a Daughter of Eve in the wood, I was to catch them and hand them over to her. And you are the first I ever met. And I've pretended to be your friend and asked you to tea, and all the time I've been meaning to wait till you were asleep and then go and tell *her*."

"Oh, but you won't, Mr. Tumnus," said Lucy. "You won't, will you? Indeed, indeed you really mustn't."

"And if I don't," said he, beginning to cry again, "she's sure to find out. And she'll have my tail cut off, and my horns sawed off, and my beard plucked out, and she'll wave her wand over my beautiful cloven hooves and turn them into horrid solid hooves like a wretched horse's.

And if she is extra and specially angry she'll turn me into stone and I shall be only a statue of a Faun in her horrible house until the four thrones at Cair Paravel are filled—and goodness knows when that will happen, or whether it will ever happen at all."

"I'm very sorry, Mr. Tumnus," said Lucy. "But please let me go home."

"Of course I will," said the Faun. "Of course I've got to. I see that now. I hadn't known what Humans were like before I met you. Of course I can't give you up to the Witch; not now that I know you. But we must be off at once. I'll see you back to the lamppost. I suppose you can find your own way from there back to Spare Oom and War Drobe?"

"I'm sure I can," said Lucy.

"We must go as quietly as we can," said Mr. Tumnus. "The whole wood is full of *her* spies. Even some of the trees are on her side."

They both got up and left the tea things on the table, and Mr. Tumnus once more put up his umbrella and gave Lucy his arm, and they went out into the snow. The journey back was not at all like the journey to the Faun's cave; they stole along as quickly as they could, without speaking a word, and Mr. Tumnus kept to the darkest places. Lucy was relieved when they reached the lamppost again.

"Do you know your way from here, Daughter of Eve?" said Tumnus.

Lucy looked very hard between the trees and could just see in the distance a patch of light that looked like daylight. "Yes," she said, "I can see the wardrobe door."

"Then be off home as quick as you can," said the Faun, "and—c-can you ever forgive me for what I meant to do?"

"Why, of course I can," said Lucy, shaking him heartily by the hand. "And I do hope you won't get into dreadful trouble on my account."

"Farewell, Daughter of Eve," said he. "Perhaps I may keep the handkerchief?"

"Rather!" said Lucy, and then ran towards the far-off patch of daylight as quickly as her legs would carry her. And presently instead of rough branches brushing past her she felt coats, and instead of crunching snow under her feet she felt wooden boards, and all at once she found herself jumping out of the wardrobe into the same empty room from which the whole adventure had started. She shut the wardrobe door tightly behind her and looked around, panting for breath. It was still raining and she could hear the voices of the others in the passage.

"I'm here," she shouted, "I'm here. I've come back, I'm all right."

ALIKI BARNSTONE

Explanations

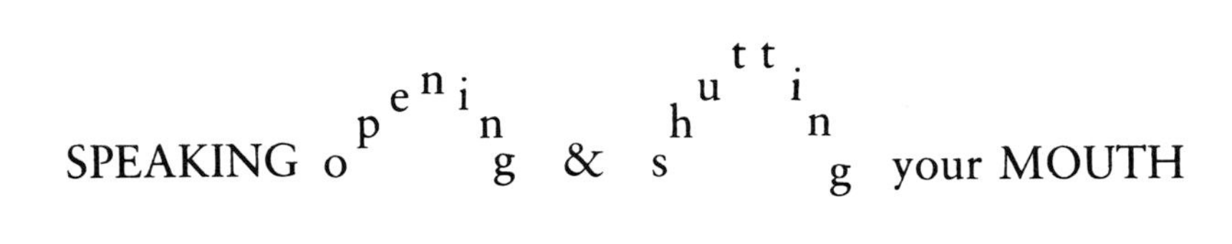

BOWL
a
cut-in-half
hollow circle

MUSIC ♫

sounds coming out of shapes

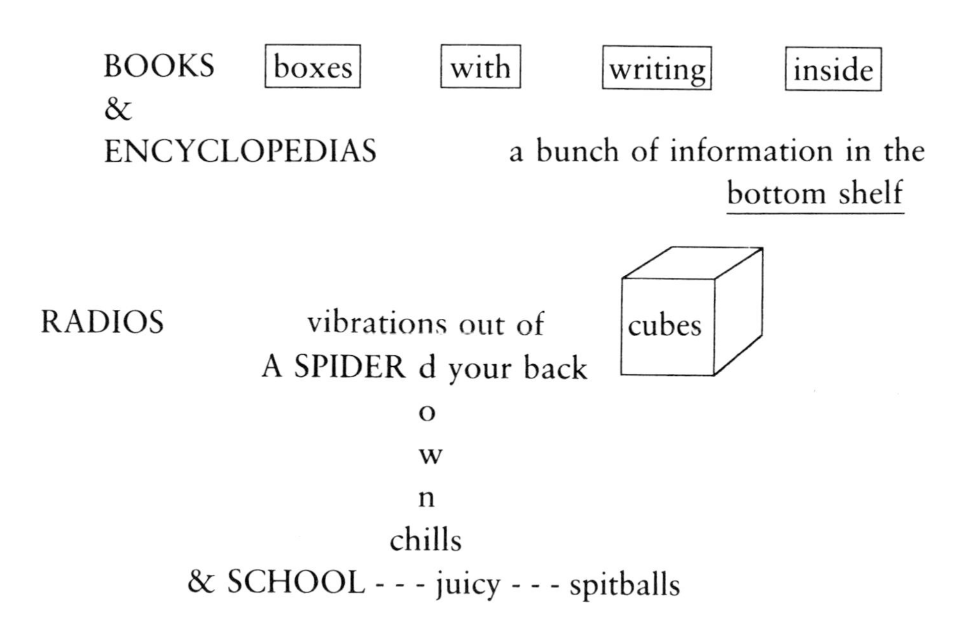

ROALD DAHL

Roald Dahl is a six foot, six inch Englishman, born of Norwegian parents. During World War I he rose to be Wing Commander in the Royal Air Force.

When young Roald was at school in England, a candy manufacturer visited the school and handed each boy a cardboard box containing nine chocolate bars, with different fillings. He asked them to tell him which they preferred. Mr. Dahl says, "It was then that I began to realize that inside those great factories there must be a secret room where fully grown men actually invent new chocolates and suddenly shout, 'I've got it!' "

Mr. Dahl thinks that's what gave him the idea for *Charlie and the Chocolate Factory*, one of the most popular children's books ever written.

Here's what the book is about. Five children are allowed into Mr. Willie Wonka's factory, where magical machines turn out wonderful candy. One of them is Charlie Bucket, who is the best kind of boy. But the other children are pretty terrible and perhaps the worst is greedy Augustus Gloop. Augustus has just knelt down to scoop up some hot melted chocolate from a river that flows right through the factory. Now read about what happens to him.

Before you start, let me say that Mr. Dahl states he still eats too much chocolate.

Augustus Gloop Goes up the Pipe

WHEN MR. WONKA turned round and saw what Augustus Gloop was doing, he cried out, "Oh, no! *Please*, Augustus, *please!* I beg of you not to do that. My chocolate must be untouched by human hands!"

"Augustus!" called out Mrs. Gloop. "Didn't you hear what the man said? Come away from that river at once!"

"This stuff is *tee*-riffic!" said Augustus, taking not the slightest notice of his mother or Mr. Wonka. "Oh boy, I need a bucket to drink it properly!"

"Augustus," cried Mr. Wonka, hopping up and down and waggling his stick in the air, "you *must* come away. You are dirtying my chocolate!"

"Augustus!" cried Mrs. Gloop.

"Augustus!" cried Mr. Gloop.

But Augustus was deaf to everything except the call of his enormous stomach. He was now lying full length on the ground with his head far out over the river, lapping up the chocolate like a dog.

"Augustus!" shouted Mrs. Gloop. "You'll be giving that nasty cold of yours to about a million people all over the country!"

"Be careful, Augustus!" shouted Mr. Gloop. "You're leaning too far out!"

Mr. Gloop was absolutely right. For suddenly there was a shriek, and then a splash, and into the river went Augustus Gloop, and in one second he had disappeared under the brown surface.

"Save him!" screamed Mrs. Gloop, going white in the face, and waving her umbrella about. "He'll drown! He can't swim a yard! Save him! Save him!"

"Good heavens, woman," said Mr. Gloop, "I'm not diving in there! I've got my best suit on!"

Augustus Gloop's face came up again to the surface, painted brown with chocolate. "Help! Help! Help!" he yelled. "Fish me out!"

"Don't just *stand* there!" Mrs. Gloop screamed at Mr. Gloop. "*Do* something!"

"I *am* doing something!" said Mr. Gloop, who was now taking off his jacket and getting ready to dive into the chocolate. But while he was doing this, the wretched boy was being sucked closer and closer toward the mouth of one of the great pipes that was dangling down into the river. Then all at once, the powerful suction took hold of him completely, and he was pulled under the surface and then into the mouth of the pipe.

The crowd on the riverbank waited breathlessly to see where he would come out.

"*There he goes!*" somebody shouted, pointing upwards.

And sure enough, because the pipe was made of glass, Augustus Gloop could be clearly seen shooting up inside it, headfirst, like a torpedo.

"Help! Murder! Police!" screamed Mrs. Gloop. "Augustus, come back at once! Where are you going?"

"It's a wonder to me," said Mr. Gloop, "how that pipe is big enough for him to go through it."

"It *isn't* big enough!" said Charlie Bucket. "Oh dear, look! He's slowing down!"

"So he is!" said Grandpa Joe.

"He's going to stick!" said Charlie.

"I think he is!" said Grandpa Joe.

"By golly, he *has* stuck!" said Charlie.

"It's his stomach that's done it!" said Mr. Gloop.

"He's blocked the whole pipe!" said Grandpa Joe.

"Smash the pipe!" yelled Mrs. Gloop, still waving her umbrella. "Augustus, come out of there at once!"

The watchers below could see the chocolate swishing around the boy in the pipe, and they could see it building up behind him in a solid mass, pushing against the blockage. The pressure was terrific. Something had to give. Something did give, and that something was Augustus. *WHOOF!* Up he shot again like a bullet in the barrel of a gun.

"He's disappeared!" yelled Mrs. Gloop. "Where does that pipe go to? Quick! Call the fire brigade!"

"Keep calm!" cried Mr. Wonka. "Keep calm, my dear lady, keep calm. There is no danger! No danger whatsoever! Augustus has gone on a little journey, that's all. A most interesting little journey. But he'll come out of it just fine, you wait and see."

"How can he possibly come out just fine!" snapped Mrs. Gloop. "He'll be made into marshmallows in five seconds!"

"Impossible!" cried Mr. Wonka. "Unthinkable! Inconceivable! Absurd! He could never be made into marshmallows!"

"And why not, may I ask?" shouted Mrs. Gloop.

"Because that pipe doesn't *go* to the Marshmallow Room!" Mr. Wonka answered. "It doesn't go anywhere near it! That pipe—the one Augustus went up—happens to lead directly to the room where I make a most delicious kind of strawberry-flavored chocolate-coated fudge. . . ."

"Then he'll be made into strawberry-flavored chocolate-coated fudge!" screamed Mrs. Gloop. "My poor Augustus! They'll be selling him by the pound all over the country tomorrow morning!"

"Quite right," said Mr. Gloop.

"I *know* I'm right," said Mrs. Gloop.

"It's beyond a joke," said Mr. Gloop.

"Mr. Wonka doesn't seem to think so!" cried Mrs. Gloop. "Just look at him! He's laughing his head off! How *dare* you laugh like that when my boy's just gone up the pipe! You monster!" she shrieked, pointing her umbrella at Mr. Wonka as though she were going to run him through. "You think it's a joke, do you? You think that sucking my boy up into your Fudge Room like that is just one great big colossal joke?"

"He'll be perfectly safe," said Mr. Wonka, giggling slightly.

"He'll be chocolate fudge!" shrieked Mrs. Gloop.

"Never!" cried Mr. Wonka.

"Of course he will!" shrieked Mrs. Gloop.

"I wouldn't allow it!" cried Mr. Wonka.

"And why not?" shrieked Mrs. Gloop.

"Because the taste would be terrible," said Mr. Wonka. "Just imagine it! Augustus-flavored chocolate-coated Gloop! No one would buy it."

"They most certainly would!" cried Mr. Gloop indignantly.

"I don't want to think about it!" shrieked Mrs. Gloop.

"Nor do I," said Mr. Wonka. "And I do promise you, madam, that your darling boy is perfectly safe."

"If he's perfectly safe, then where is he?" snapped Mrs. Gloop. "Lead me to him this instant!"

Mr. Wonka turned around and clicked his fingers sharply, *click, click, click,* three times. Immediately, an Oompa-Loompa appeared, as if from nowhere, and stood beside him.

The Oompa-Loompa bowed and smiled, showing beautiful white teeth. His skin was almost pure black, and the top of his fuzzy head came just above the height of Mr. Wonka's knee. He wore the usual deerskin slung over his shoulder.

"Now listen to me!" said Mr. Wonka, looking down at the tiny man, "I want you to take Mr. and Mrs. Gloop up to the Fudge Room and help them to find their son, Augustus. He's just gone up the pipe."

The Oompa-Loompa took one look at Mrs. Gloop and exploded into peals of laughter.

"Oh, do be quiet!" said Mr. Wonka. "Control yourself! Pull yourself together! Mrs. Gloop doesn't think it's at all funny!"

"You can say that again!" said Mrs. Gloop.

"Go straight to the Fudge Room," Mr. Wonka said to the Oompa-Loompa, "and when you get there, take a long stick and start poking around inside the big chocolate-mixing barrel. I'm almost certain you'll find him in there. But you'd better look sharp! You'll have to hurry! If you leave him in the chocolate-mixing barrel too long, he's liable to get poured into the fudge boiler, and that really *would* be a disaster, wouldn't it? My fudge would become *quite* uneatable!"

Mrs. Gloop let out a shriek of fury.

"I'm joking," said Mr. Wonka, giggling madly behind his beard. "I didn't mean it. Forgive me. I'm so sorry. Good-bye, Mrs. Gloop! And Mr. Gloop! Good-bye! Good-bye! I'll see you later. . . ."

As Mr. and Mrs. Gloop and their tiny escort hurried away, the five Oompa-Loompas on the far side of the river suddenly began hopping and dancing about and beating wildly upon a number of very small drums. "Augustus Gloop!" they chanted. "Augustus Gloop! Augustus Gloop! Augustus Gloop!"

"Grandpa!" cried Charlie. "Listen to them, Grandpa! What *are* they doing?"

"Ssshh!" whispered Grandpa Joe. "I think they're going to sing us a song!"

"*Augustus Gloop!*" chanted the Oompa-Loompas.
"*Augustus Gloop! Augustus Gloop!*
The great big greedy nincompoop!
How long could we allow this beast
To gorge and guzzle, feed and feast
On everything he wanted to?

Great Scott! It simply wouldn't do!
However long this pig might live,
We're positive he'd never give
Even the smallest bit of fun
Or happiness to anyone.
So what we do in cases such
As this, we use the gentle touch,
And carefully we take the brat
And turn him into something that
Will give great pleasure to us all—
A doll, for instance, or a ball,
Or marbles or a rocking horse.
But this revolting boy, of course,
Was so unutterably vile,
So greedy, foul, and infantile,
He left a most disgusting taste
Inside our mouths, and so in haste
We chose a thing that, come what may,
Would take the nasty taste away.
'Come on!' we cried, 'The time is ripe
To send him shooting up the pipe!
He has to go! It has to be!'
And very soon, he's going to see
Inside the room to which he's gone
Some funny things are going on.
But don't, dear children, be alarmed;
Augustus Gloop will not be harmed,
Although, of course, we must admit
He will be altered *quite a bit.*
He'll be quite changed from what he's been,
When he goes through the fudge machine:
Slowly, the wheels go round and round,

The cogs begin to grind and pound;
A hundred knives go slice, slice, slice;
We add some sugar, cream, and spice;
We boil him for a minute more,
Until we're absolutely sure
That all the greed and all the gall
Is boiled away for once and all.
Then out he comes! And now! By grace!
A miracle has taken place!
This boy, who only just before
Was loathed by men from shore to shore,
This greedy brute, this louse's ear,
Is loved by people everywhere!
For who could hate or bear a grudge
Against a luscious bit of fudge?"

"I *told* you they loved singing!" cried Mr. Wonka. "Aren't they delightful? Aren't they charming? But you mustn't believe a word they said. It's all nonsense, every bit of it!"

"Are the Oompa-Loompas really joking, Grandpa?" asked Charlie.

"Of course they're joking," answered Grandpa Joe. "They *must* be joking. At least, I hope they're joking. Don't you?"

GEORGE BARKER

What Does the Clock Say?

What does the clock say?
Nothing at all.
It hangs all day
and night on the wall
with nothing to say
with nothing to tell
except sometimes
to ting a bell.
And yet it is strange
that the short and the tall
the large, the clever,
the great and the small
will do nothing whatever
nothing at all
without asking it,
the clock on the wall.

The Cheetah, My Dearest, Is Known Not to Cheat

The cheetah, my dearest, is known not to cheat;
the tiger possesses no tie;
The horsefly, of course, was never a horse;
the lion will not tell a lie.

The turkey, though perky, was never a Turk;
nor the monkey ever a monk:
the mandrill, though like one, was never a man,
but some men are like him, when drunk.

The springbok, dear thing, was not born in the Spring;
The walrus will not build a wall.
No badger is bad; no adder can add.
There is no truth in these things at all.

ACHIM BROGER

Bruno and the Mirror

Translated by Hilda Van Stockum

BRUNO STOOD in the bathroom, brushing his teeth. As he turned away from the mirror to get his towel, he heard someone say, "Good evening, Bruno." Bruno looked around and saw Bruno in front of him. He was astonished to see himself standing there.

"Where did you come from?" he asked sternly.

The other grinned, wiped toothpaste from his lips, and pointed over his shoulder at the mirror. "From there, of course. Where else?"

At that moment the doorbell rang. A visitor? So late? Bruno looked angrily at the mirror. To his alarm, another, angry-looking Bruno stepped out.

How could hc explain to the visitor the fact that there were now three Brunos in his apartment? "Hush," he said to his pajamaed doubles. The visitor rang a few more times and went away.

Bruno took the new Brunos into the living room. One of them kept grinning; the other kept scowling. "How about changing your expressions," Bruno suggested.

"That's impossible," they said. "We can't do it. We have to keep looking exactly the way you did when you looked in the mirror."

Bruno wondered about his bathroom mirror. It looked so harmless, like any other mirror. No one would have given it credit for such clever tricks.

"Are you hungry or thirsty?" Bruno asked his doubles. Yes, they were thirsty. Bruno gave each of them a glass of milk. Then he asked the scowling one to put a record on, and he did so right away. Next Bruno asked him to tidy up the kitchen.

"Certainly," he said, and tidied up.

This is wonderful, thought Bruno. He does what I tell him to without grumbling. Let's see about the other one. "Do ten push-ups," he commanded. Immediately the other Bruno lay down on the carpet, breathed deeply, and went through the exercises—one, two, three, four, five, six, seven, eight, nine, ten.

Hmm, thought Bruno. Whenever I look in the bathroom mirror these days, new Brunos come out, and they all obey me. I should try to see how many I can get. . . .

He thought some more, and some very strange ideas came to him. If all these Brunos obey me, I needn't worry about my landlord anymore. And that Mr. Smith, who always gave me bad marks at school, I could really give it to him now. Besides, those Brunos can work for me. I have only to give them orders. With enough Brunos I could rule the whole country. Why shouldn't I become King Bruno the Greatest!

These were the kinds of ideas that came to Bruno. In the meantime, his doubles sat on the couch drinking milk.

The new Brunos would have to look tough; that was obvious. People should be afraid of them. Bruno went to the mirror in the bathroom and put his plan to work. One scowling Bruno after another came stepping out of the mirror until the bathtub was full of Brunos. He sent them into the living room and glared a few more times into the mirror.

"So, that's enough," he decided after a bit. "I can always make more tomorrow." When he took the last ones into the living room, nineteen were already there. Altogether there were twenty-three Brunos in his apartment—twenty-four, counting himself.

"Sit down," he told them. But he hadn't enough chairs, and there wasn't enough room on the couch. One of the grim ones asked, "Where are we supposed to sit?"

"Sit on the floor and talk quietly among yourselves." They did so immediately. After a while Bruno ordered them all to go to sleep. They tried, but, of course, there was far too little space in the living room.

"Where shall we lie down?" asked one.

"We need blankets and air mattresses."

"And something to eat and drink."

"I hadn't thought of that," Bruno had to admit.

"He hadn't thought of that," murmured the Brunos, and looked angrily at him. "But he *should* have thought of it!"

"Be quiet!" Bruno ordered. "Sit close together on the floor! Go to sleep! I don't want to hear another sound out of you!" They looked angrily at him and were quiet.

He couldn't go to sleep himself, for he had grown afraid of them. What if they no longer obey me, he thought. They looked at me terribly angrily just now. But he still wanted to become Bruno the Greatest.

He was the first one up in the morning, and he washed and dressed quickly. "We'll have breakfast in half an hour," he told the others. "Get up now. I'm going for rolls. Meanwhile, you can make the coffee."

"Seventy-five rolls?" the baker asked, astonished. "Why do you need so many? And what's the matter with you today, Mr. Bruno? You look so angry."

"That's none of your business," Bruno snapped. "Just give me the rolls." On the way back he bought three pounds of butter and four jars of marmalade. That would do for breakfast.

When he came home, he saw the Brunos again looked very angry.

"We need twenty-four cups, and you have only four," they complained. "Do we have to drink out of our hands? And where are you going to get enough plates and silverware?"

"I hadn't considered that my equipment is inadequate," said Bruno. "We'll have to breakfast one after the other."

"Listen to him," the others mocked. "He hadn't considered . . . perhaps he'd better do some more considering, that Mr. Bruno. What *had* he considered, anyway?"

"What about towels?" said another. "And toilet paper and toothbrushes and toothpaste? Not to mention that we'll need lunch soon after breakfast."

"I like pork best," someone shouted.

"I'd rather have beef."

"Dessert is my favorite!"

"Don't forget to buy cigarettes and chocolate!"

"I don't like coffee. Let's have tea!"

"And, of course, don't forget air mattresses and sleeping bags!"

"Do you have enough potatoes?"

"Yes, and we all need some clothes, too!"

"You'd better go right out and shop again while we have breakfast." And they pushed Bruno out the door.

I've got to get rid of them, thought Bruno, as he stood in front of his apartment house. Nothing else will do. But how shall I get rid of them?

Bruno returned empty-handed and was greeted with angry shouting. But he did not let them see how frightened he was.

"Calm down, dear friends," he said. "Everything has been ordered, but as you can imagine, there was too much to be delivered right away. We must wait until tomorrow. I suggest that, in the meantime, you all go back into the mirror. I'll call you out again tomorrow morning at ten o'clock on the dot. Then you'll find all you need, and we'll celebrate."

The Brunos talked it over among themselves. Finally they agreed. "Tomorrow early, at ten o'clock sharp, you'll call us out of the mirror again. Don't be late!"

"Absolutely," said Bruno, holding the bathroom door open. One by one they disappeared into the mirror. The last one didn't want to go, and Bruno had to push him.

As soon as he had gone, Bruno tore the mirror from the wall as quickly as he could and threw it out the window. It smashed, tinkling, into many pieces on the sidewalk below.

Somehow Bruno felt rather mean. For the first time in his life he had deliberately broken his promise. But what else could he have done?

ANON.

The human race is very odd (odder than what? you might say, and you'd be quite right). But making jokes on tombstones *is* odd, you have to admit. Some of the seven epitaphs that follow are on actual gravestones.

Epitaphs

It is so soon that I am done for,
I wonder what I was begun for.
—For a child aged three weeks,
Cheltenham Churchyard

This is the grave of Mike O'Day
Who died maintaining his right of way.
His right was clear, his will was strong,
But he's just as dead as if he'd been wrong.

Here lies the body of Mary Anne Lowder,
She burst while drinking a Seidlitz powder.
Called from this world to her heavenly rest,
She should have waited till it effervesced.

Within this grave do lie,
Back to back, my wife and I;
When the last trump the air shall fill,
If she gets up, I'll just lie still.

 ANON.

Here lies John Auricular,
Who in the ways of the Lord walked perpendicular.

Beneath this stone our baby lies,
It neither cries nor hollers,
It lived but one and twenty days,
And cost us forty dollars.

The manner of her death was thus:
She was druv over by a Bus.

J. B. S. HALDANE

J. B. S. Haldane was one of the most distinguished English scientists of his time. He was a biologist and a foremost researcher in genetics, the branch of science that deals with how living things inherit and vary the characteristics of their kind. If you're redheaded, for example, what in your ancestry is responsible for it?

This terribly learned man also wrote an absurd book for children called *My Friend Mr. Leakey*. From it I have taken and slightly shortened one story. Because I am very fond of eating, it's always been one of my favorites.

A Meal with a Magician

WHEN I first met Mr. Leakey I never guessed he was a magician. I met him like this. I was going across the Haymarket about five o'clock one afternoon. When I got to the refuge by a lamppost in the middle I stopped, but a little man who had crossed so far with me went on. Then he saw a motor bus going down the hill and jumped back, which is always a silly thing to do. He jumped right in front of a car, and if I hadn't grabbed his overcoat collar and pulled him back onto the refuge, I think the car would have knocked him down. For it was wet weather, and the road was very greasy, so it only skidded when the driver put the brakes on.

The little man was very grateful, but dreadfully frightened, so I gave him my arm across the street, and saw him back to his home, which was quite near. I won't tell you where it was, because if I did you might go there and bother him, and if he got really grumpy it might be very awkward indeed for you. I mean, he might make one of your ears as big as a cabbage leaf, or turn your hair green, or exchange your right and left feet, or something like that. And then everyone who saw you would burst out laughing, and say, "Here comes wonky Willie, or lopsided Lizzie," or whatever your name is.

"I can't bear modern traffic," he said, "the motorbuses make me so frightened. If it wasn't for my work in London I should like to live on a little island where there are no roads, or on the top of a mountain, or somewhere like that." The little man was sure I had saved his life, and insisted on my having dinner with him, so I said I would come to dinner on Wednesday week. I didn't notice anything specially odd about him then, except that his ears were rather large and that he had a little tuft of hair on the top of each of them, rather like the lynx at the Zoo. I remember I thought if I had hair there I would shave it off. He told me that his name was Leakey, and that he lived on the first floor.

Well, on Wednesday week I went to dinner with him. I went upstairs in a block of flats and knocked at a quite ordinary door, and the little hall of the flat was quite ordinary too, but when I got inside it was one of the oddest rooms I have ever seen. Instead of wallpaper there were curtains round it, embroidered with pictures of people and animals. There was a picture of two men building a house, and another of a man with a dog and a crossbow hunting rabbits. I know they were made of embroidery, because I touched them, but it must have been a very funny sort of embroidery, because the pictures were always changing. As long as you looked at them they stayed still, but if you looked away and back again they had altered. During dinner the builders had put a fresh story on the house, the hunter had shot a bird with his crossbow, and his dog had caught two rabbits.

The furniture was very funny too. There was a bookcase made out of what looked like glass with the largest books in it that I ever saw, none of them less than a foot high, and bound in leather. There were cupboards running along the tops of the bookshelves. The chairs were beautifully carved, with high wooden backs, and there were two tables. One was made of copper, and had a huge crystal globe on it. The other was a solid lump of wood about ten feet long, four feet wide, and three feet high, with holes cut in it so that you could get your knees under it. There were various odd things hanging from the ceiling. At first I couldn't make out how the room was lit. Then I saw that the light came from plants of a sort I had never seen before, growing in pots. They had red, yellow and blue fruits about as big as tomatoes, which shone. They weren't disguised electric lamps, for I touched one and it was quite cold, and soft like a fruit.

"Well," said Mr. Leakey, "what would you like for dinner?"

"Oh, whatever you've got," I said.

"You can have whatever you like," he said. "Please choose a soup."

So I thought he probably got his dinner from a restaurant, and I said, "I'll have borscht," which is a red Russian soup with cream in it.

"Right," he said, "I'll get it ready. Look here, do you mind if we have dinner served the way mine usually is? You aren't easily frightened, are you?"

"Not very easily," I said.

"All right, then, I'll call my servant, but I warn you he's rather odd."

At that Mr. Leakey flapped the tops and lobes of his ears against his head. It made a noise like when one claps one's hands, but not so loud. Out of a large copper pot about as big as the copper you wash clothes in, which was standing in one corner, came what at first I thought was a large wet snake. Then I saw it had suckers all down one side, and was really the arm of an octopus. This arm opened a cupboard and pulled out a large towel with which it wiped the next arm that came out. The dry arm then clung onto the wall with its suckers, and gradually the whole beast came out, dried itself, and crawled up the wall. It was the biggest octopus I have ever seen; every arm was about eight feet long, and its body was as big as a sack. It crawled up the wall, and then along the ceiling, holding on by its suckers like a fly. When it got above the table it held on by one arm only, and with the other seven got plates and knives and forks out of the cupboards above the bookshelves and laid the table with them.

"That's my servant Oliver," said Mr. Leakey. "He's much better than a person, because he has more arms to work with, and he can hold on to a plate with about ten suckers, so he never drops one."

When Oliver the octopus had laid the table we sat down and he offered me a choice of water, lemonade, beer, and four different kinds of wine with his seven free arms, each of which held a different bottle. I chose some water and some very good red wine from Burgundy.

All this was so odd that I was not surprised to notice that my host was wearing a top hat, but I certainly did think it a little queer when he took it off and poured two platefuls of soup out of it.

"Ah, we want some cream," he added. "Come here, Phyllis." At this a small green cow, about the size of a rabbit, ran out of a hutch, jumped onto the table, and stood in front of Mr. Leakey, who milked her into a silver cream jug which Oliver had handed down for the purpose. The cream was excellent, and I enjoyed the soup very much.

"What would you like next?" said Mr. Leakey.

"I leave it to you," I answered.

"All right," he said, "we'll have grilled turbot, and turkey to follow. Catch us a turbot, please, Oliver, and be ready to grill it, Pompey."

At this Oliver picked up a fishhook with the end of one of his arms and began making casts in the air like a fly-fisher. Meanwhile I heard a noise in the fireplace, and Pompey came out. He was a small dragon about a foot long, not counting his tail, which measured another foot. He had been lying on the burning coals, and was red-hot. So I was glad to see that as soon as he got out of the fire he put a pair of asbestos boots which were lying in the fender onto his hind feet.

"Now, Pompey," said Mr. Leakey, "hold your tail up properly. If you burn the carpet again, I'll pour a bucket of cold water over you. (Of course I wouldn't really do that, it's very cruel to pour cold water onto a dragon, especially a little one with a thin skin)," he added in a low voice, which only I could hear. But poor Pompey took the threat quite seriously. He whimpered, and the yellow flames which were coming out of his nose turned a dull blue. He waddled along rather clumsily on his hind legs, holding up his tail and the front part of his body. I think the asbestos boots made walking rather difficult for him, though they saved the carpet, and no doubt kept his hind feet warm. But of course dragons generally walk on all four feet and seldom wear boots, so I was surprised that Pompey walked as well as he did.

I was so busy watching Pompey that I never saw how Oliver caught the turbot, and by the time I looked up at him again he had just finished cleaning it, and threw it down to Pompey. Pompey caught it in his front paws, which had cooled down a bit, and were just about the right temperature for grilling things. He had long thin fingers with claws on the ends; and held the fish on each hand alternately, holding the other against his red-hot chest to warm it. By the time he had finished and put the grilled fish on to a plate which Oliver handed down Pompey was clearly feeling the cold, for his teeth were chattering, and he scampered back to the fire with evident joy.

"Yes," said Mr. Leakey, "I know some people say it is cruel to let a young dragon cool down like that, and liable to give it a bad cold. But I say a dragon can't begin to learn too soon that life isn't all fire and flames, and the world is a colder place than he'd like it to be. And they don't get colds if you give them plenty of sulphur to eat. Of course a dragon with a cold is an awful nuisance to itself and everyone else. I've known one throw flames for a hundred yards when it sneezed. But that was a full-grown one, of course. It burned down one of the Emperor of China's palaces. Besides, I really couldn't afford to keep a dragon if I didn't make use of him. Last week, for example, I used his breath to burn the old paint off the door, and his tail makes quite a good soldering iron. Then he's really much more reliable than a dog for dealing with burglars. They might shoot a dog, but leaden bullets just melt the moment they touch Pompey. Anyway, I think dragons were meant for use, not ornament. Don't you?"

"Well, do you know," I answered, "I am ashamed to say that Pompey is the first live dragon I've ever seen."

"Of course," said Mr. Leakey, "how stupid of me. I have so few guests here except professional colleagues that I forgot you were a layman. By the way," he went on, as he poured sauce out of his hat over the fish, "I don't know if you've noticed anything queer about this dinner. Of course some people are more observant than others."

"Well," I answered, "I've never seen anything like it before."

For example at that moment I was admiring an enormous rainbow-colored beetle which was crawling towards me over the table with a salt-cellar strapped on its back.

"Ah well then," said my host, "perhaps you have guessed that I'm a magician. Pompey, of course, is a real dragon, but most of the other animals here were people before I made them what they are now. Take Oliver, for example. When he was a man he had his legs cut off by a railway train. I couldn't stick them on again because my magic doesn't work against machinery. Poor Oliver was bleeding to death, so I thought the only way to save his life was to turn him into some animal with no legs. Then he wouldn't have any legs to have been cut off. I turned him into a snail, and took him home in my pocket. But whenever I tried to turn him back into something more interesting, like a dog, it had no hind legs. But an octopus has really got no legs. Those eight tentacles grow out of its head. So when I turned him into an octopus, he was all right. And he had been a waiter when he was a man, so he soon learned his job. I think he's much better than a maid because he can lift the plates from above, and doesn't stand behind one and breathe down one's neck. You may have the rest of the fish, Oliver, and a bottle of beer. I know that's what you like."

Oliver seized the fish in one of his arms and put it into an immense beak like a parrot's but much bigger, which lay in the center of the eight arms. Then he took a bottle of beer out of a cupboard, unscrewed the cork with his beak, hoisted himself up to the ceiling with two of his other arms, and turned over so that his mouth was upwards. As he emptied the bottle he winked one of his enormous eyes. Then I felt sure he must be really a man, for I never saw an ordinary octopus wink.

The turkey came in a more ordinary way. Oliver let down a large hot plate, and then a dish cover onto it. There was nothing in the cover, as I could see. Mr. Leakey got up, took a large wand out of the umbrella stand, pointed it at the dish cover, said a few words, and there was the turkey steaming hot when Oliver lifted the cover off it.

As we were finishing the turkey, Mr. Leakey looked up anxiously from time to time.

"I hope Abdu'l Makkar won't be late with the strawberries," he said.

"Strawberries?" I asked in amazement, for it was the middle of January.

"Oh yes, I've sent Abdu'l Makkar, who is a jinn, to New Zealand for some. Of course it's summer there. He oughtn't to be long now, if he has been good, but you know what jinns are, they have their faults, like the rest of us. Curiosity, especially. When one sends them on long errands they will fly too high. They like to get up quite close to Heaven to overhear what the angels are saying, and then the angels throw shooting stars at them. Then they drop their parcels, or come home half scorched. He ought to be back soon, he's been away over an hour. Meanwhile we'll have some other fruit, in case he's late."

He got up, and tapped the four corners of the table with his wand. At each corner the wood swelled; then it cracked, and a little green shoot came out and started growing. In a minute they were already about a foot high, with several leaves at the top, and the bottom quite woody. I could see from the leaves that one was a cherry, another a pear, and the third a peach, but I didn't know the fourth.

As Oliver was clearing away the remains of the turkey with four of his arms and helping himself to a sausage with a fifth, Adbu'l Makkar came in. He came feet first through the ceiling, which seemed to close behind him like water in the tank of the diving birds' house in the Zoo, when you look at it from underneath while a penguin dives in. It shook a little for a moment afterwards. He narrowly missed one of Oliver's arms, but alighted safely on the floor, bending his knees to break his fall, and bowing deeply to Mr. Leakey. He had a brown face with rather a long nose, and looked quite like a man, except that he had a pair of leathery wings folded on his back, and his nails were of gold. He were a turban and clothes of green silk.

"Oh peacock of the world and redresser of injustices," he said, "thy unworthy servant comes into the presence with rare and refreshing fruit."

"The presence deigns to express gratification at the result of thy labors."

"The joy of thy negligible slave is as the joy of King Solomon, son of David (on whom be peace, if he has not already obtained peace), when he first beheld Balkis, the queen of Sheba. May the Terminator of delights and Separator of companions be far from this dwelling."

"May the Deluder of Intelligences never trouble the profundity of thine apprehension."

"Oh dominator of demons and governor of goblins, what egregious enchanter or noble necromancer graces thy board?"

"It is written, oh Abdu'l Makkar, in the book of the sayings of the prophet Shoaib, the apostle of the Midianites, that curiosity slew the cat of Pharaoh, king of Egypt."

"That is a true word."

"Thy departure is permitted. Awaken me at the accustomed hour. But stay! My safety razor hath no more blades and the shops of London are closed. Fly therefore to Montreal, where it is even now high noon, and purchase me a packet thereof."

"I tremble and obey."

"Why dost thou tremble, oh audacious among the Ifreets?"

"Oh Emperor of enchantment, the lower air is full of airplanes, flying swifter than a magic carpet,* and each making a din like unto the bursting of the great dam of Sheba, and the upper air is infested with meteorites."

"Fly therefore at a height of five miles and thou shalt avoid both the one peril and the other. And now, oh performer of commands and executor of behests, thou hast my leave to depart."

"May the wisdom of Plato, the longevity of Shiqq, the wealth of Solomon, and the success of Alexander, be thine."

*This is of course a gross exaggeration.

"The like unto thee, with brazen knobs thereon."

The jinn now vanished, this time through the floor. While he and Mr. Leakey had been talking the trees had grown up to about four feet high, and flowered. The flowers were now falling off, and little green fruits were swelling.

"You have to talk like that to a jinn or you lose his respect. I hope you don't mind my not introducing you, but really jinns may be quite awkward at times," said my host.

We next ate the New Zealand strawberries, which were very good, with Phyllis's cream. While we did so Pompey, who acted as a sort of walking stove, came out again and melted some cheese to make a Welsh rarebit. After this we went on to dessert. The fruit was now quite ripe. The fourth tree bore half a dozen beautiful golden fruits shaped rather like apricots, but much bigger, and my host told me they were mangoes, which of course usually grow in India. In fact you can't make them grow in England except by magic. So I said I would try a mango.

"Aha," said Mr. Leakey, "this is where I have a pull over Lord Melchett or the Duke of Westminster, or any other rich man. They might be able to get mangoes here by airplane, but they couldn't give them as dessert at a smart dinner-party."

"Why not?" I asked.

"That shows you've never eaten one. The only proper place to eat a mango is in your bath. You see, it has a tough skin and a squashy inside, so when once you get through the skin all the juice squirts out. And that would make a nasty mess of people's white shirts.

"About your mango; you can eat it quite safely, if you just wait a moment while I enchant it so that it won't splash over you."

Quite a short spell and a little wiggling of his wand were enough, and then I ate the mango. It was wonderful. It was the only fruit I have ever eaten that was better than the best strawberries. I can't describe the flavor, which is a mixture of all sorts of things, including a little resin, like the smell of a pine forest in summer. There is a huge flattish stone in the middle, too big to get into your mouth, and all round it a squashy yellow pulp. To test the spell I tried to spill some down my waistcoat, but it merely jumped into my mouth. Mr. Leakey ate a pear, and gave me the other five mangoes to take home. But I had to eat them in my bath because they weren't enchanted.

While we were having coffee (out of the hat, of course) Mr. Leakey rubbed one corner of the table with his wand and it began to sprout with very fine green grass. When it was about as high as the grass on a lawn, he called Phyllis out of her hutch, and she ate some of it for her dinner. We talked for a while about magic, football, and the odder sorts of dog, such as Bedlington terriers and rough-haired Dachshunds, and then I said I must be getting home.

"I'll take you home," said Mr. Leakey, "but when you have a day to spare you must come round and spend it with me, if you'd care to see the sort of things I generally do, and we might go over to India or Java or somewhere for the afternoon. Let me know when you're free. But now just stand on this carpet, and shut your eyes, because people often get giddy the first two or three times they travel by magic carpet."

We got onto the carpet. I took a last look at the table. Then I shut my eyes, my host told the carpet my address, flapped his ears, and I felt a rush of cold air on my cheeks, and a slight giddiness. Then the air was warm again. Mr. Leakey told me to open my eyes, and I was in my sitting room at home, five miles away. As the room is small, and there were a number of books and things on the floor, the carpet could not settle down properly, and stayed about a foot up in the air. Luckily it was quite stiff, so I stepped down off it, and turned the light on.

"Good night," said Mr. Leakey, bending down to shake my hand, and then he flapped his ears and he and the carpet vanished. I was left in my room with nothing but a nice full feeling and a parcel of mangoes to persuade me that I had not been dreaming.

JOHN WALSH

The Giant Crab

Along the steep wall at the old pier's side,
The scavenging crabs come up with the tide.
"Want to catch one? It's easy! You don't need a thing
But a stone, and some fish, and some odd bits of string;
Look here now—I'll show you. First fetch that big
stone—
The one with the hole through—the cobble-shaped one;
Now join up your string—all the odd bits you've got—
Loop one end through the stone, and tie tight in a knot;
Then cram in these bits of stale fish for a bait . . .
Ready? Over she goes!
Now you've only to wait!"

Not long!

There's a tiny commotion below in the water;
There's a shout from above as the line becomes tauter;
There's a hauling up, hand over hand, until—
whee-ee-ee!—
A monster-great crab swings clear of the sea—
All legs and sharp claws, hanging desperately on,
His pincers stuck fast through the hole in the stone!
"Quick, get him!" "No hurry! He's stupid—he'll cling

Till we land him. Pull steady, and don't break the
  string . . .
Whoops! Over he comes! Give the string a sharp shake,
And he'll let go his hold and fall down on his back."

Well done!

"Now who'll pick him up?" "Not me!" "No, not me!
It's you said you fancied a crab for your tea!"
"*I* said? *I* don't want him!" "Hey, Billy, he's yours!
Come along and make friends with him!"
  "What? With those claws?
I'm not touching him yet; I'll wait till he's dead!"
"You boil them alive; that's what my mother said;
They scream in the saucepan." "This one would get out:
He'd flop to the floor and go scrambling about—
He'd crawl on the baby; he'd frighten the cat;
Why, he could do anything with claws like that!
He could jab you—"
                "Hey, somebody! Lend me that stick:
Hook him by the legs and pitch him back quick!"

Whe-e-e-ew! Sploosh! He's gone! . . .

Thank goodness!

BEN LUCIEN BURMAN

If you ever steamboat down the Mississippi you'll come to a bend near Baton Rouge where there's a river light named after Ben Lucien Burman. That's because he's written so many good books about Old Man River, especially the Catfish Bend stories. These are so famous that along the river between Memphis and New Orleans travelers often ask gas station attendants for road directions to Catfish Bend.

High Water at Catfish Bend was the first of the series and it remains the best, I think. It's about a big flood on the river and how all the animals got together to persuade the engineers down in New Orleans to take steps to prevent disaster. I got a letter once from Mr. Burman telling me why he wrote the Catfish Bend stories. He wrote: "If we don't learn to live together we'll all die together." I think of that sentence whenever I reread the adventures of the animals Mr. Burman has created.

Doc Raccoon is the wisest of the animals. Floating downriver with him is Judge Black the blacksnake, who's a vegetarian, but only some of the time; an old bullfrog who directs the Indian Bayou Glee Club; a cottontail rabbit without much brains; and J. C. Hunter, the red fox who's tricky and not altogether reliable. With the river rising, they're all in a jam together, and so they swear a pact to help each other. But the fox (who's eaten watermelons he should have shared with the others) has broken the pact of friendship, and the others—they're all huddled together on a little shanty boat—are not feeling very friendly toward him.

Doc Raccoon goes on with the story.

High Water at Catfish Bend

I WAS just starting to go ashore and ask the way of a couple of otters running around on the bank, when all of a sudden a big towboat went past, making tremendous waves. And in a minute the rope holding us to the land broke and we started racing down the river. We went faster and faster as the full current caught us, and a mole could have seen that we were heading straight for a bridge pier. We were still close to the shore, and there was a chance of saving ourselves if we could find a rope to throw over something. But there was only one rope on the shanty when we found it, and now that was gone. It certainly looked like the finish. And then, just as we were passing a little cabin on the bank, I saw Judge Black twist the end of his tail around a cleat on the shanty and shoot out his long body toward a pine tree.

He looped around it, and the boat stopped with a bump that nearly sent us all into the water. It was a wonderful thing of him to do. It must have almost pulled him in two.

He stretched three or four inches while I was watching, and I could see by his eyes how he was suffering. "You've got to get another rope," he panted. "I can't hold on but a few minutes. My whole backbone's coming apart."

And I heard a loud crack inside him.

He'd saved us and given us a new chance. But I knew it would be all wasted if we didn't do something fast. That bridge pier was still out there, with the racing water. And then I saw a rope on the porch of the cabin that was under the tree, and a dog sitting near it, a big dog, sort of like a shepherd, ragged and old, and scratching himself with both hind legs like he was crazy. I called out to him and asked him to throw me the rope.

He shook his head and scratched harder. "It's not my rope," he answered. "And I haven't got the strength to throw anything. These fleas have got me all worn out. They're worse than chiggers and measles and St. Vitus' dance put together."

I tried to make him change his mind. But the old dog was so miserable with the fleas, he didn't listen. Or maybe he couldn't hear, he was scratching so hard.

There was another loud crack inside Judge Black. "I'm breaking up," he said.

And I was sure that was the end.

Just then the fox, who hadn't spoken to anybody for days—he was feeling so bad about the watermelons—leaned way over the edge of the boat, and got as near to the old dog as he could.

"If I show you how to get rid of your fleas will you throw us the rope?" he called out.

The old dog heard that all right, and sat up fast. "I'm too old for miracles," he said.

But you could see by his ears he was interested.

"Throw it," called the fox.

The old dog waited a minute, not sure what to do, and then tossed it over. I made it fast to a stump on shore, and then Judge Black could let go.

We stretched him out on the deck, and his eyes were closed, and we thought for a while he was dead. But we kept throwing water over him, and after a while his eyes opened, and he raised his head and hissed a little, that nice, pleasant hiss you didn't mind at all. And we massaged his back, and rubbed him down with some leaves like bay leaves he told us that snakes always use for rheumatism—they get backache all the time, with such a long backbone. And then he sort of cleared his throat and took one of his cough drops, and we knew he'd be all right. And then I went off with the fox to see that he kept his promise to the dog. I was worried, too, I can tell you, because I thought maybe this was just another of his tricks. And it's no fun to make a fool of any big animal, even if he is a little old.

The fox rubbed against the dog a minute so that a few of the fleas jumped on him, and then went off a little way where there was a kind of pool by a sand bar and the water was quiet.

"Watch close," he said, and took a big leaf in his mouth and then walked into the water. He kept going forward, deeper and deeper, but very slow, so that the fleas had time to climb up to that part of his body that was still dry. And pretty soon only his head was showing, and all the fleas were collected there. And then he brought his head down lower and lower until only his nose was showing, and of course the fleas went there, too. And then he dipped his nose and there wasn't anything showing but the leaf. In no time all the fleas were out on that. And then he let the leaf go, and they all floated down the river.

The old dog couldn't wait to try it himself, and got so excited he let the leaf fall a couple of times before he did it right. And then when he found they were really gone, he was a changed animal. He ran up and down the bank, barking like a puppy, and then he raced off and told all the other dogs, and they did it, too, because the fleas were bad. The pool was full of dogs splashing everywhere. They were all as happy as the old dog afterwards, and they went off and brought us the best things that were in the houses around there to eat. We had a wonderful time. And of course we knew it was the fox that had done it, so we forgave him, and took him back in the pact.

JOHN UPDIKE

January

The days are short,
  The sun a spark
Hung thin between
  The dark and dark.

Fat snowy footsteps
  Track the floor.
Milk bottles burst
  Outside the door.

The river is
  A frozen place
Held still beneath
  The trees of lace.

The sky is low.
  The wind is gray.
The radiator
  Purrs all day.

September

The breezes taste
  Of apple peel.
The air is full
  Of smells to feel—

Ripe fruit, old footballs,
  Burning brush,
New books, erasers,
  Chalk, and such.

The bee, his hive
  Well-honeyed, hums,
And Mother cuts
  Chrysanthemums.

Like plates washed clean
  With suds, the days
Are polished with
  A morning haze.

JUDY BLUME

Judy Blume is probably one of the half-dozen most popular children's book writers in the United States. Many of her books deal with the real problems and joys faced by boys and girls aged perhaps twelve through fourteen or fifteen. They are frank and honest and sometimes they surprise parents as much as they interest young people. Generally her characters are comfortably middle-class and often they reflect life as lived in suburban New Jersey, where Judy Blume grew up. She still lives there with her husband John, who's a lawyer. They have two children—Larry and Randy.

Though most of her books are about sixth graders (and older kids) I like just as well—because it's so funny—the one called *Tales of a Fourth Grade Nothing*. "The Birthday Bash" is taken from it.

The Birthday Bash

I GOT USED to the way Fudge looked without his top front teeth. He looked like a very small first grader. Dr. Brown, our dentist, said he'd have to wait until he was six or seven to get his grown-up teeth. I started calling him Fang because when he smiles all you can see are the top two side teeth next to the big space. So it looks like he has fangs.

My mother didn't like that. "I want you to stop calling him Fang," she told me.

"What should I call him?" I asked. "Farley Drexel?"

"Just plain Fudge will be fine," my mother said.

"What's wrong with Farley Drexel?" I asked. "How come you named him that if you don't like it?"

"I like it fine," my mother said. "But right now we call him Fudge. Not Farley . . . not Drexel . . . and *not* Fang!"

"What's wrong with Fang?" I asked. "I think it sounds neat."

"Fang is an insult!"

"Oh . . . come on, Mom! He doesn't even know what a fang is!"

"But *I* know, Peter. And *I* don't like it."

"Okay . . . okay. . . ." I promised never to call my brother Fang again.

But secretly, whenever I look at him, I think it. *My brother, Fang Hatcher!* Nobody can stop me from thinking. My mind is my own.

Fudge is going to be three years old. My mother said he should have a birthday party with some of his friends. He plays with three other little kids who live in our building. There's Jennie, Ralph, and Sam. My mother invited them to Fudge's party. Grandma said she'd come over to help. My father couldn't make it. He had a Saturday business appointment. I wanted to go to Jimmy Fargo's but my mother said she needed me to supervise the games. The kids were invited from one until two-thirty.

"That's only an hour and a half," my mother reminded me. "That's not so bad, is it, Peter?"

"I don't know yet," I told her. "Ask me later."

The kitchen table was set up for the party. The cloth and napkins and paper plates and cups all matched. They had pictures of Superman on them.

Right before party time Grandma tried to change Fudge into his new suit. But he screamed his head off about it. "No suit! No suit! NO . . . NO . . . NO!"

My mother tried to reason with him. "It's your birthday, Fudgie. All your friends are coming. You want to look like a big boy, don't you?" While she was talking to him she managed to get him into his shirt and pants. But he wouldn't let her put on his shoes. He kicked and carried on until my mother and grandmother were both black and blue. Finally they decided as long as he was in his suit his feet didn't matter. So he wore his old bedroom slippers.

Ralph arrived first. He's really fat. And he isn't even four years old. He doesn't say much either. He grunts and grabs a lot, though. Usually his mouth is stuffed full of something.

So the first thing Ralph did was wander into the kitchen. He looked around for something to eat. But Grandma was guarding the place. She kept telling him "No . . . No . . . must wait until the other children come."

Jennie arrived next. She was wearing little white gloves and party shoes. She even carried a pocketbook. Besides that she had on dirty jeans and an old sweater. Her mother apologized for her clothes but said she couldn't do anything with Jennie lately—especially since she had taken to biting.

"What does she bite?" I asked, thinking about furniture or toys or stuff like that.

"She bites people," Jennie's mother said. "But you don't have to worry about it unless her teeth go through the skin. Otherwise it's perfectly safe."

I thought, *poor old Fudge! He can't even bite back since he hasn't got any top front teeth*. I looked at Jennie. She seemed so innocent. It was hard to believe she was a vampire.

Sam came last. He carried a big present for Fudge but he was crying. "It's just a stage he's going through," his mother explained. "Everything scares him. Especially birthday parties. But he'll be fine. Won't you, Sam?"

Sam grabbed onto his mother's leg and screamed, "Take me home! Take me home!" Somehow, Sam's mother untangled herself from Sam's grip and left.

So at five after one we were ready to begin. We had an eater, a biter, and a crier. I thought that two-thirty would never come. I also thought my mother was slightly crazy for dreaming up the party in the first place. "Doesn't Fudge have any normal friends?" I whispered.

"There's nothing wrong with Fudgie's friends!" my mother whispered back. "All small children are like that."

Grandma got them seated around the kitchen table. She put a party hat on each kid's head. Sam screamed, "Get it off! Get it off!" But the others wore their hats and didn't complain. My mother snapped a picture of them with her new camera.

Then Grandma turned off the lights and my mother lit the candles on Fudge's cake. It had chocolate frosting and big yellow roses. I led the singing of "Happy Birthday." My mother carried the cake across the kitchen to the party table and set it down in front of Fudge.

Sam cried, "Too dark! Too dark!" So Grandma had to turn on the kitchen lights before Fudge blew out his candles. When he was finished blowing he reached out and grabbed a rose off his cake. He shoved it into his mouth.

"Oh, Fudge!" my mother said. "Look what you did."

But Grandma said, "It's his birthday. He can do whatever he wants!"

So Fudge reached over and grabbed a second rose.

I guess fat Ralph couldn't stand seeing Fudge eat those yellow roses because he grabbed one, too. By that time the cake looked pretty messy. My mother, finally coming to her senses, took the cake away and sliced it up.

Each kid got a Dixie cup, a small piece of cake, and some milk. But Jennie hollered, "Where's my rose? Want one too!" Because her slice of birthday cake didn't happen to have one.

My mother explained that the roses were only decorations and there weren't enough to go around. Jennie seemed to accept that. But when Grandma stood over her to help open her Dixie, Jennie bit her on the hand.

"She bit me!" Grandma cried.

"Did it break the skin?" my mother asked.

"No . . . I don't think so," Grandma said, checking.

"Good. Then it's nothing to worry about," my mother told her.

Grandma went into the bathroom to put some medicine on it anyway. She wasn't taking any chances.

Ralph was the first one to finish his food. "More . . . more . . . more!" he sang, holding up his empty plate.

"I don't think you should give him any more," I whispered to my mother. "Look how fat he is now!"

"Oh, Peter . . . this is a party. Let him eat whatever he wants."

"Okay," I said. "Why should I care how fat he gets?"

My mother served Ralph a second piece of cake. He threw up right after he finished it.

Me and Grandma took the kids into the living room while my mother cleaned up the mess.

Grandma told Fudge he could open his presents while his friends watched. Jennie brought him a musical jack-in-the-box. When you turn the handle around it plays "Pop Goes the Weasel." When you reach the part of the song about Pop, the top opens and a funny clown jumps up. Fudge loved it. He clapped his hands and laughed and laughed. But Sam started to scream, "No! No more. Take it away!" He hid his face in his hands and wouldn't look up until Grandma promised to put the jack-in-the-box in another room.

Fudge opened Ralph's present next. It was a little windup car that ran all over the floor. I kind of liked it myself. So did Ralph. Because he grabbed it away from Fudge and said, "MINE."

"No!" Fudge shouted. "MINE."

When my mother heard the racket she ran in from the kitchen. She explained to Ralph that he had brought the car to Fudge because it was *his* birthday. But Ralph wouldn't listen. I guess my mother was afraid he might throw up again, and this time on the living room rug. So she begged Fudge to let Ralph play with the car for a few minutes. But Ralph kept screaming it was *his* car. So Fudge started to cry. Finally, my mother took the car away and said, "Let's see what Sam brought you."

Fudge liked that idea. He forgot about the little car as he ripped the paper and ribbon off Sam's package. It turned out to be a big picture dictionary. The same kind the Yarbys brought me a couple of months ago. Fudge got mad when he saw it.

"No!" he yelled. "NO MORE BOOK!" He threw it across the room.

"Fudge! That's terrible," my mother said. "You mustn't do that to the nice book."

"No book!" Fudge said.

Sam cried, "He doesn't like it. He doesn't like my present. I want to go home . . . I want to go home!"

Grandma tried to comfort Sam while my mother picked up the book. She gathered the wrapping paper and ribbons and cards together. Fudge didn't even look at any of the birthday cards. Oh well, he can't read, so I guess it doesn't make any difference.

"Peter," my mother said, "let's start the games . . . now . . . quick!"

I checked the time. I hoped the party was almost over. But no, it was only one-thirty. Still an hour to go. I went into my room where I had blown up a lot of balloons. My mother has this party book and it says three-year-olds like to dance around with balloons. When I got back to the living room Mom started the record player and I handed each kid a balloon.

But they just stood there looking at me. I thought, *either the guy who wrote that party book is crazy or I am!*

"Show them how, Peter," my mother said. "Take a balloon and demonstrate."

I felt like one of the world's great living fools dancing around with a balloon, but it worked. As soon as the kids saw me doing it, they started dancing too. And the more they danced the more they liked it. Until Jennie's balloon popped. That nearly scared Sam right out of his mind. He started yelling and crying. Fortunately I had blown up two dozen balloons. I was hoping they'd dance around the rest of the afternoon.

Fudge got the idea of jumping up and down on the furniture. The others liked that too. So instead of dancing with their balloons, that's what they did. And soon they were running from room to room, yelling and laughing and having a great time.

Then the doorbell rang. It was Mrs. Rudder. She lives in the apartment right under us. She wanted to know what was going on. She said it sounded like her ceiling was about to crash in on her any second.

My mother explained that Fudge was having a little birthday party and wouldn't she like to stay for a piece of cake? Sometimes my mother is really clever! So Grandma entertained Mrs. Rudder in the kitchen while Fudge and his buddies jumped up and down on his new bed.

It was delivered this morning. Fudge hasn't even slept in it yet. So naturally when my mother found out what they were up to, she was mad. "Stop it right now!" she said.

"New bed . . . big boy!" Fudge told her. Was he proud!

"You won't have a new-big-boy-bed for long if you don't stop jumping on it," my mother told him. "I know . . . let's all sit down on the floor and hear a nice story." My mother selected a picture book from Fudge's bookshelf.

"I heard that one!" Jennie said when she saw the cover.

"All right," my mother told her, "Let's hear this one." She held up another book.

"I heard that one too," Jennie said.

I think my mother was starting to lose her patience. But she chose a third book and said, "We'll all enjoy this one even if we know it by heart. And if we *do* know it by heart . . . well, we can say it together."

That's just what Jennie did. And when my mother skipped a page by mistake Jennie was right there to remind her. If you ask me, my mother felt like biting Jennie by that time!

When the story was over it was two o'clock and Ralph was sound asleep on the floor. My mother told me to put him up on Fudge's new bed while she took the rest of the children back to the living room.

I tried and tried but I couldn't lift Ralph. He must weigh a ton. So I left him sleeping on Fudge's floor and closed the door so he wouldn't hear any noise. On my way back to the living room I wished the others would fall asleep too.

"Peter," my mother suggested, "why don't you show them Dribble?"

"Mom! Dribble's my pet." You don't go around using a pet to entertain a bunch of little kids. Didn't my mother know that?

"Please, Peter," my mother said. "We've still got half an hour left and I don't know what to do with them anymore."

"Dribble!" Fudge hollered. "Dribble . . . Dribble . . . Dribble!"

I guess Sam and Jennie liked the way that sounded because they started to shout, "Dribble . . . Dribble . . . Dribble!" even though they didn't know what they were talking about.

"Oh . . . all right," I said. "I'll show you Dribble. But you've got to promise to be very quiet. You mustn't make a sound. You might scare him . . . okay?"

They all said, "Okay." My mother went into the kitchen to chat with

Grandma and Mrs. Rudder. I went into my room and came back carrying Dribble in his bowl. I put my finger over my lips to remind Fudge and his friends to be quiet. It worked. At first nobody said a word.

I put Dribble down on a table. Fudge and Sam and Jennie stood over his bowl.

"Oh . . . turtle!" Jennie said.

"Yes, Dribble's a turtle. *My* turtle," I said in a soft voice.

"See . . . see," Fudge whispered.

"They can all see," I told Fudge.

"Nice turtle," Sam said.

I wondered why he wasn't afraid this time.

"What does Dribble do?" Jennie asked.

"Do? He doesn't do anything special," I said. "He's a turtle. He does turtle things."

"Like what?" Jennie asked.

What was with this kid, anyway? "Well," I said, "he swims around a little and he sleeps on his rock and he eats."

"Does he make?" Jennie asked.

"Make?" I said.

"Make a tinkle?"

"Oh, that. Well, sure. I guess so."

Jennie laughed. So did Sam and Fudge.

"I make tinkles too. Want to see?" Jennie asked.

"No," I said.

"See . . . see," Fudge laughed, pointing at Jennie.

Jennie had a big smile on her face. Next thing I knew there was a puddle on the rug.

"Mom!" I hollered. "Come quick!"

My mother dashed in from the kitchen. "What, Peter? What is it?"

"Just look at what Jennie did," I said.

"What is that?" my mother asked, eyeing the puddle.

"She made on the floor," I said. "And on purpose!"

"Oh, Jennie!" my mother cried. "You didn't!"

"Did too," Jennie said.

"That was very naughty!" my mother told her. "You come with me." She scooped up Jennie and carried her into the bathroom.

After that Mom mopped up the puddle.

Finally the doorbell rang. It was two-thirty. The party was over. I could hardly believe it. I was beginning to think it would never end.

First Ralph's mother came. She had to wake him up to get him out of the apartment. I guess even *she* couldn't carry him.

Next Jennie's mother came. Mom gave her Jennie's wet pants in a Baggie. That was all she had to do. Jennie's mother was plenty embarrassed.

Sam's mother came last. But he didn't want to go home. Now that he was used to us I guess he liked us. He cried, "More party . . . MORE!"

"Another time," his mother said, dragging him out of our apartment by the arm.

My mother flopped down in a chair. Grandma brought her two aspirins and a glass of water. "Here, dear," she said. "Maybe these will help."

My mother swallowed the pills. She held her head.

"Three is kind of young for a party," I told my mother.

"Peter Warren Hatcher . . ." my mother began.

"Yes?" I asked.

"You are absolutely right!"

I flopped down next to my mother. She put her arm around me. Then we both watched Fudge work his new jack-in-the-box.

Later, when my father came home, he said, "How did Fudge's party go?"

My mother and I looked at each other and we laughed.

ALFRED, LORD TENNYSON

The Eagle

He clasps the crag with crooked hands;
Close to the sun in lonely lands,
Ring'd with the azure world, he stands.

The wrinkled sea beneath him crawls;
He watches from his mountain walls,
And like a thunderbolt he falls.

CARLO COLLODI

Pinocchio is the most famous piece of wood in all literature. Geppetto, a marionette maker, carved him out of a log, says the story. But he was really created by an Italian who called himself Collodi and whose actual name was Carlo Lorenzini.

Collodi is another example of a fine children's book writer who was a bachelor. The son of a cook and a lady's maid, he was a school dropout, a soldier, a journalist. But it is only as the author of *Pinocchio* that he is remembered. (Perhaps you've seen the Disney film based on this book written over a hundred years ago.)

It's about a marionette who wants badly to become a real boy, and, after a hundred adventures and misfortunes, succeeds. In *Pinocchio* something happens every minute, as in a puppet show. Collodi tells us at once that the story is not about kings and princesses, but about a block of wood that comes alive. Common people and common animals crowd its pages, with only one character—the Fairy with Azure Hair—to give it a fairy-tale touch.

Pinocchio's nose is as famous as he is and in the excerpt below you'll see what causes it to grow longer and longer. Before this, Collodi tells us, he had disobediently run away from his master Geppetto, had many adventures, met many strange creatures, was saved from hanging by the Fairy, and was put to bed to recover. Now go on with the story.

Pinocchio

Translated by Carol Della Chiesa

CHAPTER SEVENTEEN

AS SOON as the three doctors had left the room, the Fairy went to Pinocchio's bed and, touching him on the forehead, noticed that he was burning with fever.

She took a glass of water, put a white powder into it, and, handing it to the Marionette, said lovingly to him:

"Drink this, and in a few days you'll be up and well."

Pinocchio looked at the glass, made a wry face, and asked in a whining voice: "Is it sweet or bitter?"

"It is bitter, but it is good for you."

"If it is bitter, I don't want it."

"Drink it!"

"I don't like anything bitter."

"Drink it and I'll givc you a lump of sugar to take the bitter taste from your mouth."

"Where's the sugar?"

"Here it is," said the Fairy, taking a lump from a golden sugar bowl.

"I want the sugar first, then I'll drink the bitter water."

"Do you promise?"

"Yes."

The Fairy gave him the sugar and Pinocchio, after chewing and swallowing it in a twinkling, said, smacking his lips:

"If only sugar were medicine! I should take it every day."

"Now keep your promise and drink these few drops of water. They'll be good for you."

Pinocchio took the glass in both hands and stuck his nose into it. He lifted it to his mouth and once more stuck his nose into it.

"It is too bitter, much too bitter! I can't drink it."

"How do you know, when you haven't even tasted it?"

"I can imagine it. I smell it. I want another lump of sugar, then I'll drink it."

The Fairy, with all the patience of a good mother, gave him more sugar and again handed him the glass.

"I can't drink it like that," the Marionette said, making more wry faces.

"Why?"

"Because that feather pillow on my feet bothers me."

The Fairy took away the pillow.

"It's no use. I can't drink it even now."

"What's the matter now?"

"I don't like the way that door looks. It's half open."

The Fairy closed the door.

"I won't drink it," cried Pinocchio, bursting out crying. "I won't drink this awful water. I won't. I won't! No, no, no, no!"

"My boy, you'll be sorry."

"I don't care."

"You are very sick."

"I don't care."

"In a few hours the fever will take you far away to another world."

"I don't care."

"Aren't you afraid of death?"

"Not a bit. I'd rather die than drink that awful medicine."

At that moment, the door of the room flew open and in came four Rabbits as black as ink, carrying a small black coffin on their shoulders.

"What do you want from me?" asked Pinocchio.

"We have come for you," said the largest Rabbit.

"For me? But I'm not dead yet!"

"No, not dead yet; but you will be in a few moments since you have refused to take the medicine which would have made you well."

"Oh, Fairy, my Fairy," the Marionette cried out, "give me that glass! Quick, please! I don't want to die! No, no, not yet—not yet!"

And holding the glass with two hands, he swallowed the medicine at one gulp.

"Well," said the four Rabbits, "this time we have made the trip for nothing."

And turning on their heels, they marched solemnly out of the room, carrying their little black coffin and muttering and grumbling between their teeth.

In a twinkling, Pinocchio felt fine. With one leap he was out of bed and into his clothes.

The Fairy, seeing him run and jump around the room gay as a bird on wing, said to him:

"My medicine was good for you, after all, wasn't it?"

"Good indeed! It has given me new life."

"Why, then, did I have to beg you so hard to make you drink it?"

"I'm a boy, you see, and all boys hate medicine more than they do sickness."

"What a shame! Boys ought to know, after all, that medicine, taken in time, can save them from much pain and even from death."

"Next time I won't have to be begged so hard. I'll remember those black Rabbits with the black coffin on their shoulders and I'll take the glass and pouf!—down it will go!"

"Come here now and tell me how it came about that you found yourself in the hands of the Assassins."

"It happened that Fire Eater gave me five gold pieces to give to my Father, but on the way, I met a Fox and a Cat, who asked me, 'Do you want the five pieces to become two thousand?' And I said, 'Yes.' And they said, 'Come with us to the Field of Wonders.' And I said, 'Let's go.' Then they said, 'Let us stop at the Inn of the Red Lobster for dinner and after midnight we'll set out again.' We ate and went to sleep. When I awoke they were gone and I started out in the darkness all alone. On the road I met two Assassins dressed in black coal sacks, who said to me, 'Your money or your life!' and I said, 'I haven't any money'; for, you see, I had put the money under my tongue. One of them tried to put his hand in my mouth and I bit it off and spat it out; but it wasn't a hand, it was a cat's paw. And they ran after me and I ran and ran, till at last they caught me and tied my neck with a rope and hanged me to a tree, saying, 'Tomorrow we'll come back for you and you'll be dead and your mouth will be open, and then we'll take the gold pieces that you have hidden under your tongue.' "

"Where are the gold pieces now?" the Fairy asked.

"I lost them," answered Pinocchio, but he told a lie, for he had them in his pocket.

As he spoke, his nose, long though it was, became at least two inches longer.

"And where did you lose them?"

"In the wood nearby."

At this second lie, his nose grew a few more inches.

"If you lost them in the nearby wood," said the Fairy, "we'll look for them and find them, for everything that is lost there is always found."

"Ah, now I remember," replied the Marionette, becoming more and more confused. "I did not lose the gold pieces, but I swallowed them when I drank the medicine."

At this third lie, his nose became longer than ever, so long that he could not even turn around. If he turned to the right, he knocked it against the bed or into the windowpanes; if he turned to the left, he struck the walls or the door; if he raised it a bit, he almost put the Fairy's eyes out.

The Fairy sat looking at him and laughing.

"Why do you laugh?" the Marionette asked her, worried now at the sight of his growing nose.

"I am laughing at your lies."

"How do you know I am lying?"

"Lies, my boy, are known in a moment. There are two kinds of lies, lies with short legs and lies with long noses. Yours, just now, happen to have long noses."

Pinocchio, not knowing where to hide his shame, tried to escape from the room, but his nose had become so long that he could not get it out of the door.

WILLIAM SHAKESPEARE

When Icicles Hang by the Wall

When icicles hang by the wall
And Dick the shepherd blows his nail
And Tom bears logs into the hall
And milk comes frozen home in pail,
When blood is nipped and ways be foul,
Then nightly sings the staring owl,
  Tu-who!
To-whit, tu-who: a merry note,
While greasy Joan doth keel the pot.

When all aloud the wind doth blow,
And coughing drowns the parson's saw,
And birds sit brooding in the snow,
And Marian's nose looks red and raw,
When roasted crabs hiss in the bowl,
When nightly sings the staring owl,
  Tu-who!
To-whit, tu-who: a merry note,
While greasy Joan doth keel the pot.

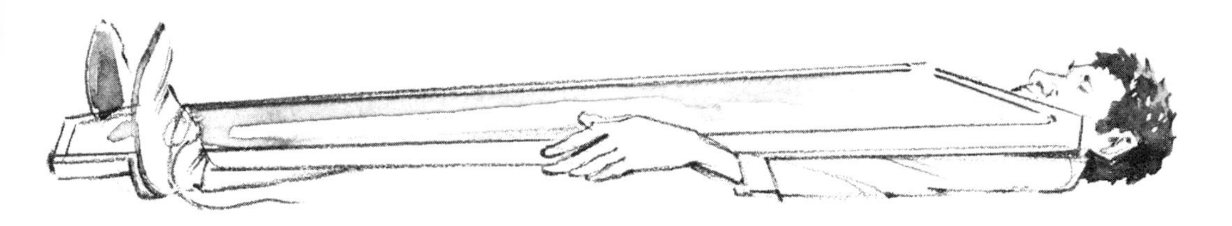

JEFF BROWN

Some Adventures of Flat Stanley

BREAKFAST was ready.

"I will go and wake the boys," Mrs. Lambchop said to her husband, George Lambchop. Just then their younger son, Arthur, called from the bedroom he shared with his brother Stanley.

"Hey! Come and look! Hey!"

Mr. and Mrs. Lambchop were both very much in favor of politeness and careful speech. "Hay is for horses, Arthur, not people," Mr. Lambchop said as they entered the bedroom. "Try to remember that."

"Excuse me," Arthur said. "But look!"

He pointed to Stanley's bed. Across it lay the enormous bulletin board that Mr. Lambchop had given the boys a Christmas ago, so that they could pin up pictures and messages and maps. It had fallen, during the night, on top of Stanley.

But Stanley was not hurt. In fact, he would still have been sleeping if he had not been woken by his brother's shout.

"What's going on here?" he called out cheerfully from beneath the enormous board.

Mr. and Mrs. Lambchop hurried to lift it from the bed.

"Heavens!" said Mrs. Lambchop.

"Gosh!" said Arthur. "Stanley's flat!"

"As a pancake," said Mr. Lambchop. "Darndest thing I've ever seen."

"Let's all have breakfast," Mrs. Lambchop said. "Then Stanley and I will go to see Doctor Dan and hear what he has to say."

The examination was almost over.

"How do you feel?" Doctor Dan asked. "Does it hurt very much?"

"I felt sort of tickly for a while after I got up," Stanley Lambchop said, "but I feel fine now."

"Well, that's mostly how it is with these cases," said Doctor Dan.

"We'll just have to keep an eye on this young fellow," he said when he had finished the examination, and he told his nurse to take Stanley's measurements.

Mrs. Lambchop wrote them down.

Stanley was four feet tall, about a foot wide, and half an inch thick.

When Stanley got used to being flat, he enjoyed it.

He could go in and out of rooms, even when the door was closed, just by lying down and sliding through the crack at the bottom.

Mr. and Mrs. Lambchop said it was silly, but they were quite proud of him.

Arthur got jealous and tried to slide under a door, but he just banged his head.

Being flat could also be helpful, Stanley found.

He was taking a walk with Mrs. Lambchop one afternoon when her favorite ring fell from her finger. The ring rolled across the sidewalk and down between the bars of a grating that covered a dark, deep shaft. Mrs. Lambchop began to cry.

"I have an idea," Stanley said.

He took the laces out of his shoes and an extra pair out of his pocket and tied them all together to make one long lace. Then he tied the end of that to the back of his belt and gave the other end to his mother.

"Lower me," he said, "and I will look for the ring."

"Thank you, Stanley," Mrs. Lambchop said. She lowered him between the bars and moved him carefully up and down and from side to side, so that he could search the whole floor of the shaft.

Two policemen came by and stared at Mrs. Lambchop as she stood holding the long lace that ran down through the grating. She pretended not to notice them.

"What's the matter, lady?" the first policeman asked. "Is your yo-yo stuck?"

"I am not playing with a yo-yo!" Mrs. Lambchop said sharply. "My son is at the other end of this lace, if you must know."

"Get the net, Harry," said the second policeman. "We have caught a cuckoo!"

Just then, down in the shaft, Stanley cried out, "Hooray!"

Mrs. Lambchop pulled him up and saw that he had the ring.

"Good for you, Stanley," she said. Then she turned angrily to the policemen. "A cuckoo, indeed!" she said. "Shame!"

The policemen apologized. "We didn't get it, lady," they said. "We have been hasty. We see that now."

"People should think twice before making rude remarks," said Mrs. Lambchop. "And then not make them at all."

The policemen realized that was a good rule and said they would try to remember it.

One day Stanley got a letter from his friend Thomas Anthony Jeffrey, whose family had moved recently to California. A school vacation was about to begin, and Stanley was invited to spend it with the Jeffreys.

"Oh, boy!" Stanley said. "I would love to go!"

Mr. Lambchop sighed. "A round-trip train or airplane ticket from New York to California is very expensive," he said. "I will have to think of some cheaper way."

When Mr. Lambchop came home from the office that evening, he brought with him an enormous brown paper envelope.

"Now then, Stanley," he said. "Try this for size."

The envelope fit Stanley very well. There was even room left over, Mrs. Lambchop discovered, for an egg-salad sandwich made with thin bread, and a flat cigarette case filled with milk.

They had to put a great many stamps on the envelope to pay for both airmail and insurance, but it was still much less expensive than a train or airplane ticket to California would have been.

The next day Mr. and Mrs. Lambchop slid Stanley into his envelope, along with the egg-salad sandwich and the cigarette case full of milk, and mailed him from the box on the corner. The envelope had to be folded to fit through the slot, but Stanley was a limber boy and inside the box he straightened right up again.

Mrs. Lambchop was nervous because Stanley had never been away from home alone before. She rapped on the box.

"Can you hear me, dear?" she called. "Are you all right?"

Stanley's voice came quite clearly. "I'm fine. Can I eat my sandwich now?"

"Wait an hour. And try not to get overheated, dear," Mrs. Lambchop said. Then she and Mr. Lambchop cried out, "Good-bye, good-bye!" and went home.

Stanley had a fine time in California. When the visit was over, the Jeffreys returned him in a beautiful white envelope they had made themselves. It had red-and-blue markings to show that it was airmail, and Thomas Jeffrey had lettered it "Valuable" and "Fragile" and "This End Up" on both sides.

Back home Stanley told his family that he had been handled so carefully he never felt a single bump. Mr. Lambchop said it proved that jet planes were wonderful, and so was the Post Office Department, and that this was a great age in which to live.

Stanley thought so, too.

After a few more weeks, however, Stanley was no longer enjoying himself. People had begun to laugh and make fun of him as he passed by. "Hello, Super-Skinny!" they would shout, and even say ruder things about the way he looked.

Stanley told his parents how he felt. "It's the other kids I mostly mind," he said. "They don't like me any more because I'm different. Flat."

"Shame on them," Mrs. Lambchop said. "It is wrong to dislike people for their shapes. Or their religion, for that matter, or the color of their skin."

"I know," Stanley said. "Only maybe it's impossible for everybody to like *everybody*."

"Perhaps," said Mrs. Lambchop. "But they can try."

Later that night Arthur Lambchop was woken by the sound of crying. In the darkness he crept across the room and knelt by Stanley's bed.

"Are you okay?" he said.

"Go away," Stanley said.

"Please let's be friends. . . ." Arthur couldn't help crying a little, too. "Oh, Stanley," he said. "Please tell me what's wrong?"

Stanley waited for a long time before he spoke. "The thing is," he said, "I'm just not happy anymore. I'm tired of being flat. I want to be a regular shape again, like other people. But I'll have to go on being flat forever. It makes me sick."

"Oh, Stanley," Arthur said. He dried his tears on a corner of Stanley's sheet and could think of nothing more to say.

"Don't talk about what I just said," Stanley told him. "I don't want the folks to worry. That would only make it worse."

"You're brave," Arthur said. "You really are."

He took hold of Stanley's hand. The two brothers sat together in the darkness, being friends. They were both still sad, but each one felt a *little* better than he had before.

And then, suddenly, though he was not even trying to think, Arthur had an idea. He jumped up and turned on the light and ran to the big storage box where toys and things were kept. He began to rummage in the box.

Stanley sat up in bed to watch.

Arthur flung aside a football and some lead soldiers and airplane models and lots of wooden blocks, and then he said, "Aha!" He had found what he wanted—an old bicycle pump. He held it up, and Stanley and he looked at each other.

"Okay," Stanley said at last. "But take it easy." He put the end of the long pump hose in his mouth and clamped his lips tightly around it so that no air could escape.

"I'll go slowly," Arthur said. "If it hurts or anything, wiggle your hand at me."

He began to pump. At first nothing happened except that Stanley's cheeks bulged a bit. Arthur watched his hand, but there was no wiggle signal, so he pumped on. Then, suddenly, Stanley's top half began to swell.

"It's working! It's working!" shouted Arthur, pumping away.

Stanley spread his arms so that the air could get around inside him more easily. He got bigger and bigger. The buttons of his pajama top burst off—*Pop! Pop! Pop!* A moment more and he was all rounded out—head and body, arms and legs. But not his right foot. That foot stayed flat.

Arthur stopped pumping. "It's like trying to do the very last bit of those long balloons," he said. "Maybe a shake would help."

Stanley shook his right foot twice, and with a little *whooshing* sound it swelled out to match the left one. There stood Stanley Lambchop as he used to be, as if he had never been flat at all!

"Thank you, Arthur," Stanley said. "Thank you very much."

The brothers were shaking hands when Mr. Lambchop strode into the room with Mrs. Lambchop right behind him. "We heard you!" said Mr. Lambchop. "Up and talking when you ought to be asleep, eh? Shame on—"

"GEORGE!" said Mrs. Lambchop. "Stanley's *round* again!"

"You're right!" said Mr. Lambchop, noticing. "Good for you, Stanley!"

"I'm the one who did it," Arthur said. "I blew him up."

Everyone was terribly excited and happy, of course. Mrs. Lambchop made hot chocolate to celebrate the occasion, and several toasts were drunk to Arthur for his cleverness.

When the little party was over, Mr. and Mrs. Lambchop tucked the boys back into their beds and kissed them, and then they turned out the light. "Good night," they said.

"Good night," said Stanley and Arthur.

It had been a long and tiring day. Very soon all the Lambchops were asleep.

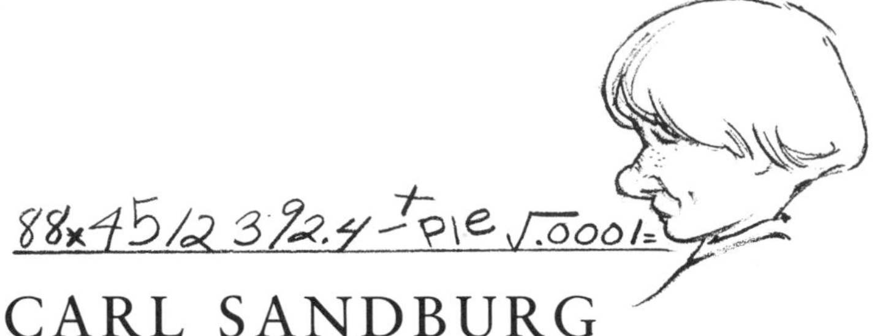

CARL SANDBURG

Arithmetic

Arithmetic is where numbers fly like pigeons in and out of your head.
Arithmetic tells you how many you lose or win if you know how many you had before you lost or won.
Arithmetic is seven eleven all good children go to heaven—or five six bundle of sticks.
Arithmetic is numbers you squeeze from your head to your hand to your pencil to your paper till you get the answer.
Arithmetic is where the answer is right and everything is nice and you can look out of the window and see the blue sky—or the answer is wrong and you have to start all over and try again and see how it comes out this time.
If you take a number and double it and double it again and then double it a few more times, the number gets bigger and bigger and goes higher and higher and only arithmetic can tell you what the number is when you decide to quit doubling.
Arithmetic is where you have to multiply—and you carry the multiplication table in your head and hope you won't lose it.

If you have two animal crackers, one good and one bad, and you eat one and a striped zebra with streaks all over him eats the other, how many animal crackers will you have if somebody offers you five six seven and you say No no no and you say Nay nay nay and you say Nix nix nix?

If you ask your mother for one fried egg for breakfast and she gives you two fried eggs and you eat both of them, who is better in arithmetic, you or your mother?

Auctioneer

Now I go down here and bring up a moon.
How much am I bid for the moon?
You see it's a bright moon and brand-new.
What can I get to start it? how much?
What! who ever ever heard such a bid for a moon?
  Come now, gentlemen, come.
This is a solid guaranteed moon.
You may never have another chance
  to make a bid on such a compact
  eighteen-carat durable gold moon.
You could shape a thousand wedding rings
  out of this moongold.
I can guarantee the gold and the weddings
  will last forever
  and then a thousand years more.
Come, gentlemen, no nonsense, make a bid.

LEILA BERG

The Woman Who Always Argued

ONCE upon a time, there was an old man and an old woman. The man was all right. It was the woman who was the trouble. Whatever anyone said, she said the opposite. If the fishmonger said, "I've some good herrings today," she said, "No, I want sprats." If the butcher said, "I've got lamb chops today," she said, "No, I want beef." If anyone opened a window, she shut it. If someone shut it, she opened it. She vowed that hens were ducks, and cats were dogs, and when it was raining she said it was snowing.

As for her poor old husband, what trouble he had. He was with her all the time, you see, because they did the farming together. So you can imagine he was very tired of it.

One morning they went across the bridge to look at their cornfield.

"Ah," said the man. "The corn will be ready by Tuesday."

"Monday," said the woman.

"Very well then, Monday," said the man. "I'll get John and Eric to help harvest it."

"No you won't," said the woman. "You'll get James and Robert."

"All right," said the man. "James and Robert. We'll start at seven."

"At six," said his wife.

"At six," agreed the man. "The weather will be good for it."

"It will be bad," she said. "It will pour."

"Well, whether it rains or shines," said the man, getting fed up, "whether we do it Monday at seven or Tuesday at six, we'll cut it with scythes."

"Shears," said his wife.

"Shears?" said the man, amazed. "Cut the corn with shears? What are you talking about! We'll cut with scythes!" (For with shears, you see, you have to bend down and go snip, snip, at one tiny bit after another. But with the lovely curved scythe, you go *swoosh!* and half the corn falls down flat.) "We'll cut with scythes!" said the man.

"Shears!" said the woman.

They went over the bridge, still arguing.

"Scythes!" said the man.

"Shears!" said the woman.

So angry was the woman that the man was arguing back, she didn't look where she was going, and she fell off the bridge into the water. When she bobbed up again, you'd think she'd shout "Help!" but not her. She shouted "Shears!" and the man only just had time to shout "Scythes!" before she bobbed back again.

Up she came again, and "Shears!" she shouted. The man yelled back "Scythes!" and she disappeared again. She came up again once more, and this time there was so much water in her mouth, because she would keep opening it to argue, that she couldn't say anything at all, so as her head went back again she stuck out her hand and with the fingers she silently went snip-snip, like shears above the water, snip-snip. Then she was gone.

"Stupid old woman!" said the man, stamping his foot. "Stupid, obstinate, argumentative old woman!"

He went to the village to get his friends to help him find her. They all came back to the bridge, and searched in the water. But she wasn't there.

"If the water has carried her away," said one of them, "she will be downstream. That is the way the river flows, and everything in the water must go with the river."

So they went downstream and looked, but they couldn't find her.

Suddenly the old man shouted, "What a fool I am! Everything else in the water would go with the river, it's true. But not my wife! She's bound to do the opposite. She'll be floating the other way, mark my words!"

So they ran up the stream, and sure enough, there she was, the opposite way to everything else. And what do you know, she was insisting on floating right *up* the waterfall!

THEODORE ROETHKE

The Bat

By day the bat is cousin to the mouse.
He likes the attic of an aging house.

His fingers make a hat about his head.
His pulse beat is so slow we think him dead.

He loops in crazy figures half the night
Among the trees that face the corner light.

But when he brushes up against a screen,
We are afraid of what our eyes have seen:

For something is amiss or out of place
When mice with wings can wear a human face.

L. FRANK BAUM

Practically everybody all over the world has heard about the Oz books. Frank Baum wrote fourteen of them and after his death the series was continued by others. There are some forty in all. In some ways the best is the first book, from which I've extracted a good long section.

Even if you haven't read any Ozes, you've probably seen the film, perhaps on TV, with Judy Garland as Dorothy, Ray Bolger as the Scarecrow, Jack Haley as the Tin Woodman, and Bert Lahr as the Cowardly Lion. It will run forever.

The Wizard of Oz was published in 1900, so its age is getting toward the century mark. Its author had been, before he started writing, a chicken breeder, an actor, a variety-store owner, a crockery salesman, and the editor of a magazine on window decorating. Once he devised for a hardware store a window featuring a man made out of pots and pans, and that may have been in his mind when he created the Tin Woodman.

Frank Baum had a three-drawer filing cabinet, with alphabetical labels. The bottom drawer was labeled O-Z and that's how he got the name for the strange country of Oz.

My own children once spent a whole summer reading all the Oz books. It can become an addiction, like eating peanuts.

The Wizard of Oz starts this way.

Dorothy is living with her Aunt Em and her Uncle Henry in the middle of a great Kansas prairie when a tremendous cyclone hits their house. Her uncle and aunt have time to save themselves by climbing down into the cyclone cellar. But Dorothy and her little dog, Toto, are whirled up into the air inside their house.

They are set down—very gently for a cyclone—"in the midst of a country of marvelous beauty." They are greeted by three queer men, about Dorothy's size, and a little old woman. They tell her she has reached the land of the Munchkins and that they are grateful to her for killing the Wicked Witch of the East. Apparently Dorothy's house, as it landed, had hit the Wicked Witch, who, as they watch, dries up, leaving nothing but a pair of magic silver shoes that now become Dorothy's.

She's anxious to return home. But first, she is told, she must visit the Emerald City in the middle of the country of Oz, ruled by the great Wizard of Oz.

And so Dorothy and Toto start on their long journey. What follows tells you how she met three odd creatures who were destined to be her companions.

If you want to know what happened afterward to Dorothy, Toto, and her three friends, and how they finally met the Wizard, get the book called *The Wizard of Oz*. Every library should have it, and there are several inexpensive editions.

The Wizard of Oz

FROM CHAPTERS THREE TO SIX

SHE BADE her friends good-bye, and again started along the road of yellow brick. When she had gone several miles she thought she would stop to rest, and so climbed to the top of the fence beside the road and sat down. There was a great cornfield beyond the fence, and not far away she saw a Scarecrow, placed high on a pole to keep the birds from the ripe corn.

Dorothy leaned her chin upon her hand and gazed thoughtfully at the Scarecrow. Its head was a small sack stuffed with straw, with eyes, nose, and mouth painted on it to represent a face. An old, pointed blue hat, that had belonged to some Munchkin, was perched on his head, and the rest of the figure was a blue suit of clothes, worn and faded, which had also been stuffed with straw. On the feet were some old boots with blue tops, such as every man wore in this country, and the figure was raised above the stalks of corn by means of the pole stuck up its back.

While Dorothy was looking earnestly into the queer, painted face of the Scarecrow, she was surprised to see one of the eyes slowly wink at her. She thought she must have been mistaken at first, for none of the scarecrows in Kansas ever wink; but presently the figure nodded its head to her in a friendly way. Then she climbed down from the fence and walked up to it, while Toto ran around the pole and barked.

"Good day," said the Scarecrow, in a rather husky voice.

"Did you speak?" asked the girl, in wonder.

"Certainly," answered the Scarecrow. "How do you do?"

"I'm pretty well, thank you," replied Dorothy politely. "How do you do?"

"I'm not feeling well," said the Scarecrow, with a smile, "for it is very tedious being perched up here night and day to scare away crows."

"Can't you get down?" asked Dorothy.

"No, for this pole is stuck up my back. If you will please take away the pole I shall be greatly obliged to you."

Dorothy reached up both arms and lifted the figure off the pole, for—being stuffed with straw—it was quite light.

"Thank you very much," said the Scarecrow, when he had been set down on the ground. "I feel like a new man."

Dorothy was puzzled at this, for it sounded queer to hear a stuffed man speak, and to see him bow and walk along beside her.

"Who are you?" asked the Scarecrow when he had stretched himself and yawned. "And where are you going?"

"My name is Dorothy," said the girl, "and I am going to the Emerald City, to ask the Great Oz to send me back to Kansas."

"Where is the Emerald City?" he inquired. "And who is Oz?"

"Why, don't you know?" she returned, in surprise.

"No, indeed. I don't know anything. You see, I am stuffed, so I have no brains at all," he answered sadly.

"Oh," said Dorothy, "I'm awfully sorry for you."

"Do you think," he asked, "if I go to the Emerald City with you, that Oz would give me some brains?"

"I cannot tell," she returned, "but you may come with me, if you like. If Oz will not give you any brains you will be no worse off than you are now."

"That is true," said the Scarecrow. "You see," he continued confidentially, "I don't mind my legs and arms and body being stuffed, because I cannot get hurt. If anyone treads on my toes or sticks a pin into me, it doesn't matter, for I can't feel it. But I do not want people to call me a fool, and if my head stays stuffed with straw instead of with brains, as yours is, how am I ever to know anything?"

"I understand how you feel," said the little girl, who was truly sorry for him. "If you will come with me I'll ask Oz to do all he can for you."

"Thank you," he answered gratefully.

They walked back to the road. Dorothy helped him over the fence, and they started along the path of yellow brick for the Emerald City.

Toto did not like this addition to the party at first. He smelled around the stuffed man as if he suspected there might be a nest of rats in the straw, and he often growled in an unfriendly way at the Scarecrow.

"Don't mind Toto," said Dorothy to her new friend. "He never bites."

"Oh, I'm not afraid," replied the Scarecrow. "He can't hurt the straw. Do let me carry that basket for you. I shall not mind it, for I can't get tired. I'll tell you a secret," he continued, as he walked along. "There is only one thing in the world I am afraid of."

"What is that?" asked Dorothy. "The Munchkin farmer who made you?"

"No," answered the Scarecrow. "It's a lighted match."

After a few hours the road began to be rough, and the walking grew so difficult that the Scarecrow often stumbled over the yellow bricks, which were here very uneven. Sometimes, indeed, they were broken or missing altogether, leaving holes that Toto jumped across and Dorothy walked around. As for the Scarecrow, having no brains, he walked straight ahead, and so stepped into the holes and fell at full length on the hard bricks. It never hurt him, however, and Dorothy would pick him up and set him upon his feet again, while he joined her in laughing merrily at his own mishap.

The farms were not nearly so well cared for here as they were farther back. There were fewer houses and fewer fruit trees, and the farther they went the more dismal and lonesome the country became.

At noon they sat down by the roadside, near a little brook, and Dorothy opened her basket and got out some bread. She offered a piece to the Scarecrow, but he refused.

"I am never hungry," he said, "and it is a lucky thing I am not, for my mouth is only painted. If I should cut a hole in it so I could eat, the straw I am stuffed with would come out, and that would spoil the shape of my head."

Dorothy saw at once that this was true, so she only nodded and went on eating her bread.

"Tell me something about yourself and the country you came from," said the Scarecrow, when she had finished her dinner. So she told him all about Kansas, and how gray everything was there, and how the cyclone had carried her to this queer Land of Oz.

The Scarecrow listened carefully, and said, "I cannot understand why you should wish to leave this beautiful country and go back to the dry, gray place you call Kansas."

"That is because you have no brains," answered the girl. "No matter how dreary and gray our homes are, we people of flesh and blood would rather live there than in any other country, be it ever so beautiful. There is no place like home."

Toward evening they came to a great forest, where the trees grew so big and close together that their branches met over the road of yellow brick. It was almost dark under the trees, for the branches shut out the daylight; but the travelers did not stop, and went on into the forest.

"If this road goes in, it must come out," said the Scarecrow, "and as the Emerald City is at the other end of the road, we must go wherever it leads us."

"Anyone would know that," said Dorothy.

"Certainly; that is why I know it," returned the Scarecrow. "If it required brains to figure it out, I never should have said it."

After an hour or so the light faded away, and they found themselves stumbling along in the darkness. Dorothy could not see at all, but Toto could, for some dogs see very well in the dark; and the Scarecrow declared he could see as well as by day. So she took hold of his arm and managed to get along fairly well.

"If you see any house, or any place where we can pass the night," she said, "you must tell me; for it is very uncomfortable walking in the dark."

Soon after the Scarecrow stopped.

"I see a little cottage at the right of us," he said, "built of logs and branches. Shall we go there?"

"Yes, indeed," answered the child. "I am all tired out."

So the Scarecrow led her through the trees until they reached the cottage, and Dorothy entered and found a bed of dried leaves in one corner. She lay down at once, and with Toto beside her soon fell into a sound sleep. The Scarecrow, who was never tired, stood up in another corner and waited patiently until morning came.

When Dorothy awoke the sun was shining through the trees and Toto had long been out chasing birds around him. There was the Scarecrow, still standing patiently in his corner, waiting for her.

"We must go and search for water," she said to him.

"Why do you want water?" he asked.

"To wash my face clean after the dust of the road, and to drink, so the dry bread will not stick in my throat."

"It must be inconvenient to be made of flesh," said the Scarecrow thoughtfully, "for you must sleep and eat and drink. However, you have brains, and it is worth a lot of bother to be able to think properly."

They left the cottage and walked through the trees until they found a little spring of clear water, where Dorothy drank and bathed and ate her breakfast. She saw there was not much bread left in the basket, and the girl was thankful the Scarecrow did not have to eat anything, for there was scarcely enough for herself and Toto for the day.

When she had finished her meal, and was about to go back to the road of yellow brick, she was startled to hear a deep groan near by.

"What was that?" she asked timidly.

"I cannot imagine," replied the Scarecrow. "But we can go and see."

Just then another groan reached their ears, and the sound seemed to come from behind them. They turned and had walked through the forest a few steps, when Dorothy discovered something shining in a ray of sunshine that fell between the trees. She ran to the place and then stopped short, with a little cry of surprise.

One of the big trees had been partly chopped through, and standing beside it, with an uplifted ax in his hands, was a man made entirely of tin. His head and arms and legs were jointed upon his body, but he stood perfectly motionless, as if he could not stir at all.

Dorothy looked at him in amazement, and so did the Scarecrow, while Toto barked sharply and made a snap at the tin legs, which hurt his teeth.

"Did you groan?" asked Dorothy.

"Yes," answered the tin man, "I did. I've been groaning for more than a year, and no one has ever heard me before or come to help me."

"What can I do for you?" she inquired softly, for she was moved by the sad voice in which the man spoke.

"Get an oilcan and oil my joints," he answered. "They are rusted so badly that I cannot move them at all. If I am well oiled I shall soon be all right again. You will find an oilcan on a shelf in my cottage."

Dorothy at once ran back to the cottage and found the oilcan, and then she returned and asked anxiously, "Where are your joints?"

"Oil my neck, first," replied the Tin Woodman. So she oiled it, and as it was quite badly rusted the Scarecrow took hold of the tin head and moved it gently from side to side until it worked freely, and then the man could turn it himself.

"Now oil the joints in my arms," he said. And Dorothy oiled them and the Scarecrow bent them carefully until they were quite free from rust and as good as new.

The Tin Woodman gave a sigh of satisfaction and lowered his ax, which he leaned against the tree.

"This is a great comfort," he said. "I have been holding that ax in the air ever since I rusted, and I'm glad to be able to put it down at last. Now, if you will oil the joints of my legs, I shall be all right once more."

So they oiled his legs until he could move them freely; and he thanked them again and again for his release, for he seemed a very polite creature, and very grateful.

"I might have stood there always if you had not come along," he said; "so you have certainly saved my life. How did you happen to be here?"

"We are on our way to the Emerald City to see the Great Oz," she answered, "and we stopped at your cottage to pass the night."

"Why do you wish to see Oz?" he asked.

"I want him to send me back to Kansas, and the Scarecrow wants him to put a few brains into his head," she replied.

The Tin Woodman appeared to think deeply for a moment. Then he said:

"Do you suppose Oz could give me a heart?"

"Why, I guess so," Dorothy answered. "It would be as easy as to give the Scarecrow brains."

"True," the Tin Woodman returned. "So, if you will allow me to join your party, I will also go to the Emerald City and ask Oz to help me."

"Come along," said the Scarecrow heartily, and Dorothy added that she would be pleased to have his company. So the Tin Woodman shouldered his ax and they all passed through the forest until they came to the road that was paved with yellow brick.

The Tin Woodman had asked Dorothy to put the oilcan in her basket. "For," he said, "if I should get caught in the rain, and rust again, I would need the oilcan badly."

It was a bit of good luck to have their new comrade join the party, for soon after they had begun their journey again they came to a place where the trees and branches grew so thick over the road that the travelers could not pass. But the Tin Woodman set to work with his ax and chopped so well that soon he cleared a passage for the entire party.

Dorothy was thinking so earnestly as they walked along that she did not notice when the Scarecrow stumbled into a hole and rolled over to the side of the road. Indeed, he was obliged to call to her to help him up again.

"Why didn't you walk around the hole?" asked the Tin Woodman.

"I don't know enough," replied the Scarecrow cheerfully. "My head is stuffed with straw, you know, and that is why I am going to Oz to ask him for some brains."

"Oh, I see," said the Tin Woodman. "But, after all, brains are not the best things in the world."

"Have you any?" inquired the Scarecrow.

"No, my head is quite empty," answered the Woodman. "But once I had brains, and a heart also. So, having tried them both, I should much rather have a heart."

"All the same," said the Scarecrow, "I shall ask for brains instead of a heart; for a fool would not know what to do with a heart if he had one."

"I shall take the heart," returned the Tin Woodman; "for brains do not make one happy, and happiness is the best thing in the world."

Dorothy did not say anything, for she was puzzled to know which of her two friends was right, and she decided if she could only get back to Kansas and Aunt Em it did not matter so much whether the Woodman had no brains and the Scarecrow no heart, or each got what he wanted.

What worried her most was that the bread was nearly gone, and another meal for herself and Toto would empty the basket. To be sure neither the Woodman nor the Scarecrow ever ate anything, but she was not made of tin or straw, and could not live unless she was fed.

All this time Dorothy and her companions had been walking through the thick woods. The road was still paved with yellow bricks, but these were much covered by dried branches and dead leaves from the trees, and the walking was not at all good.

There were few birds in this part of the forest, for birds love the open country where there is plenty of sunshine. But now and then there came a deep growl from some wild animal hidden among the trees. These sounds made the little girl's heart beat fast, for she did not know what made them; but Toto knew, and he walked close to Dorothy's side, and did not even bark in return.

"How long will it be," the child asked of the Tin Woodman, "before we are out of the forest?"

"I cannot tell," was the answer, "for I have never been to the Emerald City. But my father went there once, when I was a boy, and he said it was a long journey through a dangerous country, although nearer to the city where Oz dwells the country is beautiful. But I am not afraid so long as I have my oilcan, and nothing can hurt the Scarecrow, while you bear upon your forehead the mark of the Good Witch's kiss, and that will protect you from harm."

"But Toto!" said the girl anxiously. "What will protect him?"

"We must protect him ourselves if he is in danger," replied the Tin Woodman.

Just as he spoke there came from the forest a terrible roar, and the next moment a great Lion bounded into the road. With one blow of his paw he sent the Scarecrow spinning over and over to the edge of the road, and then he struck at the Tin Woodman with his sharp claws. But, to the Lion's surprise, he could make no impression on the tin, although the Woodman fell over in the road and lay still.

Little Toto, now that he had an enemy to face, ran barking toward the Lion, and the great beast had opened his mouth to bite the dog, when Dorothy, fearing Toto would be killed, and heedless of danger, rushed forward and slapped the Lion upon his nose as hard as she could, while she cried out:

"Don't you dare to bite Toto! You ought to be ashamed of yourself, a big beast like you, to bite a poor little dog!"

"I didn't bite him," said the Lion, as he rubbed his nose with his paw where Dorothy had hit it.

"No, but you tried to," she retorted. "You are nothing but a big coward."

"I know it," said the Lion, hanging his head in shame. "I've always known it. But how can I help it?"

"I don't know, I'm sure. To think of your striking a stuffed man, like the poor Scarecrow!"

"Is he stuffed?" asked the Lion in surprise, as he watched her pick up the Scarecrow and set him upon his feet, while she patted him into shape again.

"Of course he's stuffed," replied Dorothy, who was still angry.

"That's why he went over so easily," remarked the Lion. "It astonished me to see him whirl around so. Is the other one stuffed also?"

"No," said Dorothy, "he's made of tin." And she helped the Woodman up again.

"That's why he nearly blunted my claws," said the Lion. "When they scratched against the tin it made a cold shiver run down my back. What is that little animal you are so tender of?"

"He is my dog, Toto," answered Dorothy.

"Is he made of tin, or stuffed?" asked the Lion.

"Neither. He's a—a—a meat dog," said the girl.

"Oh! He's a curious animal and seems remarkably small, now that I look at him. No one would think of biting such a little thing except a coward like me," continued the Lion sadly.

"What makes you a coward?" asked Dorothy, looking at the great beast in wonder, for he was as big as a small horse.

"It's a mystery," replied the Lion. "I suppose I was born that way. All the other animals in the forest naturally expect me to be brave, for the Lion is everywhere thought to be the King of Beasts. I learned that if I roared very loudly every living thing was frightened and got out of my way. Whenever I've met a man I've been awfully scared. But I just roared at him, and he has always run away as fast as he could go. If the elephants and the tigers and the bears had ever tried to fight me, I should have run myself—I'm such a coward; but just as soon as they hear me roar they all try to get away from me, and of course I let them go."

"But that isn't right. The King of Beasts shouldn't be a coward," said the Scarecrow.

"I know it," returned the Lion, wiping a tear from his eye with the tip of his paw. "It is my great sorrow, and makes my life very unhappy. But whenever there is danger, my heart begins to beat fast."

"Perhaps you have heart disease," said the Tin Woodman.

"It may be," said the Lion.

"If you have," continued the Tin Woodman, "you ought to be glad, for it proves you have a heart. For my part, I have no heart, so I cannot have heart disease."

"Perhaps," said the Lion thoughtfully, "if I had no heart I should not be a coward."

"Have you brains?" asked the Scarecrow.

"I suppose so. I've never looked to see," replied the Lion.

"I am going to the Great Oz to ask him to give me some," remarked the Scarecrow, "for my head is stuffed with straw."

"And I am going to ask him to give me a heart," said the Woodman.

"And I am going to ask him to send Toto and me back to Kansas," added Dorothy.

"Do you think Oz could give me courage?" asked the Cowardly Lion.

"Just as easily as he could give me brains," said the Scarecrow.

"Or give me a heart," said the Tin Woodman.

"Or send me back to Kansas," said Dorothy.

"Then, if you don't mind, I'll go with you," said the Lion, "for my life is simply unbearable without a bit of courage."

"You will be very welcome," answered Dorothy, "for you will help to keep away the other wild beasts. It seems to me they must be more cowardly than you are if they allow you to scare them so easily."

"They really are," said the Lion, "but that doesn't make me any braver, and as long as I know myself to be a coward I shall be unhappy."

So once more the little company set off upon the journey, the Lion walking with stately strides at Dorothy's side. Toto did not approve this new comrade at first, for he could not forget how nearly he had been crushed between the Lion's great jaws. But after a time he became more at ease, and presently Toto and the Cowardly Lion had grown to be good friends.

JAMES REEVES

Slowly

Slowly the tide creeps up the sand,
Slowly the shadows cross the land.
Slowly the cart-horse pulls his mile,
Slowly the old man mounts the stile.

Slowly the hands move round the clock,
Slowly the dew dries on the dock.
Slow is the snail—but slowest of all
The green moss spreads on the old brick wall.

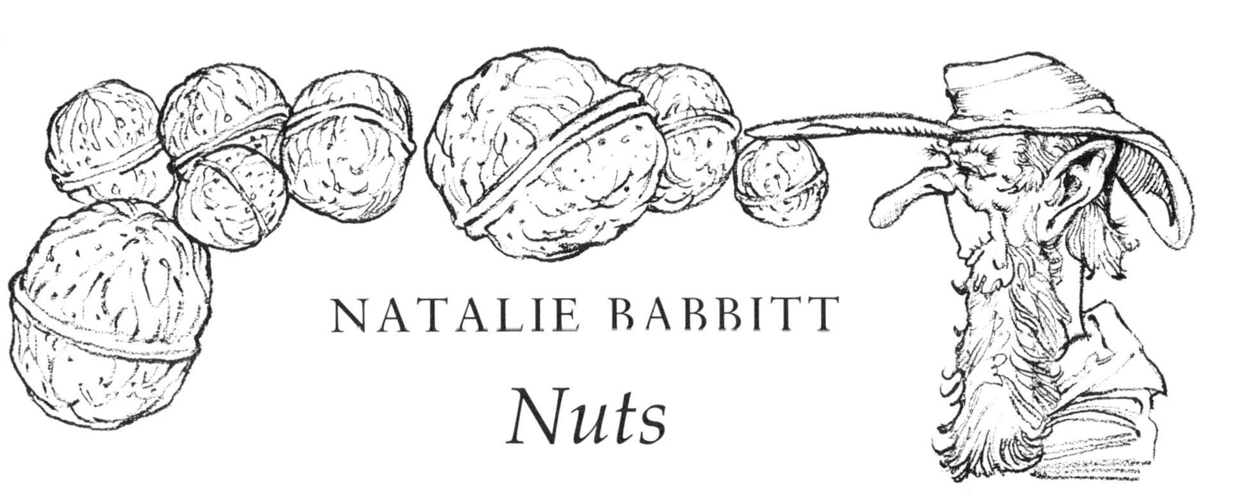

NATALIE BABBITT

Nuts

ONE DAY the Devil was sitting in his throne room eating walnuts from a large bag and complaining, as usual, about the terrible nuisance of having to crack the shells, when all at once he had an idea. "The best way to eat walnuts," he said to himself, "is to trick someone else into cracking them for you."

So he fetched a pearl from his treasure room, opened the next nut very carefully with a sharp knife so as not to spoil the shell, and put the pearl inside along with the meat. Then he glued the shell back together. "Now all I have to do," he said, "is give this walnut to some greedy soul who'll find the pearl in it and insist on opening the lot to look for more!"

So he dressed himself as an old man with a long beard and went up into the World, taking along his nutcracker and the bag of walnuts with the special nut right on top. And he sat himself down by a country road to wait.

Pretty soon a farm wife came marching along.

"Hey, there!" said the Devil. "Want a walnut?"

The farm wife looked at him shrewdly and was at once suspicious, but she didn't let on for a minute. "All right," she said. "Why not?"

"That's the way," said the Devil, chuckling to himself. And he reached into the bag and took out the special walnut and gave it to her.

However, much to his surprise, she merely cracked the nut open, picked out the meat and ate it, and threw away the shell without a single word or comment. And then she went on her way and disappeared.

"That's strange," said the Devil with a frown. "Either she swallowed my pearl or I gave her the wrong walnut to begin with."

He took out three more nuts that were lying on top of the pile, cracked them open, and ate the meat, but there was no pearl to be seen. He opened and ate four more. Still no pearl. And so it went, on and on all afternoon, till the Devil had opened every walnut in the bag, all by himself after all, and had made a terrible mess on the road with the shells. But he never did find the pearl, and in the end he said to himself, "Well, that's that. She swallowed it." And there was nothing for it but to go back down to Hell. But he took along a stomachache from eating all those nuts, and a temper that lasted for a week.

In the meantime the farm wife went on to market, where she took the pearl out from under her tongue, where she'd been saving it, and she traded it for two turnips and a butter churn and went on home again well pleased.

We are not all of us greedy.

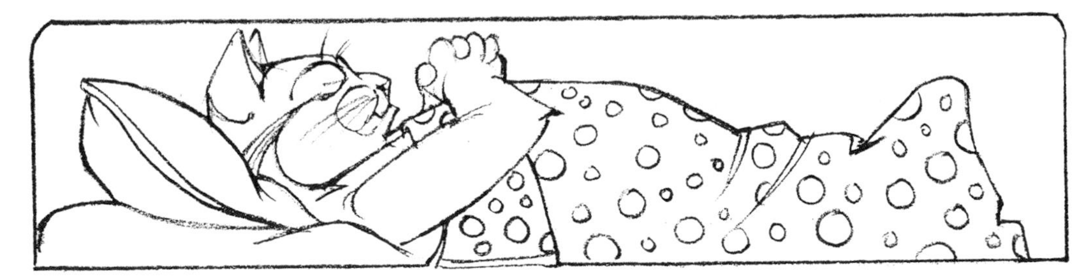

SYLVIA PLATH

Beds

Beds come in all sizes—
single or double,
cot-size or cradle,
king-size or trundle.

Most Beds are Beds
for sleeping or resting,
but the *best* Beds are much
more interesting!

Not just a white little
tucked-in-tight little
nighty-night little
turn-out-the-light little
  bed—
  instead

a Bed for Fishing,
a Bed for Cats,

a Bed for a Troupe of
Acrobats.

The *right* sort of Bed
(if you see what I mean)
is a Bed that might
be a Submarine
nosing through water
clear and green,
silver and glittery
as a sardine.

Or a Jet-Propelled Bed
for visiting Mars
with mosquito nets
for the shooting stars.

If you get hungry
in the middle of the night
a Snack Bed is good
for the appetite—
with a pillow of bread
to nibble at
and up at the head
an Automat

where you need no shillings,
just a finger to stick in
the slot, and out come
cakes and cold chicken.

On the other hand,
if you want to *move*
a Tank Bed's the Bed
most movers approve.
A Tank Bed's got cranks
and wheels and cogs
and levers to pull
if you're stuck in bogs.
A Tank Bed's treads
go upstairs or down,
through duck ponds or through
a cobbledy town.
And you're snug inside
if it rains or hails.
A Tank Bed's got
everything but sails!

Now a gentler Bed
is a good deal more
the sort of Bed
bird-watchers adore—
a kind of hammock
between two tall trees
where you can swing
in the leaves at ease.
All the birds would flock
(if I'm not mistaken)
to your berries and cherries
and bits of bacon.

In an Elephant Bed
you go where you please.
You pick bananas
right out of the trees.
An Elephant Bed
is where kings ride.
It's cool as a pool
in the shade inside.
You can climb up the trunk
and slide down behind.
Everyone knows
elephants don't mind!

Oh who cares much
if a Bed's big or small
or lumpy and bumpy—
who cares at all
as long as its springs
are bouncy and new.
From a Bounceable Bed
you bounce into the blue—
over the hollyhocks
(Toodle-oo!)
over the owls
to-whit-to-whoo,
over the moon
to Timbuktoo

with springier springs
than a kangaroo.

These are the Beds
for me and for you!
These are the Beds
to climb into.
Special and queer
and full of surprises,
Beds of amazing
shapes and sizes—

NOT just a white little
tucked-in-tight little
nighty-night little
turn-out-the-light little
bed!

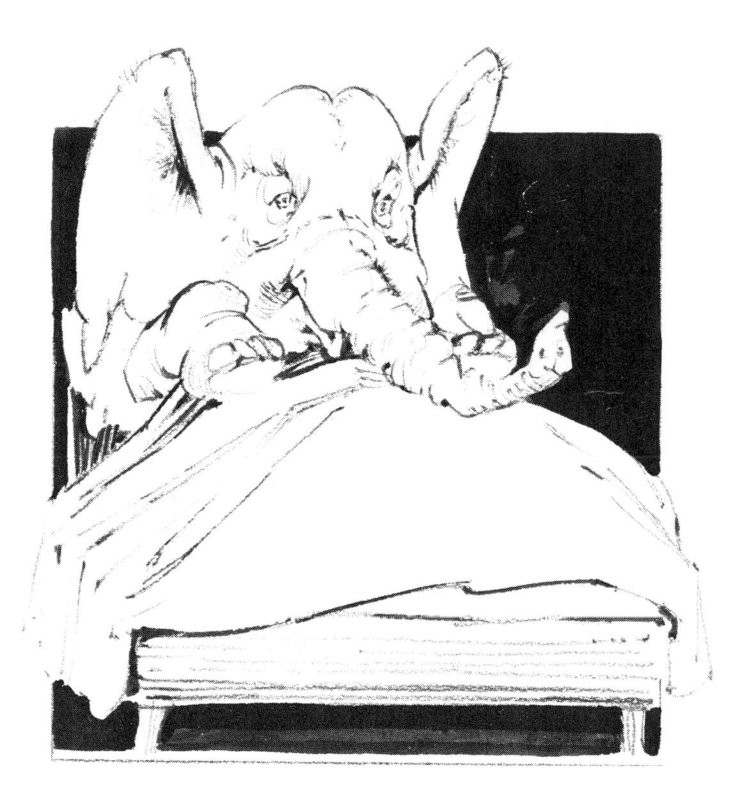

LLOYD ALEXANDER

Lloyd Alexander, slightly built, looks a little like a grown-up elf and a little like a handsomer Hans Christian Andersen. He likes cats, music, playing the violin. On his mantelpiece rests a Welsh harp with broken strings—and in his *Chronicles of Prydain* you will meet a Welsh bard the strings of whose harp break every time he embroiders on the truth.

The Prydain books are five in number: *The Book of Three, The Black Cauldron, The Castle of Llyr, Taran Wanderer,* and *The High King*. The action, of which there is plenty, takes place in Prydain, described by the author as "an imaginary, heroic, pre-medieval world." The hero, Taran, is a young Assistant Pig-Keeper, ambitious to become much more than that. In what follows (from *The Book of Three*) we are introduced to him and to the start of his marvelous adventures.

The Assistant Pig-Keeper

TARAN wanted to make a sword; but Coll, charged with the practical side of his education, decided on horseshoes. And so it had been horseshoes all morning long. Taran's arms ached, soot blackened his face. At last he dropped the hammer and turned to Coll, who was watching him critically.

"Why?" Taran cried. "Why must it be horseshoes? As if we had any horses!"

Coll was stout and round and his great bald head glowed bright pink. "Lucky for the horses," was all he said, glancing at Taran's handiwork.

"I could do better at making a sword," Taran protested. "I know I could." And before Coll could answer, he snatched the tongs, flung a strip of red-hot iron to the anvil, and began hammering away as fast as he could.

"Wait, wait!" cried Coll, "that is not the way to go after it!"

Heedless of Coll, unable even to hear him above the din, Taran pounded harder than ever. Sparks sprayed the air. But the more he pounded, the more the metal twisted and buckled, until, finally, the iron sprang from the tongs and fell to the ground. Taran stared in dismay. With the tongs, he picked up the bent iron and examined it.

"Not quite the blade for a hero," Coll remarked.

"It's ruined," Taran glumly agreed. "It looks like a sick snake," he added ruefully.

"As I tried telling you," said Coll, "you had it all wrong. You must hold the tongs—so. When you strike, the strength must flow from your shoulder and your wrist be loose. You can hear it when you do it right. There is a kind of music in it. Besides," he added, "this is not the metal for weapons."

Coll returned the crooked, half-formed blade to the furnace, where it lost its shape entirely.

"I wish I might have my own sword," Taran sighed, "and you would teach me sword-fighting."

"Wisht!" cried Coll. "Why should you want to know that? We have no battles at Caer Dallben."

"We have no horses, either," objected Taran, "but we're making horseshoes."

"Get on with you," said Coll, unmoved. "That is for practice."

"And so would this be," Taran urged. "Come, teach me the sword-fighting. You must know the art."

Coll's shining head glowed even brighter. A trace of a smile appeared on his face, as though he were savoring something pleasant. "True," he said quietly, "I have held a sword once or twice in my day."

"Teach me now," pleaded Taran. He seized a poker and brandished it, slashing at the air and dancing back and forth over the hard-packed earthen floor. "See," he called, "I know most of it already."

"Hold your hand," chuckled Coll. "If you were to come against me like that, with all your posing and bouncing, I should have you chopped into bits by this time." He hesitated a moment. "Look you," he said quickly, "at least you should know there is a right way and a wrong way to go about it."

He picked up another poker. "Here now," he ordered, with a sooty wink, "stand like a man."

Taran brought up his poker. While Coll shouted instructions, they set to parrying and thrusting, with much banging, clanking, and commotion. For a moment Taran was sure he had the better of Coll, but the old man spun away with amazing lightness of foot. Now it was Taran who strove desperately to ward off Coll's blows.

Abruptly, Coll stopped. So did Taran, his poker poised in midair. In the doorway of the forge stood the tall, bent figure of Dallben.

Dallben, master of Caer Dallben, was three hundred and seventy-nine years old. His beard covered so much of his face he seemed always to be peering over a gray cloud. On the little farm, while Taran and Coll saw to the plowing, sowing, weeding, reaping, and all the other tasks of husbandry, Dallben undertook the meditating, an occupation so exhausting he could accomplish it only by lying down and closing his eyes. He meditated an hour and a half following breakfast and again later in the day. The clatter from the forge had roused him from his morning meditation; his robe hung askew over his bony knees.

"Stop that nonsense directly," said Dallben. "I am surprised at you," he added, frowning at Coll. "There is serious work to be done."

"It wasn't Coll," Taran interrupted. "It was I who asked to learn sword play."

"I did not say I was surprised at *you*," remarked Dallben. "But perhaps I am, after all. I think you had best come with me."

Taran followed the ancient man out of the forge, across the chicken run, and into the white, thatched cottage. There, in Dallben's chamber, moldering tomes overflowed the sagging shelves and spilled onto the floor amid heaps of iron cook pots, studded belts, harps with or without strings, and other oddments.

Taran took his place on the wooden bench, as he always did when Dallben was in a mood for giving lessons or reprimands.

"I fully understand," said Dallben, settling himself behind his table, "in the use of weapons, as in everything else, there is a certain skill. But wiser heads than yours will determine when you should learn it."

"I'm sorry," Taran began, "I should not have—"

"I am not angry," Dallben said, raising a hand. "Only a little sad. Time flies quickly; things always happen sooner than one expects. And yet," he murmured, almost to himself, "it troubles me. I fear the Horned King may have some part in this."

"The Horned King?" asked Taran.

"We shall speak of him later," said Dallben. He drew a ponderous, leather-bound volume toward him, *The Book of Three*, from which he occasionally read to Taran and which, the boy believed, held in its pages everything anyone could possibly want to know.

"As I have explained to you before," Dallben went on, "—and you have very likely forgotten—Prydain is a land of many cantrevs—of small kingdoms—and many kings. And, of course, their war leaders who command the warriors."

"But there is the High King above them all," said Taran, "Math Son of Mathonwy. His war leader is the mightiest hero in Prydain. You told me of him. Prince Gwydion! Yes," Taran went on eagerly, "I know—"

"There are other things you do *not* know," Dallben said, "for the obvious reason that I have not told you. For the moment I am less concerned with the realms of the living than with the Land of the Dead, with Annuvin."

Taran shuddered at the word. Even Dallben had spoken it in a whisper.

"And with King Arawn, Lord of Annuvin," Dallben said. "Know this," he continued quickly, "Annuvin is more than a land of death. It is a treasure house, not only of gold and jewels but of all things of advantage to men. Long ago, the race of men owned these treasures. By craft and deceit, Arawn stole them, one by one, for his own evil uses. Some few of the treasures have been wrested from him, though most lie hidden deep in Annuvin, where Arawn guards them jealously."

"But Arawn did not become ruler of Prydain," Taran said.

"You may be thankful he did not," said Dallben. "He would have ruled had it not been for the Children of Don, the sons of the Lady Don and her consort Belin, King of the Sun. Long ago they voyaged to Prydain from the Summer Country and found the land rich and fair, though the race of men had little for themselves. The Sons of Don built their stronghold at Caer Dathyl, far north in the Eagle Mountains. From there, they helped regain at least a portion of what Arawn had stolen, and stood as guardians against the lurking threat of Annuvin."

"I hate to think what would have happened if the Sons of Don hadn't come," Taran said. "It was a good destiny that brought them."

"I am not always sure," said Dallben, with a wry smile. "The men of Prydain came to rely on the strength of the House of Don as a child clings to its mother. They do so even today. Math, the High King, is descended from the House of Don. So is Prince Gwydion. But that is all by the way. Prydain has been at peace—as much as men can be peaceful—until now.

"What you do not know," Dallben said, "is this: it has reached my ears that a new and mighty war lord has risen, as powerful as Gwydion; some say more powerful. But he is a man of evil for whom death is a black joy. He sports with death as you might sport with a dog."

"Who is he?" cried Taran.

Dallben shook his head. "No man knows his name, nor has any man seen his face. He wears an antlered mask, and for this reason he is called the Horned King. His purposes I do not know. I suspect the hand of Arawn, but in what manner I cannot tell. I tell you now for your own protection," Dallben added. "From what I saw this morning, your head is full of nonsense about feats of arms. Whatever notions you may have, I advise you to forget them immediately. There is unknown danger abroad. You are barely on the threshold of manhood, and I have a certain responsibility to see that you reach it, preferably with a whole skin. So, you are not to leave Caer Dallben under any circumstances, not even past the orchard, and certainly not into the forest—not for the time being."

"For the time being!" Taran burst out. "I think it will always be for the time being, and it will be vegetables and horsehoes all my life!"

"Tut," said Dallben, "there are worse things. Do you set yourself to be a glorious hero? Do you believe it is all flashing swords and galloping about on horses? As for being glorious—"

"What of Prince Gwydion?" cried Taran. "Yes! I wish I might be like him!"

"I fear," Dallben said, "that is entirely out of the question."

"But why?" Taran sprang to his feet. "I know if I had the chance—"

"Why?" Dallben interrupted. "In some cases," he said, "we learn more by looking for the answer to a question and not finding it than we do from learning the answer itself. This is one of those cases. I could tell you why, but at the moment it would only be more confusing. If you grow up with any kind of sense—which you sometimes make me doubt—you will very likely reach your own conclusions.

"They will probably be wrong," he added. "However, since they will be yours, you will feel a little more satisfied with them."

Taran sank back and sat, gloomy and silent, on the bench. Dallben had already begun meditating again. His chin gradually came to rest on his collarbone; his beard floated around his ears like a fog bank; and he began snoring peacefully.

The spring scent of apple blossom drifted through the open window. Beyond Dallben's chamber, Taran glimpsed the pale green fringe of forest. The fields, ready to cultivate, would soon turn golden with summer. *The Book of Three* lay closed on the table. Taran had never been allowed to read the volume for himself; now he was sure it held more than Dallben chose to tell him. In the sun-filled room, with Dallben still meditating and showing no sign of stopping, Taran rose and moved through the shimmering beams. From the forest came the monotonous tick of a beetle.

His hands reached for the cover. Taran gasped in pain and snatched them away. They smarted as if each of his fingers had been stung by hornets. He jumped back, stumbled against the bench, and dropped to the floor, where he put his fingers woefully into his mouth.

Dallben's eyes blinked open. He peered at Taran and yawned slowly. "You had better see Coll about a lotion for those hands," he advised. "Otherwise, I shouldn't be surprised if they blistered."

Fingers smarting, the shamefaced Taran hurried from the cottage and found Coll near the vegetable garden.

"You have been at *The Book of Three*," Coll said. "That is not hard to guess. Now you know better. Well, that is one of the three foundations of learning: see much, study much, suffer much." He led Taran to the stable where medicines for the livestock were kept, and poured a concoction over Taran's fingers.

"What is the use of studying much when I'm to see nothing at all?" Taran retorted. "I think there is a destiny laid on me that I am not to know anything interesting, go anywhere interesting, or do anything interesting. I'm certainly not to *be* anything. I'm not anything even at Caer Dallben!"

"Very well," said Coll, "if that is all that troubles you, I shall make you something. From this moment, you are Taran, Assistant Pig-Keeper. You shall help me take care of Hen Wen: see her trough is full, carry her water, and give her a good scrubbing every other day."

"That's what I do now," Taran said bitterly.

"All the better," said Coll, "for it makes things that much easier. If you want to be something with a name attached to it, I can't think of anything closer to hand. And it is not every lad who can be assistant keeper to an oracular pig. Indeed, she is the only oracular pig in Prydain, and the most valuable."

"Valuable to Dallben," Taran said. "She never tells *me* anything."

"Did you think she would?" replied Coll. "With Hen Wen, you must know how to ask—here, what was that?" Coll shaded his eyes with his hand. A black, buzzing cloud streaked from the orchard, and bore on so rapidly and passed so close to Coll's head that he had to leap out of the way.

"The bees!" Taran shouted. "They're swarming!"

"It is not their time," cried Coll. "There is something amiss."

The cloud rose high toward the sun. An instant later Taran heard a loud clucking and squawking from the chicken run. He turned to see the five hens and the rooster beating their wings. Before it occurred to him they were attempting to fly, they, too, were aloft.

Taran and Coll raced to the chicken run, too late to catch the fowls. With the rooster leading, the chickens flapped awkwardly through the air and disappeared over the brow of a hill.

From the stable the pair of oxen bellowed and rolled their eyes in terror.

Dallben's head poked out of the window. He looked irritated. "It has become absolutely impossible for any kind of meditation whatsoever," he said, with a severe glance at Taran. "I have warned you once—"

"Something frightened the animals," Taran protested. "First the bees, then the chickens flew off—"

Dallben's face turned grave. "I have been given no knowledge of this," he said to Coll. "We must ask Hen Wen about it immediately, and we shall need the letter sticks. Quickly, help me find them."

Coll moved hastily to the cottage door. "Watch Hen Wen closely," he ordered Taran. "Do not let her out of your sight."

Coll disappeared inside the cottage to search for Hen Wen's letter sticks, the long rods of ash wood carved with spells. Taran was both frightened and excited. Dallben, he knew, would consult Hen Wen only on a matter of greatest urgency. Within Taran's memory, it had never happened before. He hurried to the pen.

Hen Wen usually slept until noon. Then, trotting daintily, despite her size, she would move to a shady corner of her enclosure and settle comfortably for the rest of the day. The white pig was continually grunting and chuckling to herself, and whenever she saw Taran, she would raise her wide, cheeky face so that he could scratch under her chin. But this time, she paid no attention to him. Wheezing and whistling, Hen Wen was digging furiously in the soft earth at the far side of the pen, burrowing so rapidly she would soon be out.

Taran shouted at her, but the clods continued flying at a great rate. He swung himself over the fence. The oracular pig stopped and glanced around. As Taran approached the hole, already sizable, Hen Wen hurried to the opposite side of the pen and started a new excavation.

Taran was strong and long-legged, but, to his dismay, he saw that Hen Wen moved faster than he. As soon as he chased her from the second hole, she turned quickly on her short legs and made for the first. Both, by now, were big enough for her head and shoulders.

Taran frantically began scraping earth back into the burrow. Hen Wen dug faster than a badger, her hind legs planted firmly, her front legs plowing ahead. Taran despaired of stopping her. He scrambled back over the rails and jumped to the spot where Hen Wen was about to emerge, planning to seize her and hang on until Dallben and Coll arrived. He underestimated Hen Wen's speed and strength.

In an explosion of dirt and pebbles, the pig burst from under the fence, heaving Taran into the air. He landed with the wind knocked out of him. Hen Wen raced across the field and into the woods.

Taran followed. Ahead, the forest rose up dark and threatening. He took a breath and plunged after her.

DAVID MCCORD

This Is My Rock

This is my rock,
And here I run
To steal the secret of the sun;

This is my rock,
And here come I
Before the night has swept the sky;

This is my rock,
This is the place
I meet the evening face to face.

LOUISA MAY ALCOTT

On page 277 is the beginning of one of the most famous books for young people ever written. This first chapter of *Little Women* will enable you to decide (in case you haven't already read the book) whether you want to borrow it from the library and find out what happened to Beth, Amy, Meg, and Jo.

There must be some reason why *Little Women*, first published in 1868, is in print in dozens of editions and is read by children in China, India, and indeed almost everywhere in the world. In another form it still charms whenever that old movie with Katharine Hepburn as Jo is revived.

Louisa, who was a pretty shrewd judge of her own abilities, said of *Little Women,* "We really lived most of it, and if it succeeds, that will be the reason for it." Well, it was one reason, but only one. Many people have written true books about their own lives but their work has perished. Louisa brought to her book, not only truth, but skill in arranging the incidents, and a liveliness that still sparkles even in her old-fashioned prose. Most of all—it's hard to talk about this without seeming sentimental—she gave us a picture of a loving family, full of faults and weaknesses, but held together by what one can only call goodness. As Jo says, "Families are the most beautiful things in all the world."

I think it is this family feeling that we still respond to today when family living is more complicated than in Louisa's time. The Marches made their happiness out of themselves, out of their own characters. Too often we seem to depend on things like television.

There's something else in *Little Women* that appeals to us: the sturdy rebellious figure of Jo, standing up for her independence, a kind of pioneer of the movement for the equality of women. In a way Louisa (who is, of course, Jo) was the man of the Alcott family, worked for it, and finally redeemed it from poverty and suffering.

Her life is well worth reading about—most libraries stock Cornelia Meigs's excellent biography. She was born in 1832. Her father was an idealistic dreamer (I've always thought him a complete bore) who could not provide for his wife and their four daughters. You'll notice he hardly appears in *Little Women*. Things went hard with the Alcotts—they lived in twenty-four houses in twenty-two years, and were much poorer than the Marches in *Little*

Women. Louisa never went to school, but living in Concord, Massachusetts, at that time were many remarkable men—Thoreau, Emerson—and from them she learned a great deal.

When still a child she earned money making dolls' clothes. As a young girl she worked as a domestic, a seamstress, a teacher, and a nurse during the Civil War. But she soon found her vocation—writing. Much of it was hackwork. Then a publisher asked her to write a book for girls. Louisa replied that she didn't like girls. But she wrote *Little Women* anyway, in two and a half months. It, and its sequels, were so successful that the family was relieved from worry. In 1869 she said, "Now I think I could die in peace."

But she lived until 1888, constantly working, constantly helping others. She never married.

Playing Pilgrims

CHRISTMAS won't be Christmas without any presents," grumbled Jo, lying on the rug.

"It's so dreadful to be poor!" sighed Meg, looking down at her old dress.

"I don't think it's fair for some girls to have plenty of pretty things, and other girls nothing at all," added little Amy, with an injured sniff.

"We've got father and mother and each other," said Beth contentedly, from her corner.

The four young faces on which the firelight shone brightened at the cheerful words, but darkened again as Jo said sadly, "We haven't got father, and shall not have him for a long time." She didn't say "perhaps never," but each silently added it, thinking of father far away, where the fighting was.

Nobody spoke for a minute; then Meg said in an altered tone, "You know the reason mother proposed not having any presents this Christmas was because it is going to be a hard winter for everyone; and she thinks we ought not to spend money for pleasure, when our men are suffering so in the army. We can't do much, but we can make our little sacrifices, and ought to do it gladly. But I am afraid I don't"; and Meg shook her head, as she thought regretfully of all the pretty things she wanted.

"But I don't think the little we should spend would do any good. We've each got a dollar, and the army wouldn't be much helped by our giving that. I agree not to expect anything from mother or you, but I do want to buy Undine and Sintram for myself; I've wanted it *so* long," said Jo, who was a bookworm.

"I planned to spend mine in new music," said Beth, with a little sigh, which no one heard but the hearth brush and kettle holder.

"I shall get a nice box of Faber's drawing pencils; I really need them," said Amy decidedly.

"Mother didn't say anything about our money, and she won't wish us to give up everything. Let's each buy what we want, and have a little fun; I'm sure we work hard enough to earn it," cried Jo, examining the heels of her shoes in a gentlemanly manner.

"I know *I* do—teaching those tiresome children nearly all day, when I'm longing to enjoy myself at home," began Meg, in the complaining tone again.

"You don't have half such a hard time as I do," said Jo. "How would you like to be shut up for hours with a nervous, fussy old lady who keeps you trotting, is never satisfied, and worries you till you're ready to fly out of the window or cry?"

"It's naughty to fret; but I do think washing dishes and keeping things tidy is the worst work in the world. It makes me cross; and my hands get so stiff, I can't practice well at all"; and Beth looked at her rough hands with a sigh that anyone could hear that time.

"I don't believe any of you suffer as I do," cried Amy; "for you don't have to go to school with impertinent girls, who plague you if you don't know your lessons, and laugh at your dresses, and label your father if he isn't rich, and insult you when your nose isn't nice."

"If you mean *libel*, I'd say so, and not talk about *labels*, as if papa was a pickle bottle," advised Jo, laughing.

"I know what I mean, and you needn't be *statirical* about it. It's proper to use good words, and improve your *vocabilary*," returned Amy, with dignity.

"Don't peck at one another, children. Don't you wish we had the money papa lost when we were little, Jo? Dear me! how happy and good we'd be, if we had no worries!" said Meg, who could remember better times.

"You said the other day, you thought we were a deal happier than the King children, for they were fighting and fretting all the time, in spite of their money."

"So I did, Beth. Well, I think we are; for, though we do have to work, we make fun for ourselves, and are a pretty jolly set, as Jo would say."

"Jo does use such slang words!" observed Amy, with a reproving look at the long figure stretched on the rug. Jo immediately sat up, put her hands in her pockets, and began to whistle.

"Don't, Jo; it's so boyish!"

"That's why I do it."

"I detest rude, unladylike girls!"

"I hate affected, niminy-piminy chits!"

" 'Birds in their little nests agree,' " sang Beth, the peacemaker, with such a funny face that both sharp voices softened to a laugh, and the "pecking" ended for that time.

"Really, girls, you are both to be blamed," said Meg, beginning to lecture in her elder-sisterly fashion. "You are old enough to leave off boyish tricks, and to behave better, Josephine. It didn't matter so much when you were a little girl; but now you are so tall, and turn up your hair, you should remember that you are a young lady."

"I'm not! and if turning up my hair makes me one, I'll wear it in two tails till I'm twenty," cried Jo, pulling off her net, and shaking down a chestnut mane. "I hate to think I've got to grow up, and be Miss March, and wear long gowns, and look as prim as a China aster! It's bad enough to be a girl, anyway, when I like boys' games and work and manners! I can't get over my disappointment in not being a boy; and it's worse than ever now, for I'm dying to go and fight with papa, and I can only stay at home and knit, like a poky old woman!" And Jo shook the blue army sock till the needles rattled like castanets, and her ball bounded across the room.

"Poor Jo! It's too bad, but it can't be helped; so you must try to be contented with making your name boyish, and playing brother to us girls," said Beth, stroking the rough head at her knee with a hand that all the dishwashing and dusting in the world could not make ungentle in its touch.

"As for you, Amy," continued Meg, "you are altogether too particular and prim. Your airs are funny now; but you'll grow up an affected little goose, if you don't take care. I like your nice manners and refined ways of speaking, when you don't try to be elegant; but your absurd words are as bad as Jo's slang."

"If Jo is a tomboy and Amy a goose, what am I, please?" asked Beth, ready to share the lecture.

"You're a dear, and nothing else," answered Meg warmly; and no one contradicted her, for the "Mouse" was the pet of the family.

As young readers like to know "how people look," we will take this moment to give them a little sketch of the four sisters, who sat knitting away in the twilight, while the December snow fell quietly without, and the fire crackled cheerfully within. It was a comfortable old room, though the carpet was faded and the furniture very plain; for a good picture or two hung on the walls, books filled the recesses, chrysanthemums and Christmas roses bloomed in the windows, and a pleasant atmosphere of home-peace pervaded it.

Margaret, the eldest of the four, was sixteen, and very pretty, being plump and fair, with large eyes, plenty of soft, brown hair, a sweet mouth, and white hands, of which she was rather vain. Fifteen-year-old Jo was very tall, thin, and brown, and reminded one of a colt; for she never seemed to know what to do with her long limbs, which were very much in her way. She had a decided mouth, a comical nose, and sharp, gray eyes, which appeared to see everything, and were by turns fierce, funny, or thoughtful. Her long, thick hair was her one beauty; but it was usually bundled into a net, to be out of her way. Round shoulders had Jo, big hands and feet, a flyaway look to her clothes, and the uncomfortable appearance of a girl who was rapidly shooting up into a woman, and didn't like it. Elizabeth—or Beth, as everyone called her—was a rosy, smooth-haired, bright-eyed girl of thirteen, with a shy manner, a timid voice, and a peaceful expression, which was seldom disturbed. Her father called her "Little Tranquillity," and the name suited her excellently; for she seemed to live in a happy world of her own, only venturing out to meet the few whom she trusted and loved. Amy, though the youngest, was a most important person—in her own opinion at least. A regular snow-maiden, with blue eyes, and yellow hair, curling on her shoulders, pale and slender, and always carrying herself like a young lady mindful of her manners. What the characters of the four sisters were we will leave to be found out.

The clock struck six; and, having swept up the hearth, Beth put a pair of slippers down to warm. Somehow the sight of the old shoes had a good effect upon the girls; for mother was coming, and everyone brightened to welcome her. Meg stopped lecturing, and lighted the lamp, Amy got out of the easy chair without being asked, and Jo forgot how tired she was as she sat up to hold the slippers nearer to the blaze.

"They are quite worn out; Marmee must have a new pair."

"I thought I'd get her some with my dollar," said Beth.

"No, I shall!" cried Amy.

"I'm the oldest," began Meg, but Jo cut in with a decided—

"I'm the man of the family now papa is away, and *I* shall provide the slippers, for he told me to take special care of mother while he was gone."

"I'll tell you what we'll do," said Beth; "let's each get her something for Christmas, and not get anything for ourselves."

"That's like you, dear! What will we get?" exclaimed Jo.

Everyone thought soberly for a minute; then Meg announced, as if the idea was suggested by the sight of her own pretty hands, "I shall give her a nice pair of gloves."

"Army shoes, best to be had," cried Jo.

"Some handkerchiefs, all hemmed," said Beth.

"I'll get a little bottle of cologne; she likes it, and it won't cost much, so I'll have some left to buy my pencils," added Amy.

"How will we give the things?" asked Meg.

"Put them on the table, and bring her in and see her open the bundles. Don't you remember how we used to do on our birthdays?" answered Jo.

"I used to be *so* frightened when it was my turn to sit in the big chair with the crown on, and see you all come marching round to give the presents, with a kiss. I liked the things and the kisses, but it was dreadful to have you sit looking at me while I opened the bundles," said Beth, who was toasting her face and the bread for tea, at the same time.

"Let Marmee think we are getting things for ourselves, and then surprise her. We must go shopping tomorrow afternoon, Meg; there is so much to do about the play for Christmas night," said Jo, marching up and down, with her hands behind her back and her nose in the air.

"I don't mean to act any more after this time; I'm getting too old for such things," observed Meg, who was as much a child as ever about "dressing-up" frolics.

"You won't stop, I know, as long as you can trail round in a white gown with your hair down, and wear gold-paper jewelry. You are the best actress we've got, and there'll be an end of everything if you quit the boards," said Jo. "We ought to rehearse tonight. Come here, Amy, and do the fainting scene, for you are as stiff as a poker in that."

"I can't help it; I never saw anyone faint, and I don't choose to make myself all black and blue, tumbling flat as you do. If I can go down easily, I'll drop; if I can't, I shall fall into a chair and be graceful; I don't care if Hugo does come at me with a pistol," returned Amy, who was not gifted with dramatic power, but was chosen because she was small enough to be borne out shrieking by the villain of the piece.

"Do it this way; clasp your hands so, and stagger across the room, crying frantically, 'Roderigo! save me! save me!' " and away went Jo, with a melodramatic scream which was truly thrilling.

Amy followed, but she poked her hands out stiffly before her, and jerked herself along as if she went by machinery; and her "Ow!" was more suggestive of pins being run into her than of fear and anguish. Jo gave a despairing groan, and Meg laughed outright, while Beth let her bread burn as she watched the fun, with interest.

"It's no use! Do the best you can when the time comes, and if the audience laughs don't blame me. Come on, Meg."

Then things went smoothly, for Don Pedro defied the world in a speech of two pages without a single break; Hagar, the witch, chanted an awful incantation over her kettleful of simmering toads, with weird effect; Roderigo rent his chains asunder manfully; and Hugo died in agonies of remorse and arsenic, with a wild "Ha! ha!"

"It's the best we've had yet," said Meg, as the dead villain sat up and rubbed his elbows.

"I don't see how you can write and act such splendid things, Jo. You're a regular Shakespeare!" exclaimed Beth, who firmly believed that her sisters were gifted with wonderful genius in all things.

"Not quite," replied Jo modestly. "I do think 'The Witch's Curse, an Operatic Tragedy,' is rather a nice thing; but I'd like to try *Macbeth*, if we only had a trapdoor for Banquo. I always wanted to do the killing part. 'Is that a dagger that I see before me?' " muttered Jo, rolling her eyes and clutching at the air, as she had seen a famous tragedian do.

"No, it's the toasting fork, with mother's shoe on it instead of the bread. Beth's stagestruck!" cried Meg, and the rehearsal ended in a general burst of laughter.

"Glad to find you so merry, my girls," said a cheery voice at the door, and actors and audience turned to welcome a tall, motherly lady, with a "can-I-help-you" look about her which was truly delightful. She was not elegantly dressed, but a noble-looking woman, and the girls thought the gray cloak and unfashionable bonnet covered the most splendid mother in the world.

"Well, dearies, how have you got on today? There was so much to do, getting the boxes ready to go tomorrow, that I didn't come home to dinner. Has anyone called, Beth? How is your cold, Meg? Jo, you look tired to death. Come and kiss me, baby."

While making these maternal inquiries, Mrs. March got her wet things off, her warm slippers on, and sitting down in the easy chair, drew Amy to her lap, preparing to enjoy the happiest hour of her busy day. The girls flew about, trying to make things comfortable, each in her own way. Meg arranged the tea table; Jo brought wood and set chairs, dropping, overturning, and clattering everything she touched; Beth trotted to and fro between parlor and kitchen, quiet and busy; while Amy gave directions to everyone, as she sat with her hands folded.

As they gathered about the table, Mrs. March said, with a particularly happy face, "I've got a treat for you after supper."

A quick, bright smile went round like a streak of sunshine. Beth clapped her hands, regardless of the biscuit she held, and Jo tossed up her napkin, crying, "A letter! a letter! Three cheers for father!"

"Yes, a nice long letter. He is well, and thinks he shall get through the cold season better than we feared. He sends all sorts of loving wishes for Christmas, and an especial message to you girls," said Mrs. March, patting her pocket as if she had got a treasure there.

"Hurry and get done! Don't stop to quirk your little finger, and simper over your plate, Amy," cried Jo, choking in her tea, and dropping her bread, butter side down, on the carpet, in her haste to get at the treat.

Beth ate no more, but crept away, to sit in her shadowy corner and brood over the delight to come, till the others were ready.

"I think it was so splendid in father to go as a chaplain when he was too old to be drafted, and not strong enough for a soldier," said Meg warmly.

"Don't I wish I could go as a drummer, a *vivan*—what's its name? or a nurse, so I could be near him and help him," exclaimed Jo, with a groan.

"It must be very disagreeable to sleep in a tent, and eat all sorts of bad-tasting things, and drink out of a tin mug," sighed Amy.

"When will he come home, Marmee?" asked Beth, with a little quiver in her voice.

"Not for many months, dear, unless he is sick. He will stay and do his work faithfully as long as he can, and we won't ask for him back a minute sooner than he can be spared. Now come and hear the letter."

They all drew to the fire, mother in the big chair with Beth at her feet, Meg and Amy perched on either arm of the chair, and Jo leaning on the back, where no one would see any sign of emotion if the letter should happen to be touching.

Very few letters were written in those hard times that were not touching, especially those which fathers sent home. In this one little was said of the hardships endured, the dangers faced, or the homesickness conquered; it was a cheerful, hopeful letter, full of lively descriptions of camp life, marches, and military news; and only at the end did the writer's heart overflow with fatherly love and longing for the little girls at home.

"Give them all my dear love and a kiss. Tell them I think of them by day, pray for them by night, and find my best comfort in their affection at all times. A year seems very long to wait before I see them, but remind them that while we wait we may all work, so that these hard days need not be wasted. I know they will remember all I said to them, that they will be loving children to you, will do their duty faithfully, fight their bosom enemies bravely, and conquer themselves so beautifully, that when I come back to them I may be fonder and prouder than ever of my little women."

Everybody sniffed when they came to that part; Jo wasn't ashamed of the great tear that dropped off the end of her nose, and Amy never minded the rumpling of her curls as she hid her face on her mother's shoulder and sobbed out, "I *am* a selfish girl! but I'll truly try to be better, so he mayn't be disappointed in me by and by."

"We all will!" cried Meg. "I think too much of my looks, and hate to work, but won't any more, if I can help it."

"I'll try and be what he loves to call me, 'a little woman,' and not be rough and wild; but do my duty here instead of wanting to be somewhere else," said Jo, thinking that keeping her temper at home was a much harder task than facing a rebel or two down South.

Beth said nothing, but wiped away her tears with the blue army sock, and began to knit with all her might, losing no time in doing the duty that lay nearest her, while she resolved in her quiet little soul to be all that father hoped to find her when the year brought round the happy coming home.

Mrs. March broke the silence that followed Jo's words, by saying in her cheery voice, "Do you remember how you used to play Pilgrim's Progress when you were little things? Nothing delighted you more than to have me tie my piece-bags on your backs for burdens, give you hats and sticks and rolls of paper, and let you travel through the house from the cellar, which was the City of Destruction, up, up, to the housetop, where you had all the lovely things you could collect to make a Celestial City."

"What fun it was, especially going by the lions, fighting Apollyon, and passing through the Valley where the hobgoblins were!" said Jo.

"I liked the place where the bundles fell off and tumbled downstairs," said Meg.

"My favorite part was when we came out on the flat roof where our flowers and arbors and pretty things were, and all stood and sung for joy up there in the sunshine," said Beth, smiling, as if that pleasant moment had come back to her.

"I don't remember much about it, except that I was afraid of the cellar and the dark entry, and always liked the cake and milk we had up at the top. If I wasn't too old for such things, I'd rather like to play it over again," said Amy, who began to talk of renouncing childish things at the mature age of twelve.

"We never are too old for this, my dear, because it is a play we are playing all the time in one way or another. Our burdens are here, our road is before us, and the longing for goodness and happiness is the guide that leads us through many troubles and mistakes to the peace which is a true Celestial City. Now, my little pilgrims, suppose you begin again, not in play, but in earnest, and see how far on you can get before father comes home."

"Really, mother? Where are our bundles?" asked Amy, who was a very literal young lady.

"Each of you told what your burden was just now, except Beth; I rather think she hasn't got any," said her mother.

"Yes, I have; mine is dishes and dusters, and envying girls with nice pianos, and being afraid of people."

Beth's bundle was such a funny one that everybody wanted to laugh; but nobody did, for it would have hurt her feelings very much.

"Let us do it," said Meg thoughtfully. "It is only another name for trying to be good, and the story may help us; for though we do want to be good, it's hard work, and we forget, and don't do our best."

"We were in the Slough of Despond tonight, and mother came and pulled us out as Help did in the book. We ought to have our roll of directions, like Christian. What shall we do about that?" asked Jo, delighted with the fancy which lent a little romance to the very dull task of doing her duty.

"Look under your pillows, Christmas morning, and you will find your guidebook," replied Mrs. March.

They talked over the new plan while old Hannah cleared the table; then out came the four little workbaskets, and the needles flew as the girls made sheets for Aunt March. It was uninteresting sewing, but tonight no one grumbled. They adopted Jo's plan of dividing the long seams into four parts, and calling the quarters Europe, Asia, Africa, and America, and in that way got on capitally, especially when they talked about the different countries as they stitched their way through them.

At nine they stopped work, and sang, as usual, before they went to bed. No one but Beth could get much music out of the old piano; but she had a way of softly touching the yellow keys, and making a pleasant accompaniment to the simple songs they sang. Meg had a voice like a flute, and she and her mother led the little choir. Amy chirped like a cricket, and Jo wandered through the airs at her own sweet will, always coming out at the wrong place with a croak or a quaver that spoilt the most pensive tune. They had always done this from the time they could lisp *"Crinkle, crinkle, 'ittle 'tar,"* and it had become a household custom, for the mother was a born singer. The first sound in the morning was her voice, as she went about the house singing like a lark; and the last sound at night was the same cheery sound, for the girls never grew too old for that familiar lullaby.

JOHN MASEFIELD

Sea Fever

I must go down to the seas again, to the lonely sea and the sky,
And all I ask is a tall ship and a star to steer her by;
And the wheel's kick and the wind's song and the white sail's shaking,
And a gray mist on the sea's face and a gray dawn breaking.

I must go down to the seas again, for the call of the running tide
Is a wild call and a clear call that may not be denied;
And all I ask is a windy day with the white clouds flying,
And the flung spray and the blown spume, and the sea-gulls crying.

I must go down to the seas again, to the vagrant gypsy life,
To the gull's way and the whale's way where the wind's like a whetted
   knife;
And all I ask is a merry yarn from a laughing fellow-rover,
And quiet sleep and a sweet dream when thc long trick's over.

Cargoes

Quinquireme of Nineveh from distant Ophir
Rowing home to haven in sunny Palestine,
With a cargo of ivory,
And apes and peacocks,
Sandalwood, cedarwood, and sweet white wine.

Stately Spanish galleon coming from the Isthmus,
Dipping through the Tropics by the palm-green shores,
With a cargo of diamonds,
Emeralds, amethysts,
Topazes, and cinnamon, and gold moidores.

Dirty British coaster with a salt-caked smokestack
Butting through the Channel in the mad March days,
With a cargo of Tyne coal,
Road-rails, pig-lead,
Firewood, iron-ware, and cheap tin trays.

JOYCE COOPER ARKHURST

How Spider Got a Thin Waist
A West African Folktale

MANY dry seasons ago, before the oldest man in our village can remember, before the rain and the dry and the rain and the dry that any one of us can talk about to his children, Spider was a very big person. He did not look as he looks today, with his fat head and his fat body and his thin waist in between. Of course, he had two eyes and eight legs and he lived in a web. But none of him was thin. He was big and round, and his waistline was very fat indeed. Today, he is very different, as all of you know, and this is how it came to pass.

One day Spider was walking through the forest. It was early morning and he noticed an unusually pleasant smell. He wrinkled his nose and sniffed the wind. It was food! Goodness! He had almost forgotten. Today was the festival of the harvest. Every village in the big forest was preparing a feast. The women were cooking yams and cassava, and chicken with peanut-flavored sauce. There would be fish and peppers and rice boiling in the great pots over the fires.

Spider's heart jumped for joy. His mouth watered. His eyes sparkled and he smiled brightly. Already he could taste the food on his tongue.

Now, of course, Spider had not done any of the work to deserve such a feast, and no one had invited him to come and eat. Spider had not planted yam or potato. He had not planted rice, nor gone to sea in a long boat to catch fish. For Spider did not like to work at all. All day he played in the sun or slept, and since it is not the custom to refuse food to anyone who comes to one's door, he could eat very well by simply visiting all his friends. In fact, he ate more than they did.

Now Spider was right in the middle of the forest. Not far away there were two villages. Spider stood just in the middle, and the two were exactly the same distance away. Today each village would have a great feast.

"How lucky for me!" thought Spider.

But then he was puzzled. Since there were two dinners, he did not know which one he wanted to go to. That is, he did not know which would have the most to eat. So Spider sat under a breadfruit tree and thought and thought and thought. At last he had an idea! He could go to them both! Of course. Spider was so pleased with his good idea that he did a little dance right there and then.

But how could he know when the food was ready? He sat under the breadfruit tree again and thought and thought and thought. And then he had another idea. He did another little dance just because he was so brilliant. And then he did two things.

First, he called his eldest son, Kuma. He took a long rope and tied one end around his waist. The other end he gave to his son.

"Take this rope to the village on the east," he said to Kuma. "When the food is ready, give the rope a hard pull, and I will know it is time for me to come and eat."

And so Kuma went to the east village and took the end of the rope with him.

Then Spider called his youngest son, Kwaku. He took another long rope and tied it around his waist, just below the first one.

"Kwaku, take this rope to the village on the west," he said, "and when the food is all cooked, pull very hard on it. Then I will come and have my fill."

So Kwaku went to the west village, carrying the end of the rope with him.

My friends, can you imagine what happened? I don't think so, so I will tell you. The people in the east village and the people in the west village had their dinners at *exactly the same time*. So, of course, Kuma and Kwaku pulled on both of the ropes at the same time. Kuma pulled to the east and Kwaku pulled to the west. The ropes got tighter and tighter. Poor, greedy Spider was caught in the middle. He could go neither east nor west, nor left nor right.

Kuma and Kwaku could not understand why their father did not come, and they pulled harder all the time. And something was happening to Spider. The ropes squeezed tighter and tighter and his waist got thinner and thinner. Kuma and Kwaku waited until all the food was eaten. Then they came to look for their father. When they found him, he looked very different. His waistline was thinner than a needle! Spider never grew fat again. He stayed the same until today. He has a big head and a big body, and a tiny little waist in between.

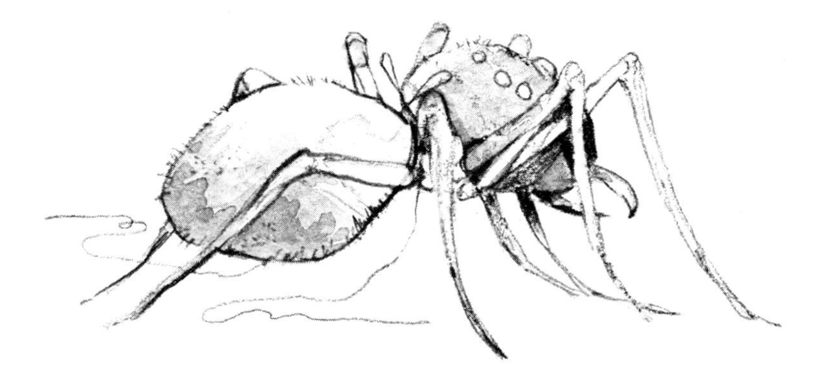

SINCLAIR LEWIS

Cat

This is a cat that sleeps at night,
That takes delight
In visions bright,
And not a vagrant that creeps at night
On boxcars by the river.
This is a sleepy cat to purr
And rarely stir
Its shining fur;
This is a cat whose softest purr
Means salmon, steaks, and liver.

That is a cat respectable,
Connectable
With selectable
Feline families respectable,
Whose names would make you quiver.
That is a cat of piety,
Not satiety,
But sobriety.
Its very purr is of piety
And thanks to its Feline Giver.

And this is how it prays:

"Ancient of days
With whiskers torrendous,
Hark to our praise,
Lick and defend us.
Lo, how we bring to Thee
Sweet breasts of mouses;
Hark how we sing to Thee,
Filling all houses
With ardent miaouses,
Until it arouses
All mankind to battery.
Thou of the golden paws,
Thou of thc silver claws,
Thy tail is the comets' cause,
King of all cattery!"

E. B. WHITE

Mr. White is a very quiet man who never says anything foolish or dull and who often says things you catch yourself thinking about much later. His books, most of them for grown-ups, are like that, too.

When he was thirty-nine years old he moved from New York City to a farm in Maine and he's stayed there ever since, writing, watching and breeding animals, looking at the natural and human world with eyes that seem to see more than most of us do. He's written three books for children. *Charlotte's Web*, I think, is the best, but the other two are almost as good. *Stuart Little* is about the adventures of a tiny boy, two inches high, who looks like a mouse and who is the son of two regular human beings, Mr. and Mrs. Little. *The Trumpet of the Swan* tells us about Louis, a cygnet who is born voiceless but who learns to play the trumpet.

Mr. White has always felt happy in his big barn in Maine and so he tried to bring it to life in *Charlotte's Web*. The story is about Fern, a girl aged eight; Templeton, a crafty, greedy rat; Wilbur, a not very aggressive pig; and Charlotte, a spider, whom we get to love even though most of us don't really go for spiders.

Fern has saved the little runt-pig Wilbur from being slaughtered. As she says to her father, "If *I* had been very small at birth, would you have killed *me?*" Wilbur is pretty comfortable in his barn, but he's also lonely; he wants someone to love and to play with. One night he hears a voice saying, "Do you want a friend, Wilbur? I'll be a friend to you." The episode that follows tells us what happened after that.

The whole story is about how Wilbur, once he has grown up, is again saved from death by Templeton the rat but mainly by Charlotte.

Mr. White writes, "Once you begin watching spiders, you haven't time for much else—the world is really loaded with them." It is Charlotte's spider-world into which he leads us, and a most interesting world it is, like our own in some ways. Perhaps that's what Mr. White wants us to feel.

Charlotte

THE NIGHT seemed long. Wilbur's stomach was empty and his mind was full. And when your stomach is empty and your mind is full, it's always hard to sleep.

A dozen times during the night Wilbur woke and stared into the blackness, listening to the sounds and trying to figure out what time it was. A barn is never perfectly quiet. Even at midnight there is usually something stirring.

The first time he woke, he heard Templeton gnawing a hole in the grain bin. Templeton's teeth scraped loudly against the wood and made quite a racket. "That crazy rat!" thought Wilbur. "Why does he have to stay up all night, grinding his clashers and destroying people's property? Why can't he go to sleep, like any decent animal?"

The second time Wilbur woke, he heard the goose turning on her nest and chuckling to herself.

"What time is it?" whispered Wilbur to the goose.

"Probably-obably-obably about half-past eleven," said the goose. "Why aren't you asleep, Wilbur?"

"Too many things on my mind," said Wilbur.

"Well," said the goose, "that's not *my* trouble. I have nothing at all on my mind, but I've too many things under my behind. Have you ever tried to sleep while sitting on eight eggs?"

"No," replied Wilbur. "I suppose it *is* uncomfortable. How long does it take a goose egg to hatch?"

"Approximately-oximately thirty days, all told," answered the goose. "But I cheat a little. On warm afternoons, I just pull a little straw over the eggs and go out for a walk."

Wilbur yawned and went back to sleep. In his dreams he heard again the voice saying, "I'll be a friend to you. Go to sleep—you'll see me in the morning."

About half an hour before dawn, Wilbur woke and listened. The barn was still dark. The sheep lay motionless. Even the goose was quiet. Overhead, on the main floor, nothing stirred: the cows were resting, the horses dozed. Templeton had quit work and gone off somewhere on an errand. The only sound was a slight scraping noise from the rooftop, where the weathervane swung back and forth. Wilbur loved the barn when it was like this—calm and quiet, waiting for light.

"Day is almost here," he thought.

Through a small window, a faint gleam appeared. One by one the stars went out. Wilbur could see the goose a few feet away. She sat with head tucked under a wing. Then he could see the sheep and the lambs. The sky lightened.

"Oh, beautiful day, it is here at last! Today I shall find my friend."

Wilbur looked everywhere. He searched his pen thoroughly. He examined the window ledge, stared up at the ceiling. But he saw nothing new. Finally he decided he would have to speak up. He hated to break the lovely stillness of dawn by using his voice, but he couldn't think of any other way to locate the mysterious new friend who was nowhere to be seen. So Wilbur cleared his throat.

"Attention, please!" He said in a loud, firm voice. "Will the party who addressed me at bedtime last night kindly make himself or herself known by giving an appropriate sign or signal!"

Wilbur paused and listened. All the other animals lifted their heads and stared at him. Wilbur blushed. But he was determined to get in touch with his unknown friend.

"Attention, please!" he said. "I will repeat the message. Will the party who addressed me at bedtime last night kindly speak up. Please tell me where you are, if you are my friend!"

The sheep looked at each other in disgust.

"Stop your nonsense, Wilbur!" said the oldest sheep. "If you have a new friend here, you are probably disturbing his rest; and the quickest way to spoil a friendship is to wake somebody up in the morning before he is ready. How can you be sure your friend is an early riser?"

"I beg everyone's pardon," whispered Wilbur. "I didn't mean to be objectionable."

He lay down meekly in the manure, facing the door. He did not know it, but his friend was very near. And the old sheep was right—the friend was still asleep.

Soon Lurvy appeared with slops for breakfast. Wilbur rushed out, ate everything in a hurry, and licked the trough. The sheep moved off down the lane, the gander waddled along behind them, pulling grass. And then, just as Wilbur was settling down for his morning nap, he heard again the thin voice that had addressed him the night before.

"Salutations!" said the voice.

Wilbur jumped to his feet. "Salu-*what?*" he cried.

"Salutations!" repeated the voice.

"What are *they*, and where are *you?*" screamed Wilbur. "Please, *please*, tell me where you are. And what are salutations?"

"Salutations are greetings," said the voice. "When I say 'salutations,' it's just my fancy way of saying hello or good morning. Actually, it's a silly expression, and I am surprised that I used it at all. As for my whereabouts, that's easy. Look up here in the corner of the doorway! Here I am. Look, I'm waving!"

At last Wilbur saw the creature that had spoken to him in such a kindly way. Stretched across the upper part of the doorway was a big spiderweb, and hanging from the top of the web, head down, was a large gray spider. She was about the size of a gumdrop. She had eight legs, and she was waving one of them at Wilbur in friendly greeting. "See me now?" she asked.

"Oh, yes indeed," said Wilbur. "Yes indeed! How are you? Good morning! Salutations! Very pleased to meet you. What is your name, please? May I have your name?"

"My name," said the spider, "is Charlotte."

"Charlotte what?" asked Wilbur, eagerly.

"Charlotte A. Cavatica. But just call me Charlotte."

"I think you're beautiful," said Wilbur.

"Well, I *am* pretty," replied Charlotte. "There's no denying that. Almost all spiders are rather nice-looking. I'm not as flashy as some, but I'll do. I wish I could see you, Wilbur, as clearly as you can see me."

"Why can't you?" asked the pig. "I'm right here."

"Yes, but I'm nearsighted," replied Charlotte. "I've always been dreadfully nearsighted. It's good in some ways, not so good in others. Watch me wrap up this fly."

A fly that had been crawling along Wilbur's trough had flown up and blundered into the lower part of Charlotte's web and was tangled in the sticky threads. The fly was beating its wings furiously, trying to break loose and free itself.

"First," said Charlotte, "I dive at him." She plunged headfirst toward the fly. As she dropped, a tiny silken thread unwound from her rear end.

"Next, I wrap him up." She grabbed the fly, threw a few jets of silk around it, and rolled it over and over, wrapping it so that it couldn't move. Wilbur watched in horror. He could hardly believe what he was seeing, and although he detested flies, he was sorry for this one.

"There!" said Charlotte. "Now I knock him out, so he'll be more comfortable." She bit the fly. "He can't feel a thing now," she remarked. "He'll make a perfect breakfast for me."

"You mean you *eat* flies?" gasped Wilbur.

"Certainly. Flies, bugs, grasshoppers, choice beetles, moths, butterflies, tasty cockroaches, gnats, midges, daddy longlegs, centipedes, mosquitoes, crickets—anything that is careless enough to get caught in my web. I have to live, don't I?"

"Why, yes, of course," said Wilbur. "Do they taste good?"

"Delicious. Of course, I don't really eat them. I drink them—drink their blood. I love blood," said Charlotte, and her pleasant, thin voice grew even thinner and more pleasant.

"Don't say that!" groaned Wilbur. "Please don't say things like that!"

"Why not? It's true, and I have to say what is true. I am not entirely happy about my diet of flies and bugs, but it's the way I'm made. A spider has to pick up a living somehow or other, and I happen to be a trapper. I just naturally build a web and trap flies and other insects. My mother was a trapper before me. Her mother was a trapper before her. All our family have been trappers. Way back for thousands and thousands of years we spiders have been laying for flies and bugs."

"It's a miserable inheritance," said Wilbur, gloomily. He was sad because his new friend was so bloodthirsty.

"Yes, it is," agreed Charlotte. "But I can't help it. I don't know how the first spider in the early days of the world happened to think up this fancy idea of spinning a web, but she did, and it was clever of her, too. And since then, all of us spiders have had to work the same trick. It's not a bad pitch, on the whole."

"It's cruel," replied Wilbur, who did not intend to be argued out of his position.

"Well, *you* can't talk," said Charlotte. "*You* have your meals brought to you in a pail. Nobody feeds me. I have to get my own living. I live by my wits. I have to be sharp and clever, lest I go hungry. I have to think things out, catch what I can, take what comes. And it just so happens, my friend, that what comes is flies and insects and bugs. And *furthermore*," said Charlotte, shaking one of her legs, "do you realize that if I didn't catch bugs and eat them, bugs would increase and multiply and get so numerous that they'd destroy the earth, wipe out everything?"

"Really?" said Wilbur. "I wouldn't want *that* to happen. Perhaps your web is a good thing after all."

The goose had been listening to this conversation and chuckling to herself. "There are a lot of things Wilbur doesn't know about life," she thought. "He's really a very innocent little pig. He doesn't even know what's going to happen to him around Christmastime; he has no idea that Mr. Zuckerman and Lurvy are plotting to kill him." And the goose raised herself a bit and poked her eggs a little further under her so that they would receive the full heat from her warm body and soft feathers.

Charlotte stood quietly over the fly, preparing to eat it. Wilbur lay down and closed his eyes. He was tired from his wakeful night and from the excitement of meeting someone for the first time. A breeze brought him the smell of clover—the sweet-smelling world beyond his fence. "Well," he thought, "I've got a new friend, all right. But what a gamble friendship is! Charlotte is fierce, brutal, scheming, bloodthirsty—everything I don't like. How can I learn to like her, even though she is pretty and, of course, clever?"

Wilbur was merely suffering the doubts and fears that often go with finding a new friend. In good time he was to discover that he was mistaken about Charlotte. Underneath her rather bold and cruel exterior, she had a kind heart, and she was to prove loyal and true to the very end.

KARLA KUSKIN

Rules

Do not jump on ancient uncles.
Do not yell at average mice.
Do not wear a broom to breakfast.
Do not ask a snake's advice.
Do not bathe in chocolate pudding.
Do not talk to bearded bears.
Do not smoke cigars on sofas.
Do not dance on velvet chairs.
Do not take a whale to visit
Russell's mother's cousin's yacht.
And whatever else you do do
It is better you
Do not.

MARK TWAIN

Sometimes I think that if Mark Twain had stuck to his real name, Samuel Langhorne Clemens, he might not have become quite so famous. As a young man, he worked as a steamboat pilot on the Mississippi River. One of the crew, taking soundings, would call up to Sam, "By the mark, twain," which meant that at that particular moment the depth happened to be two fathoms, or twelve feet. And so in 1863, after he had become a newspaper correspondent in the Far West, he appropriated the two words and made out of them a name that today is known throughout the world.

He lived a long and varied life as printer, pilot, soldier (briefly), journalist, silver miner, traveler, lecturer, humorist, unsuccessful businessman, and very successful writer. Halley's comet appeared during the year of his birth and he was fond of saying that when it came round again it would signalize his death. It was an eerily correct prophecy. In 1910 the comet reappeared and Mark Twain disappeared, leaving behind him one great book and many good ones.

The great one is *Huckleberry Finn,* which you may want to tackle after reading *Tom Sawyer*. It's from the latter novel that I've drawn the selection printed below. *Tom Sawyer* is made up of memories of Mark's own boyhood, spent in the sleepy little hamlet of Hannibal, Missouri, where the romantic sights and sounds of Old Man River dominated the lives of its inhabitants almost a century and a half ago.

Humor tends to date but I think the story of Tom and the pinch-bug is still funny.

The Pinch-bug and His Prey

ABOUT half past ten the cracked bell of the small church began to ring, and presently the people began to gather for the morning sermon. The Sunday-school children distributed themselves about the house and occupied pews with their parents, so as to be under supervision. Aunt Polly came, and Tom and Sid and Mary sat with her—Tom being placed next the aisle, in order that he might be as far away from the open window and the seductive outside summer scenes as possible. The crowd filed up the aisles: the aged and needy postmaster, who had seen better days; the mayor and his wife—for they had a mayor there, among other unnecessaries; the justice of the peace; the widow Douglas, fair, smart, and forty, a generous, good-hearted soul and well-to-do, her hill mansion the only palace in the town, and the most hospitable and much the most lavish in the matter of festivities that St. Petersburg could boast; the bent and venerable Major and Mrs. Ward; lawyer Riverson, the new notable from a distance; next the belle of the village, followed by a troop of lawn-clad and ribbon-decked young heartbreakers; then all the young clerks in town in a body—for they had stood in the vestibule sucking their cane-heads, a circling wall of oiled and simpering admirers, till the last girl had run their gantlet; and last of all came the Model Boy, Willie Mufferson, taking as heedful care of his mother as if she were cut glass. He always brought his mother to church, and was the pride of all the matrons. The boys all hated him, he was so good. And besides, he had been "thrown up to them" so much. His white handkerchief was hanging out of his pocket behind, as usual on Sundays—accidentally. Tom had no handkerchief, and he looked upon boys who had, as snobs.

The congregation being fully assembled, now, the bell rang once more, to warn laggards and stragglers, and then a solemn hush fell upon the church which was only broken by the tittering and whispering of the choir in the gallery. The choir always tittered and whispered all through service. There was once a church choir that was not ill-bred, but I have forgotten where it was, now. It was a great many years ago, and I can scarcely remember anything about it, but I think it was in some foreign country.

The minister gave out the hymn, and read it through with a relish in a peculiar style which was much admired in that part of the country. His voice began on a medium key and climbed steadily up till it reached a certain point, where it bore with strong emphasis upon the topmost word and then plunged down as if from a springboard:

> *Shall I be car-ri-ed to the skies, on flow'ry* beds
> *of ease,*
> *Whilst others fight to win the prize, and sail thro'* blood-
> *y seas?*

He was regarded as a wonderful reader. At church "sociables" he was always called upon to read poetry; and when he was through, the ladies would lift up their hands and let them fall helplessly in their laps, and "wall" their eyes, and shake their heads, as much as to say, "Words cannot express it; it is *too* beautiful for this mortal earth."

After the hymn had been sung, the Reverend Mr. Sprague turned himself into a bulletin board, and read off "notices" of meetings and societies and things till it seemed that the list would stretch out to the crack of doom—a queer custom which is still kept up in America, even in cities, away here in this age of abundant newspapers. Often, the less there is to justify a traditional custom, the harder it is to get rid of it.

And now the minister prayed. A good, generous prayer it was, and went into details: it pleaded for the church, and the little children of the church; for the other churches of the village; for the village itself; for the country; for the state; for the state officers; for the United States; for the churches of the United States; for Congress; for the President; for the officers of the government; for poor sailors, tossed by stormy seas; for the oppressed millions groaning under the heel of European monarchies and Oriental despotisms; for such as have the light and the good tidings, and yet have not eyes to see nor ears to hear withal; for the heathen in the far islands of the sea; and closed with a supplication that the words he was about to speak might find grace and favor, and be as seed sown in fertile ground, yielding in time a grateful harvest of good. Amen.

There was a rustling of dresses, and the standing congregation sat down. The boy whose history this book relates did not enjoy the prayer, he only endured it—if he even did that much. He was restive all through it; he kept tally of the details of the prayer, unconsciously—for he was not listening, but he knew the ground of old, and the clergyman's regular route over it—and when a little trifle of new matter was interlarded, his ear detected it and his whole nature resented it; he considered additions unfair, and scoundrelly. In the midst of the prayer a fly had lit on the back of the pew in front of him and tortured his spirit by calmly rubbing its hands together, embracing its head with its arms, and polishing it so vigorously that it seemed to almost part company with the body, and the slender thread of a neck was exposed to view; scraping its wings with its hind legs and smoothing them to its body as if they had been coattails; going through its whole toilet as tranquilly as if it knew it was perfectly safe. As indeed it was; for as sorely as Tom's hands itched to grab for it they did not dare—he believed his soul would be instantly destroyed if he did such a thing while the prayer was going on. But with the closing sentence his hand began to curve and steal forward; and the instant the "Amen" was out the fly was a prisoner of war. His aunt detected the act and made him let it go.

The minister gave out his text and droned along monotonously through an argument that was so prosy that many a head by and by began to nod—and yet it was an argument that dealt in limitless fire and brimstone and thinned the predestined elect down to a company so small as to be hardly worth the saving. Tom counted the pages of the sermon; after church he always knew how many pages there had been, but he seldom knew anything else about the discourse. However, this time he was really interested for a little while. The minister made a grand and moving picture of the assembling together of the world's hosts at the millennium when the lion and the lamb should lie down together and a little child should lead them. But the pathos, the lesson, the moral of the great spectacle were lost upon the boy; he only thought of the conspicuousness of the principal character before the onlooking nations; his face lit with the thought, and he said to himself that he wished he could be that child, if it was a tame lion.

Now he lapsed into suffering again, as the dry argument was resumed. Presently he bethought him of a treasure he had and got it out. It was a large black beetle with formidable jaws—a "pinch-bug," he called it. It was in a percussion-cap box. The first thing the beetle did was to take him by the finger. A natural fillip followed, the beetle went floundering into the aisle and lit on its back, and the hurt finger went into the boy's mouth. The beetle lay there working its helpless legs, unable to turn over. Tom eyed it, and longed for it; but it was safe out of his reach. Other people uninterested in the sermon found relief in the beetle, and they eyed it too. Presently a vagrant poodle-dog came idling along, sad at heart, lazy with the summer softness and the quiet, weary of captivity, sighing for change. He spied the beetle; the drooping tail lifted and wagged. He surveyed the prize; walked around it; smelled at it from a safe distance; walked around it again; grew bolder, and took a closer smell; then lifted his lip and made a gingerly snatch at it, just missing it; made another, and another; began to enjoy the diversion; subsided to his stomach with the beetle between his paws, and continued his experiments; grew weary at last, and then indifferent and absentminded. His head nodded, and little by little his chin descended and touched the enemy, who seized it. There was a sharp yelp, a flirt of the poodle's head, and the beetle fell a couple of yards away, and lit on its back once more. The neighboring spectators shook with a gentle inward joy, several faces went behind fans and handkerchiefs, and Tom was entirely happy. The dog looked foolish, and probably felt so; but there was resentment in his heart, too, and a craving for revenge. So he went to the beetle and began a wary attack on it again; jumping at it from every point of a circle, lighting with his forepaws within an inch of the creature, making even closer snatches at it with his teeth, and jerking his head till his ears flapped again. But he grew tired once more, after a while; tried to amuse himself with a fly but found no relief; followed an ant around, with his nose close to the floor, and quickly wearied of that; yawned, sighed, forgot the beetle entirely, and sat down on it. Then there was a wild yelp of agony and the poodle went sailing up the aisle; the yelps continued, and so did the dog; he crossed the house in front of the altar; he flew down the other aisle; he crossed before the doors; he clamored up the homestretch; his anguish grew with his progress; till presently he was but a woolly comet moving in its orbit with the gleam and the speed of light. At last the frantic sufferer sheered from its course, and sprang into its master's lap; he flung it out of the window, and the voice of distress quickly thinned away and died in the distance.

By this time the whole church was red-faced and suffocating with suppressed laughter, and the sermon had come to a dead standstill. The discourse was resumed presently, but it went lame and halting, all possibility of impressiveness being at an end; for even the gravest sentiments were constantly being received with a smothered burst of unholy mirth, under cover of some remote pew-back, as if the poor parson had said a rarely facetious thing. It was a genuine relief to the whole congregation when the ordeal was over and the benediction pronounced.

Tom Sawyer went home quite cheerful, thinking to himself that there was some satisfaction about divine service when there was a bit of variety in it. He had but one marring thought; he was willing that the dog should play with his pinch-bug, but he did not think it was upright in him to carry it off.

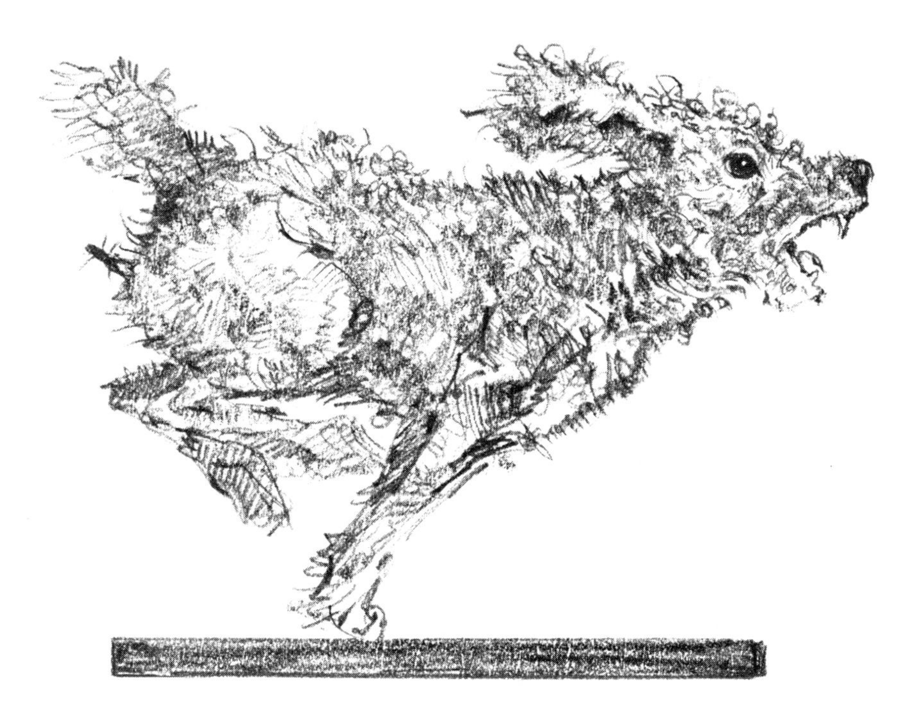

MAXINE W. KUMIN

Snail

No one writes a letter to the snail.
He does not have a mailbox for his mail.
He does not have a bathtub or a rug.
There's no one in his house that he can hug.
There isn't any room when he's inside.

And yet they say the snail is satisfied.

ROSEMARY SUTCLIFF

When I was young it was hard for me to realize that countries, nations, races were also young at some time or other, that they began just as I did and grew older just as I did. Then I began to read about the past and had a curious feeling—I still have it—that the more I knew about the history of the human race, the larger I felt *myself* to be.

A good, easy way to feel the past is by reading historical novels and stories. Rosemary Sutcliff has written many fine novels about the youth of our own mother country, Britain. About two thousand years ago the ancient Romans conquered Britain and ruled it for about five hundred years. Here is a story drawn from those early times of Britain's morning years. Perhaps it will lead you on to her many novels that make the past present.

The Fugitives

THE SHADOWS were lengthening across the terrace, but the thick beech hedge that divided it from the next garden made a sheltered corner, and Lucian, sitting on the broad stone bench that followed the curve of the hedge, did not really need the striped native blanket round his legs. But he knew that if he threw it off, Marcipor, his father's body-slave, who had carried him out there, would fuss like an old woman.

He leaned sideways, frowning in concentration at the lump of clay on the broad raised bench-end—Marcipor had begged it for him from his friend who worked for a potter by the East Gate—which he was trying to work up into the likeness of a sleeping hound. The trouble was that he couldn't remember quite how a hound's muzzle went when it was flattened by resting across the paws. He must notice, next time he saw Syrius lying beside Father's feet in the evening.

The little spring wind blowing across the cantonment brought the thin silver crowing of trumpets from the fort; brought, too, the sound of boys' voices and the barking of a dog. The Senior Centurion's house was the last in the cantonment, and beyond the terrace wall open land dropped gently to the slow silver loop of the river. And looking up from the clay hound, Lucian could see three boys and a half-grown sheepdog pup racing across the hillside, the boys whooping as they ran, the pup circling ahead of them with streaming ears and tail.

Lucian could remember how it felt to run like that. He was twelve now, and he had been seven when the strange sickness came; other children had had it, too, and mostly they had died. Lucian hadn't died, but when the sickness passed, he had not been able to run any more.

The boys and the dog had disappeared now, and he returned to the clay hound. Despite his uncertainty about the muzzle, it seemed to him that it had begun to look like Syrius, and also that there was a liveness about it. Not just cold clay any more but with something of Syrius in it—or maybe something of himself. It was not very long ago that he had discovered that he could make clay do that; and it still surprised him and gave him a rather odd sensation in the pit of his stomach.

A brushing and crashing in the midst of the beech hedge made him look up again, twisting round on the bench, just in time to see a man diving through. A man who half fell, gathered himself again, and stumbled forward a pace or two, then checked, snatching a glance behind him at the torn twigs and scatter of last year's brown leaves that marked the way he had come.

Lucian gave a sharp gasp, and the intruder whipped round, his hand leaping to the dagger at his belt, and their eyes met.

The odd thing was that the boy was not in the least frightened, and after that first startled moment, he simply sat and looked at the man, while the stranger stood and stared back out of strained gray eyes in a very young gray face. Rough hair clung wetly to his sweating forehead, and his breast panted in and out like the flanks of a hunted animal.

Lucian was the first to speak. "What is it? Are you running away from something?—A runaway slave?"

The man swallowed thickly, and steadied his sobbing breath, and for an instant, unlikely as it seemed, there was a flicker of reckless laughter in his face. "You could call it that."

"And they are after you?"

The man nodded.

But Lucian was noticing that the tattered tunic with the brown of last year's leaves clinging to it was the regulation red cloth tunic that the Auxiliaries wore under their leather jerkins. "It's the Eagles you're running away from! You're a deserter!"

"Right second time—and they're hunting the cantonment for me."

Scorn blazed up in Lucian. "I hope they catch you and drag you back!"

"I'm not going back. I've had enough," the deserter said slowly. "I'll die first—and so will you!" He was close to Lucian now, and the point of the dagger just kissed against the boy's throat.

Lucian looked at the hand that held it, and up the arm, and came again to the gray, desperate face. His mouth was dry, and he licked his lower lip.

"Now listen. You haven't seen anybody pass this way."

"I have! And you can't stop me telling as soon as you're gone!"

The deserter said, "Not unless I kill you now, and I don't want to do that if I can help it. But if I am retaken, I'll live long enough to escape once more, and then I shall come and kill you."

"I'll shout!" Lucian said, desperately. "There are people quite near!" And all the while he was listening, listening for the sounds of the hunt.

"They'd need to be very near to come before this blade was in your throat! It is too late for shouting; it's too late to run now, too; the time for running was when I first broke through the hedge."

"I—if you kill me now, they'll crucify you when they do catch you." Lucian heard his own voice not sounding quite like his own. "And if you don't, I shall tell which way you went, and you can talk big, but you won't get your chance to escape again. That's bairn's talk."

For the first time he saw a flicker of uncertainty in the man's eyes and slowly the dagger was withdrawn a thumbnail's breadth from his throat. "If I take this away, will you promise not to bolt?" the man said, in a changed tone.

"Yes." Not for anything in the world would he have admitted that he couldn't.

The dagger was withdrawn and sheathed. The man hesitated still an instant and glanced back again the way he had come, listening for sounds of the hunt. Then he seemed to come to a decision and spoke quickly and urgently. "I've twisted my ankle and I'm just about done, or

I'd not be telling you this, but it seems I've not much choice. And I shan't have time to tell you more than once, so listen . . . I'm carrying secret dispatches for Caesar—so secret and so deadly that to get them past our enemies, I've had to play the deserter. They know nothing of that up at the fort; to them I'm just a deserter like any other, and if they catch up with me—"

He broke off with a small, one-shouldered shrug.

Lucian's heart, which had not quickened much, even with the dagger at his throat, fell over itself and began to pound like a runner's at the end of a race. "If they catch up with you?"

"I can't tell you. It would—be disaster for the whole province. I can't tell you any more."

And at that moment the little wind brought the first rumor of the sounds they had both been listening for: a small smother of sounds that if they had been made by hounds instead of men, would have been a pack giving tongue on a hot scent.

Despite the drubbing of his heart, Lucian's head had started to feel cold and clear, as though it were set far above the level of what was happening around him. "Get under the bench! I'll pull the blanket over the front of it, and if you get close up this end, behind my legs—"

The man looked at him for one instant, as though testing for a trap, and then in another way, as though he were puzzled, maybe, by the blanket and the way the boy had never attempted to get up or dive clear. Then he nodded, and without a word dropped on hands and knees and was gone under cover.

Lucian dragged the rug from his legs in frantic haste, and flung the free half of it out along the bench so that it trailed down in front and made a small dark hiding-place for the desperate man he could feel crouching there. Then he began with great care and concentration to do something—he never knew what—about the way the hound's muzzle was pressed up by the paws.

Everything had happened at racing speed, and now there was a sudden blankness of nothing happening at all, and all the while he was terrified that Syrius, who was in the kitchen hoping for a bone, would come trotting down the garden and smell the stranger under the bench, or that Marcipor would come and fetch him in.

And then the search party was in the very next garden, and the old garden-slave was scolding like an angry hen because somebody's great feet were in his herb patch. Someone only a few feet away called, "Sir! Here's a broken place in the hedge; he's gone this way!" and there was a sharp exclamation and footsteps on gravel, and then:

"No, not through the hedge, too, you fool! It's the Pilus Prior's garden. Over the wall at the bottom," and the half-running tramp of feet going down beyond the hedge.

Lucian caught a deep breath, and looked up from the little clay figure as half a dozen Legionaries led by a young Centurion came scrambling over the terrace wall.

The Centurion saw the boy on the bench and called out to him almost before both feet were on the terrace: "There's been a man through here. Which way did he go?"

"What man? There hasn't been any man." Lucian's voice wobbled a little and the Centurion, a cheerful-looking, freckled individual, came over to him while his men scattered at once to search the garden.

"Then why are you looking as though you'd seen a ghost?" he asked.

Lucian managed a grin. "Six—no, seven ghosts. You and your lot made me jump. I didn't hear you coming."

"Fair enough. Look now, we're hunting a deserter, and we know he came this way. Where did he go?"

"No one has been through the garden while I've been out here."

"How long is that?"

"An hour or more."

"And no one passed?"

"I told you!"

The Centurion jerked his chin towards the broken place in the hedge.

"Who made that, then?"

"That?" Lucian gazed blankly in the direction indicated.

"Gap in the hedge."

"Oh that! Syrius our dog made it. They throw out their meat bones because it's good for the roses, and he's always breaking through."

The Centurion eyed him consideringly, and was silent a moment.

"Don't you believe me?" Lucian said, as haughtily as he could manage. "My father is Lucius Lycinius, the Pilus Prior of the Legion! Do you d-dare to think I'd go hiding a deserter?"

The Centurion threw back his head with a crack of laughter. "Roma Dea! I'd know you for the Old Man's son anywhere, when you put on that tone—even if I hadn't known this was his garden. . . . But we're searching all this quarter till we find him. He twisted an ankle dropping over the bathhouse wall, and he was going as lame as a duck when we lost him. He can't have—got—far."

His voice trailed off awkwardly, and Lucian realized that the friendly freckle-faced young Centurion knew about him, had probably known all along, and was wishing that he hadn't said that about being lame as a duck and not getting far.

He had always hated strangers knowing about him not being able to walk. He hated it now. He felt shamed and a little sick and in the usual way of things he would have glared at the young Centurion to show how much he didn't care; but this time it didn't matter whether he cared or not; all that mattered was to keep them from discovering the man under the bench. And if he could hold the Centurion here standing right against the bench while his men finished their search, they would be less likely to go peering under it.

"Perhaps he's managed to hide in one of the market carts," he suggested.

"The carts are being checked. Any sign, Rufrius?"

"Not yet, sir." The shout came back, slightly muffled from among tangled rose and elder bushes that shut off all view of the house.

"Push on farther up that way."

Lucian searched desperately for something else to say, and found it. "Why did he desert?"

The Centurion shrugged. "There are always a few deserters among the Auxiliaries at this time of year. Maybe the homesickness catches them more sharply in the springtime. Poor stupid devils. Even if he's not caught, there's not much life for a deserter; you can't spend all your life running away."

Lucian gave a little shiver, and covered it by saying, "It gets cold still, once the sun is behind the hills."

The Centurion nodded. "Hadn't you better have that blanket round you?"

"No!" said Lucian quickly, and then, "It makes my legs stronger to have the air all round them."

"Ah well, that's the way then," the Centurion said bracingly. "You get them good and strong, and we'll have you in the Legion yet." His eyes were with his men among the bushes; he hitched at his sword-belt; in another instant he would have gone to join them.

And then Lucian heard the sound that he had been dreading. Syrius had winded strangers and was baying his head off in the kitchen quarters; the baying loudened and changed tempo as a door was opened and he could hear Marcipor cursing. Another moment and the great hound would come flying down from the house. He knew Legionaries and would not bother much about them once he saw what they were, but a man with the hunted smell on him, hiding under the bench. . . .

One blunt stab of hopelessness shot through Lucian. The affair was out of his hands now; only the gods could hold back the terrible thing from happening. In desperation, with no time to think, he did the one thing that was left. He made a sacrifice to the gods. It was an odd sacrifice, but strong, for it meant giving up old dreams that he had not known until that instant he was still clinging on to; it meant doing the hardest and bravest thing he had ever done in his life. He caught the young Centurion's eye in the instant before he turned away, and managed a grin. "Tell that to the wild geese! My head works well enough, it's only my legs that don't and I've got sense enough to know there's not much room for you in the Legion if you can't walk."

Syrius and Marcipor appeared where the path curved through the bushes, the slave clinging to the bronze-studded collar of the huge hound who dragged forward, snarling, his hackles raised in a great comb along his back.

Marcipor checked as the Centurion went striding to meet him, and inquired in the coolly respectful tone that could be more blighting than the Pilus Prior's when he chose, whether it was by his Master's orders that half the Legion was in his garden.

Lucian could not hear properly what passed after that, for the two men spoke together quietly, and they were a little way off. But Syrius had stopped snarling, and he saw Marcipor let go the hound's collar and give him an open-palmed slap on the rump to send him back to the house.

Syrius hesitated an instant, looking back, and Lucian, his mouth dry and the palms of his hands sweating, did not dare to look at him direct, lest that should bring him over. Then out of the corner of his eye he saw the hound look away, his ears suddenly pricked, and knew that in the nick of time his father had turned the corner of the street. Syrius always heard him as he turned that corner, every evening. An instant later the hound gave a pleased bark, and went bounding back towards the house.

Relief broke over Lucian in a wave, and he scarcely knew what was happening in the next few moments, until suddenly the search was over, and the Legionaries were going. The Centurion checked beside him in passing, and said, "My legs are all right, but maybe my head's not so good. I'm sorry we'll not be having you in the Legion."

Then they were gone, but almost before Lucian could draw breath the next danger was there to be faced, as Marcipor came along the terrace, saying, "Time you were indoors."

"No!" Lucian said. "Not just yet, Marcipor. It feels so good out here after being shut in all the winter." Then, as the big gray-haired slave hesitated, "Listen—there's Father calling for you."

"I didn't hear him."

"I'm sure I did. Please, Marcipor!"

"Very well, if you have the blanket round you again. Just while I get the Commander out of his harness and see to his bath."

Lucian hardly knew how to bear it as the slave, still fussing, pulled the blanket back into place and tucked it in. He only had to stoop just a little lower, he only had to look back once as he went up towards the house. . . .

But neither of these things happened and in a little while, when the last sounds of the hunt had died away, the man who carried Caesar's dispatches was crouching with his shoulders propped against the bench, rubbing his swollen ankle to ease the stiffness, and pulling in slow gasps of air as though he had been half stifled in his hiding-place. "That was valiantly done. Do you know, I was wondering, when I crawled under that bench, whether I was crawling into a trap," he said at last.

"But you had told me about the secret dispatches."

"Och yes—the dispatches for Caesar." The man looked up with a a wry flicker of something that might have been laughter.

"You must go," Lucian said. "You can hide among the rough stuff under the terrace until full dusk, and then make for the river woods. Marcipor will be out soon to carry me back to the house." He never noticed that he did not mind this man whom he had hidden from the search party knowing about him.

The man had got up, wincing as his ankle took the strain. "Like our good friend the Centurion, I'm sorry the Legion will be having to do without you," he said. "Maybe it's the Legion's loss."

"Oh, I don't suppose I'd have made much of a soldier anyway—not like my father."

"I—wonder." The young man put out a forefinger and touched the little clay hound. "One thing I will tell you: maybe you would not have made as good a soldier as your father, but I am very sure your father could not make a lump of potter's clay breathe warm and heavy like a sleeping hound."

He turned towards the low terrace wall, swung a leg over, and dropped from sight.

Lucian heard the grunt of pain, as he landed, and sat looking at the place where he had been, suddenly very tired. He picked up the little hound, but the clay was getting dry. He couldn't work it much more, and he thought he knew now what was wrong with the muzzle. He would keep it, all the same; it was part of something very important. But as soon as he could get some more clay he would make another hound, or maybe something else. And he knew that it would be better than this one.

Somehow he did not think much about Caesar's dispatches. It wasn't until years later that he understood that he had never quite believed that story, and it was simply because the man was being hunted, that he had hidden him.

The deserter crouched among the docks and hazel-scrub under the terrace wall, waiting for the light to go.

He had stuck two years of the Auxiliaries—two years out of twenty-five—and for most of them he had not even been able to remember what had made him join; unless it was simply that the chieftain his grandfather had been so determined that he should head the young men of their valley when they went down to join the draft. Two years of the rigid discipline, the bullying of the Decurion, the loss of freedom, and today, quite suddenly, it had all been more than he could bear. So he had gone out over the bath-house wall.

If he had not twisted his ankle, he'd have been well into the woods, by now. But what was it the Centurion had said?—"You can't spend all your life running away." The boy had been running away too, in his own fashion, but then he had stopped. Sweating in the dark under the bench, the deserter had known when the boy stopped running away.

Below him the river woods were blurring into the twilight.

Probably it would not be death, if he gave himself up of his own accord. It would be flogging; it would be cells and bread-and-water and shame; and when all that was over, the cage of discipline and the bullying Decurion, just as before. But maybe one could make some kind of a fresh start?

He felt in an odd way that he had company on his road, when he got up, stumbling on his wrenched ankle, and turned back towards the fort.

JOHN KIERAN

There's This That I Like about Hockey, My Lad

There's this that I like about hockey, my lad;
  It's a clattering, battering sport.
As a popular pastime it isn't half bad
  For chaps of the sturdier sort.
You step on the gas and you let in the clutch;
You start on a skate and come back on a crutch;
Your chance of surviving is really not much;
  It's something like storming a fort.

There's this that I like about hockey, my boy;
  There's nothing about it that's tame.
The whistle is blown and the players deploy;
  They start in to maul and to maim.
There's a dash at the goal and a crash on the ice;
The left wing goes down when you've swatted him twice;
And your teeth by a stick are removed in a trice;
  It's really a rollicking game.

There's this that I like about hockey, old chap;
  I think you'll agree that I'm right,
Although you may get an occasional rap,
  There's always good fun in the fight.
So toss in the puck, for the players are set,
Sing ho! for the dash on the enemy net;
And ho! for the smash as the challenge is met;
  And hey! for a glorious night!

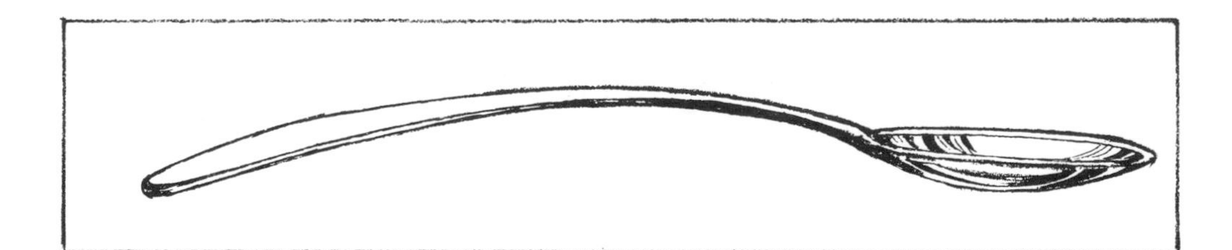

ISAAC BASHEVIS SINGER

Shrewd Todie and Lyzer the Miser

Translated by the author and Elizabeth Shub

IN A VILLAGE somewhere in the Ukraine there lived a poor man called Todie. Todie had a wife, Shaindel, and seven children, but he could never earn enough to feed them properly. He tried many trades and failed in all of them. It was said of Todie that if he decided to deal in candles the sun would never set. He was nicknamed Shrewd Todie because whenever he managed to make some money, it was always by trickery.

This winter was an especially cold one. The snowfall was heavy and Todie had no money to buy wood for the stove. His seven children stayed in bed all day to keep warm. When the frost burns outside, hunger is stronger than ever, but Shaindel's larder was empty. She reproached Todie bitterly, wailing, "If you can't feed your wife and children, I will go to the rabbi and get a divorce."

"And what will you do with it, eat it?" Todie retorted.

In the same village there lived a rich man called Lyzer. Because of his stinginess he was known as Lyzer the Miser. He permitted his wife to bake bread only once in four weeks because he had discovered that fresh bread is eaten up more quickly than stale.

Todie had more than once gone to Lyzer for a loan of a few gulden, but Lyzer had always replied: "I sleep better when the money lies in my strongbox rather than in your pocket."

Lyzer had a goat, but he never fed her. The goat had learned to visit the houses of the neighbors, who pitied her and gave her potato peelings. Sometimes, when there were not enough peelings, she would gnaw on the old straw of the thatched roofs. She also had a liking for tree bark. Nevertheless, each year the goat gave birth to a kid. Lyzer milked her but, miser that he was, did not drink the milk himself. Instead he sold it to others.

Todie decided that he would take revenge on Lyzer and at the same time make some much-needed money for himself.

One day, as Lyzer was sitting on a box eating borscht and dry bread (he used his chairs only on holidays so that the upholstery would not wear out), the door opened and Todie came in.

"Reb Lyzer," he said, "I would like to ask you a favor. My oldest daughter, Basha, is already fifteen and she's about to become engaged. A young man is coming from Janev to look her over. My cutlery is tin, and my wife is ashamed to ask the young man to eat soup with a tin spoon. Would you lend me one of your silver spoons? I give you my holy word that I will return it to you tomorrow."

Lyzer knew that Todie would not dare to break a holy oath and he lent him the spoon.

No young man came to see Basha that evening. As usual, the girl walked around barefoot and in rags, and the silver spoon lay hidden under Todie's shirt. In the early years of his marriage Todie had possessed a set of silver tableware himself. He had, however, long since sold it all, with the exception of three silver teaspoons that were used only on Passover.

The following day, as Lyzer, his feet bare (in order to save his shoes), sat on his box eating borscht and dry bread, Todie returned.

"Here is the spoon I borrowed yesterday," he said, placing it on the table together with one of his own teaspoons.

"What is the teaspoon for?" Lyzer asked.

And Todie said: "Your tablespoon gave birth to a teaspoon. It is her child. Since I am an honest man, I'm returning both mother and child to you."

Lyzer looked at Todie in astonishment. He had never heard of a silver spoon giving birth to another. Nevertheless, his greed overcame his doubt and he happily accepted both spoons. Such an unexpected piece of good fortune! He was overjoyed that he had lent Todie the spoon.

A few days later, as Lyzer (without his coat, to save it) was again sitting on his box eating borscht with dry bread, the door opened and Todie appeared.

"The young man from Janev did not please Basha because he had donkey ears, but this evening another young man is coming to look her over. Shaindel is cooking soup for him, but she's ashamed to serve him with a tin spoon. Would you lend me . . ."

Even before Todie could finish the sentence, Lyzer interrupted. "You want to borrow a silver spoon? Take it with pleasure."

The following day Todie once more returned the spoon and with it one of his own silver teaspoons. He again explained that during the night the large spoon had given birth to a small one and in all good conscience he was bringing back the mother and newborn baby. As for the young man who had come to look Basha over, she hadn't liked him either, because his nose was so long that it reached to his chin. Needless to say that Lyzer the Miser was overjoyed.

Exactly the same thing happened a third time. Todie related that this time his daughter had rejected her suitor because he stammered. He also reported that Lyzer's silver spoon had again given birth to a baby spoon.

"Does it ever happen that a spoon has twins?" Lyzer inquired.

Todie thought it over for a moment. "Why not? I've even heard of a case where a spoon had triplets."

Almost a week passed by and Todie did not go to see Lyzer. But on Friday morning, as Lyzer (in his underdrawers to save his pants) sat on his box eating borscht and dry bread, Todie came in and said, "Good day to you, Reb Lyzer."

"A good morning and many more to you," Lyzer replied in his friendliest manner. "What good fortune brings you here? Did you perhaps come to borrow a silver spoon? If so, help yourself."

"Today I have a very special favor to ask. This evening a young man from the big city of Lublin is coming to look Basha over. He is the son of a rich man and I'm told he is clever and handsome as well. Not only do I need a silver spoon, but since he will remain with us over the Sabbath I need a pair of silver candlesticks, because mine are brass and my wife is ashamed to place them on the Sabbath table. Would you lend me your candlesticks? Immediately after the Sabbath, I will return them to you."

Silver candlesticks are of great value and Lyzer the Miser hesitated, but only for a moment.

Remembering his good fortune with the spoons, he said: "I have eight silver candlesticks in my house. Take them all. I know you will return them to me just as you say. And if it should happen that any of them give birth, I have no doubt that you will be as honest as you have been in the past."

"Certainly," Todie said. "Let's hope for the best."

The silver spoon, Todie hid beneath his shirt as usual. But taking the candlesticks, he went directly to a merchant, sold them for a considerable sum, and brought the money to Shaindel. When Shaindel saw so much money, she demanded to know where he had gotten such a treasure.

"When I went out, a cow flew over our roof and dropped a dozen silver eggs," Todie replied. "I sold them and here is the money."

"I have never heard of a cow flying over a roof and laying silver eggs," Shaindel said doubtingly.

"There is always a first time," Todie answered. "If you don't want the money, give it back to me."

"There'll be no talk about giving it back," Shaindel said. She knew that her husband was full of cunning and tricks—but when the children are hungry and the larder is empty, it is better not to ask too many questions. Shaindel went to the marketplace and bought meat, fish, white flour, and even some nuts and raisins for a pudding. And since a lot of money still remained, she bought shoes and clothes for the children.

It was a very gay Sabbath in Todie's house. The boys sang and the girls danced. When the children asked their father where he had gotten the money, he replied: "It is forbidden to mention money during the Sabbath."

Sunday, as Lyzer (barefoot and almost naked to save his clothes) sat on his box finishing up a dry crust of bread with borscht, Todie arrived and, handing him his silver spoon, said: "It's too bad. This time your spoon did not give birth to a baby."

"What about the candlesticks?" Lyzer inquired anxiously.

Todie sighed deeply. "The candlesticks died."

Lyzer got up from his box so hastily that he overturned his plate of borscht.

"You fool! How can candlesticks die?" he screamed.

"If spoons can give birth, candlesticks can die."

Lyzer raised a great hue and cry and had Todie called before the rabbi. When the rabbi heard both sides of the story, he burst out laughing. "It serves you right," he said to Lyzer. "If you hadn't chosen to believe that spoons give birth, now you would not be forced to believe that your candlesticks died."

"But it's all nonsense," Lyzer objected.

"Did you not expect the candlesticks to give birth to other candlesticks?" the rabbi said admonishingly. "If you accept nonsense when it brings you profit, you must also accept nonsense when it brings you loss." And he dismissed the case.

The following day, when Lyzer the Miser's wife brought him his borscht and dry bread, Lyzer said to her, "I will eat only the bread. Borscht is too expensive a food, even without sour cream."

The story of the silver spoons that gave birth and the candlesticks that died spread quickly through the town. All the people enjoyed Todie's victory and Lyzer the Miser's defeat. The shoemaker's and tailor's apprentices, as was their custom whenever there was an important happening, made up a song about it:

Lyzer, put your grief aside.
What if your candlesticks have died?
You're the richest man on earth
With silver spoons that can give birth
And silver eggs as living proof
Of flying cows above your roof.
Don't sit there eating crusts of bread—
To silver grandsons look ahead.

However, time passed and Lyzer's silver spoons never gave birth again.

JOHN KEATS

There Was a Naughty Boy

There was a naughty boy,
  A naughty boy was he,
He would not stop at home,
  He could not quiet be—
    He took
    In his knapsack
    A book
    Full of vowels
    And a shirt
    With some towels,
    A slight cap
    For night cap,
    A hair brush,
    Comb ditto,
    New stockings—
    For old ones
    Would split O!
    This knapsack
    Tight at's back
    He riveted close
  And followed his nose

To the North,
To the North,
And followed his nose
To the North.

There was a naughty boy,
And a naughty boy was he,
He ran away to Scotland
The people for to see—
There he found
That the ground
Was as hard,
That a yard
Was as long,
That a song
Was as merry,
That a cherry
Was as red—
That lead
Was as weighty
That fourscore
Was as eighty,
That a door
Was as wooden
As in England—
So he stood in his shoes
And he wondered,
He wondered,
He stood in his shoes
And he wondered.

J. R. R. TOLKIEN

What is a Hobbit? Hobbits are beings between three and four feet tall who inhabit an imaginary region called the Shire. They live in cozy, nicely furnished, roomy holes and are fond of food, tobacco, comfort, presents, and parties. They are not terribly fond of hardship or adventure, but one of them, Bilbo Baggins by name, found himself undergoing both. His story is told in Professor Tolkien's *Hobbit* and also, in greater detail, in his three-volume epic fantasy, *The Lord of the Rings*, which has sold over three million copies in nine languages.

The selection below is from the fifth chapter of *The Hobbit*, which grew out of stories Professor Tolkien originally told his children.

Bilbo, the Wizard Gandalf, and thirteen dwarfs set forth on a quest for the treasure guarded in his cave by Smaug the Dragon. Bilbo has just escaped from a band of evil goblins and finds himself in an underground tunnel. On the floor of the tunnel his groping hand picks up a tiny metal ring—and this is going to prove important, as you will see. He makes his way in darkness, holding his little magic sword before him, till he comes to a subterranean lake. And here he meets Gollum, the most interesting and certainly the most evil character in the whole book. I'm sorry I've had to end the extract below just at a moment of high suspense, but you can find *The Hobbit* in the library or buy it cheaply, in paperback, and then you can discover how Bilbo made out in his quest for the treasure, how he faced wolves and giant spiders and evil orcs, and finally the terrible dragon Smaug. It's a great story.

Well, here's how he meets Gollum.

The Hobbit

FROM CHAPTER FIVE

DEEP DOWN HERE by the dark water lived old Gollum, a small slimy creature. I don't know where he came from, nor who or what he was. He was Gollum—as dark as darkness, except for two big round pale eyes in his thin face. He had a little boat, and he rowed about quite quietly on the lake; for lake it was, wide and deep and deadly cold. He paddled it with large feet dangling over the side, but never a ripple did he make. Not he. He was looking out of his pale lamplike eyes for blind fish, which he grabbed with his long fingers as quick as thinking. He liked meat too. Goblin he thought good, when he could get it; but he took care they never found him out. He just throttled them from behind, if they ever came down alone anywhere near the edge of the water, while he was prowling about. They very seldom did, for they had a feeling that something unpleasant was lurking down there, down at the very roots of the mountain. They had come on the lake, when they were tunneling down long ago, and they found they could go no further; so there their road ended in that direction, and there was no reason to go that way—unless the Great Goblin sent them. Sometimes he took a fancy for fish from the lake, and sometimes neither goblin nor fish came back.

Actually Gollum lived on a slimy island of rock in the middle of the lake. He was watching Bilbo now from the distance with his pale eyes like telescopes. Bilbo could not see him, but he was wondering a lot about Bilbo, for he could see that he was no goblin at all.

Gollum got into his boat and shot off from the island, while Bilbo was sitting on the brink altogether flummoxed and at the end of his way and his wits. Suddenly up came Gollum and whispered and hissed:

"Bless us and splash us, my preciousssss! I guess it's a choice feast; at least a tasty morsel it'd make us, gollum!" And when he said *gollum* he made a horrible swallowing noise in his throat. That is how he got his name, though he always called himself "my precious."

The hobbit jumped nearly out of his skin when the hiss came in his ears, and he suddenly saw the pale eyes sticking out at him.

"Who are you?" he said, thrusting his dagger in front of him.

"What iss he, my preciouss?" whispered Gollum (who always spoke to himself through never having anyone else to speak to). This is what he had come to find out, for he was not really very hungry at the moment, only curious; otherwise he would have grabbed first and whispered afterwards.

"I am Mr. Bilbo Baggins. I have lost the dwarves and I have lost the wizard, and I don't know where I am; and I don't want to know, if only I can get away."

"What's he got in his handses?" said Gollum, looking at the sword, which he did not quite like.

"A sword, a blade which came out of Gondolin!"

"Sssss," said Gollum, and became quite polite. "Praps ye sits here and chats with it a bitsy, my preciousss. It like riddles, praps it does, does it?" He was anxious to appear friendly, at any rate for the moment, and until he found out more about the sword and the hobbit, whether he was quite alone really, whether he was good to eat, and whether Gollum was really hungry. Riddles were all he could think of. Asking them, and sometimes guessing them, had been the only game he had ever played with other funny creatures sitting in their holes in the long, long ago, before he lost all his friends and was driven away, alone, and crept down, down, into the dark under the mountains.

"Very well," said Bilbo, who was anxious to agree, until he found out more about the creature, whether he was quite alone, whether he was fierce or hungry, and whether he was a friend of the goblins.

"You ask first," he said, because he had not had time to think of a riddle.

So Gollum hissed:

What has roots as nobody sees,
Is taller than trees,
Up, up it goes,
And yet never grows?

"Easy!" said Bilbo. "Mountain, I suppose."

"Does it guess easy? It must have a competition with us, my preciouss! If precious asks, and it doesn't answer, we eats it, my preciousss. If it asks us, and we don't answer, then we does what it wants, eh? We show it the way out, yes!"

"All right!" said Bilbo, not daring to disagree, and nearly bursting his brain to think of riddles that could save him from being eaten.

Thirty white horses on a red hill,
First they champ,
Then they stamp,
Then they stand still.

That was all he could think of to ask—the idea of eating was rather on his mind. It was rather an old one, too, and Gollum knew the answer as well as you do.

"Chestnuts, chestnuts," he hissed. "Teeth! teeth! my preciousss; but we has only six!" [Bilbo and Gollum ask and answer a few more riddles. By sheer accident Bilbo guesses a very tough one that Gollum propounds.]

Gollum was disappointed once more; and now he was getting angry, and also tired of the game. It had made him very hungry indeed. This time he did not go back to the boat. He sat down in the dark by Bilbo. That made the hobbit most dreadfully uncomfortable and scattered his wits.

"It's got to ask uss a quesstion, my preciouss, yes, yess, yesss. Jusst one more quesstion to guess, yes, yess," said Gollum.

But Bilbo simply could not think of any question with that nasty wet cold thing sitting next to him, and pawing and poking him. He scratched himself, he pinched himself; still he could not think of anything.

"Ask us! ask us!" said Gollum.

Bilbo pinched himself and slapped himself; he gripped on his little sword; he even felt in his pocket with his other hand. There he found the ring he had picked up in the passage and forgotten about.

"What have I got in my pocket?" he said aloud. He was talking to himself, but Gollum thought it was a riddle, and he was frightfully upset.

"Not fair! not fair!" he hissed. "It isn't fair, my precious, is it, to ask us what it's got in its nassty little pocketses?"

Bilbo, seeing what had happened and having nothing better to ask, stuck to his question. "What have I got in my pocket?" he said louder.

"S-s-s-s-s," hissed Gollum. "It must give us three guesseses, my preciouss, three guesseses."

"Very well! Guess away!" said Bilbo.

"Handses!" said Gollum.

"Wrong," said Bilbo, who had luckily just taken his hand out again. "Guess again!"

"S-s-s-s-s," said Gollum more upset than ever. He thought of all the things he kept in his own pockets: fishbones, goblins' teeth, wet shells, a bit of bat-wing, a sharp stone to sharpen his fangs on, and other nasty things. He tried to think what other people kept in their pockets.

"Knife!" he said at last.

"Wrong!" said Bilbo, who had lost his some time ago. "Last guess!"

Now Gollum was in a much worse state than when Bilbo had asked him the egg question. He hissed and spluttered and rocked himself backwards and forwards, and slapped his feet on the floor, and wriggled and squirmed; but still he did not dare to waste his last guess.

"Come on!" said Bilbo. "I am waiting!" He tried to sound bold and cheerful, but he did not feel at all sure how the game was going to end, whether Gollum guessed right or not.

"Time's up!" he said.

"String, or nothing!" shrieked Gollum, which was not quite fair—working in two guesses at once.

"Both wrong," cried Bilbo, very much relieved; and he jumped at once to his feet, put his back to the nearest wall, and held out his little sword. He knew, of course, that the riddle game was sacred and of immense antiquity, and even wicked creatures were afraid to cheat when they played at it. But he felt he could not trust this slimy thing to keep any promise at a pinch. Any excuse would do for him to slide out of it. And after all that last question had not been a genuine riddle according to the ancient laws.

But at any rate Gollum did not at once attack him. He could see the sword in Bilbo's hand. He sat still, shivering and whispering. At last Bilbo could wait no longer.

"Well?" he said. "What about your promise? I want to go. You must show me the way."

"Did we say so, precious? Show the nassty little Baggins the way out, yes, yes. But what has it got in its pocketses, eh? Not string, precious, but not nothing. Oh no! gollum!"

"Never you mind," said Bilbo. "A promise is a promise."

"Cross it is, impatient, precious," hissed Gollum. "But it must wait, yes it must. We can't go up the tunnels so hasty. We must go and get some things first, yes, things to help us."

"Well, hurry up!" said Bilbo, relieved to think of Gollum going away.

He thought he was just making an excuse and did not mean to come back. What was Gollum talking about? What useful thing could he keep out on the dark lake? But he was wrong. Gollum did mean to come back. He was angry now and hungry. And he was a miserable wicked creature, and already he had a plan.

Not far away was his island, of which Bilbo knew nothing, and there in his hiding place he kept a few wretched oddments, and one very beautiful thing, very beautiful, very wonderful. He had a ring, a golden ring, a precious ring.

"My birthday present!" he whispered to himself, as he had often done in the endless dark days. "That's what we wants now, yes; we wants it!"

He wanted it because it was a ring of power, and if you slipped that ring on your finger, you were invisible; only in the full sunlight could you be seen, and then only by your shadow, and that would be shaky and faint.

"My birthday present! It came to me on my birthday, my precious." So he had always said to himself. But who knows how Gollum came by that present, ages ago in the old days when such rings were still at large in the world? Perhaps even the Master who ruled them could not have said. Gollum used to wear it at first, till it tired him; and then he kept it in a pouch next his skin, till it galled him; and now usually he hid it in a hole in the rock on his island, and was always going back to look at it. And still sometimes he put it on, when he could not bear to be parted from it any longer, or when he was very, very, hungry, and tired of fish. Then he would creep along dark passages looking for stray goblins. He might even venture into places where the torches were lit and made his eyes blink and smart; for he would be safe. Oh yes, quite safe. No one would see him, no one would notice him, till he had his fingers on their throat. Only a few hours ago he had worn it, and caught a small goblin-imp. How it squeaked! He still had a bone or two left to gnaw, but he wanted something softer.

"Quite safe, yes," he whispered to himself. "It won't see us, will it, my precious? No. It won't see us, and its nassty little sword will be useless, yes quite."

That is what was in his wicked little mind, as he slipped suddenly from Bilbo's side, and flapped back to his boat, and went off into the dark. Bilbo thought he had heard the last of him. Still he waited a while; for he had no idea how to find his way out alone.

Suddenly he heard a screech. It sent a shiver down his back. Gollum was cursing and wailing away in the gloom, not very far off by the sound of it. He was on his island, scrabbling here and there, searching and seeking in vain.

"Where is it? Where iss it?" Bilbo heard him crying. "Losst it is, my precious, lost, lost! Curse us and crush us, my precious is lost!"

"What's the matter?" Bilbo called. "What have you lost?"

"It mustn't ask us," shrieked Gollum. "Not its business, no, gollum! It's losst, gollum, gollum, gollum."

"Well, so am I," cried Bilbo, "and I want to get unlost. And I won the game, and you promised. So come along! Come and let me out, and then go on with your looking!" Utterly miserable as Gollum sounded, Bilbo could not find much pity in his heart, and he had a feeling that anything Gollum wanted so much could hardly be something good. "Come along!" he shouted.

"No, not yet, precious!" Gollum answered. "We must search for it, it's lost, gollum."

"But you never guessed my last question, and you promised," said Bilbo.

"Never guessed!" said Gollum. Then suddenly out of the gloom came a sharp hiss. "What has it got in its pocketses? Tell us that. It must tell first."

As far as Bilbo knew, there was no particular reason why he should not tell. Gollum's mind had jumped to a guess quicker than his; naturally, for Gollum had brooded for ages on this one thing, and he was always afraid of its being stolen. But Bilbo was annoyed at the delay. After all, he had won the game, pretty fairly, at a horrible risk. "Answers were to be guessed not given," he said.

"But it wasn't a fair question," said Gollum. "Not a riddle, precious, no."

"Oh well, if it's a matter of ordinary questions," Bilbo replied, "then I asked one first. What have you lost? Tell me that!"

"What has it got in its pocketses?" The sound came hissing louder and sharper, and as he looked towards it, to his alarm Bilbo now saw two small points of light peering at him. As suspicion grew in Gollum's mind, the light of his eyes burned with a pale flame.

"What have you lost?" Bilbo persisted.

But now the light in Gollum's eyes had become a green fire, and it was coming swiftly nearer. Gollum was in his boat again, paddling wildly back to the dark shore; and such a rage of loss and suspicion was in his heart that no sword had any more terror for him.

Bilbo could not guess what had maddened the wretched creature, but he saw that all was up, and that Gollum meant to murder him at any rate. Just in time he turned and ran blindly back up the dark passage down which he had come, keeping close to the wall and feeling it with his left hand.

"What has it got in its pocketses?" he heard the hiss loud behind him, and the splash as Gollum leapt from his boat. "What have I, I wonder?" he said to himself, as he panted and stumbled along. He put his left hand in his pocket. The ring felt very cold as it quietly slipped on to his groping forefinger.

The hiss was close behind him. He turned now and saw Gollum's eyes like small green lamps coming up the slope. Terrified, he tried to run faster, but suddenly he struck his toes on a snag in the floor, and fell flat with his little sword under him.

In a moment Gollum was on him. But before Bilbo could do anything, recover his breath, pick himself up, or wave his sword, Gollum passed by, taking no notice of him, cursing and whispering as he ran.

What could it mean? Gollum could see in the dark. Bilbo could see the light of his eyes palely shining even from behind. Painfully he got up, and sheathed his sword, which was now glowing faintly again, then very cautiously he followed. There seemed nothing else to do. It was no good crawling back down to Gollum's water. Perhaps if he followed him, Gollum might lead him to some way of escape without meaning to.

"Curse it! curse it! curse it!" hissed Gollum. "Curse the Baggins! It's gone! What has it got in its pocketses? Oh we guess, we guess, my precious. He's found it, yes he must have. My birthday present."

There are many verses by Tolkien scattered through *The Hobbit* and *The Lord of the Rings*. The one that follows seems to me the most successful.

Cat

The fat cat on the mat
  may seem to dream
of nice mice that suffice
  for him, or cream;
but he free, maybe,
  walks in thought
unbowed, proud, where loud
  roared and fought
his kin, lean and slim,
  or deep in den
in the East feasted on beasts
  and tender men.

The giant lion with iron
  claw in paw,
and huge ruthless tooth
  in gory jaw;
the pard dark-starred,
  fleet upon feet,
that oft soft from aloft
  leaps on his meat
where woods loom in gloom—
  far now they be,
  fierce and free,
  and tamed is he;
but fat cat on the mat
  kept as a pet,
  he does not forget.

ROBERT McCLOSKEY

The Doughnuts

ONE FRIDAY night in November Homer overheard his mother talking on the telephone to Aunt Agnes over in Centerburg. "I'll stop by with the car in about half an hour and we can go to the meeting together," she said, because tonight was the night the Ladies' Club was meeting to discuss plans for a box social and to knit and sew for the Red Cross.

"I think I'll come along and keep Uncle Ulysses company while you and Aunt Agnes are at the meeting," said Homer.

So after Homer had combed his hair and his mother had looked to see if she had her knitting instructions and the right size needles, they started for town.

Homer's Uncle Ulysses and Aunt Agnes have a very up and coming lunchroom over in Centerburg, just across from the courthouse on the town square. Uncle Ulysses is a man with advanced ideas and a weakness for labor-saving devices. He equipped the lunchroom with automatic toasters, automatic coffee maker, automatic dishwasher, and an automatic doughnut maker. All just the latest thing in labor-saving devices. Aunt Agnes would throw up her hands and sigh every time Uncle Ulysses bought a new labor-saving device. Sometimes she became unkindly disposed toward him for days and days. She was of the opinion that Uncle Ulysses just frittered away his spare time over at the barbershop with the sheriff and the boys, so, what was the good of a labor-saving device that gave you more time to fritter?

When Homer and his mother got to Centerburg they stopped at the lunchroom, and after Aunt Agnes had come out and said, "My, how that boy does grow!" which was what she always said, she went off with Homer's mother in the car. Homer went into the lunchroom and said, "Howdy, Uncle Ulysses!"

"Oh, hello, Homer. You're just in time," said Uncle Ulysses. "I've been going over this automatic doughnut machine, oiling the machinery and cleaning the works . . . wonderful things, these labor-saving devices."

"Yep," agreed Homer, and he picked up a cloth and started polishing the metal trimmings while Uncle Ulysses tinkered with the inside workings.

"Opfwo-oof!!" sighed Uncle Ulysses and, "Look here, Homer, you've got a mechanical mind. See if you can find where these two pieces fit in. I'm going across to the barbershop for a spell, 'cause there's somethin' I've got to talk to the sheriff about. There won't be much business here until the double feature is over and I'll be back before then."

Then as Uncle Ulysses went out the door he said, "Uh, Homer, after you get the pieces in place, would you mind mixing up a batch of doughnut batter and put it in the machine? You could turn the switch and make a few doughnuts to have on hand for the crowd after the movie . . . if you don't mind."

"O.K.," said Homer, "I'll take care of everything."

A few minutes later a customer came in and said, "Good evening, bud."

Homer looked up from putting the last piece in the doughnut machine and said, "Good evening, sir, what can I do for you?"

"Well, young feller, I'd like a cup o' coffee and some doughnuts," said the customer.

"I'm sorry, mister, but we won't have any doughnuts for about half an hour, until I can mix some dough and start this machine. I could give you some very fine sugar rolls instead."

"Well, bud, I'm in no real hurry so I'll just have a cup o' coffee and wait around a bit for the doughnuts. Fresh doughnuts are always worth waiting for is what I always say."

"O.K.," said Homer, and he drew a cup of coffee from Uncle Ulysses' super automatic coffee maker.

"Nice place you've got here," said the customer.

"Oh, yes," replied Homer, "this is a very up and coming lunchroom with all the latest improvements."

"Yes," said the stranger, "must be a good business. I'm in business too. A traveling man in outdoor advertising. I'm a sandwich man, Mr. Gabby's my name."

"My name is Homer. I'm glad to meet you, Mr. Gabby. It must be a fine profession, traveling and advertising sandwiches."

"Oh no," said Mr. Gabby, "I don't advertise sandwiches, I just wear any kind of an ad, one sign on front and one sign on behind, this way. . . . Like a sandwich. Ya know what I mean?"

"Oh, I see. That must be fun, and you travel too?" asked Homer as he got out the flour and the baking powder.

"Yeah, I ride the rods between jobs, on freight trains, ya know what I mean?"

"Yes, but isn't that dangerous?" asked Homer.

"Of course there's a certain amount a risk, but you take any method a travel these days, it's all dangerous. Ya know what I mean? Now take airplanes for instance . . ."

Just then a large shiny black car stopped in front of the lunchroom and a chauffeur helped a lady out of the rear door. They both came inside and the lady smiled at Homer and said, "We've stopped for a light snack. Some doughnuts and coffee would be simply marvelous."

Then Homer said, "I'm sorry, ma'am, but the doughnuts won't be ready until I make this batter and start Uncle Ulysses' doughnut machine."

"Well now aren't *you* a clever young man to know how to make *doughnuts!*"

"Well," blushed Homer, "I've really never done it before but I've got a receipt to follow."

"Now, young man, you simply must allow me to help. You know, I haven't made doughnuts for years, but I know the best receipt for doughnuts. It's marvelous, and we really must use it."

"But, ma'am . . ." said Homer.

"Now just *wait* till you taste these doughnuts," said the lady. "Do you have an apron?" she asked, as she took off her fur coat and her rings and her jewelry and rolled up her sleeves. "Charles," she said to the chauffeur, "hand me that baking powder, that's right, and, young man, we'll need some nutmeg."

So Homer and the chauffeur stood by and handed things and cracked the eggs while the lady mixed and stirred. Mr. Gabby sat on his stool, sipped his coffee, and looked on with great interest.

"There!" said the lady when all of the ingredients were mixed. "Just *wait* till you taste these doughnuts!"

"It looks like an awful lot of batter," said Homer as he stood on a chair and poured it into the doughnut machine with the help of the chauffeur. "It's about *ten* times as much as Uncle Ulysses ever makes."

"But wait till you taste them!" said the lady with an eager look and a smile.

Homer got down from the chair and pushed a button on the machine marked "*Start.*" Rings of batter started dropping into the hot fat. After a ring of batter was cooked on one side an automatic gadget turned it over and the other side would cook. Then another automatic gadget gave the doughnut a little push and it rolled neatly down a little chute, all ready to eat.

"That's a simply *fascinating* machine," said the lady as she waited for the first doughnut to roll out.

"Here, young man, *you* must have the first one. Now isn't that just *too* delicious!? Isn't it simply marvelous?"

"Yes, ma'am, it's very good," replied Homer as the lady handed doughnuts to Charles and to Mr. Gabby and asked if they didn't think they were simply divine doughnuts.

"It's an old family receipt!" said the lady with pride.

Homer poured some coffee for the lady and her chauffeur and for Mr. Gabby, and a glass of milk for himself. Then they all sat down at the lunch counter to enjoy another few doughnuts apiece.

"I'm so glad you enjoy my doughnuts," said the lady. "But now, Charles, we really must be going. If you will just take this apron, Homer, and put two dozen doughnuts in a bag to take along, we'll be on our way. And, Charles, don't forget to pay the young man." She rolled down her sleeves and put on her jewelry, then Charles managed to get her into her big fur coat.

"Good night, young man, I haven't had so much fun in years. I *really* haven't!" said the lady, as she went out the door and into the big shiny car.

"Those are sure good doughnuts," said Mr. Gabby as the car moved off.

"You bet!" said Homer. Then he and Mr. Gabby stood and watched the automatic doughnut machine make doughnuts.

After a few dozen more doughnuts had rolled down the little chute, Homer said, "I guess that's about enough doughnuts to sell to the after-theater customers. I'd better turn the machine off for a while."

Homer pushed the button marked *"Stop"* and there was a little click, but nothing happened. The rings of batter kept right on dropping into the hot fat, and an automatic gadget kept right on turning them over, and another automatic gadget kept right on giving them a little push, and the doughnuts kept right on rolling down the little chute, all ready to eat.

"That's funny," said Homer, "I'm sure that's the right button!" He pushed it again but the automatic doughnut maker kept right on making doughnuts.

"Well, I guess I must have put one of those pieces in backwards," said Homer.

"Then it might stop if you push the button marked *'Start,'* " said Mr. Gabby.

Homer did, and the doughnuts still kept rolling down the little chute, just as regular as a clock can tick.

"I guess we could sell a few more doughnuts," said Homer, "but I'd better telephone Uncle Ulysses over at the barbershop." Homer gave the number and while he waited for someone to answer he counted thirty-seven doughnuts roll down the little chute.

Finally someone answered, "Hello! This is the sarberbhop, I mean the barbershop."

"Oh, hello, sheriff. This is Homer. Could I speak to Uncle Ulysses?"

"Well, he's playing pinochle right now," said the sheriff. "Anythin' I can tell 'im?"

"Yes," said Homer. "I pushed the button marked *'Stop'* on the doughnut machine but the rings of batter keep right on dropping into the hot fat, and an automatic gadget keeps right on turning them over, and another automatic gadget keeps giving them a little push, and the doughnuts keep right on rolling down the little chute! It won't stop!"

"O.K. Wold the hire, I mean, hold the wire and I'll tell 'im." Then Homer looked over his shoulder and counted another twenty-one doughnuts roll down the little chute, all ready to eat. Then the sheriff said, "He'll be right over. . . . Just gotta finish this hand."

"That's good," said Homer. "G'by, sheriff."

The window was full of doughnuts by now so Homer and Mr. Gabby had to hustle around and start stacking them on plates and trays and lining them up on the counter.

"Sure are a lot of doughnuts!" said Homer.

"You bet!" said Mr. Gabby. "I lost count at twelve hundred and two and that was quite a while back."

People had begun to gather outside the lunchroom window, and someone was saying, "There are almost as many doughnuts as there are people in Centerburg, and I wonder how in tarnation Ulysses thinks he can sell all of 'em!"

Every once in a while somebody would come inside and buy some, but while somebody bought two to eat and a dozen to take home, the machine made three dozen more.

By the time Uncle Ulysses and the sheriff arrived and pushed through the crowd, the lunchroom was a calamity of doughnuts! Doughnuts in the window, doughnuts piled high on the shelves, doughnuts stacked on plates, doughnuts lined up twelve deep all along the counter, and doughnuts still rolling down the little chute, just as regular as a clock can tick.

"Hello, sheriff, hello, Uncle Ulysses, we're having a little trouble here," said Homer.

"Well, I'll be dunked!!" said Uncle Ulysses.

"Dernd ef you won't be when Aggy gits home," said the sheriff.

"Mighty fine doughnuts though. What'll you do with 'em all, Ulysses?"

Uncle Ulysses groaned and said, "What will Aggy say? We'll never sell 'em all."

Then Mr. Gabby, who hadn't said anything for a long time, stopped piling doughnuts and said, "What you need is an advertising man. Ya know what I mean? You got the doughnuts, ya gotta create a market . . . understand? . . . It's balancing the demand with the supply. . . . That sort of thing."

"Yep!" said Homer. "Mr. Gabby's right. We have to enlarge our market. He's an advertising sandwich man, so if we hire him, he can walk up and down in front of the theater and get the customers."

"You're hired, Mr. Gabby!" said Uncle Ulysses.

Then everybody pitched in to paint the signs and to get Mr. Gabby sandwiched between. They painted "SALE ON DOUGHNUTS" in big letters on the window too.

Meanwhile the rings of batter kept right on dropping into the hot fat, and an automatic gadget kept right on turning them over, and another automatic gadget kept right on giving them a little push, and the doughnuts kept right on rolling down the little chute, just as regular as a clock can tick.

"I certainly hope this advertising works," said Uncle Ulysses, wagging his head. "Aggy'll certainly throw a fit if it don't."

The sheriff went outside to keep order, because there was quite a crowd by now—all looking at the doughnuts and guessing how many thousand there were, and watching new ones roll down the little chute, just as regular as a clock can tick. Homer and Uncle Ulysses kept stacking doughnuts. Once in a while somebody bought a few, but not very often.

Then Mr. Gabby came back and said, "Say, you know there's not much use o' me advertisin' at the theater. The show's all over, and besides almost everybody in town is out front watching that machine make doughnuts!"

"Zeus!" said Uncle Ulysses. "We must get rid of these doughnuts before Aggy gets here!"

"Looks like you will have ta hire a truck ta waul 'em ahay, I mean haul 'em away!!" said the sheriff, who had just come in. Just then there was a noise and a shoving out front and the lady from the shiny black car and her chauffeur came pushing through the crowd and into the lunchroom.

"Oh, gracious!" she gasped, ignoring the doughnuts, "I've lost my diamond bracelet, and I know I left it here on the counter," she said, pointing to a place where the doughnuts were piled in stacks of two dozen.

"Yes, ma'am, I guess you forgot it when you helped make the batter," said Homer.

Then they moved all the doughnuts around and looked for the diamond bracelet, but they couldn't find it anywhere. Meanwhile the doughnuts kept rolling down the little chute, just as regular as a clock can tick.

After they had looked all around the sheriff cast a suspicious eye on Mr. Gabby, but Homer said, "He's all right, sheriff, he didn't take it. He's a friend of mine."

Then the lady said, "I'll offer a reward of one hundred dollars for that bracelet! It really *must* be found! . . . it *really* must!"

"Now don't you worry, lady," said the sheriff. "I'll get your bracelet back!"

"Zeus! This is terrible!" said Uncle Ulysses. "First all of these doughnuts and then on top of all that, a lost diamond bracelet . . ."

Mr. Gabby tried to comfort him, and he said, "There's always a bright side. That machine'll probably run outta batter in an hour or two."

If Mr. Gabby hadn't been quick on his feet Uncle Ulysses would have knocked him down, sure as fate.

Then while the lady wrung her hands and said, "We must find it, we *must!*" and Uncle Ulysses was moaning about what Aunt Agnes would say, and the sheriff was eyeing Mr. Gabby, Homer sat down and thought hard.

Before twenty more doughnuts could roll down the little chute he shouted, "SAY! I know where the bracelet is! It was lying here on the counter and got mixed up in the batter by mistake! The bracelet is cooked inside one of these doughnuts!"

"Why . . . I really believe you're right," said the lady through her tears. "Isn't that *amazing?* Simply *amazing!*"

"I'll be durn'd!" said the sheriff.

"Ohh-h!" moaned Uncle Ulysses. "Now we have to break up all of these doughnuts to find it. Think of the *pieces!* Think of the *crumbs!* Think of what *Aggy* will say!"

"Nope," said Homer. "We won't have to break them up. I've got a plan."

So Homer and the advertising man took some cardboard and some paint and printed another sign. They put this sign in the window, and the sandwich man wore two more signs that said the same thing and walked around in the crowd out front.

FRESH DOUGHNUTS
2 for 5¢
WHILE THEY LAST
$100.00 PRIZE
FOR FINDING
A BRACELET
INSIDE A DOUGHNUT
P.S. YOU HAVE TO GIVE
THE BRACELET BACK

THEN . . .the doughnuts began to sell! *Everybody* wanted to buy doughnuts, *dozens* of doughnuts!

And that's not all. Everybody bought coffee to dunk the doughnuts in too. Those that didn't buy coffee bought milk or soda. It kept Homer and the lady and the chauffeur and Uncle Ulysses and the sheriff busy waiting on the people who wanted to buy doughnuts.

When all but the last couple of hundred doughnuts had been sold, Rupert Black shouted, "I GAWT IT!!" and sure enough . . . there was the diamond bracelet inside of his doughnut!

Then Rupert went home with a hundred dollars, the citizens of Centerburg went home full of doughnuts, the lady and her chauffeur drove off with the diamond bracelet, and Homer went home with his mother when she stopped by with Aunt Aggy.

As Homer went out of the door he heard Mr. Gabby say, "Neatest trick of merchandising I ever seen," and Aunt Aggy was looking skeptical while Uncle Ulysses was saying, "The rings of batter kept right on dropping into the hot fat, and the automatic gadget kept right on turning them over, and the other automatic gadget kept right on giving them a little push, and the doughnuts kept right on rolling down the little chute just as regular as a clock can tick—they just kept right on a comin', an' a comin', an' a comin', an' a comin'."

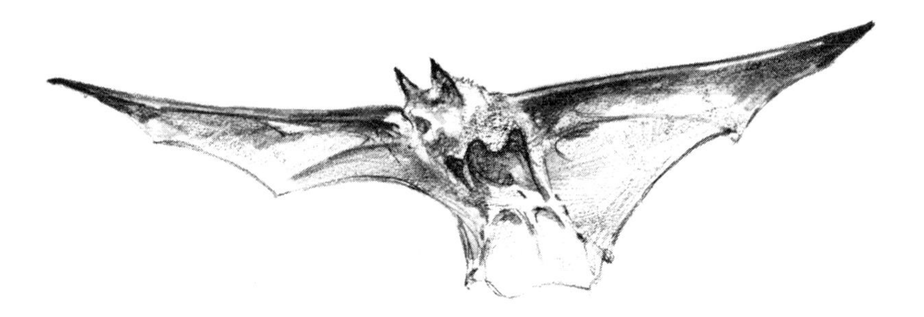

RANDALL JARRELL

Bats

A bat is born
Naked and blind and pale.
His mother makes a pocket of her tail
And catches him. He clings to her long fur
By his thumbs and toes and teeth.
And then the mother dances through the night
Doubling and looping, soaring, somersaulting—
Her baby hangs on underneath.
All night, in happiness, she hunts and flies.
Her high sharp cries
Like shining needlepoints of sound
Go out into the night and, echoing back,
Tell her what they have touched.
She hears how far it is, how big it is,
Which way it's going:
She lives by hearing.
The mother eats the moths and gnats she catches
In full flight; in full flight
The mother drinks the water of the pond
She skims across. Her baby hangs on tight.
Her baby drinks the milk she makes him
In moonlight or starlight, in midair.
Their single shadow, printed on the moon
Or fluttering across the stars,

Whirls on all night; at daybreak
The tired mother flaps home to her rafter.
The others all are there.
They hang themselves up by their toes,
They wrap themselves in their brown wings.
Bunched upside down, they sleep in air.
Their sharp ears, their sharp teeth, their
quick sharp faces
Are dull and slow and mild.
All the bright day, as the mother sleeps,
She folds her wings about her sleeping child.

PHILIPPA PEARCE

Philippa Pearce's father and grandfather were both flour-millers. As a child she lived next door to the mill and to the river that partly powered it, in the lovely flat countryside near Cambridge, England. The garden of her house, as it was in her father's time, reappears in her finest book, *Tom's Midnight Garden*. In that same book there's a skating scene that recalls the skating she herself did as a girl on the flooded water-meadows of Cambridgeshire.

Tom's Midnight Garden is about one of the greatest of mysteries: Time. We human beings, especially when young, have always felt that Time was something more or other than what is measured on a clock. Physicists, especially since Einstein, are sure that this is so. At any rate, in Philippa Pearce's story, young Tom, who's staying with his aunt and uncle, hears the clock strike thirteen, after midnight. Exploring the house's backyard, he finds himself in a strange garden. The garden, it seems, belongs to a past time of perhaps sixty or seventy years ago. In it he meets a girl, Hatty, who also seems to belong to a past age.

But the story, though it turns on the idea of a "time warp," is not really science fiction. There's a mystery in it and a clever reader may be able to solve it before the book's end; but it's not a mystery story, either. Or a fantasy. Indeed, I know of nothing in all of children's literature quite like it. It stays with you like certain dreams.

The excerpt that follows tells us about one of Tom's many meetings with Hatty in the midnight garden. It's printed below only to make you want to read the whole book.

Tom's Midnight Garden

FROM CHAPTER THIRTEEN

THE POSSIBILITY of Hatty's being a ghost stayed in his mind, however—at the back of his mind. He was not even aware of the presence of the idea, until one day in the garden it became the cause of a quarrel with Hatty herself. It was the only real quarrel that ever took place between them.

They were beginning to build their tree house, in the Steps of St. Paul's; as usual, Tom was directing, while Hatty did the work of pulling and plaiting branches together, to make the walls. The floor—of old pieces of boarding that Hatty had found in the potting shed—was already in place.

Hatty, as she worked, was singing to herself from hymns and songs and ballads. Now she was singing the end of the ballad of Sweet Molly Malone:

> *"Her ghost wheels her barrow*
> *Through streets broad and narrow,*
> *Singing, 'Cockles and Mussels,*
> *Alive—alive-oh!' "*

And Hatty continued to hum and murmur, under her breath, the refrain: "Alive—alive-oh! Alive—alive-oh!"

Suddenly Tom said—he blurted it out before he could help himself:

"What's it like—I mean, I wonder what it's like to be dead and a ghost?"

Hatty stopped singing at once, and looked at him slyly over her shoulder, and laughed. Tom repeated the question: "What is it like to be a ghost?"

"Like?" said Hatty. She turned fully to face him, and laid a hand upon his knee, and looked eagerly into his face. "Ah, tell me, Tom!"

For a moment, Tom did not understand her; then he jumped to his feet and shouted: "I'm not a ghost!"

"Don't be silly, Tom," Hatty said. "You forget that I saw you go right through the orchard door when it was shut."

"That proves what I say!" said Tom. "I'm not a ghost, but the orchard door is, and that was why I could go through it. The door's a ghost, and the garden's a ghost; and so are you, too!"

"Indeed I'm not; you are!"

They were glaring at each other now; Hatty was trembling. "You're a silly little boy!" she said (and Tom thought resentfully that she seemed to have been growing up a good deal too much recently). "And you make a silly little ghost! Why do you think you wear those clothes of yours? None of my cousins ever played in the garden in clothes like that. Such outdoor clothes can't belong to nowadays, *I* know! Such clothes!"

"They're my pajamas," said Tom, indignantly, "my best visiting pajamas! I sleep in them. And this is my bedroom slipper." His second slipper had been left, as usual, to wedge the flat-door upstairs.

"And you go about so, in the daytime, always in your nightclothes!" Hatty said scornfully. "And it's the fashion nowadays, is it, to wear only one slipper? Really, you are silly to give such excuses! You wear strange clothes that no one wears nowadays, because you're a ghost. Why, I'm the only person in the garden who sees you! I can see a ghost."

Hatty would never believe the real explanation of his clothes, and Tom chose what he thought was a shorter counter-argument: "Do you know I could put my hand through you—now—just as if you weren't there?"

Hatty laughed.

"I could—I could!" shouted Tom.

She pointed at him: "You're a ghost!"

In a passion, Tom hit her a blow upon the outstretched wrist. There was great force of will as well as of muscle behind the blow, and his hand went right through—not quite as through thin air, for Tom felt a something, and Hatty snatched back her wrist and nursed it in her other hand. She looked as if she might cry, but that could not have been for any pain, for the sensation had not been strong enough. In a wild defense of herself, Hatty still goaded him: "Your hand didn't go through my wrist; my wrist went through your hand! You're a ghost, with a cruel, ghostly hand!"

"Do you hear me?" Tom shouted. "You're a ghost, and I've proved it! You're dead and gone and a ghost!"

There was a quietness, then, in which could be heard a cuckoo's stuttering cry from the wood beyond the garden; and then the sound of Hatty's beginning softly to weep. "I'm not dead—oh, please, Tom, I'm not dead!" Now that the shouting had stopped, Tom was not sure of the truth, after all, but only sure that Hatty was crying as he had never seen her cry since she had been a very little girl, wearing mourning-black and weeping her way along the sundial path—weeping for death so early.

He put his arm round her: "All right, then, Hatty! You're not a ghost—I take it all back—all of it. Only don't cry!"

He calmed her; and she consented at last to dry her tears and go back to plaiting the branches, only sniffing occasionally. Tom did not reopen a subject that upset her so deeply, although he felt that he owed it to himself to say, some time later, "Mind you, I'm not a ghost either!" This, by her silence, Hatty seemed to allow.

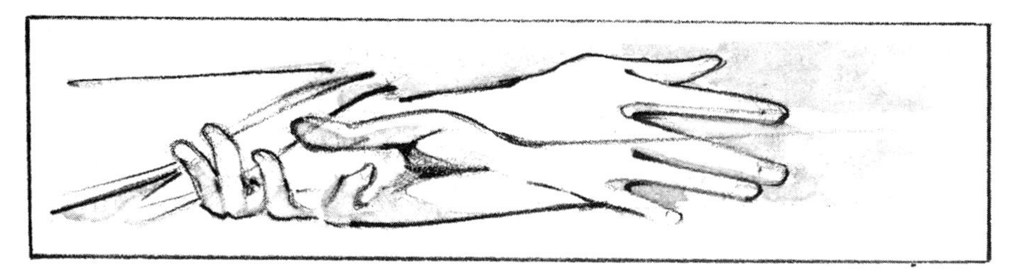

TED HUGHES

My Uncle Dan

My Uncle Dan's an inventor, you may think that's very fine.
You may wish he was your uncle instead of being mine—
If he wanted he could make a watch that bounces when it drops,
He could make a helicopter out of string and bottle tops
Or any really useful thing you can't get in the shops.

But Uncle Dan has other ideas:
The bottomless glass for ginger beers,
The toothless saw that's safe for the tree,
A special word for a spelling bee
(Like Lionocerangoutangadder),
Or the roll-uppable rubber ladder,
The mystery pie that bites when it's bit—
My Uncle Dan invented it.

My Uncle Dan sits in his den inventing night and day.
His eyes peer from his hair and beard like mice from a load of hay.
And does he make the shoes that will go walks without your feet?
A shrinker to shrink instantly the elephants you meet?
A carver that just carves from the air steaks cooked and ready to eat?

No, no, he has other intentions—
Only perfectly useless inventions:

Glassless windows (they never break),
A medicine to cure the earthquake,
The unspillable screwed-down cup,
The stairs that go neither down nor up,
The door you simply paint on a wall—
Uncle Dan invented them all.

SAM LEVENSON

Many years ago I used to be on TV and radio. One show I worked on was called "This Is Show Business." We introduced many fine performers on this show, and one of the best of them was a young comedian named Sam Levenson, who became famous. He and I grew to be great friends, partly because we had both been high-school teachers when we were younger, and partly because our childhoods were very much alike. It's for that last reason I enjoyed reading "A Hike in New York City." I hope you will, too.

A Hike in New York City

AT LEAST once each summer we kids went off on a hike, but never without strong opposition from Mama. When it came to the open road, Mama had a closed mind.

Her method of discouraging us from venturing into the unknown was to make the entire project appear ridiculous:

"You're going on a what?"

"We're going on a hike."

"What's a hike?" Mama would ask.

When we started to explain it, the whole idea did in fact become ridiculous.

"We go walking, Ma."

"Walking? For that you have to leave home? What's the matter with walking right here? You walk; I'll watch."

"You don't understand, Ma. We take lunch along."

"I'll give you lunch here, and you can march right around the table," and she would start singing a march, clapping her hands rhythmically.

"Ma, we climb mountains in the woods."

She couldn't understand why it was so much more enjoyable to fall off a mountain than off a fire escape.

"And how about the wild animals in the woods?"

"Wild animals? What kind of wild animals?"

"A bear, for instance. A bear could eat you up."

"Ma. Bears don't eat little children."

"Okay. So he won't eat you, but he could take a bite and spit out! I'm telling you now, if a wild animal eats you up don't come running to me. And who's going with you?"

"Well, there's Georgie—"

"Georgie! Not him! He's a real wild animal!" She then went on to list all the conditions for the trip. "And remember one thing, don't tear your pants, and remember one thing, don't eat wild berries and bring me home the cramps, and remember one thing, don't tell me tomorrow morning that you're too tired to go to school, and remember one thing, wear rubbers, a sweater, warm underwear, and an umbrella, and a hat, and remember one thing, if you should get lost in the jungle, call up so I'll know you're all right. And don't dare come home without color in your cheeks. I wish I was young and free like you. Take soap."

Since the consent was specifically granted for the next day only, that night none of us slept. There was always a chance that it might rain. Brother Albert stayed at the crystal set all night like a ship's radio operator with his earphones on, listening to weather bulletins and repeating them aloud for the rest of us. "It's clearing in Nebraska. Hot air masses coming up from the Gulf. They say it's good for planting alfalfa. Storm warning off the coast of Newfoundland. It's drizzling in Montreal."

At 6:00 A.M. we were ready for Operation Hike, rain or shine, but we had to wait for Papa to get up. We didn't need his permission, but we did need his blanket.

Into the valley of Central Park marched the six hundred, bowed down with knapsacks, flashlights, a Cracker-Jack box compass-mirror (so you could tell not only where you were lost but who was lost), a thermos bottle (semiautomatic—you had to fill it but it emptied by itself), and an ax. Onward! Forward! Upward! Philip was always the leader. He was the one to get lost first. Jerry was the lookout. He would yell, "Look out!" and fall off the cliff. None of us knew how long we were supposed to march. We went on because we didn't know what to do if we stopped. One brave coward finally spoke up. "I can't go on anymore. The heat is killing me. Let's start the fire here."

No hike was complete without Georgie and his Uncle Bernie's World War I bugle. This kid had lungs like a vacuum cleaner. With him outside the walls of Jericho, they could have sent the rest of the army home. He used to stand on a hill and let go a blast that had the Staten Island ferries running into each other.

Lunch, naturally, had been packed in a shoe box—sandwiches, fruit, cheese, and napkins all squashed together neatly. The lid would open by itself every twenty minutes for air.

It happened every time, the Miracle of the Sandwiches. One kid always got a "brilliant idea." "Hey. I got a brilliant idea. I'm tired of my mother's sandwiches. Let's everybody trade sandwiches." All the kids exchanged sandwiches, and miraculously we all ended up with salami.

Albert was the true nature lover. "You know, you can learn a lot about human nature from the ants," he always said as he lifted up rock after rock to study his favorite insects. And he was right. While he was studying the ants, someone swiped his apple.

We came home with color in our cheeks—green. To make sure we could go again, we didn't forget Mama. We brought her a bouquet. She took one whiff and broke out in red blotches. Papa yelled but didn't lay a hand on us. He was afraid it was catching.

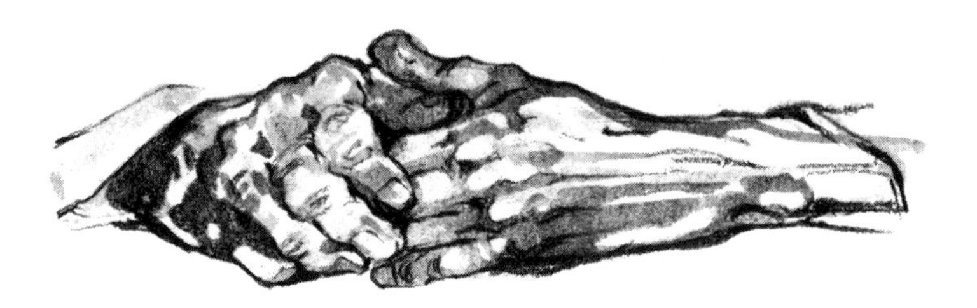

LANGSTON HUGHES

Mother to Son

Well, son, I'll tell you:
Life for me ain't been no crystal stair.
It's had tacks in it,
And splinters,
And boards torn up,
And places with no carpet on the floor—
Bare.
But all the time
I'se been a-climbin' on,
And reachin' landin's,
And turnin' corners,
And sometimes goin' in the dark
Where there ain't been no light.
So, boy, don't you turn back.
Don't you set down on the steps
'Cause you finds it kinder hard.
Don't you fall now—
For I'se still goin', honey,
I'se still climbin'
And life for me ain't been no crystal stair.

MARY NORTON

Mary Norton is nearsighted. She writes, "When others saw the far hills, the distant woods, the soaring pheasant, I, as a child, would turn sideways to the close bank, the tree roots, and the tangled grasses." This may help to explain why she has written four books about people six inches tall or less. Here are the titles of the books: *The Borrowers, The Borrowers Afield, The Borrowers Afloat,* and *The Borrowers Aloft.*

These books, which I admire as much as anything in this *Treasury*, are *not* fantasy. We have to accept just one impossibility—that the Borrowers exist. Once that's done, everything that happens is as real, as true, and as interesting almost as our own lives.

Mary Norton is an Englishwoman (she's been an actress as well as a writer) and the *Borrowers* series is very English. But everything's perfectly comprehensible to American readers.

"Poor Stainless," the story that follows, is complete in itself and wasn't originally part of the series. But two of the main characters, Homily and her daughter Arrietty, appear in all the books. Before you start the story, let Mary Norton tell you about the Borrowers.

> Where, we sometimes ask ourselves, do all the sewing needles go? And the drawing pins, the matchboxes, the hairpins, the thimbles, the safety pins? Factories go on making safety pins, and people go on buying safety pins, and yet there never is a safety pin just when you want one. Where are they all? Now, at this minute? They cannot all just be lying somewhere about the house. Who takes them and why? It must—one begins to realize—be something or someone who is living quite close beside us, under the same roof; something or someone with human tastes and almost human needs; something (or someone) very secret, very hidden—under the floorboards, maybe, or behind the wall paneling. Very small, of course—that stands to reason—and very busy, always improvising, always "making do." And brave—they must be very brave to venture out into the vast human rooms (as dangerous to them as such rooms are to mice) seeking the wherewithal on which to sustain their lives. Who could grudge them the odd

pencil stub, the occasional bottle top, the used postage stamp, or the leftover sliver of cheese? No (it takes all kinds, as they say, to make a world): we should accept their hidden presence and gently leave them alone. Children call them "the Borrowers."

Poor Stainless

AND NOW," said Arrietty to Homily, "tell me what-you-used-to-do. . . ."

The phrase, run together in one eager breath, had lost its meaning as words—it described an activity, a way of passing the time while engaged in monotonous tasks. They were unpicking sequins from a square of yellowed chiffon: Homily unpicked while Arrietty threaded the glimmering circles on a string of pale blue silk. It was a fine spring day and they sat beside the grating let into the outside wall. The sunlight fell across them in crisscross squares, and the soft air moved their hair.

"Well," said Homily, after a moment, "did I ever tell you about the time when I lit the big candle?"

"And burned a hole in the floorboards—and in the carpet upstairs? And human beings shrieked—and your father beat you with a wax matchstick? Yes, you've told me."

"It was a candle my father borrowed to melt down for dips. It shined lovely," said Homily.

"Tell me about the time when the cook upstairs upset the boiling marmalade and it all leaked down between the cracks—"

"Oh, that was dreadful," said Homily, "but we bottled it, or most of it, in acorn cups and an empty tube called morphia. But the mess, oh dear, the mess—my mother was beside herself. There was a corner of our carpet," added Homily reflectively, "which tasted sweet for months." With a work-worn hand she smoothed down the gleaming chiffon which billowed smokelike on the moving air.

"I know what," cried Arrietty suddenly, "tell me about the rat!"

"Oh, not again," said Homily.

She glanced at herself in a sequin which—to her—was about the size of a hand-mirror. "I'm going very gray," she said. She polished up the sequin with a corner of her apron and stared again, patting her hair at the temples. "Did I ever tell you about Poor Stainless?"

"Who was he?" asked Arrietty.

"One of the Knife Machine boys."

"No . . ." said Arrietty, uncertainly.

"That was the first time I went upstairs. To look for Stainless." Homily, staring into the sequin, lifted her hair a little at the temples. "Oh, dear," she said, in a slightly dispirited voice.

"I like it gray," said Arrietty warmly, gently retrieving the sequin; "it suits you. What about Poor Stainless—"

"He was lost, you see. And we were all to go up and look for him. It was an order," said Homily. "Some people thought it wrong that the women should go, too, but there it was: it was an order."

"Who gave it?" asked Arrietty.

"The grandfathers, of course. It was the first time I ever saw the scullery. After that, once I knew the way, I used to sneak up there now and again but no one ever knew. Oh, dear, I shouldn't say this to you!"

"Never mind," said Arrietty.

"Poor Stainless. He was the youngest of that family. They used to live down a hole in the plaster on a level with the table where the knife machine used to stand. They did all their borrowing in the scullery. Practically vegetarians they were—carrots, turnips, watercress, celery, peas, beans—the lot. All the stuff Crampfurl, the gardener, used to bring in in baskets. Lovely complexions they had, every one of them. Especially Stainless. Stainless had cheeks like apple blossom. 'Merry little angel' my mother used to call him. All the grown-ups were mad about Stainless—he had a kind of way with them. But not with us. We didn't like him."

"Why not?" asked Arrietty, suddenly interested.

"I don't know," said Homily, "he had mean ways—well, more like teasing kind of ways; and he never got found out. He'd coax black beetles down our chute—great things with horns they were—and we'd know it was him but we couldn't prove it. And many a time he'd creep along above our floorboards, with a bent pin on a string, and hook at me through a crack in our ceiling: if we had a party, he'd do it, because he was too young to be asked. But it wasn't any fun, getting hooked by Stainless—caught me by the hair, once he did. And in those days—" said Homily complacently, taking up another sequin, "my hair was my crowning glory." She stared into the sequin reflectively, then put it down with a sigh.

"Well, anyway," she went on briskly, "Stainless disappeared. What a to-do!—His mother, it seemed, had sent him out to borrow parsley. Eleven-fifteen in the morning it was and, by evening, he hadn't returned. And he didn't return that night.

"Now you must understand about parsley—it's a perfectly simple borrow and a quick one. Five minutes, it should have taken him: all you had to do was to walk along the knife machine table onto a ledge at the top of the wainscot, drop down (quite a small drop) onto the draining board and the parsley always stood in an old jam jar at the back of the sink—on a zinc shelf, like, with worn holes in it.

"Some said, afterwards, Stainless was too young to be sent for parsley. They blamed the parents. But there was his mother, single-handed behind the knife machine getting a meal for all the family and the elder ones off borrowing with their father and, as I told you, Stainless was always out anyway directly his mother's back was turned—plaguing us and what not and whispering down the cracks: 'I see you,' he'd say—there was no privacy with Stainless until my father wallpapered our ceiling. Well, anyway," went on Homily, pausing to get her breath, "Stainless had disappeared and the next day, a lovely sunny afternoon, at three o'clock sharp, we were all to go up and look for him. It was Mrs. Driver's afternoon out, and the maids would be having their rest.

"We all had our orders: some were to look among the garden boots and the blacking brushes; others in the vegetable bins; my father and your Uncle Hendreary's father and several of the stronger men had to carry a spanner with a wooden spoon lashed across it to unscrew the trap in the drain below the sink.

"I stopped to watch this, I remember. Several of us did. Round and round they went—like Crampfurl does with the cider-press—on the bottom of an upturned bucket under the sink. Suddenly, there was a great clatter and the screw came tumbling off and there was a rush of greasy water all over the bucket top. Oh dear, oh dear," exclaimed Homily, laughing a little but half ashamed of doing so, "those poor men! None of their wives would have them home again until they had climbed up into the sink proper and had the tap turned on them. *Then* it was the hot tap, which was meant to be lukewarm. Oh dear, oh dear, what a to-do! But still no Stainless.

"We young ones were taken home then, but it was a good four hours before the men abandoned the search. We ate our tea in silence, I remember, while our mothers sniffed and wiped their eyes. After tea, my younger brother started playing marbles with three old dried peas he had, and my mother rebuked him and said, 'Quiet now—have you no respect? Think of your father and of all those brave men Upstairs!' The way she said 'Upstairs' made your hair stand on end.

"And, yet, you know, Arrietty, I liked the scullery, what I'd seen of it—with the sunshine coming through the yard door and falling warm on that old brick floor. And the bunches of bay-leaf and dried thyme. But I did remember there had been a mousetrap under the sink and another under the boot cupboard. Not that these were dangerous—except for those who did not know—our father would roll a potato at them and then they would go click. But they'd jump a bit when they did it and that's what startled you. No, the real danger was Crampfurl, the gardener, coming in suddenly through the yard door with the vegetables for dinner; or Mrs. Driver, the cook, back from her afternoon out, to fill a kettle. And there were other maids then in the house who might take a fancy to a radish or an apple from the barrel behind the scullery door.

"Anyway, when darkness came the rescue party was called off. Our mothers made a great fuss of the men, thankful to see them back, and brought them their suppers and fetched their slippers. And no one spoke above a whisper. And we were sent to bed.

"By that time, we too felt grave. As we lay cozily under the warm covers, we could not help but think of Stainless. Poor Stainless. Perhaps he'd gone *past* the trap and down the drain of the sink into the sewers. We knew there were borrowers who lived in sewers and that they were dreadful people, wild and fierce like rats. Once, my little brother played with one and got bitten in the arm and his shirt stolen. And he got a dreadful rash.

"Next day, the two grandfathers called another meeting: they were the elders, like, and always made the decisions. One grandfather was my father's great-uncle. I forget now who the other was . . ."

"Never mind," said Arrietty.

"Well," said Homily, "the long and short of it was—we were all to go Upstairs, and go throughout every room. Firbank was full of borrowers, in those days—or so it seemed—and some we never knew. But we was to seek them out, any we could find, and ask about Poor Stainless. A house-to-house search they called it."

"Goodness!" gasped Arrietty.

"We was all to go," said Homily.

"Women and children, too?"

"*All,*" said Homily, "except the little 'uns."

She sat still, frowning into space; her face seemed graven by the memory. "Some said the old men were mad," she went on, after a moment. "But it was wonderfully organized: we were to go in twos—

two to each room. The elder ones and the young girls for the ground floor, the younger men and some quite young boys for the creepers."

"What creepers?"

"The creepers up the house front, of course: they had to search the bedrooms!"

"Yes, I see," said Arrietty.

"That was the only way you could get up to the first floor in those days. It was long before your father invented his hatpin. There was no one could tackle the stairs—the height of the treads, you see, and nothing to grip on . . ."

"Yes. Go on about the creepers."

"Early dawn it was, barely light, when the young lads were lined up on the gravel, marking from below which of the windows was open. One, two, three, GO—and they was off—all the ivy and wisteria leaves shaking like a palsy! Oh, the stories they had to tell about what they found in those bedrooms but never a sign of Stainless! One poor little lad slipped on a windowsill and gripped on a cord to save himself: it was the cord of a roller blind and the roller blind went clattering up to the ceiling and there he was—hanging on a thing like a wooden acorn. He got down in the end—swung himself back and forth until he got a grip on the pelmet, then down the curtain by the bobbles. Not much fun, though, with two great human beings in nightcaps, snoring away on the bed.

"We women and girls took the downstairs rooms, each with a man who knew the ropes, like. We had orders to be back by teatime, because of the little 'uns, but the men were to search on until dusk. I had my Uncle Bolty and they'd given us the morning room. And it was on that spring day, just after it became light—" Homily paused significantly—"that I first saw the Overmantels!"

"Oh," exclaimed Arrietty, "I remember—those proud kind of borrowers who lived above the chimney piece?"

"Yes," said Homily, "them." She thought for a moment. "You never could tell how many of them there were because you always saw them doubled in the looking glass. The overmantel went right up to the ceiling, filled with shelves and twisty pillars and plush-framed photographs. You saw them always gliding about behind the cape-gooseberries, or the jars of pipe cleaners or the Japanese fans. They smelled of cigars and brandy and—something else. But perhaps that was the smell of the room. Russian leather—yes, that was it. . . ."

"Go on," said Arrietty; "did they speak to you?"

"Speak to us! Did the Overmantels speak to us!" Homily gave a short laugh, then shook her head grimly as though dismissing a memory. Her cheeks had become very pink.

"But," said Arrietty, breaking the odd silence, "at least, you saw them!"

"Oh, we saw them right enough. And heard them. There was plenty of them about that morning. It was early, you see, and they knew the human beings were asleep. There they all were, gliding about, talking and laughing among themselves—and dressed up to kill for a mouse hunt. And they saw us all right, as we stood beside the door, but would they look at us? No, not they. Not straight, that is: their eyes slid about all the time, as they laughed and talked among themselves. They looked past us and over us and under us but never quite at us. Long, long eyes they had, and funny light tinkling voices. You couldn't make out what they said.

"After a while, my Uncle Bolty stepped forward: he cleared his throat and put on his very best voice (he could do this voice, you see, that's why they chose him for the morning room). 'Excuse and pardon me,' he said (it was lovely the way he said it) 'for troubling and disturbing you, but have you by any chance seen—' and he went on to describe Poor Stainless, lovely complexion and all.

"Not a sign of notice did he get. Those Overmantels just went on laughing and talking and putting on airs like as if they were acting on a stage. And beautiful they looked, too (you couldn't deny it), some of the women, in their long-necked Overmantel way. The early morning sunlight shining on all that looking glass lit them all up, like, to a kind of pinky gold. Lovely it was. You couldn't help but notice. . . .

"My Uncle Bolty began to look angry and his face grew very red. 'High or low, we're borrowers all,' he said in a loud voice, 'and this little lad—' he almost shouted it— 'was the apple of his mother's eye!' But the Overmantels went on talking in a silly, flustered way, laughing a little still, and sliding their long eyes sideways.

"My Uncle Bolty suddenly lost his temper. 'All right,' he thundered, forgetting his special voice and going back to his country one, 'you silly feckless lot. High you may be but remember this—them as dwells below the kitchen floor has solid earth to build on and we'll outlast you yet!'

"With that he turns away, and I go after him, crying a little—I wouldn't know for why. Knee-high we were in the pile of the morning-room carpet. As we passed through the doorway a silence fell behind us. We waited in the hall and listened for a while. It was a long, long silence."

Arrietty did not speak. She sat there lost in thought and gazing at her mother. After a moment, Homily sighed and said, "Somehow, I don't seem to forget that morning, though nothing much happened really—when you come to think of it. Some of the others had terrible adventures, especially them who was sent to search the bedrooms. But your Great-uncle Bolty was right. When they closed up most of the house, after Her Ladyship's accident, the morning room wasn't used any more. Starved out, they must have been, those Overmantels. Or frozen out." She sighed again and shook her head. "You can't help but feel sorry for them. . . .

"We all stayed up that night, even us young ones, waiting and hoping for news. The search parties kept arriving back in ones and twos. There was hot soup for all and some were given brandy. Some of the mothers looked quite gray with worry but they kept up a good front, caring for all and sundry as they came tumbling in down the chute. By morning, all the searchers were home. The last to arrive were three young lads who had got trapped in the bedrooms when the housemaids came up at dusk to close the windows and draw the curtains. It had come on to rain, you see. They had to crouch inside the fender for over an hour while two great human beings changed for dinner. It was a lady and gentleman and, as they dressed, they quarreled—and it was all to do with someone called 'Algy.' Algy this and Algy that . . . on and on. Scorched and perspiring as these poor boys were, they peered out through the brass curlicues of the fender, and took careful note of everything. At one point, the lady took off most of her hair and hung it on a chair back. The borrowers were astonished. At another point, the gentleman—taking off his socks—flung them across the room and one landed in the fireplace. The borrowers were terrified and pulled it out of sight; it was a woolen sock and might begin to singe; they couldn't risk the smell."

"How did they get away?"

"Oh, that was easy enough once the room was empty, and the guests were safely at dinner. They unraveled the sock, which had a hole in the toe, and let themselves down through the bannisters on the landing. The first two got down all right. But the last, the littlest one, was hanging in air when the butler came by with a soufflé. All was well, though, the butler didn't look up, and the little one didn't let go.

"Well, that was that. The search was called off and, for us younger ones at least, life seemed to return to normal. Then one afternoon—it must have been a week later because it was a Saturday, I remember, and that was the day our mother always took a walk down the drainpipe to have tea with the Rain-Barrels and on this particular Saturday she took our little brother with her. Yes, that was it—anyway, we two girls, my sister and I, found ourselves alone in the house. Our mother always left us jobs to do and that afternoon it was to cut up a length of black shoelace to make armbands in memory of Stainless. Everybody was making them—it was an order 'to show respect'—and we were all to put them on together in three days' time. After a while, we forgot to be sad and chattered and laughed as we sewed. It was so peaceful, you see, sitting there together and with no fear any more of black beetles.

"Suddenly my sister looked up, as though she had heard a noise. 'What's that?' she said, and she looked kind of frightened.

"We both of us looked round the room, then I heard her let out a cry: she was staring at a knothole in the ceiling. Then I saw it too —something moving in the knothole. It seemed to be black but it wasn't a beetle. We could neither of us speak or move: we just sat there riveted—watching this thing come winding down towards us out of the ceiling. It was a shiny snaky sort of thing, and it had a twist or curl in it which, as it got lower, swung round in a blind kind of way and drove us shrieking into a corner. We clung together, crying and staring, until suddenly my sister said 'Hush!' We waited, listening. 'Someone spoke,' she whispered, staring towards the ceiling. Then we heard it—a hoarse voice, rather breathy and horribly familiar. 'I can see you!' it said.

"We were furious. We called him all sorts of names. We threatened him with every kind of punishment. We implored him to take the Thing away. But all he did was to giggle a little, and keep on saying, in that silly singsong voice: "Taste it . . . taste it . . . it's lovely!"

"Oh," breathed Arrietty, "did you dare?"

Homily frowned. "Yes. In the end. And it was lovely," she admitted grudgingly, "it was a liquorice boot-lace."

"But where had he been all that time?"

"In the village shop."

"But—" Arrietty looked incredulous, "how did he get there?"

"It was all quite simple really. Mrs. Driver had left her shopping basket on the scullery table, with a pair of shoes to be heeled. Stainless, on his way to the parsley, heard her coming, and nipped inside a shoe. Mrs. Driver put the shoes in the basket and carried them off to the village. She put down the basket on the shop counter while she gossiped awhile with the postmistress and, seizing the right opportunity, Stainless scrambled out."

"But how did he get back home again?"

"The next time Mrs. Driver went in for the groceries, of course. He was in a box of hair-combs at the time but he recognized the basket."

Arrietty looked thoughtful. "Poor Stainless," she said, after a moment, "what an experience! He must have been terrified."

"Terrified! Stainless! Not he! He'd enjoyed every minute of it!" Homily's voice rose. "He'd had one wild, wicked, wonderful, never-to-be-forgotten week of absolute, glorious freedom—living on jujubes, walnut whips, chocolate bars, bull's-eyes, hundreds and thousands, and still lemonade. And what had he done to deserve it?" The chiffon between Homily's fingers seemed to dance with indignation. "That's what we asked ourselves! We didn't like it. Not after all we'd been through: we never did think it was fair!" Crossly, she shook out the chiffon, and with lips set, began to fold it. But gradually, as she smoothed her hands across the frail silk, her movements became more gentle: she looked thoughtful suddenly and, as Arrietty watched, a little smile began to form at the corners of her mouth. "There was one thing, though, that we all noticed . . ." she said after a moment.

"What was that?" asked Arrietty.

"He'd lost his wonderful complexion."

EDWIN A. HOEY

"Foul Shot"

With two 60's stuck on the scoreboard
And two seconds hanging on the clock,
The solemn boy in the center of eyes,
Squeezed by silence,
Seeks out the line with his feet,
Soothes his hands along his uniform,
Gently drums the ball against the floor,
Then measures the waiting net,
Raises the ball on his right hand,
Balances it with his left,
Calms it with fingertips,
Breathes,
Crouches,
Waits,
And then through a stretching of stillness,
Nudges it upward.

The ball slides up and out,
Lands,
Leans,
Wobbles,

Wavers,
Hesitates,
Exasperates,
Plays it coy
Until every face begs with unsounding
screams—
And then
And then
And then
Right before ROAR-UP,
Dives down and through.

E. L. KONIGSBURG

Most small children, especially if they live in a big city, fear getting lost. When I was very young I used to have nightmares about being accidentally locked up in a museum or department store after closing hours. When I first read Mrs. Konigsburg's *From the Mixed-up Files of Mrs. Basil E. Frankweiler* I was in my sixties. After finishing it I wondered why I should suddenly feel a sense of great relief. Then I realized why. This book is about two children who spend a whole week living and *sleeping* in New York's Metropolitan Museum of Art—and having a pretty good time doing it. My childish nightmare had come back to me as I read the book, and had been dispelled or cured or something by this funny and comforting story.

If you read the whole book you'll see that the adventures of Claudia (twelve) and Jamie (nine) are all mixed up with a very rich lady named Mrs. Frankweiler. It is she who tells the story in a long letter to her lawyer, Mr. Saxonberg.

The brother and sister decided to run away from their comfortable suburban home not because they're miserable but just in order to make their parents appreciate them. They settle on the museum as a good place to stay—it's comfortable and it's free. They take a train to New York and emerge from Grand Central Station. The episode that follows tells what happened next.

From the Mixed-up Files of Mrs. Basil E. Frankweiler

CHAPTER THREE

AS SOON as they reached the sidewalk, Jamie made his first decision as treasurer. "We'll walk from here to the museum."

"Walk?" Claudia asked. "Do you realize that it is over forty blocks from here?"

"Well, how much does the bus cost?"

"The bus!" Claudia exclaimed. "Who said anything about taking a bus? I want to take a taxi."

"Claudia," Jamie said, "you are quietly out of your mind. How can you even think of a taxi? We have no more allowance. No more income. You can't be extravagant any longer. It's not my money we're spending. It's *our* money. We're in this together, remember?"

"You're right," Claudia answered. "A taxi is expensive. The bus is cheaper. It's only twenty cents each. We'll take the bus."

"*Only* twenty cents each. That's forty cents total. No bus. We'll walk."

"We'll wear out forty cent's worth of shoe leather," Claudia mumbled. "You're sure we have to walk?"

"Positive," Jamie answered. "Which way do we go?"

"Sure you won't change your mind?" The look on Jamie's face gave her the answer. She sighed. No wonder Jamie had more than twenty-four dollars; he was a gambler and a cheapskate. If that's the way he wants to be, she thought, I'll never ask him for bus fare; I'll suffer and never, let him know about it. But he'll regret it when I simply collapse from exhaustion. I'll collapse quietly.

"We'd better walk up Madison Avenue," she told her brother. "I'll see too many ways to spend *our* precious money if we walk on Fifth Avenue. All those gorgeous stores."

She and Jamie did not walk exactly side by side. Her violin case kept bumping him, and he began to walk a few steps ahead of her. As Claudia's pace slowed down from what she was sure was an accumulation of carbon dioxide in her system (she had not yet learned about muscle fatigue in science class even though she was in sixth grade honors class), Jamie's pace quickened. Soon he was walking a block and a half ahead of her. They would meet when a red light held him up. At one of these mutual stops Claudia instructed Jamie to wait for her on the corner of Madison Avenue and Eightieth Street, for there they would turn left to Fifth Avenue.

She found Jamie standing on the corner, probably one of the most civilized street corners in the whole world, consulting a compass and announcing that when they turned left, they would be heading "due northwest." Claudia was tired and cold at the tips; her fingers, her toes, her nose were all cold while the rest of her was perspiring under the weight of her winter clothes. She never liked feeling either very hot or very cold, and she hated feeling both at the same time. "Head due northwest. Head due northwest," she mimicked. "Can't you simply say turn right or turn left as everyone else does? Who do you think you are? Daniel Boone? I'll bet no one's used a compass in Manhattan since Henry Hudson."

Jamie didn't answer. He briskly rounded the corner of Eightieth Street and made his hand into a sun visor as he peered down the street. Claudia needed an argument. Her internal heat, the heat of anger, was cooking that accumulated carbon dioxide. It would soon explode out of her if she didn't give it some vent. "Don't you realize that we must try to be inconspicuous?" she demanded of her brother.

"What's inconspicuous?"

"Un-noticeable."

Jamie looked all around. "I think you're brilliant, Claude. New York is a great place to hide out. No one notices no one."

"Anyone," Claudia corrected. She looked at Jamie and found him smiling. She softened. She had to agree with her brother. She was brilliant. New York was a great place, and being called brilliant had cooled her down. The bubbles dissolved. By the time they reached the museum, she no longer needed an argument.

As they entered the main door on Fifth Avenue, the guard clicked off two numbers on his people counter. Guards always count the people going into the museum, but they don't count them going out. (My chauffeur, Sheldon, has a friend named Morris who is a guard at the Metropolitan. I've kept Sheldon busy getting information from Morris. It's not hard to do since Morris loves to talk about his work. He'll tell about anything except security. Ask him a question he won't or can't answer, and he says, "I'm not at liberty to tell. Security.")

By the time Claudia and Jamie reached their destination, it was one o'clock, and the museum was busy. On any ordinary Wednesday over twenty-six thousand people come. They spread out over the twenty acres of floor space; they roam from room to room to room to room to room. On Wednesday come the gentle old ladies who are using the time before the Broadway matinee begins. They walk around in pairs. You can tell they are a set because they wear matching pairs of orthopedic shoes, the kind that lace on the side. Tourists visit the museum on Wednesdays. You can tell them because the men carry cameras, and the women look as if their feet hurt; they wear high heeled shoes. (I always say that those who wear'em deserve 'em.) And there are art students. Any day of the week. They also walk around in pairs. You can tell that they are a set because they carry matching black sketchbooks.

(You've missed all this, Saxonberg. Shame on you! You've never set your well-polished shoe inside that museum. More than a quarter of a million people come to that museum every week. They come from Mankato, Kansas, where they have no museums and from Paris, France, where they have lots. And they all enter free of charge because that's what the musuem is: great and large and wonderful and free to all. And complicated. Complicated enough even for Jamie Kincaid.)

No one thought it strange that a boy and a girl, each carrying a book bag and an instrument case and who would normally be in school, were visiting a museum. After all, about a thousand schoolchildren visit the museum every day. The guard at the entrance merely stopped them and told them to check their cases and book bags. A museum rule: no bags, food, or umbrellas. None that the guards can see. Rule or no rule, Claudia decided it was a good idea. A big sign in the checking room said NO TIPPING, so she knew that Jamie couldn't object. Jamie did object, however; he pulled his sister aside and asked her how she expected him to change into his pajamas. His pajamas, he explained, were rolled into a tiny ball in his trumpet case.

Claudia told him that she fully expected to check out at 4:30. They would then leave the museum by the front door and within five minutes would re-enter from the back, through the door that leads from the parking lot to the Children's Museum. After all, didn't that solve all their problems? (1) They would be seen leaving the museum. (2) They would be free of their baggage while they scouted around for a place to spend the night. And (3) it was free.

Claudia checked her coat as well as her packages. Jamie was condemned to walking around in his ski jacket. When the jacket was on and zippered, the Orlon plush lining did a great deal to muffle his twenty-four-dollar rattle. Claudia would never have permitted herself to become so overheated, but Jamie liked perspiration, a little bit of dirt, and complications.

Right now, however, he wanted lunch. Claudia wished to eat in the restaurant on the main floor, but Jamie wished to eat in the snack bar downstairs; he thought it would be less glamorous, but cheaper, and as chancellor of the exchequer, as holder of the veto power, and as tightwad of the year, he got his wish. Claudia didn't really mind too much when she saw the snack bar. It was plain but clean.

Jamie was dismayed at the prices. They had $28.61 when they went into the cafeteria, and only $27.11 when they came out still feeling hungry. "Claudia," he demanded, "did you know food would cost so much? Now, aren't you glad we didn't take a bus?"

Claudia was no such thing. She was not glad that they hadn't taken a bus. She was merely furious that her parents, and Jamie's too, had been so stingy that she had been away from home for less than one whole day and was already worried about survival money. She chose not to answer Jamie. Jamie didn't notice; he was completely wrapped up in problems of finance.

"Do you think I could get one of the guards to play me a game of war?" he asked.

"That's ridiculous," Claudia said.

"Why? I brought my cards along. A whole deck."

Claudia said, "*Inconspicuous* is exactly the opposite of that. Even a guard at the Metropolitan who sees thousands of people every day would remember a boy who played him a game of cards."

Jamie's pride was involved. "I cheated Bruce through all second grade and through all third grade so far, and he still isn't wise."

"Jamie! Is that how you knew you'd win?"

Jamic bowed his head and answered, "Well, yeah. Besides, Brucie has trouble keeping straight the jacks, queens, and kings. He gets mixed up."

"Why do you cheat your best friend?"

"I sure don't know. I guess I like complications."

"Well, quit worrying about money now. Worry about where we're going to hide while they're locking up this place."

They took a map from the information stand; for free. Claudia selected where they would hide during that dangerous time immediately after the museum was closed to the public and before all the guards and helpers left. She decided that she would go to the ladies' room, and Jamie would go to the men's room just before the museum closed. "Go to the one near the restaurant on the main floor," she told Jamie.

"I'm not spending a night in a men's room. All that tile. It's cold. And besides, men's rooms make noises sound louder. And I rattle enough now."

Claudia explained to Jamie that he was to enter a booth in the men's room. "And then stand on it," she continued.

"Stand on it? Stand on what?" Jamie demanded.

"You know," Claudia insisted. "Stand on it!"

"You mean stand on the toilet?" Jamie needed everything spelled out.

"Well, what else would I mean? What else is there in a booth in the men's room? And keep your head down. And keep the door to the booth very slightly open," Claudia finished.

"Feet up. Head down. Door open. Why?"

"Because I'm certain that when they check the ladies' room and the men's room, they peek under the door and check only to see if there are feet. We must stay there until we're sure all the people and guards have gone home."

"How about the night watchman?" Jamie asked.

Claudia displayed a lot more confidence than she really felt. "Oh! there'll be a night watchman, I'm sure. But he mostly walks around the roof trying to keep people from breaking in. We'll already be in. They call what he walks, a catwalk. We'll learn his habits soon enough. They must mostly use burglar alarms in the inside. We'll just never touch a window, a door, or a valuable painting. Now, let's find a place to spend the night."

They wandered back to the rooms of fine French and English furniture. It was here Claudia knew for sure that she had chosen the most elegant place in the world to hide. She wanted to sit on the lounge chair that had been made for Marie Antoinette or at least sit at her writing table. But signs everywhere said not to step on the platform. And some of the chairs had silken ropes strung across the arms to keep you from even trying to sit down. She would have to wait until after lights out to be Marie Antoinette.

At last she found a bed that she considered perfectly wonderful, and she told Jamie that they would spend the night there. The bed had a tall canopy, supported by an ornately carved headboard at one end and by two gigantic posts at the other. (I'm familiar with that bed, Saxonberg. It is as enormous and fussy as mine. And it dates from the sixteenth century like mine. I once considered donating my bed to the museum, but Mr. Untermyer gave them this one first. I was somewhat relieved when he did. Now I can enjoy my bed without feeling guilty because the museum doesn't have one. Besides, I'm not that fond of donating things.)

Claudia had always known that she was meant for such fine things. Jamie, on the other hand, thought that running away from home to sleep in just another bed was really no challenge at all. He, James, would rather sleep on the bathroom floor, after all. Claudia then pulled him around to the foot of the bed and told him to read what the card said.

Jamie read, "Please do not step on the platform."

Claudia knew that he was being difficult on purpose; therefore, she read for him, "State bed—scene of the alleged murder of Amy Robsart, first wife of Lord Robert Dudley, later Earl of . . ."

Jamic couldn't control his smile. He said "You know, Claude, for a sister and a fussbudget, you're not too bad."

Claudia replied, "You know, Jamie, for a brother and a cheapskate, you're not too bad."

Something happened at precisely that moment. Both Claudia and Jamie tried to explain to me about it, but they couldn't quite. I know what happened, though I never told them. Having words and explanations for everything is too modern. I especially wouldn't tell Claudia. She has too many explanations already.

What happened was: they became a team, a family of two. There had been times before they ran away when they had acted like a team, but those were very different from *feeling* like a team. Becoming a team didn't mean the end of their arguments. But it did mean that the arguments became a part of the adventure, became discussions not threats. To an outsider the arguments would appear to be the same because feeling like part of a team is something that happens invisibly. You might call it *caring*. You could even call it *love*. And it is very rarely, indeed, that it happens to two people at the same time—especially a brother and a sister who had always spent more time with activities than they had with each other.

They followed their plan: checked out of the museum and re-entered through a back door. When the guard at that entrance told them to check their instrument cases, Claudia told him that they were just passing through on their way to meet their mother. The guard let them go, knowing that if they went very far, some other guard would stop them again. However, they managed to avoid other guards for the remaining minutes until the bell rang. The bell meant that the museum was closing in five minutes. They then entered the booths of the rest rooms.

They waited in the booths until five-thirty, when they felt certain that everyone had gone. Then they came out and met. Five-thirty in winter is dark, but nowhere seems as dark as the Metropolitan Museum of Art. The ceilings are so high that they fill up with a lot of darkness. It seemed to Jamie and Claudia that they walked through miles of corridors. Fortunately, the corridors were wide, and they were spared bumping into things.

At last they came to the hall of the English Renaissance. Jamie quickly threw himself upon the bed, forgetting that it was only about six o'clock and thinking that he would be so exhausted that he would immediately fall asleep. He didn't. He was hungry. That was one reason he didn't fall asleep immediately. He was uncomfortable, too. So he got up from bed, changed into his pajamas, and got back into bed. He felt a little better.

Claudia had already changed into her pajamas. She, too, was hungry, and she, too, was uncomfortable. How could so elegant and romantic a bed smell so musty? She would have liked to wash everything in a good, strong sweet-smelling detergent.

As Jamie got into bed, he still felt uneasy, and it wasn't because he was worried about being caught. Claudia had planned everything so well that he didn't concern himself about that. The strange way he felt had little to do with the strange place in which they were sleeping. Claudia felt it, too. Jamie lay there thinking. Finally, realization came.

"You know, Claude," he whispered, "I didn't brush my teeth."

Claudia answered, "Well, Jamie, you can't always brush after every meal." They both laughed very quietly. "Tomorrow," Claudia reassured him "we'll be even better organized."

It was much earlier than her bedtime at home, but still Claudia felt tired. She thought she might have an iron deficiency anemia: tired blood. Perhaps, the pressures of everyday stress and strain had gotten her down. Maybe she was light-headed from hunger; her brain cells were being robbed of vitally needed oxygen for good growth and, and . . . yawn.

She shouldn't have worried. It had been an unusually busy day. A busy and unusual day. So she lay there in the great quiet of the museum next to the warm quiet of her brother and allowed the soft stillness to settle around them: a comforter of quiet. The silence seeped from their heads to their soles and into their souls. They stretched out and relaxed. Instead of oxygen and stress, Claudia thought now of hushed and quiet words: glide, fur, banana, peace. Even the footsteps of the night watchman added only an accented quarter-note to the silence that had become a hum, a lullaby.

They lay perfectly still even long after he passed. Then they whispered good night to each other and fell asleep. They were quiet sleepers, and hidden by the heaviness of the dark, they were easily not discovered.

(Of course, Saxonberg, the draperies of that bed helped, too.)

GELETT BURGESS

I Wish That My Room Had a Floor

I wish that my room had a floor;
I don't so much care for a door,
  But this walking around
  Without touching the ground
Is getting to be such a bore.

RUDYARD KIPLING

The English author Rudyard Kipling wrote many books for children and young boys and girls. For younger children (and for his little daughter Josephine) he wrote the *Just So Stories.* These are famous but I find them self-conscious and pretentious, so I don't include any. Older boys and girls should try his masterpiece, *Kim,* about the adventures of an English boy in India more than a hundred years ago.

His best-known work for children is *The Jungle Books* (there are two of them) but, though they are wonderfully written, I find something unpleasantly "authoritarian" in them. They concern Mowgli, an English boy who is brought up by wolves and other jungle animals. Reminds you of Tarzan, doesn't it? Try *The Jungle Books;* maybe my dislike of them is a weakness in me, or a blindness of some sort.

The story below is usually included in *The Jungle Books* even though it's not about Mowgli and his animal companions but about one of the greatest fights in animal-story literature, between a mongoose and a cobra. A mongoose is not a goose at all, but a small mammal that looks partly like a weasel, partly like a cat. It's found in India, the scene of the story, and feeds on snakes and rodents. When it's angry its eyes get very red.

Our mongoose in the story is called Rikki-tikki-tavi from the sound it makes. Washed out of its burrow by a flood, it's rescued by an Englishman ("the big man") and his wife. It becomes a house pet, particularly beloved by the little son, Teddy. Mongooses are very curious, the family motto being "Run and find out." One day, poking around in the garden of the bungalow, Rikki meets Darzee the Tailorbird and his wife. He also narrowly avoids death from the big black cobra Nag and his wife, Nagaina. Even more dangerous is the small dusty snakeling Karait, whom he encounters and paralyzes with one bite. Teddy's father finishes off Karait, but it is Rikki who has really saved Teddy from death. Here's how the story continues.

Rikki-tikki-tavi

THAT NIGHT at dinner, walking to and fro among the wine-glasses on the table, he might have stuffed himself three times over with nice things. But he remembered Nag and Nagaina, and though it was very pleasant to be patted and petted by Teddy's mother, and to sit on Teddy's shoulder, his eyes would get red from time to time, and he would go off into his long war-cry of "*Rikk-tikk-tikki-tikki-tchk!*"

Teddy carried him off to bed, and insisted on Rikki-tikki sleeping under his chin. Rikki-tikki was too well bred to bite or scratch, but as soon as Teddy was asleep he went off for his nightly walk round the house, and in the dark he ran up against Chuchundra the Muskrat creeping round by the wall. Chuchundra is a brokenhearted little beast. He whimpers and cheeps all the night, trying to make up his mind to run into the middle of the room, but he never gets there.

"Don't kill me," said Chuchundra, almost weeping. "Rikki-tikki don't kill me!"

"Do you think a snake-killer kills muskrats?" said Rikki-tikki scornfully.

"Those who kill snakes get killed by snakes," said Chuchundra, more sorrowfully than ever. "And how am I to be sure that Nag won't mistake me for you some dark night?"

"There's not the least danger," said Rikki-tikki, "but Nag is in the garden, and I know you don't go there."

"My cousin Chua the Rat told me—" said Chuchundra, and then he stopped.

"Told you what?"

"*Hsh!* Nag is everywhere, Rikki-tikki. You should have talked to Chua in the garden."

"I didn't—so you must tell me. Quick, Chuchundra, or I'll bite you!"

Chuchundra sat down and cried till the tears rolled off his whiskers. "I am a very poor man," he sobbed. "I never had spirit enough to run out into the middle of the room. *Hsh!* I mustn't tell you anything. Can't you *hear,* Rikki-tikki?"

Rikki-tikki listened. The house was as still as still, but he thought he could just catch the faintest *scratch-scratch* in the world—a noise as faint as that of a wasp walking on a windowpane—the dry scratch of a snake's scales on brickwork.

"That's Nag or Nagaina," he said to himself, "and he is crawling into the bathroom sluice. You're right, Chuchundra. I should have talked to Chua."

He stole off to Teddy's bathroom, but there was nothing there, and then to Teddy's mother's bathroom. At the bottom of the smooth plaster wall there was a brick pulled out to make a sluice for the bathwater, and as Rikki-tikki stole in by the masonry curb where the bath is put, he heard Nag and Nagaina whispering together outside in the moonlight.

"When the house is emptied of people," said Nagaina to her husband, "*he* will have to go away, and then the garden will be our own again. Go in quietly, and remember that the big man who killed Karait is the first one to bite. Then come out and tell me, and we will hunt for Rikki-tikki together."

"But are you sure that there is anything to be gained by killing the people?" said Nag.

"Everything. When there were no people in the bungalow, did we have any mongoose in the garden? So long as the bungalow is empty, we are king and queen of the garden. And remember that as soon as our eggs in the melon-bed hatch (as they may tomorrow), our children will need room and quiet."

"I had not thought of that," said Nag. "I will go, but there is no need that we should hunt for Rikki-tikki afterwards. I will kill the big man and his wife, and the child if I can, and come away quietly. Then the bungalow will be empty, and Rikki-tikki will go."

Rikki-tikki tingled all over with rage and hatred at this, and then Nag's head came through the sluice, and his five feet of cold body followed it. Angry as he was, Rikki-tikki was very frightened as he saw the size of the big cobra. Nag coiled himself up, raised his head, and looked into the bathroom in the dark, and Rikki could see his eyes glitter.

"Now, if I kill him here, Nagaina will know, and if I fight him on the open floor, the odds are in his favor. What am I to do?" said Rikki-tikki-tavi.

Nag waved to and fro, and then Rikki-tikki heard him drinking from the biggest water-jar that was used to fill the bath. "That is good," said the snake. "Now, when Karait was killed, the big man had a stick. He may have that stick still, but when he comes in to bathe in the morning he will not have a stick. I shall wait here till he comes. Nagaina—do you hear me?—I shall wait here in the cool till daytime."

There was no answer from outside, so Rikki-tikki knew Nagaina had gone away. Nag coiled himself down, coil by coil, round the bulge at the bottom of the water-jar, and Rikki-tikki stayed still as death. After an hour he began to move, muscle by muscle, towards the jar. Nag was asleep, and Rikki-tikki looked at his big back, wondering which would be the best place for a good hold. "If I don't break his back at the first jump," said Rikki, "he can still fight, and if he fights—O Rikki!" He looked at the thickness of the neck below the hood, but that was too much for him, and a bite near the tail would only make Nag savage.

"It must be the head," he said at last, "the head above the hood. And, when I am once there, I must not let go."

Then he jumped. The head was lying a little clear of the water-jar, under the curve of it, and, as his teeth met, Rikki braced his back against the bulge of the red earthenware to hold down the head. This gave him just one second's purchase, and he made the most of it. Then he was battered to and fro as a rat is shaken by a dog—to and fro on the floor, up and down, and round in great circles, but his eyes were red and he held on as the body cart-whipped over the floor, upsetting the tin dipper and the soap dish and the flesh-brush, and banged against the tin side of the bath. As he held he closed his jaws tighter and tighter, for he made sure he would be banged to death, and, for the honor of his family, he preferred to be found with his teeth locked. He was dizzy, aching, and felt shaken to pieces when something went off like a thunderclap just behind him; a hot wind knocked him senseless and red fire singed his fur. The big man had been wakened by the noise, and had fired both barrels of a shotgun into Nag just behind the hood.

Rikki-tikki held on with his eyes shut, for now he was quite sure he was dead, but the head did not move, and the big man picked him up and said: "It's the mongoose again, Alice. The little chap has saved *our* lives now." Then Teddy's mother came in with a very white face, and saw what was left of Nag, and Rikki-tikki dragged himself to Teddy's bedroom and spent half the rest of the night shaking himself tenderly to find out whether he really was broken into forty pieces, as he fancied.

When morning came he was very stiff, but well pleased with his doings. "Now I have Nagaina to settle with, and she will be worse than five Nags, and there's no knowing when the eggs she spoke of will hatch. Goodness! I must go and see Darzee," he said.

Without waiting for breakfast, Rikki-tikki ran to the thornbush where Darzee was singing a song of triumph at the top of his voice. The news of Nag's death was all over the garden, for the sweeper had thrown the body on the rubbish heap.

"Oh, you stupid tuft of feathers!" said Rikki-tikki angrily. "Is this the time to sing?"

"Nag is dead—is dead—is dead!" sang Darzee. "The valiant Rikki-tikki caught him by the head and held fast. The big man brought the bang-stick, and Nag fell in two pieces! He will never eat my babies again."

"All that's true enough, but where's Nagaina?" said Rikki-tikki, looking carefully round him.

"Nagaina came to the bathroom sluice and called for Nag," Darzee went on, "and Nag came out on the end of a stick—the sweeper picked him up on the end of a stick and threw him upon the rubbish heap. Let us sing about the great, the red-eyed Rikki-tikki!" And Darzee filled his throat and sang.

"If I could get up to your nest, I'd roll your babies out!" said Rikki-tikki. "You don't know when to do the right thing at the right time. You're safe enough in your nest there, but it's war for me down here. Stop singing a minute, Darzee."

"For the great, the beautiful Rikki-tikki's sake I will stop," said Darzee. "What is it, O killer of the terrible Nag?"

"Where is Nagaina, for the third time?"

"On the rubbish heap by the stables, mourning for Nag. Great is Rikki-tikki with the white teeth."

"Bother my white teeth! Have you ever heard where she keeps her eggs?"

"In the melon-bed, on the end nearest the wall, where the sun strikes nearly all day. She hid them there weeks ago."

"And you never thought it worthwhile to tell me? The end nearest the wall, you said?"

"Rikki-tikki, you are not going to eat her eggs?"

"Not eat exactly—no. Darzee, if you have a grain of sense you will fly off to the stables and pretend that your wing is broken, and let Nagaina chase you away to this bush. I must get to the melon-bed, and if I went there now she'd see me."

Darzee was a feather-brained little fellow who could never hold more than one idea at a time in his head, and just because he knew that Nagaina's children were born in eggs like his own, he didn't think at first that it was fair to kill them. But his wife was a sensible bird, and she knew that cobra's eggs meant young cobras later on. So she flew off from the nest, and left Darzee to keep the babies warm, and continue his song about the death of Nag. Darzee was very like a man in some ways.

She fluttered in front of Nagaina by the rubbish heap, and cried out: "Oh, my wing is broken! The boy in the house threw a stone at me and broke it." Then she fluttered more desperately than ever.

Nagaina lifted up her head and hissed: "You warned Rikki-tikki when I would have killed him. Indeed and truly, you've chosen a bad place to be lame in." And she moved towards Darzee's wife, slipping along over the dust.

"The boy broke it with a stone!" shrieked Darzee's wife.

"Well! It may be some consolation to you when you're dead to know that I shall settle accounts with the boy. My husband lies on the rubbish heap this morning, but before night the boy in the house will lie very still. What is the use of running away? I am sure to catch you. Little fool, look at me!"

Darzee's wife knew better than to do *that,* for a bird who looks at a snake's eyes gets so frightened that she cannot move. Darzee's wife fluttered on, piping sorrowfully, and never leaving the ground, and Nagaina quickened her pace.

Rikki-tikki heard them going up the path from the stables, and he raced for the end of the melon-patch near the wall. There, in the warm litter above the melons, very cunningly hidden, he found twenty-five eggs, about the size of a bantam's eggs, but with whitish skins instead of shells.

"I was not a day too soon," he said, for he could see the baby cobras curled up inside the skin, and he knew that the minute they were hatched they could each kill a man or a mongoose. He bit off the tops of the eggs as fast as he could, taking care to crush the young cobras, and turned over the litter from time to time to see whether he had missed any. At last there were only three eggs left, and Rikki-tikki began to chuckle to himself, when he heard Darzee's wife screaming:

"Rikki-tikki, I led Nagaina towards the house, and she has gone into the veranda, and—oh, come quickly—she means killing!"

Rikki-tikki smashed two eggs, and tumbled backwards down the melon-bed with the third egg in his mouth, and scuttled to the veranda as hard as he could put foot to the ground. Teddy and his mother and father were there at early breakfast, but Rikki-tikki saw that they were not eating anything. They sat stone-still, and their faces were white. Nagaina was coiled up on the matting by Teddy's chair, within easy striking distance of Teddy's bare leg, and she was swaying to and fro, singing a song of triumph.

"Son of the big man that killed Nag," she hissed, "stay still. I am not ready yet. Wait a little. Keep very still, all you three! If you move I strike, and if you do not move I strike. Oh, foolish people, who killed my Nag!"

Teddy's eyes were fixed on his father, and all his father could do was to whisper: "Sit still, Teddy. You mustn't move. Teddy, keep still."

Then Rikki-tikki came up and cried: "Turn round, Nagaina, turn and fight!"

"All in good time," said she, without moving her eyes. "I will settle my account with *you* presently. Look at your friends, Rikki-tikki. They are still and white. They are afraid. They dare not move, and if you come a step nearer I strike."

"Look at your eggs," said Rikki-tikki, "in the melon-bed near the wall. Go and look, Nagaina!"

The big snake turned half round, and saw the egg on the veranda. "Ah-h! Give it to me," she said.

Rikki-tikki put his paw on each side of the egg, and his eyes were blood-red. "What price for a snake's egg? For a young cobra? For a young king-cobra? For the last—the very last of the brood? The ants are eating all the others down by the melon-bed."

Nagaina spun clear round, forgetting everything for the sake of the one egg, and Rikki-tikki saw Teddy's father shoot out a big hand, catch Teddy by the shoulder, and drag him across the little table with the teacups, safe and out of reach of Nagaina.

"Tricked! Tricked! Tricked! *Rikk-tck-tck!*" chuckled Rikki-tikki. "The boy is safe, and it was I—I—I that caught Nag by the hood last night in the bathroom." Then he began to jump up and down, all four feet together, his head close to the floor. "He threw me to and fro, but he could not shake me off. He was dead before the big man blew him in two. I did it! *Rikki-tikki-tck-tck!* Come then, Nagaina. Come and fight with me. You shall not be a widow for long."

Nagaina saw that she had lost her chance of killing Teddy, and the egg lay between Rikki-tikki's paws. "Give me the egg, Rikki-tikki. Give me the last of my eggs, and I will go away and never come back," she said, lowering her hood.

"Yes, you will go away, and you will never come back, for you will go to the rubbish heap with Nag. Fight, widow! The big man has gone for his gun! Fight!"

Rikki-tikki was bounding all round Nagaina, keeping just out of reach of her stroke, his little eyes like hot coals. Nagaina gathered herself together, and flung out at him. Rikki-tikki jumped up and backwards. Again and again and again she struck, and each time her head came with a whack on the matting of the veranda and she gathered herself together like a watch spring. Then Rikki-tikki danced in a circle to get behind her, and Nagaina spun round to keep her head to his head, so that the rustle of her tail on the matting sounded like dry leaves blown along by the wind.

He had forgotten the egg. It still lay on the veranda, and Nagaina came nearer and nearer to it, till at last, while Rikki-tikki was drawing breath, she caught it in her mouth, turned to the veranda steps, and flew like an arrow down the path, with Rikki-tikki behind her. When the cobra runs for her life, she goes like a whiplash flicked across a horse's neck. Rikki-tikki knew that he must catch her, or all the trouble would begin again. She headed straight for the long grass by the thornbush, and as he was running Rikki-tikki heard Darzee still singing his foolish little song of triumph. But Darzee's wife was wiser. She flew off her nest as Nagaina came along, and flapped her wings about Nagaina's head. If Darzee had helped they might have turned her, but Nagaina only lowered her hood and went on. Still, the instant's delay brought Rikki-tikki up to her, and as she plunged into the rathole where she and Nag used to live, his little white teeth were clenched to her tail, and he went down with her—and very few mongooses, however wise and old they may be, care to follow a cobra into its hole. It was dark in the hole, and Rikki-tikki never knew when it might open out and give Nagaina room to turn and strike at him. He held on savagely, and stuck out his feet to act as brakes on the dark slope of the hot, moist earth. Then the grass by the mouth of the hole stopped waving, and Darzee said: "It's all over with Rikki-tikki! We must sing his death-song. Valiant Rikki-tikki is dead! For Nagaina will surely kill him underground."

So he sang a very mournful song that he made up on the spur of the minute, and just as he got to the most touching part the grass quivered again, and Rikki-tikki, covered with dirt, dragged himself out of the hole leg by leg, licking his whiskers. Darzee stopped with a little shout. Rikki-tikki shook some of the dust out of his fur and sneezed. "It is all over," he said. "The widow will never come out again." And the red ants that live between the grass stems heard him, and began to troop down one after another to see if he had spoken the truth.

Rikki-tikki curled himself up in the grass and slept where he was—slept and slept till it was late in the afternoon, for he had done a hard day's work.

"Now," he said when he awoke, "I will go back to the house. Tell the coppersmith, Darzee, and he will tell the garden that Nagaina is dead."

The coppersmith is a bird who makes a noise exactly like the beating of a little hammer on a copperpot, and the reason he is always making it is because he is the town crier to every Indian garden, and tells all the news to everybody who cares to listen. As Rikki-tikki went up the path, he heard his "attention" notes like a tiny dinner gong, and then the steady *"Ding-dong-tock!* Nag is dead—*dong!* Nagaina is dead! *Ding-*

dong-tock!" That set all the birds in the garden singing, and the frogs croaking, for Nag and Nagaina used to eat frogs as well as little birds.

When Rikki got to the house, Teddy and Teddy's mother (she looked very white still, for she had been fainting) and Teddy's father came out and almost cried over him. And that night he ate all that was given him till he could eat no more, and went to bed on Teddy's shoulder, where Teddy's mother saw him when she came to look late at night.

"He saved our lives and Teddy's life," she said to her husband. "Just think, he saved all our lives."

Rikki-tikki woke up with a jump, for the mongooses are light sleepers.

"Oh, it's you," said he. "What are you bothering for? All the cobras are dead, and if they weren't, I'm here."

Rikki-tikki had a right to be proud of himself. But he did not grow too proud, and he kept that garden as a mongoose should keep it, with tooth and jump and spring and bite, till never a cobra dared show its head inside the walls.

Kipling also wrote some extraordinary verse, much of which is still quoted today. Here are two examples. It doesn't matter, but "The Way Through the Woods" is, of all the verse contained in this *Treasury,* the one I love best.

The Way Through the Woods

They shut the road through the woods
Seventy years ago.
Weather and rain have undone it again,
And now you would never know
There was once a road through the woods
Before they planted the trees.
It is underneath the coppice and heath,
And the thin anemones.
Only the keeper sees
That, where the ring-dove broods,
And the badgers roll at ease,
There was once a road through the woods.

Yet, if you enter the woods
Of a summer evening late,
When the night-air cools on the trout-ringed pools
Where the otter whistles his mate,
(They fear not men in the woods,
Because they see so few.)
You will hear the beat of a horse's feet,
And the swish of a skirt in the dew,
Steadily cantering through
The misty solitudes,
As though they perfectly knew
The old lost road through the woods . . .
But there is no road through the woods.

Six Honest Servingmen

I keep six honest servingmen;
(They taught me all I knew)
Their names are What and Why and When
And How and Where and Who
I send them over land and sea,
I send them east and west;
But after they have worked for me,
I give them all a rest.
I let them rest from nine till five,
For I am busy then,
As well as breakfast, lunch, and tea,
For they are hungry men:
But different folk have different views:
I know a person small—
She keeps ten million servingmen,
Who get no rest at all
She sends 'em abroad on her own affairs,
From the second she opens her eyes—
One million Hows, two million Wheres
And seven million Whys!

M. E. KERR

M. E. Kerr's novels are usually about teenagers (*some* teenagers) as they were in the 1970s and, I guess, still are. M. E. Kerr, Elaine Konigsburg, and Louise Fitzhugh are my favorite "realistic" writers—that is, storytellers who write truly about people, young and old, whom you recognize or somehow find near and familiar.

Dinky Hocker Shoots Smack! is not really about a junkie but about a fat girl whose parents don't give her the attention she needs and deserves. As Tucker, one of the main characters, says to Mr. Hocker, trying to explain poor Dinky's trouble, "I think it's about having your feelings shoved aside."

If you don't know M. E. Kerr's wry, tough, funny book, give this first chapter a try and see whether you don't feel like going on with *Dinky Hocker Shoots Smack!*

Dinky Hocker Shoots Smack!

CHAPTER ONE

DON'T TELL PEOPLE we've moved to Brooklyn," Tucker Woolf's father always told him. "Tell them we've moved to Brooklyn *Heights*."

"Why? Brooklyn Heights is Brooklyn."

"Believe me, Tucker, you'll make a better impression."

Which was very important to Tucker's father—making a good impression. That fact was one of the reasons Tucker felt sorry for his father now. It was hard to make a good impression when you'd just been fired.

No sooner had they moved from Gramercy Park in Manhattan to Joralemon Street in Brooklyn Heights, than Tucker's father lost his job. At the same time, he developed an allergy to cats. That meant Tucker had to give away Nader.

Nader was a nine-month-old calico cat Tucker had found under a Chevrolet the first night they moved into their new Heights town house. Tucker had named the cat Ralph Nader, who had done his own time under Chevrolets. But when Tucker discovered he was a she, he had shortened her name to Nader.

Nader had lived for three months with the Woolfs, until Tucker's father began wheezing and sneezing at the sight of her.

In Brooklyn Heights when you wanted to find something or get rid of something, you put a sign up on a tree.

Tucker's sign read:

> DO YOU FEEL UNWANTED, IN THE WAY, AND THE CAUSE OF EVERYONE'S MISERY? ARE YOU TALKED ABOUT BEHIND YOUR BACK AND PLOTTED AGAINST? THEN YOU KNOW HOW I FEEL. I AM A CALICO KITTEN PUTTING MYSELF UP FOR ADOPTION. I HAVE ALREADY BEEN SPAYED BY DR. WASSERMAN OF HICKS STREET, AND I AM IN GOOD CONDITION PHYSICALLY. MENTALLY I AM ON A DOWNER, THOUGH, UNTIL I RELOCATE. IF YOU KNOW HOW A LOSER FEELS AND WANT TO HELP, CALL MAIN 4-8415.

The only one who called was Dinky Hocker of Remsen Street. She came waddling down to Joralemon and took Nader away in a plaid carrying case, telling Tucker to visit the cat whenever he felt like it.

At first Tucker went there often. But after a while he stopped going, because of what was happening to Nader. Dinky, who was fourteen, a year younger than Tucker, ate all the time. She fed Nader all the time, too. Dinky was five foot four and weighed around 165. Now Nader was toddling around like something that had had too much air pumped into it. Her eyes were glazed over with too many memories of too much mackerel, steak, raw egg, hamburger, milk, and tuna fish.

Nader knew how to retrieve empty, wadded-up cigarette packages. But on Tucker's last visit to her, she had refused even to get up on her feet at the sound of cellophane crinkling. She had cocked one eye, looked at Tucker forlornly, and sunk back into a calorie-drugged sleep.

Although Tucker stopped visiting Nader, he didn't stop thinking about her. He had never owned a pet, and to have found this one huddled under a car, flea-ridden and runny-eyed, made him feel all the more responsible toward her.

"Somehow," Tucker's mother had commented, "you identify with that cat, and I don't see why. You've never been a stray. You've always been loved. Is there anything you've ever really wanted that you couldn't have?"

"I guess not."

"Then why all the concern over this animal? She has a perfectly good home now."

"I just don't think a cat should weigh about two tons, that's all!"

"Hey, Tucker," his father said. "What did the two-ton canary say as he prowled down the dark alley late at night?"

"I don't know," Tucker said. "What *did* the two-ton canary say?" But he knew. It was such an old joke.

Tucker's father said, "Here Kitty, Kitty. Here Kitty, Kitty."

Tucker's mother laughed unusually hard at the joke. She had been overdoing everything where Tucker's father was concerned, ever since he'd lost his job. She pretended it took great effort to stop laughing. Then she told Tucker, "You're probably right to just put that cat out of your mind. Don't go over to the Hockers' anymore. I thought Dinky would be a nice new friend for you, but don't go if it gets you worrying about the cat!"

Tucker attended private school in Manhattan. Afternoons, when he got back to Brooklyn, he often went directly to the Heights branch of the Brooklyn Public Library. It was easier to study there. Tucker's father and uncle spent their afternoons at the town house dreaming up some new scheme that was supposed to make them both millionaires in five years. They hadn't said yet what the scheme was. Their discussions were noisy and argumentative. Around four-thirty, they always began "the official cocktail hour," which made them noisier and lasted until Tucker's mother returned from her temporary job.

Tucker was an authority on libraries. He went to them as often as drunks did to dry out and read up on their symptoms in the medical books; and as often as crazies did to talk to themselves in corners and warm themselves by radiators.

As a small boy, Tucker had been allowed to watch only fourteen hours of television a week. He could watch whatever he chose to watch, and if he wanted to spend one day watching television for fourteen hours straight, he could do that. But he could never watch more than fourteen hours a week.

He had become a reader and a sketcher. In the libraries of New York he found he could do both easier than anywhere else.

As a reader, he was what his mother called a "dilettante." A dabbler. He often didn't finish books and magazines he started. If he checked six books out of the library to take home to read, he never got around to reading any of them. It was the way his father was about their eating in neighborhood restaurants. They never ate in them. His father always said, "We'll get around to them eventually. Let's try something not so close at hand."

But *in* the library, Tucker could read parts of as many books as he wanted to. It was a smorgasbord.

As an artist, Tucker was what his mother called "a depressing Bosch." The first time she had called him that, he had asked why. She had answered, "Bosch, as in Hieronymus Bosch. Look it up." His mother was a great researcher on every subject, but she never did anyone else's research for him. This was what Tucker found under Bosch, Hieronymus: *A Dutch painter known for his scenes of nightmarish tortures in hell at the hands of weird monsters.*

Tucker had looked up the paintings of Bosch. With his mother's special talent for overstatement, he could see why she would say that. Tucker's scenes of library life were odd imaginings: the prissy-looking, middle-aged woman with seams in her stockings, checking out a book with "corpse" in the title, should be sketched with a limp hand hanging out of her purse. In a balloon above her head would be a line of handless people marching into a hand laundry. The nervous-looking man back by the law books, reading up on leases with his overcoat on and necktie loosened, would be sketched reading in a chair before an apartment house, with all his furniture piled around him on the sidewalk, in a snowstorm.

As a sketcher, Tucker could find a face smorgasbord in the libraries, too. It seemed to him sometimes that anyone with any trouble at all eventually found his way to a city library, and the really troubled ones became regulars. Their features were wrecked with disappointment and forbearance. Tucker would look for them at the Epiphany branch on East Twenty-third, back near the religious books; in the basement reference room at the Jefferson in Greenwich Village; in the lobby at Donnell in the West Fifties; the whole of Tompkins Square, and Circulating in the Forty-second Street main branch. Tucker loved wrecked faces, sad smiles, and soft tones, and the libraries of New York abounded in them.

But of all the libraries Tucker had ever visited, the one in Brooklyn Heights was hands down the winner.

Tucker had intended to write a long poem about it and how it wasn't phony like many. It didn't pull something like putting books almost as old as *My Ántonia* in the Pay Duplicate section and charging you five cents a day to read it. It had no Pay Duplicate section, in fact. It was air-conditioned. It had bathrooms and telephone booths and lockers. It was like what someone had once said about the difference between being rich and poor: rich was better. It was plush.

One afternoon, a week before Thanksgiving, Tucker had gone there to work on a poem for his Creative Writing class. The poem was supposed to have a theme of "thanks for something out-of-the-ordinary."

Tucker's poem was about the library. For that reason he would never finish it or show it to anyone. He was aware that a male cat-lover, who was also a lover of libraries, was better off keeping all that to himself. Another fact he kept to himself was his ambition to be a librarian. He figured he'd announce it one day in college, after he'd scored the winning touchdown in a football game or won high honors in some course like Outer Space Cartography.

His poem began:

> *I never thought that anything I'd like best,*
> *Would be located on Cadman Plaza West,*
> *In Brooklyn.*

He jotted it down on the outside of his spiral notebook, saw its promise, abandoned it, and put on his coat. It was five o'clock. In the days when he was still visiting Nader, it was the time he'd start over to Remsen Street.

Instead, he headed down Clinton and turned into Pierrepont, and because Brooklyn Heights was the way he'd heard the English were about animals, he saw cats on stoops, with bells and nametags around their necks, saucers left on windowsills for cats, cats looking down from windows, and cats sunning themselves under lamps in people's parlors. There were dogs everywhere, too, but Tucker had become a cat man.

Tucker had to pass the First Unitarian Church. On the lawn in front was a sermon board behind glass. Instead of the Sunday sermon title and the names of the ministers, there was always a saying on the board: a line from a poem or book.

That afternoon there was something taken from *The Little Prince* by Antoine de Saint-Exupéry.

> *If you tame me, then we shall need each other.*
> *To me, you will be unique in all the world. To*
> *you, I shall be unique in all the world.*

Tucker got a sudden flash of Nader sitting under the Chevrolet on Henry Street the evening he found her. He could remember taking her home under his jacket and telling her not to be wild, everything was going to be okay for her. In fact, he told her, she had walked into a very good deal. That was the truth, too, because Tucker's father hadn't been fired yet. He hadn't been allergic yet. He'd simply been this professional fund-raiser Tucker'd always known him to be. No sweat about money problems. No postnasal drip. He hadn't even minded Nader's litter pan in the bathroom.

Tucker got another flash, not of the past, but of the future: Nader keeling over one day, finished from a massive coronary at nine months. Dr. Wasserman, the Heights vet, told the assembled mourners, "This kitten was stuffed to death." That was what Tucker's father had once said about a client: "His wife stuffed him to death until he suffered a massive coronary."

Tucker's mother had corrected the statement. "His wife stuffed him until he had a massive coronary and died," she said. "He didn't have the massive coronary after he died, dear."

Tucker's mother had her PhD in English Lit. She had once been an editor. Now she was working as one again, temporarily. Just as Tucker was not supposed to say they had moved to Brooklyn, and was supposed to say Brooklyn *Heights,* so was Tucker not supposed to say his mother worked on *Stirring Romances*, and was supposed to say she worked for Arrow Publications. *If you tame me, then we shall need each other.*

Tucker Woolf was tall for his age, with a certain way of standing which had landed him in Corrective Posture two years in a row. He was blue-eyed and bespectacled, with chin-length straight black hair. He shifted his book bag from his right hand to his left. He straightened his shoulders and stopped looking down at the street. It was time to take a stand.

If it would make his father feel better, he was willing to remember to add Heights to Brooklyn when he said where he lived. If it would make his father feel better, he was willing to say his mother's temporary job was at Arrow Publications, never mentioning the crummy magazine which employed her. He was willing, in life, to be discreet, diplomatic, subtle, gentle and forgiving; but there were times when this behavior was wrong.

Tucker Woolf marched across Pierrepont past the Appellate Division of the State Supreme Court, down Henry Street past the Church of Our Lady of Lebanon, and across and down Remsen Street almost to the river. He thought of how he had forced himself to concentrate in Dinky Hocker's presence, so he would never even say something accidental like "fat chance" or "fathead" or "the fat's in the fire." He had handled the whole enormous problem with kid gloves and kindness; but there were times when this behavior was wrong.

He stopped before a red brownstone with a yellow door, went up the stone steps, and lifted the brass knocker.

Dinky herself answered.

Dinky had dusty blond hair, and her cheeks flushed from the slightest exertion. She favored ersatz articles of clothing, like her father's tweed-suit vest worn over a T-shirt, with green cotton pajama bottoms and old white tennis socks.

That was the way she was dressed as she answered the door.

"I thought you weren't going to exercise your visiting rights anymore," she said. Dinky's father was a lawyer, and her conversation was sometimes peppered with legal jargon.

"I just dropped by to tell you I doubt that Nader's happy having a weight problem," Tucker said. "I doubt that you are, either. But you've given her your problem and it isn't fair."

"She's given me a problem, too," Dinky said, undaunted by this sudden pronouncement. "She's scratched her claws on our Hide-A-Bed and ruined it, just when we need it."

"You didn't even listen," Tucker said, walking into the foyer and setting down his book bag. "I'm going to stay until it sinks in, Dinky! Nader doesn't deserve your problems."

"*No one* deserves my problems," Dinky said.

"Why do you have to feed her so much?"

"Don't worry," Dinky said. "We've got another mouth to feed, suddenly. We'll be lucky if there's enough to go around."

"What are you talking about?"

"I'm talking about my cousin."

Then suddenly from behind Dinky this girl appeared.

The first thing Tucker noticed was her eyes. They were very bright, and Tucker found himself wanting to smile at the girl, as though they both had some sort of mischief as a secret between them, maybe on Dinky, maybe not. But there was a definite vibration, an exchange, and Tucker almost did smile, except Tucker rarely smiled. He smiled to himself, usually; no one could tell. But he had an idea this girl could tell. Her own smile grew all the broader.

"This is the other mouth," Dinky said, her hand sweeping grandly and cynically toward the girl. There was something old-fashioned-looking about the girl. She was wearing a navy-blue jumper and a white blouse with long, billowing sleeves. She was wearing a string of pearls, white stockings, and black shoes. The girl was how old? Older than Tucker? Younger? The same age? He wasn't sure. Her hair was black and it spilled down past her shoulders. Her eyes were green like Nader's, and her skin was very smooth and very white.

"I'm Tucker Woolf," Tucker said, because Dinky forgot to introduce them beyond announcing that the girl was the other mouth.

"I'm Natalia Line."

"Fine," Tucker said, embarrased because it rhymed.

"Natalia has a fine line," the girl laughed. "Natalia has a fine, divine line," she continued, laughing all the harder, "a fine divine line, that's mine," and her eyes were flashing.

Tucker didn't laugh easily. He didn't like silly girls. He wouldn't have liked the whole scene at any other time, but somehow it was different because of the girl. He smiled at her. Then he laughed out loud.

Tucker's mother often used to say whenever he laughed, "Oh, don't tell me you're going to choke up some youthful laughter, Tucker!" because he was usually so solemn.

Dinky Hocker was the only one who wasn't amused. "We have a walking, talking, rhyming dictionary living with us," she said very sarcastically, "and I can tell you I'm thrilled about *that.*"

ROBERT FROST

The Pasture

I'm going out to clean the pasture spring;
I'll only stop to rake the leaves away
(And wait to watch the water clear, I may):
I sha'n't be gone long.—You come too.

I'm going out to fetch the little calf
That's standing by the mother. It's so young,
It totters when she licks it with her tongue.
I sha'n't be gone long.—You come too.

Stopping by Woods on a Snowy Evening

Whose woods these are I think I know.
His house is in the village though;
He will not see me stopping here
To watch his woods fill up with snow.

My little horse must think it queer
To stop without a farmhouse near
Between the woods and frozen lake
The darkest evening of the year.

He gives his harness bells a shake
To ask if there is some mistake.
The only other sound's the sweep
Of easy wind and downy flake.

The woods are lovely, dark and deep.
But I have promises to keep,
And miles to go before I sleep,
And miles to go before I sleep.

NORTON JUSTER

Norton Juster is an architect who also writes children's books. The best one, I think, is *The Phantom Tollbooth.* An eleven-year-old girl reader once remarked, "It's very good for a sophisticated laugh," which is a pretty sophisticated judgment.

It's about the quite impossible, quite convincing adventures of a boy named Milo who didn't know what to do with himself. He goes through a magic tollbooth into a queer country called Dictionopolis populated by creatures such as Tock the watchdog, whose body is an alarm clock and who becomes Milo's companion; a Letter Man who sells words and letters; a Spelling Bee who naturally spells out much of what he says; a large beetlelike insect called a Humbug; a politician known as Officer Shrift, a short man of course—you must have heard about short shrift; and five advisers to the king—a duke, a minister, a count, an earl, and an undersecretary—who have their own special manner of talking. Milo, Tock, and the five cabinet members make their way to the palace where the Royal Banquet is about to begin.

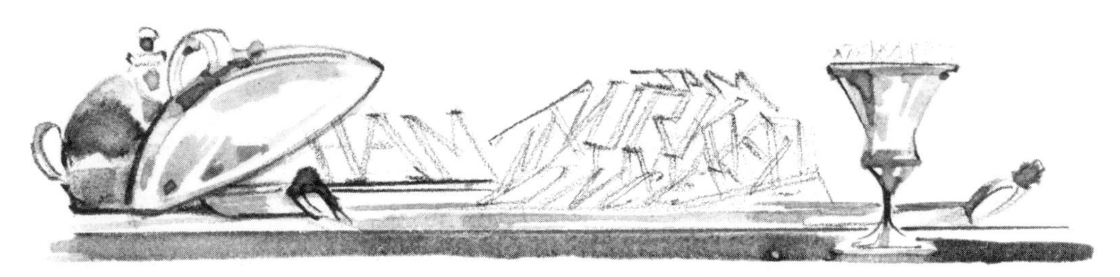

The Royal Banquet

"RIGHT this way."

"Follow us."

"Come along."

"Step lively."

"Here we go," they shouted, hopping from the wagon and bounding up the broad marble stairway. Milo and Tock followed close behind. It was a strange-looking palace, and if he didn't know better he would have said it looked exactly like an enormous book, standing on end, with its front door in the lower part of the binding just where they usually place the publisher's name.

Once inside, they hurried down a long hallway, which glittered with crystal chandeliers and echoed with their footsteps. The walls and ceiling were covered with mirrors, whose reflections danced dizzily along with them, and the footmen bowed coldly.

"We must be terribly late," gasped the earl nervously as they reached the tall doors of the banquet hall.

It was a vast room, full of people loudly talking and arguing. The long table was carefully set with gold plates and linen napkins. An attendant stood behind each chair, and at the center, raised slightly above the others, was a throne covered in crimson cloth. Directly behind, on the wall, was the royal coat of arms, flanked by the flags of Dictionopolis.

Milo noticed many of the people he had seen in the marketplace. The Letter Man was busy explaining to an interested group the history of the W, and off in a corner the Humbug and the Spelling Bee were arguing fiercely about nothing at all. Officer Shrift wandered through the crowd, suspiciously muttering, "Guilty, guilty, they're all guilty," and, on noticing Milo, brightened visibly and commented in passing, "Is it six million years already? My, how time flies."

Everyone seemed quite grumpy about having to wait for lunch, and they were all relieved to see the tardy guests arrive.

"Certainly glad you finally made it, old man," said the Humbug, cordially pumping Milo's hand. "As guest of honor you must choose the menu of course."

"Oh, my," he thought, not knowing what to say.

"Be quick about it," suggested the Spelling Bee. "I'm famished—f-a-m-i-s-h-e-d."

As Milo tried to think, there was an ear-shattering blast of trumpets, entirely off key, and a page announced to the startled guests:

"KING AZAZ THE UNABRIDGED."

The king strode through the door and over to the table and settled his great bulk onto the throne, calling irritably, "Places, everyone. Take your places."

He was the largest man Milo had ever seen, with a great stomach, large piercing eyes, a gray beard that reached to his waist, and a silver signet ring on the little finger of his left hand. He also wore a small crown and a robe with the letters of the alphabet beautifully embroidered all over it.

"What have we here?" he said, staring down at Tock and Milo as everyone else took his place.

"If you please," said Milo, "my name is Milo and this is Tock. Thank you very much for inviting us to your banquet, and I think your palace is beautiful."

"Exquisite," corrected the duke.

"Lovely," counseled the minister.

"Handsome," recommended the count.

"Pretty," hinted the earl.

"Charming," submitted the undersecretary.

"SILENCE," suggested the king. "Now, young man, what can you do to entertain us? Sing songs? Tell stories? Compose sonnets? Juggle plates? Do tumbling tricks? Which is it?"

"I can't do any of those things," admitted Milo.

"What an ordinary little boy," commented the king. "Why, my cabinet members can do all sorts of things. The duke here can make mountains out of molehills. The minister splits hairs. The count makes hay while the sun shines. The earl leaves no stone unturned. And the undersecretary," he finished ominously, "hangs by a thread. Can't you do anything at all?"

"I can count to a thousand," offered Milo.

"A-A-R-G-H, numbers! Never mention numbers here. Only use them when we absolutely have to," growled Azaz disgustedly. "Now, why don't you and Tock come up here and sit next to me, and we'll have some dinner?"

"Are you ready with the menu?" reminded the Humbug.

"Well," said Milo, remembering that his mother had always told him to eat lightly when he was a guest, "why don't we have a light meal?"

"A light meal it shall be," roared the bug, waving his arms.

The waiters rushed in carrying large serving platters and set them on the table in front of the king. When he lifted the covers, shafts of brilliant-colored light leaped from the plates and bounced around the ceiling, the walls, across the floor, and out the windows.

"Not a very substantial meal," said the Humbug, rubbing his eyes, "but quite an attractive one. Perhaps you can suggest something a little more filling."

The king clapped his hands, the platters were removed, and, without thinking, Milo quickly suggested, "Well, in that case, I think we ought to have a square meal of—"

"A square meal it is," shouted the Humbug again. The king clapped his hands once more and the waiters reappeared carrying plates heaped high with steaming squares of all sizes and colors.

"Ugh," said the Spelling Bee, tasting one, "these are awful."

No one else seemed to like them very much either, and the Humbug got one caught in his throat and almost choked.

"Time for the speeches," announced the king as the plates were again removed and everyone looked glum. "You first," he commanded, pointing to Milo.

"Your Majesty, ladies and gentlemen," started Milo timidly, "I would like to take this opportunity to say that in all the—"

"That's quite enough," snapped the king. "Mustn't talk all day."

"But I'd just begun," objected Milo.

"NEXT!" bellowed the king.

"Roast turkey, mashed potatoes, vanilla ice cream," recited the Humbug, bouncing up and down quickly.

"What a strange speech," thought Milo, for he'd heard many in the past and knew that they were supposed to be long and dull.

"Hamburgers, corn on the cob, chocolate pudding—p-u-d-d-i-n-g," said the Spelling Bee in his turn.

"Frankfurters, sour pickles, strawberry jam," shouted Officer Shrift from his chair. Since he was taller sitting than standing, he didn't bother to get up.

And so down the line it went, with each guest rising briefly, making a short speech, and then resuming his place. When everyone had finished, the king rose.

"Pâté de foie gras, soupe à l'oignon, faisan sous cloche, salade endive, fromages et fruits et demi-tasse," he said carefully and clapped his hands again.

The waiters reappeared immediately, carrying heavy, hot trays, which they set on the table. Each one contained the exact words spoken by the various guests, and they all began eating immediately with great gusto.

"Dig in," said the king, poking Milo with his elbow and looking disapprovingly at his plate. "I can't say that I think much of your choice."

"I didn't know that I was going to have to eat my words," objected Milo.

"Of course, of course, everyone here does," the king grunted. "You should have made a tastier speech."

Milo looked around at everyone busily stuffing himself and then back at his own unappetizing plate. It certainly didn't look worth eating, and he was so very hungry.

"Here, try some somersault," suggested the duke. "It improves the flavor."

"Have a rigmarole," offered the count, passing the breadbasket.

"Or a ragamuffin," seconded the minister.

"Perhaps you'd care for a synonym bun," suggested the duke.

"Why not wait for your just desserts?" mumbled the earl indistinctly, his mouth full of food.

"How many times must I tell you not to bite off more than you can chew?" snapped the undersecretary, patting the distressed earl on the back.

"In one ear and out the other," scolded the duke, attempting to stuff one of his words through the earl's head.

"If it isn't one thing, it's another," chided the minister.

"Out of the frying pan into the fire," shouted the count, burning himself badly.

"Well, you don't have to bite my head off," screamed the terrified earl, and flew at the others in a rage.

The five of them scuffled wildly under the table.

"STOP THAT AT ONCE," thundered Azaz, "or I'll banish the lot of you!"

"Sorry."

"Excuse me."

"Forgive us."

"Pardon."

"Regrets," they apologized in turn, and sat down glaring at each other.

The rest of the meal was finished in silence until the king, wiping the gravy stains from his vest, called for dessert. Milo, who had not eaten anything, looked up eagerly.

"We're having a special treat today," said the king as the delicious smells of homemade pastry filled the banquet hall. "By royal command the pastry chefs have worked all night in the half bakery to make sure that—"

"The half bakery?" questioned Milo.

"Of course, the half bakery," snapped the king. "Where do you think half-baked ideas come from? Now, please don't interrupt. By royal command the pastry chefs have worked all night to—"

"What's a half-baked idea?" asked Milo again.

"Will you be quiet?" growled Azaz angrily; but before he could begin again, three large serving carts were wheeled into the hall and everyone jumped up to help himself.

"They're very tasty," explained the Humbug, "but they don't always agree with you. Here's one that's very good." He handed it to Milo and, through the icing and nuts, Milo saw that it said THE EARTH IS FLAT.

"People swallowed that one for years," commented the Spelling Bee, "but it's not very popular these days—d-a-y-s." He picked up a long one that stated THE MOON IS MADE OF GREEN CHEESE and hungrily bit off the part that said CHEESE. "Now *there's* a half-baked idea," he said, smiling.

Milo looked at the great assortment of cakes, which were being eaten almost as quickly as anyone could read them. The count was munching contentedly on IT NEVER RAINS BUT IT POURS and the king was busy slicing one that stated NIGHT AIR IS BAD AIR.

"I wouldn't eat too many of those if I were you," advised Tock. "They may look good, but you can get terribly sick of them."

"Don't worry," Milo replied; "I'll just wrap one up for later," and he folded his napkin around EVERYTHING HAPPENS FOR THE BEST.

T. S. ELIOT

The Song of the Jellicles

Jellicle Cats come out tonight
Jellicle Cats come one come all:
The Jellicle Moon is shining bright—
Jellicles come to the Jellicle Ball.

Jellicle Cats are black and white,
Jellicle Cats are rather small;
Jellicle Cats are merry and bright,
And pleasant to hear when they caterwaul.
Jellicle Cats have cheerful faces,
Jellicle Cats have bright black eyes;
They like to practice their airs and graces
And wait for the Jellicle Moon to rise.

Jellicle Cats develop slowly,
Jellicle Cats are not too big;
Jellicle Cats are roly-poly,
They know how to dance a gavotte and a jig.
Until the Jellicle Moon appears
They make their toilet and take their repose:
Jellicles wash behind their ears,
Jellicles dry between their toes.

Jellicle Cats are white and black,
Jellicle Cats are of moderate size;
Jellicles jump like a jumping-jack,
Jellicle Cats have moonlit eyes.
They're quiet enough in the morning hours,
They're quiet enough in the afternoon,
Reserving their terpsichorean powers
To dance by the light of the Jellicle Moon.

Jellicle Cats are black and white,
Jellicle Cats (as I said) are small;
If it happens to be a stormy night
They will practice a caper or two in the hall.
If it happens the sun is shining bright
You would say they had nothing to do at all:
They are resting and saving themselves to be right
For the Jellicle Moon and the Jellicle Ball.

KENNETH GRAHAME

Kenneth Grahame was descended from Robert of Bruce, the Scottish king who at the famous battle of Bannockburn in 1314 freed Scotland from English rule. Except for his handsome presence Grahame did not inherit his remote ancestor's kingly or martial qualities. Entering the Bank of England when he was nineteen, he became its secretary in 1898, retiring in 1907. His real life, however, was not that of a businessman but that of a dreamer in love with the English countryside, with the happier memories of his childhood, with books, with his own fancies. You can get a dim idea of his personality from the titles of three of his books (not written for children): *Dream Days, Pagan Papers, The Golden Age.*

Abandoned by his father early in life, he was reared by his maternal grandmother. He married unhappily, his physically handicapped and only child Alastair committed suicide at twenty, and he himself suffered from poor health for the last twenty-five years of his life. Yet in *The Wind in the Willows* (1908) he wrote a book that, though a certain sadness can be felt between the lines, shines with joy, humor, and delight in the quick life of river, wood, field, moor, meadow, and the byways of an England that was passing away even as he sat writing.

The Wind in the Willows grew out of stories that he told or wrote to his unfortunate little son. It is about animals—Mole, Water Rat, Badger, Toad, Otter—but of course the animals are also human beings. They lived in a world Grahame himself would have liked to inhabit—a snug, peaceful world in which, as Rat says, "There is *nothing*— absolutely nothing—half so much worth doing as simply messing about in boats."

Friendship, food and drink, jokes, sunlight—these are some of the pleasant things that form the atmosphere of the book—though, if you read it all, you will find that the characters are threatened by enemies and endangered by the comical vanity and recklessness of the irrepressible Toad. What *The Wind in the Willows* is really about, I think, is freedom, which Grahame possessed only when he was a child.

When the book first came out a London reviewer wrote: "As a contribution to natural history the work is negligible." This statement is funnier than anything in the book itself.

The first chapter, printed below, introduces us to the main characters and, I hope, will want to make you read the rest of *The Wind in the Willows.*

The Riverbank

THE MOLE had been working very hard all the morning, spring-cleaning his little home. First with brooms, then with dusters; then on ladders and steps and chairs, with a brush and a pail of whitewash; till he had dust in his throat and eyes, and splashes of whitewash all over his black fur, and an aching back and weary arms. Spring was moving in the air above and in the earth below and around him, penetrating even his dark and lowly little house with its spirit of divine discontent and longing. It was small wonder, then, that he suddenly flung down his brush on the floor, said "Bother!" and "Oh blow!" and also "Hang spring cleaning!" and bolted out of the house without even waiting to put on his coat. Something up above was calling him imperiously, and he made for the steep little tunnel which answered in his case to the graveled carriage-drive owned by animals whose residences are nearer to the sun and air. So he scraped and scratched and scrabbled and scrooged, and then he scrooged again and scrabbled and scratched and scraped, working busily with his little paws and muttering to himself, "Up we go! Up we go!" till at last, pop! his snout came out into the sunlight, and he found himself rolling in the warm grass of a great meadow.

"This is fine!" he said to himself. "This is better than whitewashing!" The sunshine struck hot on his fur, soft breezes caressed his heated brow, and after the seclusion of the cellarage he had lived in so long the carol of happy birds fell on his dulled hearing almost like a shout.

Jumping off all his four legs at once, in the joy of living and the delight of spring without its cleaning, he pursued his way across the meadow till he reached the hedge on the further side.

"Hold up!" said an elderly rabbit at the gap. "Sixpence for the privilege of passing by the private road!" He was bowled over in an instant by the impatient and contemptuous Mole, who trotted along the side of the hedge chaffing the other rabbits as they peeped hurriedly from their holes to see what the row was about. "Onion-sauce! Onion-sauce!" he remarked jeeringly, and was gone before they could think of a thoroughly satisfactory reply. Then they all started grumbling at each other. "How *stupid* you are! Why didn't you tell him—" "Well, why didn't *you* say—" "You might have reminded him—" and so on, in the usual way; but, of course, it was then much too late, as is always the case.

It all seemed too good to be true. Hither and thither through the meadows he rambled busily, along the hedgerows, across the copses, finding everywhere birds building, flowers budding, leaves thrusting—everything happy, and progressive, and occupied. And instead of having an uneasy conscience pricking him and whispering, "White-wash!" he somehow could only feel how jolly it was to be the only idle dog among all these busy citizens. After all, the best part of a holiday is perhaps not so much to be resting yourself, as to see all the other fellows busy working.

He thought his happiness was complete when, as he meandered aimlessly along, suddenly he stood by the edge of a full-fed river. Never in his life had he seen a river before—this sleek, sinuous, full-bodied animal, chasing and chuckling, gripping things with a gurgle and leaving them with a laugh, to fling itself on fresh playmates that shook themselves free, and were caught and held again. All was a-shake and a-shiver—glints and gleams and sparkles, rustle and swirl, chatter and bubble. The Mole was bewitched, entranced, fascinated. By the side of the river he trotted as one trots, when very small, by the side of a man who holds one spellbound by exciting stories; and when tired at last, he sat on the bank, while the river still chattered on to him, a babbling procession of the best stories in the world, sent from the heart of the earth to be told at last to the insatiable sea.

As he sat on the grass and looked across the river, a dark hole in the bank opposite, just above the water's edge, caught his eye, and dreamily he fell to considering what a nice snug dwelling-place it would make for an animal with few wants and fond of a bijou riverside residence, above flood level and remote from noise and dust. As he gazed, something bright and small seemed to twinkle down in the heart of it, vanished, then twinkled once more like a tiny star. But it could hardly be a star in such an unlikely situation; and it was too glittering and small for a glowworm. Then, as he looked, it winked at him, and so declared itself to be an eye; and a small face began gradually to grow up round it, like a frame round a picture.

A brown little face, with whiskers.

A grave round face, with the same twinkle in its eye that had first attracted his notice.

Small neat ears and thick silky hair.

It was the Water Rat!

Then the two animals stood and regarded each other cautiously.

"Hullo, Mole!" said the Water Rat.

"Hullo, Rat!" said the Mole.

"Would you like to come over?" inquired the Rat presently.

"Oh, it's all very well to *talk,*" said the Mole rather pettishly, he being new to a river and riverside life and its ways.

The Rat said nothing, but stooped and unfastened a rope and hauled on it; then lightly stepped into a little boat which the Mole had not observed. It was painted blue outside and white within, and was just the size for two animals; and the Mole's whole heart went out to it at once, even though he did not yet fully understand its uses.

The Rat sculled smartly across and made fast. Then he held up his forepaw as the Mole stepped gingerly down. "Lean on that!" he said. "Now then, step lively!" and the Mole to his surprise and rapture found himself actually seated in the stern of a real boat.

"This has been a wonderful day!" said he, as the Rat shoved off and took to the sculls again. "Do you know, I've never been in a boat before in all my life."

"What?" cried the Rat, openmouthed: "Never been in a—you never—well, I—what have you been doing, then?"

"Is it so nice as all that?" asked the Mole shyly, though he was quite prepared to believe it as he leaned back in his seat and surveyed the cushions, the oars, the rowlocks, and all the fascinating fittings, and felt the boat sway lightly under him.

"Nice? It's the *only* thing," said the Water Rat solemnly, as he leaned forward for his stroke. "Believe me, my young friend, there is *nothing*—absolutely nothing—half so much worth doing as simply messing about in boats. Simply messing," he went on dreamily: "messing—about—in—boats; messing—"

"Look ahead, Rat!" cried the Mole suddenly.

It was too late. The boat struck the bank full tilt. The dreamer, the joyous oarsman, lay on his back at the bottom of the boat, his heels in the air.

"—about in boats—or *with* boats," the Rat went on composedly, picking himself up with a pleasant laugh. "In or out of 'em, it doesn't matter. Nothing seems really to matter, that's the charm of it. Whether you get away, or whether you don't; whether you arrive at your destination or whether you reach somewhere else, or whether you never get anywhere at all, you're always busy, and you never do anything in particular; and when you've done it there's always something else to do, and you can do it if you like, but you'd much better not. Look here! If you've really nothing else on hand this morning, supposing we drop down the river together, and have a long day of it?"

The Mole waggled his toes from sheer happiness, spread his chest with a sigh of full contentment, and leaned back blissfully into the soft cushions. "*What* a day I'm having!" he said. "Let us start at once!"

"Hold hard a minute, then!" said the Rat. He looped the painter through a ring in his landing-stage, climbed up into his hole above, and after a short interval reappeared staggering under a fat, wicker luncheon-basket.

"Shove that under your feet," he observed to the Mole, as he passed it down into the boat. Then he untied the painter and took the sculls again.

"What's inside it?" asked the Mole, wiggling with curiosity.

"There's cold chicken inside it," replied the Rat briefly; "coldtongue-coldhamcoldbeefpickledgherkinssaladfrenchrollscresssandwidgespotted meatgingerbeerlemonadesodawater—"

"Oh stop, stop," cried the Mole in ecstasies: "This is too much!"

"Do you really think so?" inquired the Rat seriously. "It's only what I always take on these little excursions; and the other animals are always telling me that I'm a mean beast and cut it *very* fine!"

The Mole never heard a word he was saying. Absorbed in the new life he was entering upon, intoxicated with the sparkle, the ripple, the scents and the sounds and the sunlight, he trailed a paw in the water and dreamed long waking dreams. The Water Rat, like the good little fellow he was, sculled steadily on and forbore to disturb him.

"I like your clothes awfully, old chap," he remarked after some half an hour or so had passed. "I'm going to get a black velvet smoking suit myself someday, as soon as I can afford it."

"I beg your pardon," said the Mole, pulling himself together with an effort. "You must think me very rude; but all this is so new to me. So—this—is—a—River!"

"*The* River," corrected the Rat.

"And you really live by the river? What a jolly life!"

"By it and with it and on it and in it," said the Rat. "It's brother and sister to me, and aunts, and company, and food and drink, and (naturally) washing. It's my world, and I don't want any other. What it hasn't got is not worth having, and what it doesn't know is not worth knowing. Lord! the times we've had together! Whether in winter or summer, spring or autumn, it's always got its fun and its excitements. When the floods are on in February, and my cellars and basement are brimming with drink that's no good to me, and the brown water runs by my best bedroom window; or again when it all drops away and shows patches of mud that smells like plum cake, and the rushes and weed clog the channels, and I can potter about dry-shod over most of the bed of it and find fresh food to eat, and things careless people have dropped out of boats!"

"But isn't it a bit dull at times?" the Mole ventured to ask. "Just you and the river, and no one else to pass a word with?"

"No one else to—well, I mustn't be hard on you," said the Rat with forbearance. "You're new to it, and of course you don't know. The bank is so crowded nowadays that many people are moving away altogether. Oh no, it isn't what it used to be, at all. Otters, kingfishers, dabchicks, moorhens, all of them about all day long and always wanting you to *do* something—as if a fellow had no business of his own to attend to!"

"What lies over *there?*" asked the Mole, waving a paw towards a background of woodland that darkly framed the water meadows on one side of the river.

"That? Oh that's just the Wild Wood," said the Rat shortly. "We don't go there very much, we riverbankers."

"Aren't they—aren't they very *nice* people in there?" said the Mole a trifle nervously.

"W-e-ll," replied the Rat, "let me see. The squirrels are all right. *And* the rabbits—some of 'em, but rabbits are a mixed lot. And then there's Badger, of course. He lives right in the heart of it; wouldn't live anywhere else, either, if you paid him to do it. Dear old Badger! Nobody interferes with *him*. They'd better not," he added significantly.

"Why, who *should* interfere with him?" asked the Mole.

"Well, of course—there—are others," explained the Rat in a hesitating sort of way. "Weasels—and stoats—and foxes—and so on. They're all right in a way—I'm very good friends with them—pass the time of day when we meet, and all that—but they break out sometimes, there's no denying it, and then—well, you can't really trust them, and that's the fact."

The Mole knew well that it is quite against animal etiquette to dwell on possible trouble ahead, or even to allude to it; so he dropped the subject.

"And beyond the Wild Wood again?" he asked: "Where it's all blue and dim, and one sees what may be hills or perhaps they mayn't and something like the smoke of towns, or is it only cloud-drift?"

"Beyond the Wild Wood comes the Wide World," said the Rat. "And that's something that doesn't matter, either to you or to me. I've never been there, and I'm never going, nor you either, if you've got any sense at all. Don't ever refer to it again, please. Now then! Here's our backwater at last, where we're going to lunch."

Leaving the main stream, they now passed into what seemed at first sight like a little landlocked lake. Green turf sloped down to either edge, brown snaky tree-roots gleamed below the surface of the quiet water, while ahead of them the silvery shoulder and foamy tumble of a weir, arm-in-arm with a restless dripping mill wheel, that held up in its turn a gray-gabled mill house, filled the air with a soothing murmur of sound, dull and smothery, yet with little clear voices speaking up cheerfully out of it at intervals. It was so very beautiful that the Mole could only hold up both forepaws and gasp, "Oh my! Oh my! Oh my!"

The Rat brought the boat alongside the bank, made her fast, helped the still awkward Mole safely ashore, and swung out the luncheon-basket.

The Mole begged as a favor to be allowed to unpack it all by himself; and the Rat was very pleased to indulge him, and to sprawl at full length on the grass and rest, while his excited friend shook out the tablecloth and spread it, took out all the mysterious packets one by one and arranged their contents in due order, still gasping, "Oh my! Oh my!" at each fresh revelation. When all was ready, the Rat said, "Now, pitch in, old fellow!" and the Mole was indeed very glad to obey, for he had started his spring cleaning at a very early hour that morning, as people *will* do, and had not paused for bite or sup; and he had been through a very great deal since that distant time which now seemed so many days ago.

"What are you looking at?" said the Rat presently, when the edge of their hunger was somewhat dulled, and the Mole's eyes were able to wander off the tablecloth a little.

"I am looking," said the Mole, "at a streak of bubbles that I see traveling along the surface of the water. That is a thing that strikes me as funny."

"Bubbles? Oho!" said the Rat, and chirruped cheerily in an inviting sort of way.

A broad glistening muzzle showed itself above the edge of the bank, and the Otter hauled himself out and shook the water from his coat.

"Greedy beggars!" he observed, making for the provender. "Why didn't you invite me, Ratty?"

"This was an impromptu affair," explained the Rat. "By the way—my friend Mr. Mole."

"Proud, I'm sure," said the Otter, and the two animals were friends forthwith.

"Such a rumpus everywhere!" continued the Otter. "All the world seems out on the river today. I came up this backwater to try and get a moment's peace, and then stumble upon you fellows!—At least—I beg pardon—I don't exactly mean that, you know."

There was a rustle behind them, proceeding from a hedge wherein last year's leaves still clung thick, and a stripy head, with high shoulders behind it, peered forth on them.

"Come on, old Badger," shouted the Rat.

The Badger trotted forward a pace or two; then grunted, "H'm! Company," and turned his back and disappeared from view.

"That's *just* the sort of fellow he is!" observed the disappointed Rat. "Simply hates Society! Now we shan't see any more of him today. Well, tell us *who's* out on the river?"

"Toad's out, for one," replied the Otter. "In his brand-new wager-boat; new togs, new everything!"

The two animals looked at each other and laughed.

"Once, it was nothing but sailing," said the Rat. "Then he tired of that and took to punting. Nothing would please him but to punt all day and every day, and a nice mess he made of it. Last year it was house-boating, and we all had to go and stay with him in his houseboat, and pretend we liked it. He was going to spend the rest of his life in a houseboat. It's all the same whatever he takes up; he gets tired of it, and starts on something fresh."

"Such a good fellow, too," remarked the Otter reflectively: "But no stability—especially in a boat!"

From where they sat they could get a glimpse of the main stream across the island that separated them; and just then a wager-boat flashed into view, the rower—a short, stout figure—splashing badly and rolling a good deal, but working his hardest. The Rat stood up and hailed him, but Toad—for it was he—shook his head and settled sternly to his work.

"He'll be out of the boat in a minute if he rolls like that," said the Rat, sitting down again.

"Of course he will," chuckled the Otter. "Did I ever tell you that good story about Toad and the lock keeper? It happened this way. Toad . . ."

An errant mayfly swerved unsteadily athwart the current in the intoxicated fashion affected by young bloods of mayflies seeing life. A swirl of water and a "cloop!" and the mayfly was visible no more.

Neither was the Otter.

The Mole looked down. The voice was still in his ears, but the turf whereon he had sprawled was clearly vacant. Not an Otter to be seen, as far as the distant horizon.

But again there was a streak of bubbles on the surface of the river.

The Rat hummed a tune, and the Mole recollected that animal etiquette forbade any sort of comment on the sudden disappearance of one's friends at any moment, for any reason or no reason whatever.

"Well, well," said the Rat, "I suppose we ought to be moving. I wonder which of us had better pack the luncheon-basket?" He did not speak as if he was frightfully eager for the treat.

"Oh, please let me," said the Mole. So, of course, the Rat let him.

Packing the basket was not quite such pleasant work as unpacking the basket. It never is. But the Mole was bent on enjoying everything, and although just when he had got the basket packed and strapped up tightly he saw a plate staring up at him from the grass, and when the job had been done again the Rat pointed out a fork which anybody ought to have seen, and last of all, behold! the mustard pot, which he had been sitting on without knowing it—still, somehow, the thing got finished at last, without much loss of temper.

The afternoon sun was getting low as the Rat sculled gently homewards in a dreamy mood, murmuring poetry-things over to himself, and not paying much attention to Mole. But the Mole was very full of lunch, and self-satisfaction, and pride, and already quite at home in a boat (so he thought) and was getting a bit restless besides: and presently he said, "Ratty! Please, *I* want to row, now!"

The Rat shook his head with a smile. "Not yet, my young friend," he said—"wait till you've had a few lessons. It's not so easy as it looks."

The Mole was quiet for a minute or two. But he began to feel more and more jealous of Rat, sculling so strongly and so easily along, and his pride began to whisper that he could do it every bit as well. He jumped up and seized the sculls so suddenly, that the Rat, who was gazing out over the water and saying more poetry-things to himself, was taken by surprise and fell backwards off his seat with his legs in the air for the second time, while the triumphant Mole took his place and grabbed the sculls with entire confidence.

"Stop it, you *silly* ass!" cried the Rat, from the bottom of the boat. "You can't do it! You'll have us over!"

The Mole flung his sculls back with a flourish, and made a great dig at the water. He missed the surface altogether, his legs flew up above his head, and he found himself lying on the top of the prostrate Rat. Greatly alarmed, he made a grab at the side of the boat, and the next moment—sploosh!

Over went the boat, and he found himself struggling in the river.

Oh my, how cold the water was, and Oh, how *very* wet it felt. How it sang in his ears as he went down, down, down! How bright and welcome the sun looked as he rose to the surface coughing and spluttering! How black was his despair when he felt himself sinking again! Then a firm paw gripped him by the back of his neck. It was the Rat, and he was evidently laughing—the Mole could *feel* him laughing, right down his arm and through his paw, and so into his—the Mole's—neck.

The Rat got hold of a scull and shoved it under the Mole's arm; then he did the same by the other side of him and, swimming behind, propelled the helpless animal to shore, hauled him out, and set him down on the bank, a squashy, pulpy lump of misery.

When the Rat had rubbed him down a bit, and wrung some of the wet out of him, he said, "Now, then, old fellow! Trot up and down the towing-path as hard as you can, till you're warm and dry again, while I dive for the luncheon-basket."

So the dismal Mole, wet without and ashamed within, trotted about till he was fairly dry, while the Rat plunged into the water again, recovered the boat, righted her and made her fast, fetched his floating property to shore by degrees, and finally dived successfully for the luncheon-basket and struggled to land with it.

When all was ready for a start once more, the Mole, limp and dejected, took his seat in the stern of the boat; and as they set off, he said in a low voice, broken with emotion, "Ratty, my generous friend! I am very sorry indeed for my foolish and ungrateful conduct. My heart quite fails me when I think how I might have lost that beautiful luncheon-basket. Indeed, I have been a complete ass, and I know it. Will you overlook it this once and forgive me, and let things go on as before?"

"That's all right, bless you!" responded the Rat cheerily. "What's a little wet to a Water Rat? I'm more in the water than out of it most days. Don't you think any more about it; and, look here! I really think you had better come and stop with me for a little time. It's very plain and rough, you know—not like Toad's house at all—but you haven't seen that yet; still, I can make you comfortable. And I'll teach you to row, and to swim, and you'll soon be as handy on the water as any of us."

The Mole was so touched by his kind manner of speaking that he could find no voice to answer him; and he had to brush away a tear or two with the back of his paw. But the Rat kindly looked in another direction, and presently the Mole's spirits revived again, and he was even able to give some straight back-talk to a couple of moorhens who were sniggering to each other about his bedraggled appearance.

When they got home, the Rat made a bright fire in the parlor, and planted the Mole in an armchair in front of it, having fetched down a dressing gown and slippers for him, and told him river stories till suppertime. Very thrilling stories they were, too, to an earth-dwelling animal like Mole. Stories about weirs, and sudden floods, and leaping pike, and steamers that flung hard bottles—at least bottles were certainly flung, and *from* steamers, so presumably *by* them; and about herons, and how particular they were whom they spoke to; and about adventures down drains, and night fishings with Otter, or excursions far afield with Badger. Supper was a most cheerful meal; but very shortly afterwards a terribly sleepy Mole had to be escorted upstairs by his considerate host, to the best bedroom, where he soon laid his head on his pillow in great peace and contentment, knowing that his newfound friend the River was lapping the sill of his window.

This day was only the first of many similar ones for the emancipated Mole, each of them longer and fuller of interest as the ripening summer moved onward. He learned to swim and to row, and entered into the joy of running water; and with his ear to the reed-stems he caught, at intervals, something of what the wind went whispering so constantly among them.

The poem that follows is sung by Mr. Toad himself. Kenneth Grahame remarks: "It was perhaps the most conceited song that any animal ever composed."

The Song of Mr. Toad

The world has held great Heroes,
As history books have showed;
But never a name to go down to fame
Compared with that of Toad!

The clever men at Oxford
Know all that there is to be knowed.
But they none of them knew one half as much
As intelligent Mr. Toad!

The animals sat in the Ark and cried,
Their tears in torrents flowed.
Who was it said, "There's land ahead"?
Encouraging Mr. Toad!

The Army all saluted
As they marched along the road.
Was it the King? Or Kitchener?
No. It was Mr. Toad!

The Queen and her Ladies-in-waiting
Sat at the window and sewed.
She cried, "Look! who's that *handsome* man?"
They answered, "Mr. Toad."

JEAN CRAIGHEAD GEORGE

The phone rang at Mrs. George's house and a friendly voice notified her that her book *Julie of the Wolves* had won the John Newbery Medal, given every year for the most distinguished contribution to American literature for children. She reports: "I was electrified and then unbelievably calm. I serenely opened a can of dog food and handed it to a guest who dropped in, put the book I had been reading in the refrigerator, and washed a batch of clean clothes."

Many of the authors in this *Treasury* have won the Newbery Medal but that's not why I've chosen them. Not all good books win prizes and not all prizes go to good books. But there's no doubt about *Julie*. Mrs. George deserved the medal.

The science of observing and interpreting animals in their natural habitat is called ethology. It's a fairly recent science and that's why even fine animal stories like Kipling's *Jungle Book* don't always reflect the actual behavior of animals. Mrs. George spent a summer at the Arctic Research Laboratory at Barrow, Alaska. All her family are naturalists and ecologists. When she writes about animals, she doesn't have to fake it.

Julie is an Eskimo girl whose real name is Miyax. Julie is her "gussak," or white man's name. When the story opens she is alone and starving in the bleak tundra of the North Slope of Alaska. She is only thirteen but has been recently married to a boy named Daniel. Too young for married life, she has run away and finds herself on the tundra with only a wolf pack for company.

From her hunter-father Kapugen she has learned that humans who are willing to learn can communicate with wolves. And so she hopes that Amaroq, the leader of the pack, will somehow help her to survive in the wilderness. So far she hasn't been able to make him understand. Here's how the story continues.

Julie of the Wolves

IT HAD NEVER OCCURRED to her that she would not reach Point Hope before her food ran out.

A dull pain seized her stomach. She pulled blades of grass from their sheaths and ate the sweet ends. They were not very satisfying, so she picked a handful of caribou moss, a lichen. If the deer could survive in winter on this food, why not she? She munched, decided the plant might taste better if cooked, and went to the pond for water.

As she dipped her pot in, she thought about Amaroq. Why had he bared his teeth at her? Because she was young and he knew she couldn't hurt him? No, she said to herself, it was because he was speaking to her! He had told her to lie down. She had even understood and obeyed him. He had talked to her not with his voice, but with his ears, eyes, and lips; and he had even commended her with a wag of his tail.

She dropped her pot, scrambled up the frost heave, and stretched out on her stomach.

"Amaroq," she called softly, "I understand what you said. Can you understand me? I'm hungry—very, very hungry. Please bring me some meat."

The great wolf did not look her way and she began to doubt her reasoning. After all, flattened ears and a tail-wag were scarcely a conversation. She dropped her forehead against the lichens and re-thought what had gone between them.

"Then why did I lie down?" she asked, lifting her head and looking at Amaroq. "Why did I?" she called to the yawning wolves. Not one turned her way.

Amaroq got to his feet, and as he slowly arose he seemed to fill the sky and blot out the sun. He was enormous. He could swallow her without even chewing.

"But he won't," she reminded herself. "Wolves do not eat people. That's gussak talk. Kapugen said wolves are gentle brothers."

The black puppy was looking at her and wagging his tail. Hopefully, Miyax held out a pleading hand to him. His tail wagged harder. The mother rushed to him and stood above him sternly. When he licked her cheek apologetically, she pulled back her lips from her fine white teeth. They flashed as she smiled and forgave her cub.

"But don't let it happen again," said Miyax sarcastically, mimicking her own elders. The mother walked toward Amaroq.

"I should call you Martha after my stepmother," Miyax whispered. "But you're much too beautiful. I shall call you Silver instead."

Silver moved in a halo of light, for the sun sparkled on the guard hairs that grew out over the dense underfur and she seemed to glow.

The reprimanded pup snapped at a crane fly and shook himself. Bits of lichen and grass spun off his fur. He reeled unsteadily, took a wider stance, and looked down at his sleeping sister. With a yap he jumped on her and rolled her to her feet. She whined. He barked and picked up a bone. When he was sure she was watching, he ran down the slope with it. The sister tagged after him. He stopped and she grabbed the bone, too. She pulled; he pulled; then he pulled and she yanked.

Miyax could not help laughing. The puppies played with bones like Eskimo children played with leather ropes.

"I understand *that,*" she said to the pups. "That's tug-of-war. Now how do you say, 'I'm hungry'?"

Amaroq was pacing restlessly along the crest of the frost heave as if something were about to happen. His eyes shot to Silver, then to the gray wolf Miyax had named Nails. These glances seemed to be a summons, for Silver and Nails glided to him, spanked the ground with their forepaws, and bit him gently under the chin. He wagged his tail furiously and took Silver's slender nose in his mouth. She crouched before him, licked his cheek, and lovingly bit his lower jaw. Amaroq's tail flashed high as her mouthing charged him with vitality. He nosed her affectionately. Unlike the fox who met his mate only in the breeding season, Amaroq lived with his mate all year.

Next, Nails took Amaroq's jaw in his mouth and the leader bit the top of his nose. A third adult, a small male, came slinking up. He got down on his belly before Amaroq, rolled trembling to his back, and wriggled.

"Hello, Jello," Miyax whispered, for he reminded her of the quivering gussak dessert her mother-in-law made.

She had seen the wolves mouth Amaroq's chin twice before and so she concluded that it was a ceremony, a sort of "Hail to the Chief." He must indeed be their leader for he was clearly the wealthy wolf; that is, wealthy as she had known the meaning of the word on Nunivak Island. There the old Eskimo hunters she had known in her childhood thought the riches of life were intelligence, fearlessness, and love. A man with these gifts was rich and was a great spirit who was admired in the same way that the gussaks admired a man with money and goods.

The three adults paid tribute to Amaroq until he was almost smothered with love; then he bayed a wild note that sounded like the wind on the frozen sea. With that the others sat around him, the puppies scattered between them. Jello hunched forward and Silver shot a fierce glance at him. Intimidated, Jello pulled his ears together and back. He drew himself down until he looked smaller than ever.

Amaroq wailed again, stretching his neck until his head was high above the others. They gazed at him affectionately and it was plain to see that he was their great spirit, a royal leader who held his group together with love and wisdom.

Any fear Miyax had of the wolves was dispelled by their affection for each other. They were friendly animals and so devoted to Amaroq that she needed only to be accepted by him to be accepted by all. She even knew how to achieve this—bite him under the chin. But how was she going to do that?

She studied the pups, hoping they had a simpler way of expressing their love for him. The black puppy approached the leader, sat, then lay down and wagged his tail vigorously. He gazed up at Amaroq in pure adoration, and the royal eyes softened.

Well, that's what I'm doing! Miyax thought. She called to Amaroq. "I'm lying down gazing at you, too, but you don't look at *me* that way!"

When all the puppies were wagging his praises, Amaroq yipped, hit a high note, and crooned. As his voice rose and fell, the other adults sang out and the puppies yipped and bounced.

The song ended abruptly. Amaroq arose and trotted swiftly down the slope. Nails followed, and behind him ran Silver, then Jello. But Jello did not run far. Silver turned and looked him straight in the eye. She pressed her ears forward aggressively and lifted her tail. With that, Jello went back to the puppies and the three sped away like dark birds.

Miyax hunched forward on her elbows, the better to see and learn. She now knew how to be a good puppy, pay tribute to the leader, and even to be a leader by biting others on the top of the nose. She also knew how to tell Jello to baby-sit. If only she had big ears and a tail, she could lecture and talk to them all.

Flapping her hands on her head for ears, she flattened her fingers to make friends, pulled them together and back to express fear, and shot them forward to display her aggression and dominance. Then she folded her arms and studied the puppies again.

The black one greeted Jello by tackling his feet. Another jumped on his tail, and before he could discipline either, all five were upon him. He rolled and tumbled with them for almost an hour; then he ran down the slope, turned, and stopped. The pursuing pups plowed into him, tumbled, fell, and lay still. During a minute of surprised recovery there was no action. Then the black pup flashed his tail like a semaphore signal and they all jumped on Jello again.

Miyax rolled over and laughed aloud. "That's funny. They're really like kids."

When she looked back, Jello's tongue was hanging from his mouth and his sides were heaving. Four of the puppies had collapsed at his feet and were asleep. Jello flopped down, too, but the black pup still looked around. He was not the least bit tired. Miyax watched him, for there was something special about him.

He ran to the top of the den and barked. The smallest pup, whom Miyax called Sister, lifted her head, saw her favorite brother in action, and, struggling to her feet, followed him devotedly. While they romped, Jello took the opportunity to rest behind a clump of sedge, a moisture-loving plant of the tundra. But hardly was he settled before a pup tracked him to his hideout and pounced on him. Jello narrowed his eyes, pressed his ears forward, and showed his teeth.

"I know what you're saying," she called to him. "You're saying, 'lie down.' " The puppy lay down, and Miyax got on all fours and looked for the nearest pup to speak to. It was Sister.

"Ummmm," she whined, and when Sister turned around she narrowed her eyes and showed her white teeth. Obediently, Sister lay down.

"I'm talking wolf! I'm talking wolf!" Miyax clapped, and tossing her head like a pup, crawled in a happy circle. As she was coming back she saw all five puppies sitting in a row watching her, their heads cocked in curiosity. Boldly the black pup came toward her, his fat backside swinging as he trotted to the bottom of her frost heave, and barked.

"You are *very* fearless, and *very* smart," she said. "Now I know why you are special. You are wealthy and the leader of the puppies. There is no doubt what you'll grow up to be. So I shall name you after my father Kapugen, and I shall call you Kapu for short."

Kapu wrinkled his brow and turned an ear to tune in more acutely on her voice.

"You don't understand, do you?"

Hardly had she spoken than his tail went up, his mouth opened slightly, and he fairly grinned.

"Ee-lie!" she gasped. "You do understand. And that scares me." She perched on her heels. Jello whined an undulating note and Kapu turned back to the den.

Miyax imitated the call to come home. Kapu looked back over his shoulder in surprise. She giggled. He wagged his tail and jumped on Jello.

She clapped her hands and settled down to watch this language of jumps and tumbles, elated that she was at last breaking the wolf code. After a long time she decided they were not talking but roughhousing, and so she started home. Later she changed her mind. Roughhousing was very important to wolves. It occupied almost the entire night for the pups.

"Ee-lie, okay," she said. "I'll learn to roughhouse. Maybe then you'll accept me and feed me." She pranced, jumped, and whimpered; she growled, snarled, and rolled. But nobody came to roughhouse.

Sliding back to her camp, she heard the grass swish and looked up to see Amaroq and his hunters sweep around her frost heave and stop about five feet away. She could smell the sweet scent of their fur.

The hairs on her neck rose and her eyes widened. Amaroq's ears went forward aggressively and she remembered that wide eyes meant fear to him. It was not good to show him she was afraid. Animals attacked the fearful. She tried to narrow them, but remembered that was not right either. Narrowed eyes were mean. In desperation she recalled that Kapu had moved forward when challenged. She pranced right up to Amaroq. Her heart beat furiously as she grunt-whined the sound of the puppy begging adoringly for attention. Then she got down on her belly and gazed at him with fondness.

The great wolf backed up and avoided her eyes. She had said something wrong! Perhaps even offended him. Some slight gesture that meant nothing to her had apparently meant something to the wolf. His ears shot forward angrily and it seemed all was lost. She wanted to get up and run, but she gathered her courage and pranced closer to him. Swiftly she patted him under the chin.

The signal went off. It sped through his body and triggered emotions of love. Amaroq's ears flattened and his tail wagged in friendship. He could not react in any other way to the chin pat, for the roots of this signal lay deep in wolf history. It was inherited from generations and generations of leaders before him. As his eyes softened, the sweet odor of ambrosia arose from the gland on the top of his tail and she was drenched lightly in wolf scent. Miyax was one of the pack.

ANON.

Here's an African poem (by our old friend Anon.) that I found in a good collection of such poems: *A Crocodile Has Me by the Leg,* edited by Leonard W. Doob. You might want to track it down.

Song of an Unlucky Man

Translated by Merlin Ennis

Chaff is in my eye,
A crocodile has me by the leg,
A goat is in the garden,
A porcupine is cooking in the pot,
Meal is drying on the pounding rock,
The King has summoned me to court,
And I must go to the funeral of my mother-in-law:
In short, I am busy.

NORMAN HUNTER

Below is one of the stories from Mr. Hunter's book called *The Incredible Adventures of Professor Branestawm.* We see so many scary TV stories about Mad Scientists that I'm always happy to meet one who's just plain funny.

The Too-Many Professors

LOR' BLESS my heart, whatever can that awful smell be?" gasped Mrs. Flittersnoop, coming out of the kitchen all of a dither, with a smudge of flour on her nose because she was making cakes and her hair all over the place because she was making haste. "Can't be the drains, for the man was here only yesterday to see to them. Can't be something gone bad, for I turned out the larder with my own hands this very morning."

Sniff, sniff, pw-o-o-ugh—it certainly was an extreme sort of smell. Much worse than drains, not so bearable as something gone bad, utterly unlike any kind of smell anyone has ever smelled.

"It's the Professor I'll be bound," said Mrs. Flittersnoop, wiping her hands on her apron.

And it certainly was the Professor, for before Mrs. Flittersnoop had time to get to the door of his inventory out he burst with a little bottle in one hand, a garden syringe in the other, and his clothes stained all the colors of the rainbow and some more besides.

"Amazing! astounding!" he shouted, pushing Mrs. Flittersnoop aside, dashing into his study, and then coming back to fetch her in as well.

"Begging your pardon, sir, but if it's illegible spirits you're making I must give notice," she said, putting her hands on her hips, where they slipped off again because she was a bit thinnish.

"Listen," gasped the Professor getting his five pairs of spectacles so mixed up that he could see four Mrs. Flittersnoops all different sizes and one upside down. "World will resound with discovery. Name a household word. Branestawm's bewildering bacteria, the secret of life revealed! I never used to think I was as clever as I thought I was, but now I see I'm much cleverer than I dared to hope I might be."

Mrs. Flittersnoop didn't answer. The Professor had just uncorked the bottle and the simply awful smellish odor immediately became so bad she had to bury her nose in her apron, which unfortunately only buried half of it, because it was a long nose and a short apron.

"This liquid," said the Professor, all of a tremble with excitement, "will bring to life any picture to which it is applied. Look at this."

He poured some of the sparkling liquid into a glass jar, drew some up in the syringe, and squirted it over a picture of some apples on the cover of a book. Nothing happened, except that the picture got wet.

"Very good, sir, I'm sure," said Mrs. Flittersnoop in a muffled sort of voice from inside the apron. "And now I must be getting back to my cakes." She was out of the room and halfway to the kitchen before the Professor could stop her and drag her back.

"Wait, wait, wait, wait," he shouted excitedly. "It takes time. Look, look!" he pointed with a quivering finger at the picture.

"Oo—er," said his housekeeper. "It's going all lumpy like."

It certainly was. The apples began to swell up, the picture went all nobbly. Green smoke rose from the paper. The smell would have got worse only it couldn't. Then suddenly four lovely rosy apples rolled out of the picture onto the table, as real and solid as you please.

"Oh my!" exclaimed Mrs. Flittersnoop.

"Try one," said the Professor, and together they munched the apples. And except for a rather papery flavor and a funny feeling they gave you as if you were eating an apple in a dream that wasn't there at all but only seemed to be, the apples were certainly a success.

"It is rather a pity," said the Professor, spraying a picture of a box of chocolates to life, "that it costs more to make the liquid for doing this than it would cost to buy the things."

"You don't say!" said Mrs. Flittersnoop, taking a handful of the chocolates and not bothering about her cakes anymore, which had burned themselves into cinders in the meantime, only neither of them could smell them because of the other smell, and thinking the Professor could just spray a few cakes out of a book if he wanted them.

"Yes," said the Professor, hunting about among his books and papers, "and there are certain limitations to the power of the liquid. The things it brings to life go back as they were when the liquid dries off."

"Oo—er," said Mrs. Flittersnoop, thinking of the apples and chocolates she had eaten. But the Professor was pulling out a book with a picture of a cat in it.

"Let me try this," he said, "I don't know yet whether it will work with animals or people."

He filled the syringe again while Mrs. Flittersnoop hid behind the door in case the cat was a scratchy sort of one, which it was quite likely to be, because most of the Professor's books were about wildish kinds of animals.

"Phiz-z-z-z-z-," went the spray. They waited, the paper bulged, the picture smoked, the smell didn't get worse, just as before. Then—"Meow!"—out jumped the cat.

But oh good gracious and heavens above, the next minute with a terrific whoosh of a zoom the whole room was full of an elephant!

"Amazing!" gasped the Professor, struggling out of the wastepaper basket where the elephant had knocked him. But Mrs. Flittersnoop slammed the door and rushed screaming all the way to her sister Aggie's in Lower Pagwell without even stopping to wipe the flour off her nose.

The cat jumped out of the window and followed her, still meowing because the picture of it had showed it meowing and it didn't seem to be able to stop. But most definitely awkward of all, the elephant squeezed its big self through the French windows and followed her too.

"Heavens!" gasped the Professor, getting so worked up that his socks came down. And he dashed after the elephant, dropping his glasses all over the place and holding his handkerchief hoping to be able to catch it and dry the wonderful liquid off it and make it go back into a picture, but not hoping so very much.

But while the Professor was chasing the elephant who was running after the cat who seemed to want to catch up with Mrs. Flittersnoop, who definitely did want to get to her sister Aggie's, the most absolute things were going on in the Professor's room. Voices could have been heard if there had been anyone about to hear them. Rumblings and rustlings were occurring. Chatterings went up. People started talking round the place like goodness knows what.

When the elephant had come out of the picture so suddenly he'd upset the jar of wonderful liquid all over the Professor's photograph album. Good gracious, what a thing to do! Liquid that could make things come to life and all! And upset on a photograph album of all places!

When the Professor, who had given up the chase at Pagwell Gardens, came staggering back all out of breath the first thing he noticed was himself opening the door to himself.

"Good afternoon," said the Professor, not recognizing himself.

"Don't take it for a moment, the sun's in my eyes," said the other one of him.

The Professor was just wondering what the answer to that was when two more of himself, one at sixteen and one at twenty-two, came out of the study, followed by three of Mrs. Flittersnoop in different hats of her sister Aggie's, two of Colonel Dedshott, one before he joined the Catapult Cavaliers and one just after.

"Heavens!" cried the Professor. Pushing past them he dashed up the stairs, nearly falling over three more of himself aged eighteen months, cannoned into another Mrs. Flittersnoop at fifteen, in fancy dress as Bo-Peep, on the landing. Feverishly he searched the rooms. Everywhere were more and more of himself, at all ages and in all sorts of clothes including one of him extra specially young with nothing on at all but a big smile.

Everywhere there were duplicate Mrs. Flittersnoops and spare Colonel Dedshotts and extra copies of various friends and relations. The wonderful liquid had brought every single one of the photographs in the album to life. And they were all saying the same things over and over again.

"Don't take it yet, I've got the sun in my eyes," and "Had I better take my hat off first?" and "Hurry up and take it, I must go in and get tea," and "I say, what a ripping camera!" and "Baby want petty sing," and "Goo goo." All of them were saying whatever they were saying when the photograph was taken and couldn't say anything else. But as they were all saying it together it began to get awful. Worst of all, there was half of a policeman who had got taken in one of the photos by mistake, and he kept hopping about on his one leg saying in a half sort of voice "Pass along p——" which was all he could manage of "Pass along please."

"Terrible! terrible!" gasped the Professor, guessing what had happened although he hadn't any of his pairs of spectacles on and everyone looked a bit hazy, especially one of Mrs. Flittersnoop that had been taken out of focus and was all hazy anyway and kept saying "Ploof woo woo muffn plith a woogle," because of course her voice was out of focus too.

"Oh dear," gasped the Professor, "supposing I get mixed up with all these come-to-life-photo sort of people and forget which is really me?"

Just then there was a loud bang from the inventory, where one of the Professors, age sixteen, had been fiddling about trying to invent something and done an explosion instead.

Out dashed the Professor nearly in time to be hit by a piece of roof. But immediately a rumblety bump followed by loud wowing from inside the house made him dash back. Three of them, aged eighteen months, had fallen down the stairs together. A thing he had done himself just after those particular photographs were taken.

"Ploof woo woo muffn plith a woogle," shouted the out-of-focus hazy Mrs. Flittersnoop rushing down the stairs. "Pass along p—— Pass along p—— Pass along p——" cried the half policeman hopping along from the kitchen, where he had been trying to eat half a pie he had found.

Then pr-r-r-ing-g went the doorbell and in came the real Colonel Dedshott.

"Ha! hullo, Branestawm!" he said to one of the photo Professors, aged twenty or so. "Party on and all that, what! Sorry to intrude, you know."

"Hold it perfectly still while you press the lever," said the photo Professor, who had been telling someone how to take the photo.

"Ha, ha! yes, of course," said the Colonel, not understanding a bit of course but thinking the Professor was talking some of his professorish stuff, which he wouldn't have understood anyway. "Been for a holiday? You're looking well, 'pon my word you look ten years younger."

"Hold it perfectly still while you press the lever," retorted the photo Professor, who of course looked very much more than ten years younger than the real Professor.

"Ploof woo woo muffn plith a woogle," said the hazy Mrs. Flittersnoop, bustling up.

"Goo goo," said the very young nothing-on-at-all Professor, trying to climb up the Colonel's trousers.

"How will my uniform come out?" said one of the photo sort of Colonels clanking out of the dining room.

"What's this? what's this!" roared the real Colonel, catching sight of him. "Impostor, scoundrel! That is not me at all, I'm me here," he shouted and chased his photograph up the stairs. "Impostor, scoundrel!" "Will my uniform come out all right?" "Wait till I catch you. Police,

police!" "Pass along p—— Pass along p——" "Goo goo," "Ploof woo woo muffn plith a woogle."

It was more awful than ever. The real Professor dashed round a corner slap into the real Colonel, and each of them thought the other wasn't him at all, and while they were getting explained to each other three of the Mrs. Flittersnoops changed hats, which probably made things no worse.

"Quick," gasped the Professor after he had told the Colonel what had happened, so rapidly that the Colonel's head was nearly as fuzzy as the out-of-focus Mrs. Flittersnoop. "Must get blotting paper, dry liquid off photos, then will go back into album."

Round the house they dashed, brandishing blotters right and left. The little Professors were caught and blotted up quite easily, but Colonel Dedshott got away from himself three times, and the Mrs. Flittersnoop in fancy dress kept dodging the Professor round the banisters.

Slap slap, bump bang, scuffle biff. "Don't take it yet, I've got the sun in my eyes." "Hold it perfectly still . . ." "How will my uniform come out?" "Ploof woo woo muffn . . ." Round and round the house, up and down the stairs. The real Professor and Colonel caught each other eight times. The half policeman was hopping about like a canary shouting his half piece half at the top of his voice. Some of the Professors had got hold of blotting paper and were joining in the chase. Then a window blew open and the draft from the open front door blew them all out of it and down the road, for they were beginning to get a bit light now that the effects of the liquid were wearing off.

"After them!" panted the Colonel, drawing his sword and falling over it.

Out they dashed and down the road. Clouds of Professors and Mrs. Flittersnoops were all over the place. A real policeman stopped and gaped at the half policeman, who shouted "Pass along p——" for the last time and them went zzzzzzzzp back into the photograph he had come from, with the Professor aged twenty.

"Hurray, hurray!" roared the Colonel, throwing his hat in the air and not bothering to catch it, when it landed on the real Professor's head. "Victory! the enemy is routed."

And so they were, for the sun had come out and quickly dried the wonderful liquid off the unreasonable crowd of extra sort of people and soon the road was strewn with photographs, which the Colonel and the Professor carefully burned, making an awful smoke all over the place, but never mind.

Next day a note came up from Mrs. Flittersnoop, written on the back of a picture of an elephant, to say that if the Professor would promise not to do it again she would come back.

"Well, well, well," he said. "All the liquid has been used up and I've forgotten the recipe so I shan't be able to do it again, thank goodness. But it was most instructive."

So back came Mrs. Flittersnoop, and the Professor wrote a book about his wonderful liquid but nobody believed it.

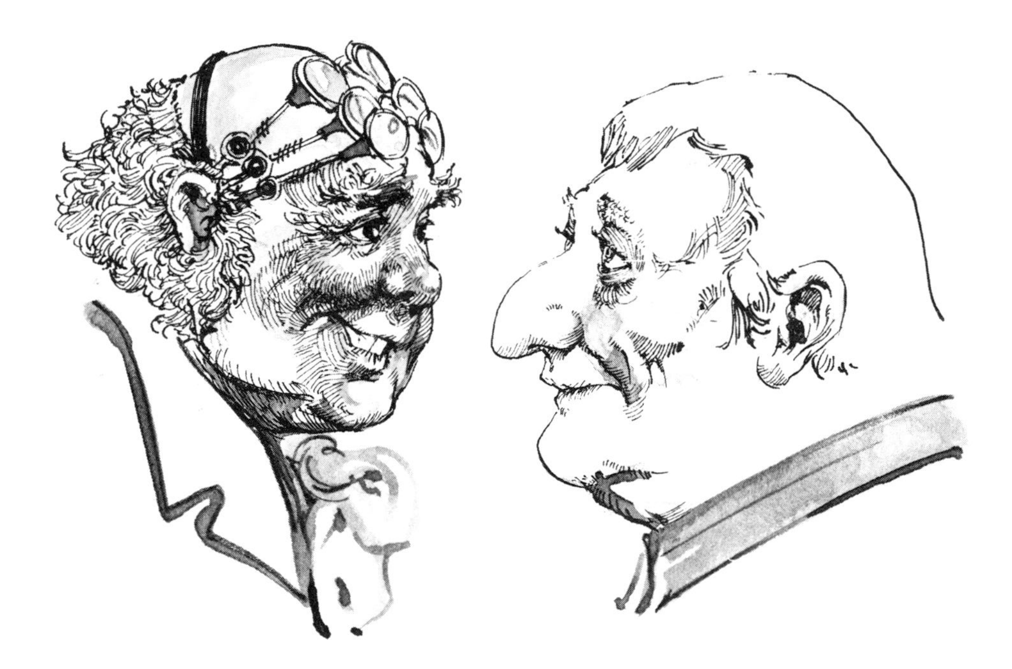

WALTER DE LA MARE

Silver

Slowly, silently, now the moon
Walks the night in her silver shoon;
This way, and that, she peers, and sees
Silver fruit upon silver trees;
One by one the casements catch
Her beams beneath the silvery thatch;
Couched in his kennel, like a log,
With paws of silver sleeps the dog;
From their shadowy cote the white breasts peep
Of doves in a silver-feathered sleep;
A harvest mouse goes scampering by,
With silver claws, and silver eye;
And moveless fish in the water gleam,
By silver reeds in a silver stream.

Bones

Said Mr. Smith, "I really cannot
  Tell you, Dr. Jones—
The most peculiar pain I'm in—
  I think it's in my bones."

Said Dr. Jones, "Oh, Mr. Smith,
  That's nothing. Without doubt
We have a simple cure for that;
  It is to take them out."

He laid forthwith poor Mr. Smith
  Close-clamped upon the table,
And, cold as stone, took out his bone
  As fast as he was able.

And Smith said, "Thank you, thank you, thank you,"
  And wished him a Good-day;
And with his parcel 'neath his arm
  He slowly moved away.

Jim Jay

Do diddle di do,
  Poor Jim Jay
Got stuck fast
  In Yesterday.
Squinting he was,
  On cross-legs bent,
Never heeding
  The wind was spent.
Round veered the weathercock,
  The sun drew in—
And stuck was Jim
  Like a rusty pin. . . .

We pulled and we pulled
  From seven till twelve,
Jim, too frightened
  To help himself.
But all in vain.
  The clock struck one,
And there was Jim
  A little bit gone.
At half-past five
  You scarce could see
A glimpse of his flapping
  Handkerchee.

And when came noon,
  And we climbed sky-high,
Jim was a speck
  Slip-slipping by.

Come tomorrow,
  The neighbors say,
He'll be past crying for:
  Poor Jim Jay.

LOUISE FITZHUGH

When Louise Fitzhugh's *Harriet the Spy* first came out there was a big fuss about it. It was something absolutely new in books for children. Some teachers and parents were shocked by it because it doesn't always present grown-ups and school in a favorable light, and also because Harriet herself, though very smart, is a snooper, too, and even a little mean. Besides, the book and its sequel, *The Long Secret,* often deal with matters not ordinarily found in children's books. There isn't a sentimental word or episode in them. I doubt, however, that they'll shock you.

Harriet Welsch, aged eleven, is the only child of rather rich parents living on Manhattan's Upper East Side. She's a curious girl, intensely interested in what people, especially older ones, do and feel and think. And so she becomes a spy—that is, she keeps secret notebooks in which she records everything she notices about her parents, her friends, her neighbors. This eventually gets her into trouble, as you'll find out if you read this funny, surprising, and very "sophisticated" book.

The extract I've chosen makes fun of the fancy school she attends. The reference to "Ole Golly" is to her beloved nursemaid who has just gone to be married, leaving Harriet feeling rather lost.

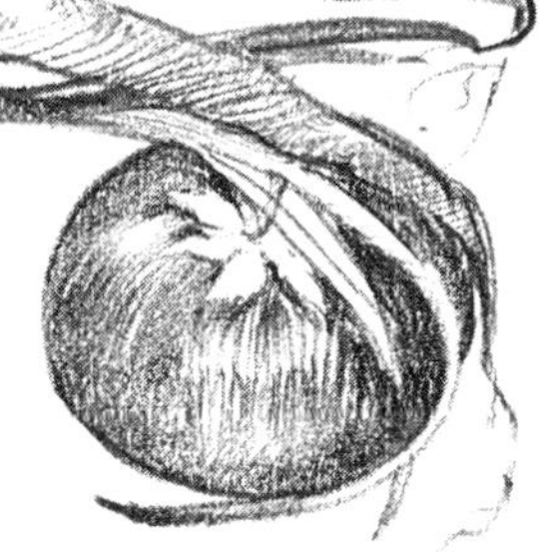

Harriet the Spy

FROM CHAPTER SEVEN

SHE SUDDENLY REMEMBERED that today was the day for parts to be chosen for the Christmas pageant. She wanted to be on time because otherwise she would get a rotten part. Last year she had been late and had ended up being one of the sheep.

Even though she hurried she still went through the same routine she went through every morning. She loved routine so much that Ole Golly had always had to watch her to see that she didn't put on the same clothes as the day before. They always seemed to Harriet to fit better after she had worn them for a while.

As soon as she was dressed she bounced down the steps into the dining room, where her mother sent her back upstairs immediately to wash her face. How could she remember all these things, she wondered. Ole Golly always remembered everything. After breakfast she took a few cursory notes—comments on the weather, the cook, her father's choice of tie, etc.—then got her books and walked to school. She took a few more notes as she watched people pouring into the school. Everyone always sidled up to her and asked, "What are you writing in that notebook?" Harriet would just smile slyly. It drove them crazy.

Harriet always did her work swiftly and in a very routine way, signing everything *Harriet M. Welsch* with a big flourish. She loved to write her name. She loved to write anything for that matter. Today she was about to write her name at the top of the page when she remembered again that today was the day for discussion on the Christmas pageant.

Miss Elson came into the room and they all stood up and said, "Good morning, Miss Elson." Miss Elson bowed and said, "Good morning, children." Then they all sat down and punched each other.

Sport threw Harriet a note which said: *I hear there's a dance about pirates. Let's try and get that one, that is if we have to do it.*

Harriet wrote back a note which said: *We have to do it, they throw you out otherwise.*

Sport wrote back: *I have no Christmas spirit.*

Harriet wrote back: *We'll have to fake it.*

Miss Elson stood in the middle of the room and called for order. No one paid the slightest bit of attention, so she hit the blackboard with the eraser which sent up a cloud of smoke, making her sneeze and everyone else laugh. Then she grew very stern and stared a long time at a spot somewhere down the middle aisle. That always worked.

"Now, children," she began when there was silence, "today is the day to plan our Christmas pageant. First, let's have some ideas from the floor about what we would like to do. I don't think I need bother explaining what this day means to us. There is only one new child here who might wonder." The Boy with the Purple Socks looked horribly embarrassed. "And I think I can simplify this by saying that at the Christmas pageant we get a chance to show the parents what we have been learning. Now each one hold up your hand when you have a suggestion."

Sport's arm shot up. "What about pirates?"

"Well, that's a thought. I'll write that down, Simon, but I think I heard something about the fourth grade being pirates. Next?"

Marion Hawthorne stood up. Harriet and Sport looked at each other with pained expressions. Marion said, "I think, Miss Elson, that we should do a spectacular of the Trojan War. That would show everyone exactly what we have been learning." She sat down again.

Miss Elson smiled. "That's a lovely idea, Marion. I shall certainly write that down." Harriet, Sport, and Janie groaned loudly. Janie stood up. "Miss Elson. Don't you think there will be certain difficulties about building a Trojan horse, much less getting us all in there?"

"Well, I don't think we'll go that far in realism, Janie. This is still open for discussion anyway, so let's hear the other ideas before we discuss the details. I don't know how big a spectacular we could have in the time allotted us. Anyway, I think I should remind you that we are not supposed to give a play. The sixth grade is supposed to dance. We are due in the gymnasium in thirty minutes to discuss this dance with Miss Berry, the dance teacher, then be measured for costumes by Miss Dodge. Now you know that once the subject is chosen you all improvise your dances. But this year you will be allowed to choose your subject, whereas always before Miss Berry has chosen it."

"SOLDIERS," screamed Sport.

"Now, not out of turn, Simon. I'll go down the line and each one gets a chance." Miss Elson then called the roll. "Andrews?" she said, and Carrie got up and said that she thought it would be nice to have a dance about Dr. Kildare and Ben Casey. Miss Elson wrote it down. There was a great deal of whispering around the room as people started trying to get their gang to agree on something.

"Gibbs?"

"I think that a dance about the Curies discovering radium would be nice. We could all be particles except me and Sport, and we could be Monsieur and Madame Curie."

"Hansen?"

Beth Ellen shot a terrified glance at Marion Hawthorne, who had been sending her a barrage of notes. Finally she said softly, "I think we should all be things you eat at Christmas dinner."

"Hawthorne?"

Marion stood up. "I think that's an excellent suggestion on Beth Ellen Hansen's part. I think we should be Christmas dinner too."

"Hennessey?"

Rachel stood up. "I agree with Marion and Beth Ellen. I think that's a good idea."

"Peters?"

Laura Peters was terribly shy, so shy that she smiled at everybody all the time, as though they were about to hit her. "I think that's a good idea too," she quavered, and sank gratefully back into her seat.

"Matthews?"

The Boy with the Purple Socks stood up and said in an offhand way, "Why not? I'd just as soon be a Christmas dinner as anything else."

"Rocque?"

Simon looked at Harriet. She knew what that look meant. She was becoming aware of the same thing. They were surrounded. They should have gotten together and now it was too late. In a minute they would all be assigned to things like giblet gravy. Simon stood up. "I don't know why we don't do the Trojan War like Marion Hawthorne said first. I would a whole lot rather be a soldier than some carrots and peas."

Very clever, thought Harriet. Maybe Marion would consent to her own idea. How bright Sport is, she thought.

"Welsch?"

"I think Sport's absolutely right," and sat down, intercepting a glare from Marion Hawthorne as she did so. Uh-oh, thought Harriet, she's on to us.

"Whitehead?"

Pinky's was the only name left. Sport threw a pencil right in his face. At first Harriet couldn't see why. Then she saw Pinky look at Sport, then stand up and say sadly, "I agree with Harriet and Simon."

Well, thought Harriet, that's three against the world. Too bad Janie had to be in such a hurry about the Curies.

There was a vote but they knew they had lost even before it happened.

Miss Elson said, "I think that's a lovely idea. Now we can have a little discussion with Miss Berry about which parts of the dinner we will take, and then you can start making up your dances at home. Now let's go to the gym."

Everyone but Marion Hawthorne and Rachel Hennessey looked terribly disgruntled. They all got up and filed after Miss Elson out of the classroom, down the stairs, into the courtyard, through the courtyard with the little patch of green called the back lawn, and into the gymnasium, where a scene of utter pandemonium greeted them.

It was obvious that everyone in the school was in the gym. There were all sizes and shapes of girls from little ones to older ones just about to graduate. Miss Berry was screeching frantically, and Miss Dodge was measuring so fast she looked as though she might fly right out the window. Hairpins were falling out and her glasses were askew as she whipped through waist after waist, hip after hip. Miss Berry's leotards looked baggy.

Sport looked around wildly. "I've never been so terrified in my life. Look at all these girls." He began to edge his way toward Pinky Whitehead and the Boy with the Purple Socks.

Harriet grabbed him by the collar. "You stay right here. Suppose something happens and we have to have partners." She pushed her face close to his. He began to sweat nervously but stayed next to her after that.

"Now, children, sixth grade over here, please." Miss Elson was gesturing frantically.

Marion Hawthorne looked around pompously at everyone who didn't move instantly. She always seemed to be laboring under the impression that she was Miss Elson's understudy. "Come along there, Harriet," she said imperiously. Harriet had a sudden vision of Marion grown up, and decided she wouldn't look a bit different, just taller and more pinched.

"Boy, does she tee me off," said Sport, digging his hands in his pockets and his sneakers against the floor as though he would never move.

"Simon." Miss Elson spoke quite sharply, and Sport jumped a mile. "Simon, Harriet, Jane, come along now." They moved. "Now we'll stand here and wait our turn with Miss Berry and I don't want any talking. The din in this place is unbearable."

"Isn't it awful?" said Marion Hawthorne in a falsetto.

Harriet thought, Marion Hawthorne is going to grow up and play bridge a lot.

Pinky Whitehead looked as though he might faint. He ran to Miss Elson frantically and whispered something in her ear. She looked down at him. "Oh, Pinky, can't you wait?"

"No," said Pinky loudly.

"But it's so far!"

Pinky shook his head again, was dismissed by Miss Elson, and ran out. Sport laughed. There weren't any bathrooms for boys in the gym.

"Thought he'd never leave," said Janie. She had gotten this from her mother.

Harriet looked at Beth Ellen staring into space. Harriet was under the impression that Beth Ellen had a mother in an insane asylum, because Mrs. Welsch had once said, "That poor child. Her mother is always at Biarritz."

"All right, children, Miss Berry is ready now." They marched over with flat feet, like prisoners. Harriet felt like Sergeant York.

Miss Berry was in her usual state of hysteria. Her hair was pulled into a wispy ponytail, as though it were pulling her eyes back.

She looked at them wildly. "Sixth grade, yes, sixth grade, let's see. What have you decided? Well? What have you decided?"

Marion Hawthorne spoke for them, naturally. "We've decided to be a whole Christmas dinner," she said brightly.

"Lovely, lovely. Now let's see, vegetables first, vegetables . . ." Sport started to sprint for the door. Miss Elson pulled him back by the ear. Pinky Whitehead arrived back. Miss Berry turned to him, enchanted. "*You* will make a *wonderful* stalk of celery."

"What?" said Pinky stupidly.

"And *you*"—she pointed to Harriet—"are an ONION."

This was too much. "I refuse. I absolutely REFUSE to be an onion."

She stood her ground. She could hear Sport whispering his support behind her. Her ears began to burn as they all turned and looked at her. It was the first time she had ever really refused to do anything.

"Oh, dear." Miss Berry looked as though she might run out the door.

"Harriet, that's ridiculous. An onion is a beautiful thing. Have you ever really looked at an onion?" Miss Elson was losing all touch with reality.

"I will NOT do it."

"Harriet, that's enough. We won't have any more of this impudence. You ARE an onion."

"I am not."

"Harriet, that is QUITE enough."

"I won't do it. I quit."

Sport was pulling at her sleeve. He whispered frantically, "You can't quit. This is a SCHOOL." But it was too late. A roar of laughter went up from the group. Even that mild thing, Beth Ellen, was laughing her head off. Harriet felt her face turning red.

Miss Berry seemed to come back to life. "Now, children. I think it would be nice to take each thing from its inception to the time it arrives on the table. We must have some more vegetables. You, there"—she pointed to Janie—"you're squash. And you"—she pointed to Beth Ellen—"are a pea." Beth Ellen looked as though tears were close. "You two"—she pointed to Marion Hawthorne and Rachel Hennessey—"can be the gravy. . . ." At this Harriet, Sport, and Janie broke into hysterical peals of laughter and had to be quieted by Miss Elson before Miss Berry could continue. "I don't see what's funny. We have to have gravy. You"—she pointed to Sport—"and you"—she pointed to Pinky Whitehead—"are the turkey." "Well, of all the . . ." began Sport and was shushed by Miss Elson.

After she had made the Boy with the Purple Socks into a bowl of cranberries, she turned to the class.

"Now all the vegetables, listen to me," said Miss Berry, planting her feet firmly in the fifth position. Harriet made a mental note to make a note of the fact that Miss Berry always wore, even on the street, those flat, mouse-gray practice shoes. They were always terribly old ones with the cross bar curling away from the arch.

". . . I want you to feel—to the very best of your endeavor—I want you to feel that one morning you *woke up* as one of these vegetables, one of these *dear* vegetables, nestling in the earth, warm in the heat and power and magic of growth, or striving tall above the ground, pushing through, bit by bit in the miracle of birth, waiting for the glorious moment when you will be . . ."

"Eaten," Harriet whispered to Sport.

". . . once and for all, your essential and beautiful self, full-grown, radiant." Miss Berry's eyes were beginning to glaze. One arm was outstretched toward the skylight; half of her hair had fallen over one ear. She held the pose in silence.

Miss Elson coughed. It was a things-are-getting-altogether-out-of-hand cough.

Miss Berry jumped. She looked as though she had just come up out of a subway and didn't know east from west. She gave an embarrassed titter, then started afresh. "We'll start with the tenderest moment of these little vegetables, for you know, children, this dance has a story, a story, a lovely story." She trilled a bit of laughter to let them know she was still there. "It starts, as do all stories, with the moment of conception." She looked around in a delighted way. Miss Elson turned pale.

"It starts, naturally, with the farmer—"

"Hey, I want to be the farmer," Sport yelled.

"Do not say 'hey' to a teacher." Miss Elson was losing patience.

"Oh, but, dear boy, one of the older girls will be the farmer. A farmer must be taller, after all, than vegetables. Vegetables are very *short.*" She looked annoyed that he didn't know this. Sport turned away in disgust.

"Well, the farmer comes in on this lovely morning when the ground is freshly broken, open and yielding, waiting to receive. When he enters, you will all be piled in a corner like seed waiting to be planted. You will just lie there in lumps like this—" and she fell abruptly to the ground. She lay there like a heap of old clothes.

"Come on, let's split; she's gone." Sport turned to go.

"Miss Berry, I think they've got the position," said Miss Elson loudly. Miss Berry turned one inquiring eye over her shoulder to face a royal snub from Miss Elson. She scrambled to her feet.

"All right, children"—she was suddenly crisp—"I want you to start improvising your dances, and I will see what you've done next dance class." The change in her was so remarkable that the children all stared in silence. "Please file over there and be fitted." She turned her back. It was all so swift that Miss Elson stood gaping a minute before she started to herd them toward the costume corner. They all looked back curiously at Miss Berry, who stood, feet planted flatly, her misunderstood nose high in the air.

The costume corner looked like Macy's on sale day. Quantities of tulle flew through the air.

Sport wilted. "Boy, this is a scene I *really* can't make."

It *was* dreary. Harriet remembered it from last year as a long wait with your feet hurting while a terribly flustered Miss Dodge measured you in a sweaty way and, likely as not, stuck you full of pins.

"One day," said Janie, "I am going to come in here with a vial and blow this place sky-high."

The three of them stood glumly, staring at the tulle.

"How do you practice being an onion?" Harriet looked over at Miss Berry, who was falling into another pile of rags on the floor. Evidently all the dances were the same.

Sport got an evil look. "I think I'll scream as loud as I can when she measures me."

Janie's turn came. "Here goes nothing," she said loudly.

KORNEI CHUKOVSKY

I do not read Russian so I am not sure if there are many good Russian writers for children. Those who have been translated into English for the most part sound pretty bad. Kornei Chukovsky is the great exception. Two interesting facts about Chukovsky are that he was also a magician and that he died a millionaire, which is hard to do in Soviet Russia.

He knew English well and admired Hugh Lofting's Doctor Dolittle stories, an example of which you will find on page 126. But even before he became acquainted with Lofting, he had conceived for Russian children a Doctor Dolittle of his own. In Russia, Doctor Concocter is called Doctor Aybolit, which means Ouch-it-hurts.

I have shortened Richard N. Coe's wonderful translation of "Doctor Concocter" a little. Try reading it aloud—that's the best way.

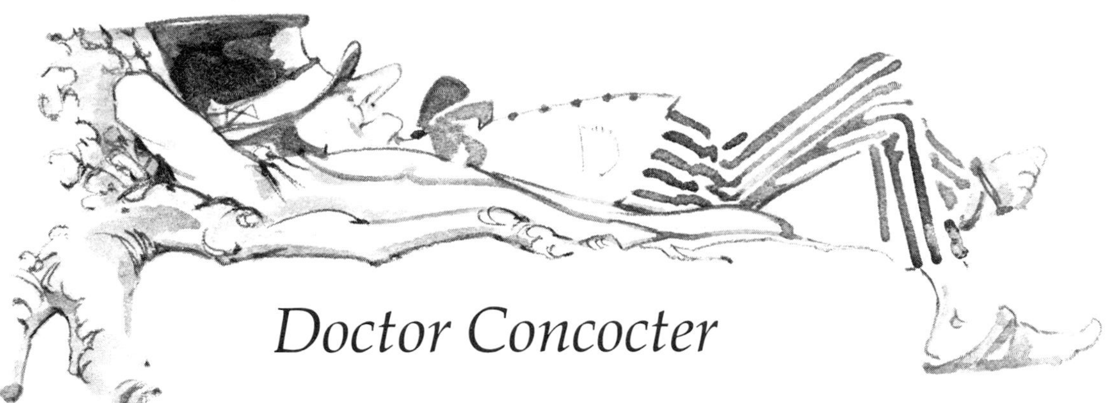

Doctor Concocter

Translated by Richard N. Coe

Doctor
Concocter
sits under a tree;
He's ever
so clever.
(He has a *Degree!*)
All the Hares,
and the Bears,
and the Snakes,
and the Weasels
Are sure
of a cure
for their headaches
and measles.
Hippo,
or Rhino,
or Otter,
or Setter . . .
Doctor
Concocter
will make them all
better.

One windy day,
One day in May,
When the West wind blew from the North,
The telegraph-pup
Came galloping up
With a telegram held in his mouth:
"Doctor, get dressed,
Here's an urgent request
From the Hippos who live in the South!"

"Come to Africa!
To Africa . . . !
As quick as quick can be!
Come and save
our Hippo-babies,
who are sick as sick can be!"

"You don't mean it?"
"Yes, we do . . .
They've got chickenpox and 'flu,
They've got cholera and mumps,
And they've all come out in lumps;
They've got gastroenteritis,
dermatitis
and bronchitis,
Poli-
oli-
myelitis . . .
Come and tell us what to do!
Come and tell us . . .
Come and tell us . . .
Oh, we don't know what to do."

"Don't you worry!
  I shall hurry,
I'll be round to see you soon.
  Shall I find you near the river,
    Near the old Limpopo River,
  Where the rains come down forever
From the Mountains of the Moon?"
"Oh, our home lies hidden far
  Beyond the Isles of Zanzibar,
    Where the Hills of Ruwenzori
  Touch the Coast of Cinnabar . . .
Where the empty Kalahari
  Sighs forever and forever . . .
    Where the jungle twines like ivy
  Round the great Limpopo River . . .

"In the river,
  In the river,
    In the great Limpopo River,
  In the pale Limpopo River
  Lie the islands where we are."

So . . .
    The Doctor grabbed his bag,
  Set off running like a stag,
Through the hedges,
    Through the sedges,
He ran busy as a Beaver;
And he whispered as he ran:
  "I must get there if I can!
I must get there,
                    quickly,
                              quickly,

To the great Limpopo River."

But the rain turned into snow,
  And the gales began to blow,
    And they shouted: "Doctor, Doctor,
  You'll be turned to ice, you know!"

And the Doctor tripped and fell,
  And he lay there very still,
    And he said: "I can't go on,
  And I don't feel very well . . .
And I *really* can't go on . . .
  And I *really* don't feel well . . .
    I shall never
                never
                    NEVER
Reach the pale Limpopo River!"
Then from out behind a tree
  Slid a Wolf, all gray and black:
"Doctor, jump upon my back,"
                                        he said,
"*I*'ll take you to the sea . . ."

So . . .
    With the Doctor on his back,
He went ambling down the track,
    He went lurching down the track
  Like a Retriever.

And the Doctor, as he ran,
  Said: "I must get there if I can,

I must get there,
quickly,
quickly,
To the great Limpopo River!"

[The Doctor reaches the sea, almost drowns, is saved by a whale, comes ashore, climbs peak after peak until he's pretty tired. Then—]

Then an Eagle came and cried:
"Doctor, would you like a ride?
What's a mountain range or two?
I could fly you to Peru!"

So . . .
The Doctor sat astride
On the Eagle's back, and cried:
"I never met an Eagle
More intelligent and clever!"
And he whispered as he flew:
"Well, no matter what I do,
I shall get there,
quickly,
quickly,
To the great Limpopo River."

Far, far away
In Africa,
In tropical
Black Africa,
A lonely Hippopotamus
Sits weeping
By the sea . . .

Beneath a palm
He sits forlorn,
From dawn to dusk,
From dusk to dawn,
Seeking the ship
That should be borne
Across the silver sea . . .

And far away
In Africa,
In tropical
Black Africa,
The great Limpopo River
Winds forever
To the sea.

Vociferous,
Belligerent,
Rhinoceros
And Elephant
Fill the forest hollows
With their bellows
Of complaint.

Rows of Hip-
popotami
grip
their tummies dismally,
Shiver-shaking,
Tummy-aching,
Feeling sick and faint.

Six-and-sixty
Ostrich-chicks
Have ricked their backs
And cricked their necks,
And from their beaks
Come squawks and squeaks
Of protest and disaster . . .

They've all got gout
And dysentery,
And athlete's foot,
And housemaid's knee;
Their heads are sore,
Their throats are raw,
Their toes done up in plaster.

Five baby sharks
Have aching teeth
(Six rows on top
And six beneath) . . .
Five baby basking-
Sharks are asking,
Asking for the Doctor . . .

. . .

From the rim of the sea,
From a castle of cloud,
Came a rushing of wings,
Beating low, beating loud . . .

And a speck appeared
Where the sea began,
And the speck took the shape
Of a bird and a man . . .

Of a man who sat
On an Eagle's back,
And waved with his stick
And his bag and his hat,
Crying: "Africa! *Africa! AFRICA!*"

And the Beasts and the Birds
In herds on the shore,
Answered: "Welcome to Africa!
Welcome once more
To Africa! *Africa! AFRICA!*"
The Hippos
lie glum,
each clutching his tum
(Doctor
Concocter
lands safe on the ground.)
They grumble
and mumble:
"Why *doesn't* he come?"
(Doctor
Concocter
has started his round.)
Doctor
Concocter
sets off like a rocket,

With thirty
varieties
of cures in his pocket;
He orders them
cod-liver oil
by the plateful,
And pills
by the boxful,
although they taste hateful,
And drops
by the mugful,
and lint by the fistful,
For any young patient
who's fretful
or wistful.
He's dosed
all the Tigers
with liquorice slices,
With cinnamon-cake
and
with passion-fruit ices;
He's sounded
their chests
and he's tested their lungs,
He's stuck
his thermometer
under their tongues,
Over
And over
Again!

He's treated
the Vultures
for hiccups and mumps;
He's treated
the Camels
for bumps on their humps;
He's dosed
all the Puffins
with truffles and muffins,
With muffins and truffles
and truffles
and muffins,
With buttery
muffles
and waffle-y truffins . . .
Over
And over
Again!

Doctor
Concocter
is busy all night!
Doctor
Concocter
is busy for weeks!
Not resting,
not eating,
just testing and treating
Their feet
and their teeth
and their beaks.

Just patching their humps
and spring-cleaning
their lungs,
Over
And over
Again . . .

Just popping
thermometers
under their tongues
(Rhinoceros-tongues
and
Great-Anteater-tongues),
Just sticking
thermometers
under their tongues,
Over
And over
Again!

There's no whining,
There's no groaning,
By the river,
By the river . . .
No more Hippos
Lie a-moaning
By the great Limpopo River . . .
The Rhinoceros
Is dancing
By the great Limpopo River,

And the Elephant
Is prancing
Where the river
Meets the sea.

All the Sharks
Are basking idly,
Showing rows of teeth
And grinning;
The Tarantulas
Are spinning;
The Giraffes
Are smirking widely . . .

And each Hippo-baby
wallows
In the swamps
and in the shallows . . .
Oh,
the Hippo-potto-pippos
Are as happy as can be.

The Hartebeests
are wallowing
and bellowing and hollering
(Oh, you can hear the trumpeting
from Zanzibar
to Crete!)
"Thank you,
Doctor,
for your ices,

For your nice
vanilla-slices!
You have helped
us
through our crisis!
You have set
us
on our feet!
We've been lapping
up
your lotions,
We've enjoyed
your pills
and potions,
And we thank you,
thank you,
THANK YOU,
For your visit
was
a treat."

LUCRETIA P. HALE

I've put these two little bits of nonsense in as a kind of experiment. If your great-great-grandparents happened to be living in the United States about a century ago they might have laughed over *The Peterkin Papers* (1880). It's the first American nonsense classic. I wonder how many of you will still find these pieces funny, as I do. (A "carter" is, of course, an old word for what today we might call a moving man.)

About Elizabeth Eliza's Piano

ELIZABETH ELIZA had a present of a piano, and she was to take lessons of the postmaster's daughter.

They decided to have the piano set across thc window in the parlor, and the carters brought it in, and went away.

After they had gone the family all came in to look at the piano; but they found the carters had placed it with its back turned towards the middle of the room, standing close against the window.

How could Elizabeth Eliza open it? How could she reach the keys to play upon it?

Solomon John proposed that they should open the window, which Agamemnon could do with his long arms. Then Elizabeth Eliza should go round upon the piazza, and open the piano. Then she could have her music-stool on the piazza, and play upon the piano there.

So they tried this; and they all thought it was a very pretty sight to see Elizabeth Eliza playing on the piano, while she sat on the piazza, with the honeysuckle vines behind her.

It was very pleasant, too, moonlight evenings. Mr. Peterkin liked to take a doze on his sofa in the room; but the rest of the family liked to sit on the piazza. So did Elizabeth Eliza, only she had to have her back to the moon.

All this did very well through the summer; but, when the fall came, Mr. Peterkin thought the air was too cold from the open window, and the family did not want to sit out on the piazza.

Elizabeth Eliza practiced in the mornings with her cloak on; but she was obliged to give up her music in the evenings, the family shivered so.

One day, when she was talking with the lady from Philadelphia, she spoke of this trouble.

The lady from Philadelphia looked surprised, and then said, "But why don't you turn the piano round?"

One of the little boys pertly said, "It is a square piano."

But Elizabeth Eliza went home directly, and, with the help of Agamemnon and Solomon John, turned the piano round.

"Why did we not think of that before?" said Mrs. Peterkin. "What shall we do when the lady from Philadelphia goes home again?"

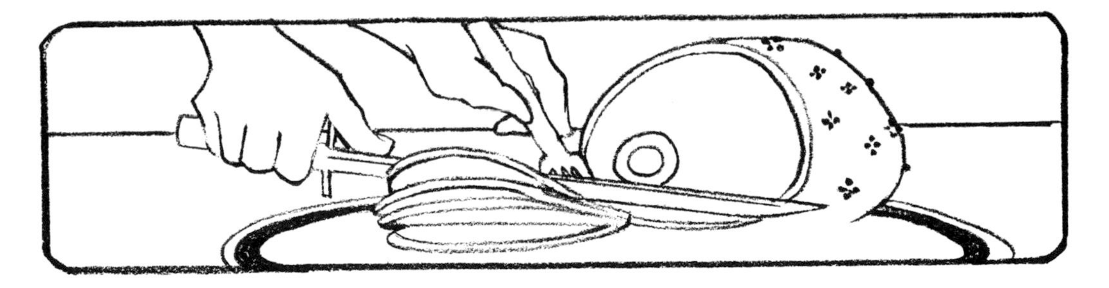

At Dinner

ANOTHER little incident occurred in the Peterkin family. This was at dinnertime.

They sat down to a dish of boiled ham. Now it was a peculiarity of the children of the family that half of them liked fat, and half liked lean. Mr. Peterkin sat down to cut the ham. But the ham turned out to be a very remarkable one. The fat and the lean came in separate slices—first one of lean, then one of fat, then two slices of lean, and so on. Mr. Peterkin began as usual by helping the children first, according to their age. Now Agamemnon, who liked lean, got a fat slice; and Elizabeth Eliza, who preferred fat, had a lean slice. Solomon John, who could eat nothing but lean, was helped to fat, and so on. Nobody had what he could eat.

It was a rule of the Peterkin family that no one should eat any of the vegetables without some of the meat; so now, although the children saw upon their plates applesauce, and squash and tomato, and sweet potato and sour potato, not one of them could eat a mouthful, because not one was satisfied with the meat. Mr. and Mrs. Peterkin, however, liked both fat and lean, and were making a very good meal, when they looked up and saw the children all sitting eating nothing, and looking dissatisfied into their plates.

"What is the matter now?" said Mr. Peterkin.

But the children were taught not to speak at table. Agamemnon, however, made a sign of disgust at his fat, and Elizabeth Eliza at her lean, and so on; and they presently discovered what was the difficulty.

"What shall be done now?" said Mrs. Peterkin.

They all sat and thought for a little while.

At last said Mrs. Peterkin, rather uncertainly, "Suppose we ask the lady from Philadelphia what is best to be done."

But Mr. Peterkin said he didn't like to go to her for everything; let the children try and eat their dinner as it was.

And they all tried, but they couldn't. "Very well, then," said Mr. Peterkin, "let them go and ask the lady from Philadelphia."

"All of us?" cried one of the little boys, in the excitement of the moment.

"Yes," said Mrs. Peterkin, "only put on your india-rubber boots." And they hurried out of the house.

The lady from Philadelphia was just going in to her dinner; but she kindly stopped in the entry to hear what the trouble was. Agamemnon and Elizabeth Eliza told her all the difficulty, and the lady from Philadelphia said, "But why don't you give the slices of fat to those who like the fat, and the slices of lean to those who like the lean?"

They looked at one another. Agamemnon looked at Elizabeth Eliza, and Solomon John looked at the little boys. "Why didn't we think of that?" said they, and ran home to tell their mother.

JOHN CIARDI

All About Boys and Girls

I know all about boys, I do,
And I know all about little girls, too.
I know what they eat. I know what they drink.
I know what they like. I know what they think.

And so I'm writing this to say,
Don't let children out to play.
It makes them sad. They'd rather go
To school or to the dentist. Oh,

I know they're bashful about saying
How much it hurts to be out playing
When they could go to school and spell
And mind their manners. They won't tell

How tired they are of games and toys.
But I know girls, and I know boys.
They like to sweep floors, chop the wood,
And practice being very good.

They'd rather sit and study hard
Than waste the whole day in the yard.
What good is fun and making noise?
That's not for girls! That's not for boys!

Warning

The inside of a whirlpool
Is not a place to stop,
Or you'll find you reach the bottom
Before you reach the top.

WALTER FARLEY

Walter Farley was crazy about horses from the time he was a small boy. He wanted to become a jockey, a vet, or a breeder of horses. With *The Black Stallion,* his first book, it became clear that he was not destined to doctor horses or ride them professionally, but rather to write about them. His books became so popular, however, that he could afford to breed horses for fun. So he achieved part of his boyhood ambition.

The Black Stallion opens aboard the tramp steamer *Drake,* bound for England. Alec Ramsay is aboard, his final destination being his home in the United States. In India his uncle Ralph had taught him the one thing he had always wanted to do—ride. His uncle had also given him as a going-away present a pearl pocketknife. The *Drake* stops at a small Arabian port to take aboard, in the care of a dark-skinned man, a magnificent, untamed black stallion. Every night Alec steals up to the stallion's stall and leaves some sugar for him.

The chapter that follows tells us what happens next. If you want to know what happens *after* the storm, get the book out of your library. You may have to wait for it, because it's a great favorite. (Some of you may have seen the movie made from the book.)

The Storm

THE *DRAKE* stopped at Alexandria, Bengasi, Tripoli, Tunis and Algiers, passed the Rock of Gibraltar, and turned north up the coast of Portugal. Now they were off Cape Finisterre on the coast of Spain, and in a few days, Captain Watson told Alec, they would be in England.

Alec wondered why the Black was being shipped to England—perhaps for stud, perhaps to race. The slanting shoulders, the deep broad chest, the powerful legs, the knees not too high nor too low—these, his uncle had taught him, were marks of speed and endurance.

That night Alec made his customary trip to the stall, his pockets bulging with sugar. The night was hot and still; heavy clouds blacked out the stars; in the distance long streaks of lightning raced through the sky. The Black had his head out the window. Again he was looking out to sea, his nostrils quivering more than ever. He turned, whistled as he saw the boy, then again faced the water.

Alec felt elated—it was the first time that the stallion hadn't drawn back into the stall at sight of him. He moved closer. He put the sugar in the palm of his hand and hesitantly held it out to the stallion. The Black turned and once again whistled—softer this time. Alec stood his ground. Neither he nor anyone else had been this close to the stallion since he came on board. But he did not care to take the chance of extending his arm any nearer the bared teeth, the curled nostrils. Instead he placed the sugar on the sill. The Black looked at it, then back at the boy. Slowly he moved over and began to eat the sugar. Alec watched him for a moment, satisfied; then as the rain began to fall, he went back to his cabin.

He was awakened with amazing suddenness in the middle of the night. The *Drake* lurched crazily and he was thrown onto the floor. Outside there were loud rolls of thunder, and streaks of lightning made his cabin as light as day.

His first storm at sea! He pulled the light cord—it was dead. Then a flash of lightning again illuminated the cabin. The top of his bureau had been swept clear and the floor was covered with broken glass. Hurriedly he put on his pants, shirt and slippers and started for the door; then he stopped. Back he went to the bed, fell on his knees, and reached under. He withdrew a life belt and strapped it around him. He hoped that he wouldn't need it.

He opened the door and made his way, staggering, to the deck. The fury of the storm drove him back into the passageway; he hung on to the stair rail and peered into the black void. He heard the shouts of Captain Watson and the crew faintly above the roar of the winds. Huge waves swept from one end of the *Drake* to the other. Hysterical passengers crowded into the corridor. Alec was genuinely scared now; never had he seen a storm like this!

For what seemed hours to him, the *Drake* plowed through wave after wave, trembling, careening on its side, yet somehow managing to stay afloat. The long streaks of lightning never diminished; they zigzagged through the sky, their sharp cracks resounding on the water.

From the passageway, Alec saw one of the crew make his way along the deck in his direction, desperately fighting to hold on to the rail. The *Drake* rolled sideways and a huge wave swept over the boat. When it had passed, the sailor was gone. The boy closed his eyes and prayed.

The storm began to subside a little and Alec felt new hope. Then suddenly a bolt of fire seemed to fall from the heavens above them. A sharp crack and the boat shook. Alec was thrown flat on his face, stunned. Slowly he regained consciousness. He was lying on his stomach; his face felt hot and sticky. He raised his hand, and withdrew it covered with blood. Then he became conscious of feet stepping on him. The passengers, yelling and screaming, were climbing, crawling over him! The *Drake* was still—its engines dead.

Struggling, Alec pushed himself to his feet. Slowly he made his way onto the deck. His startled eyes took in the scene about him. The *Drake*, struck by lightning, seemed almost cut in half! They were sinking! Strange, with what seemed the end so near, he should feel so cool. They were manning the lifeboats, and Captain Watson was there shouting directions. One boat was being lowered into the water. A large wave caught it in the side and turned it over—its occupants disappeared beneath the water.

The second lifeboat was being filled and Alec waited his turn. But when it came, the boat had reached its quota.

"Wait for the next one, lad," Captain Watson said sternly. He put his arm on the boy's shoulder. Alec did his best to smile.

As they watched the second lifeboat being lowered, the dark-skinned man appeared and rushed up to the captain, waving his arms and babbling hysterically.

"Under the bed, under the bed!" Captain Watson shouted at him.

Then Alec saw the man had no life belt. Terror in his eyes, he turned away from the captain toward Alec. Frantically he rushed at the boy and tried to tear the life belt from his back. Alec struggled, but he was no match for the half-crazed man. Then Captain Watson had his hands on him and threw him against the rail.

Alec saw the man's eyes turn to the lifeboat that was being lowered. Before the captain could stop him, he was climbing over the rail. He was going to jump into the boat! Suddenly the *Drake* lurched. The man lost his balance and, screaming, fell into the water. He never rose to the surface.

The dark-skinned man was drowned. Immediately Alec thought of the Black. What was happening to him? Was he still in his stall? Driven by an irresistible impulse, Alec fought his way out of line and toward the stern of the boat. If the stallion was alive, he was going to set him free and give him his chance to fight for life.

The stall was still standing. Alec heard a shrill whistle rise above the storm. He rushed to the door, lifted the heavy bar, and swung it open. For a second the mighty hooves stopped pounding and there was silence. Alec backed slowly away.

Then he saw the Black, his head held high, his nostrils blown out with excitement. Suddenly he snorted and plunged straight for the rail and Alec. Alec was paralyzed, he couldn't move. One hand was on the rail, which was broken at this point, leaving nothing between him and the open water. The Black swerved as he came near him, and the boy realized that the stallion was making for the hole. The horse's shoulder grazed him as he swerved, and Alec went flying into space. He felt the water close over his head.

When he came up, his first thought was of the ship; then he heard an explosion, and he saw the *Drake* settling deep into the water. Frantically he looked around for a lifeboat, but there was none in sight. Then he saw the Black swimming not more than ten yards away. Something swished by him—a rope, and it was attached to the Black's halter! The same rope that they had used to bring the stallion aboard the boat, and which they had never been able to get close enough to the horse to untie. Without stopping to think, Alec grabbed hold of it. Then he was pulled through the water, out into the open sea.

The waves were still large, but with the aid of his life belt, Alec was able to stay on top. He was too far gone now to give much thought to what he had done. He only knew that he had had his choice of remaining in the water alone or being pulled by the Black. If he was to die, he would rather die with the mighty stallion than alone. He took one last look behind and saw the *Drake* sink into the depths.

For hours Alec battled the waves. He had tied the rope securely around his life belt. He could hardly hold his head up. Suddenly he felt the rope slacken. The Black had stopped swimming! Alec anxiously waited; peering into the darkness he could just make out the head of the stallion. The Black's whistle pierced the air! After a few minutes, the rope became taut again. The horse had changed his direction. Another hour passed, then the storm diminished to high rolling swells. The first streaks of dawn appeared on the horizon.

The Black had stopped four times during the night, and each time he had altered his course. Alec wondered whether the stallion's wild instinct was leading him to land. The sun rose and shone down brightly on the boy's head; the salt water he had swallowed during the night made him almost mad with thirst. But when Alec felt that he could hold out no longer, he looked ahead at the struggling, fighting animal in front of him, and new courage came to him.

Suddenly he realized that they were going with the waves, instead of against them. He shook his head, trying to clear his brain. Yes, they were riding in; they must be approaching land! Eagerly he strained his salt-filled eyes and looked into the distance. And then he saw it—about a quarter of a mile away was a beach. Only an island, but there might be food and water, and a chance to survive! Faster and faster they approached the white sand. They were in the breakers. The Black's scream shattered the stillness. He was able to walk; he staggered a little and shook his black head. Then his action shifted marvelously, and he went faster through the shallow water.

Alec's head whirled—what stamina and endurance this horse had! He was being drawn toward the beach with ever-increasing speed. Suddenly he realized the danger of his position. He must untie this rope from around his waist, or else he would be dragged to death over the sand! Desperately his fingers flew to the knot; it was tight, he had made sure of that. Frantically he worked on it as the shore drew closer and closer.

The Black was now on the beach. Thunder began to roll from beneath his hooves as he broke out of the water. Hours in the water had swelled the knot—Alec couldn't untie it! Then he remembered his pocketknife. Could it still be there? His hand darted to his rear pants pocket; luckily he had buttoned it. Alec's fingers reached inside and came out grasping the knife.

He was now on the beach being dragged by the stallion; the sand flew in his face. Quickly he opened the knife and began to cut the rope. His body burned from the sand, his clothes were being torn off of him! His speed was increasing every second! Madly he sawed away at the rope. With one final thrust he was through! His outflung hands caressed the sand. As he closed his eyes, his parched lips murmured, "Yes—Uncle Ralph—it did—come in handy."

MALCOLM CRAGG

Shame

Alone on Monday night, walking away
  from a fight I never had.
I feel lonely walking down the
  murky lane.
I can't feel my feet prodding along
  the road because I have other
  things to think about.
Why, why was I so terrified
  of somebody who was no bigger
  then me?
Whose face I'll never forget, his eyes
  pounding into my face.
Whose voice was so sharp and
  clear, that it made me shiver.
I walk away ashamed.

WILLIAM PÈNE DU BOIS

Mr. du Bois believes the best way to travel is in a balloon and that is what the hero of his book *The Twenty-one Balloons* does. At age sixty-six, Professor William Waterman Sherman stopped teaching arithmetic, built himself a huge balloon, and decided to just float around for a year. This was about one hundred years ago when balloons were most popular.

Well, on the seventh day of his trip (he started west from San Francisco) a hole in his balloon forced him to descend on a small volcanic Pacific island called Krakatoa.

Now, Krakatoa is a real island and in 1883 it blew up with an explosion heard three thousand miles away. That true incident is part of the tale of Professor Sherman's fantastic adventures. But before he escapes from the island he spends some time on Krakatoa and finds it to be one of the strangest places imaginable. For instance, it's so full of diamond mines that every Krakatoan owns a fortune one hundred times as big as the United States Treasury.

Professor Sherman, tired after his day's exploration of the mines in the company of a citizen called Mr. F., goes to sleep. What follows tells us about the Gourmet Government.

The Gourmet Government

I WOKE UP the next morning after a night of peaceful and heavy sleep. I knew I had slept well and in complete comfort because I am a great dreamer; and when all is well at night I dream pleasant dreams. On uncomfortable nights, I have nightmares. That night I dreamt I was back on my inflated mattress in the *Globe*. You can well imagine my surprise when I woke up in a big and beautiful antique canopied bed in an exquisite bedroom, furnished in Louis the Fourteenth style. The wallpaper of my room was pale blue with gold fleurs-de-lis. The curtains were red velvet, each trimmed with a large gold cloth sunburst, symbolizing the opulence and extravagance of the "Sun King," Louis the Fourteenth of France. I hadn't noticed the room at all the night before. While eating my supper in bed by the light of one candle, I had seen that I was in a canopied bed; but I suppose that my mind, in an effort to put my body at ease, tired as I was by the excitement of the day, had pictured the room as the sort of simple American Colonial bedroom I had become so used to at home.

I got up and put on my clothes. I found that someone had taken away the slightly wrinkled suit I had worn but a few hours the day before, and replaced it with a complete fresh one. This was quite to my liking. As I was dressing, I heard a knock at my door and Mr. F. walked in. We exchanged greetings and I assured him that I had spent a most comfortable night. While we were talking, I heard the sinister rumbling noise coming from the direction of the mountain. I went to the window, looked out, and saw that the ground below had started to move again. It didn't go up and down with the violence it had the day before near the mountain, but rather looked like animated furrows in a plowed field. Mr. F. explained that the ground didn't move much in the village which was situated as far as possible from the mountain. I asked him why it was that the house we were in didn't move when the earth did. His answer was extraordinary:

"The Bible tells us to build our houses on foundations of stone," he said; "on Krakatoa we have found it necessary to use an even stronger foundation. Our houses are built on a substructure of solid diamond boulders. Come," he added, "I'll take you out to breakfast."

On my way downstairs, I noticed that Mr. F.'s house wasn't consistently Louis Fourteenth in style, but was furnished in the best French tastes of many different periods. I saw other rooms, some Louis Fifteenth, some Empire.

As I left the house I turned around to take a look at its outside appearance. The building was the same as the Petit Trianon in Versailles, a building which I have always considered one of my favorite pieces of architecture. This was all an unbelievable dream—to think of finding such a building on a small island in the Pacific.

I looked around at other buildings. They were equally fabulous. As I stumbled along the rippling ground I noticed, in this order: a replica of George Washington's Mount Vernon house; a typical British cottage with a thick thatched roof; a lovely Chinese pagoda; a building of typical Dutch architecture; a small copy of Shepheard's Hotel in Cairo; Mr. F.'s French house; and about a dozen other houses all representing different nations. We were heading for the British cottage. We entered the cottage, walked into the dining room where some eighty other people were eating breakfast. As we walked in, Mr. F. announced in a loud, clear voice, "Ladies and gentlemen, may I present Professor Sherman, the new citizen of Krakatoa." I was given a most cordial welcome. Everyone in the room stood up and applauded; then the men came toward me, their hands extended. I was introduced in order to a Mr. A., a Mr. B., a Mr. C., right on through to a Mr. T. The man named

Mr. B. was evidently my host at this British cottage. He led us to a table. We sat down. I immediately turned to my companion and said, "Mr. F., before I become any more confused, if such a thing is possible, will you please start from the beginning and tell me the history of Krakatoa? Will you please tell me how all of these lovely people got here? Will you please explain why each house is entirely different in architecture, why the two houses I have visited so far both have gigantic dining rooms? Will you please tell me why all of the men here have the names of the letters of the alphabet? I have never thought there could be a country in the world so foreign and confusing as to customs as this one appears to be."

Mr. F. laughed. "First of all, let's get some breakfast," he said. We went to a huge table where in large silver chafing dishes could be found large quantities of the deliciously prepared kidneys, mutton chops, and bacon which make up the hearty British breakfasts. We helped ourselves and returned to our table and Mr. F. told me the story of Krakatoa:

"Eight years ago, a young sailor now known as Mr. M. was shipwrecked off the island of Krakatoa in a tremendous hurricane. He landed on the island in good physical condition, which was extremely fortunate for him because the rest of the crew of the ship he was on were drowned in the ocean. As soon as he felt the earth rumbling beneath his feet, he knew he was on the most dreaded of islands, Krakatoa. He didn't want to go near the mountain, for he knew that the volcanic action of the mountain caused all of that violent shaking in the earth. He couldn't stay on the beach, though, because the winds of the hurricane caused a blinding and extremely dangerous sandstorm which would destroy any man. He instinctively made his way for the shelter of the jungle. He crawled through the jungle toward the mountain, trying to get as far away from the beach as he possibly could. He must have had a horrible time of it, for he was not only being thrashed by the bending trees and wind-whipped underbrush of the jungle, but was also going up and down with the sickening motion of Krakatoa's surface. Sometime during the night he crawled up on that peaceful plot of ground near the mines where the earth doesn't move. He groped around in the dark looking for shelter and finally found a hole in the wall of the mountain which he thought to be a cave. He crawled in and slept in comparative peace but in great discomfort. He woke up, of course, in the diamond mines.

"His first thoughts, upon suddenly discovering that he was the richest man in the world, were naturally of how to get off Krakatoa and back to civilization with a sizable load of diamonds. At that time, getting off Krakatoa was a difficult thing to do. It is hard to leave a place no outsider dares to approach. This was a good thing in a way, because it gave him a chance to get used to living on Krakatoa, to realize that one could live on Krakatoa, and to think out carefully the best way of taking full advantage of the enormous wealth attached to the mines.

"He built himself a raft which took him a month to complete because at first he didn't have any tools. He found a diamond in the mines the shape of an ax head and made an ax of this. It was a crude tool, but one which never needed to be sharpened. He finished the raft and set out to sea one afternoon when he sighted a ship in the distance. He took with him only four diamonds, three small ones about the size of marbles and one large one about the size of a baseball. The ship picked him up. It was headed for the United States. He told the captain of the ship that he had been shipwrecked on Krakatoa, invented horrible stories about how terrible the place was to live on. The captain, however, needed no convincing, for he had no desire whatsoever to go to Krakatoa.

"When Mr. M. arrived in San Francisco, he sold the three smaller diamonds to three different diamond brokers for approximately ten thousand dollars apiece. Then he picked twenty families, the twenty families you see here; and using the huge diamond the size of a baseball as bait, lured them into taking a trip with him back to this fabulous island. He picked the families with care. Each family was required to have two things in order to be chosen. They had to have: (a) one boy and one girl between the ages of three and eight; and (b) definite creative interests, such as interests in painting, writing, the sciences, music, architecture, medicine. These two requirements would not only assure future generations of Krakatoa citizens; but also he assumed that people with creative interests are not liable to be too bored on a small desolate island; and people with inventive interests can more easily cope with unusual situations and form a stronger foundation for a cultured heredity.

"With the thirty thousand dollars Mr. M. made by selling the small diamonds, he bought himself a ship. Mr. M. was the only man of the selected families chosen who was a sailor. He proceeded to make sailors out of all the other men by carefully training them on cruises on the ship he had bought. We were soon a capable crew. We loaded the ship with our families and supplies, and sailed away. That was about seven years ago.

"Krakatoa is situated between Java and Sumatra. It is in a small group of three supposedly uninhabited islands named Krakatoa, Verlaten, and Lang. Verlaten Island hides a small inlet of Krakatoa from possible sight from Sumatra and also protects the inlet from the rough sea. We planned to dock our ship in this inlet. We did this in the middle of the night.

"Our first year on Krakatoa was pretty horrible. Upon seeing the mines, we all became rather piggish. There was no way of actually dividing the diamonds except by making twenty shares; that is, twenty pieces of paper each entitling its owner to an equal part of the mines. A greedy desire seemed to be in each of us at that time to become the one and only owner of all of the diamonds. Some of the families were made up of architects and builders. They built themselves comfortable little huts and settled down to a rather normal way of living. We were sleeping either on the ground or in the shelter of the mines. We asked the builders to make us houses too. They agreed to do it only if we gave them our shares in the mines. We refused at first, then found out (after months of uncomfortable living in the height of the rainy season) that we all simply had to have huts. We gave our diamond shares to the four building families. They made us our huts in return for which they became the owners of the diamond mines.

"Now that we all had houses, we all started thinking of ways of getting our diamonds back. There was nothing to buy on Krakatoa. We lived mostly off of the abundant vegetation on the island. The climate is humid, warm, and steady; the earth, due to its volcanic nature, is full of phosphoric acids and potassium, and everything grows well here. One of the families opened a restaurant. This was an excellent idea. The four families who owned all the diamonds were anxious to show their power. There was no way of spending their diamonds here. There was no way of getting to another country either, except in our ship. It took all of the men on the island to make up the ship's crew, and none of the families without diamonds had any desire to take the families with diamonds back to the United States. So the families with diamonds showed their power by 'eating out' every night at the restaurant. The restaurant owners charged a fabulous price for their meals; I think it was three meals to the share. In spite of this the restaurant idea seemed to work. Soon another family opened a restaurant which was just a little better, and then another house was turned into a restaurant, and after a while every house was turned into a restaurant and the diamonds started to become equally divided again. After about four months of fierce competition in which we all became excellent cooks, we found that we each had our shares back and that we were all considerably happier. There was a tremendous variety of cooking to be had from house to house, and we decided to celebrate the regaining of our shares with a big banquet in which each family would contribute its favorite dish. It was a sumptuous affair and we ended it by drawing up a Constitution for the Government of Krakatoa.

"We have an unusual Constitution. It's sort of a Restaurant Government. There are twenty families on the island, each running a restaurant. We made it a law here that every family shall go to a different restaurant every night of the month, around the village square in rotation. In this way no family of Krakatoa has to work more than once every twenty days, and every family is assured a great variety of food."

I understood now why the two houses I had visited were both apparently restaurants, so I asked Mr. F. to explain to me how the families got their alphabetic names.

"That's quite simple," said Mr. F. "There are twenty restaurants around the village square here. We lettered them, A, B, C, D, E, and F, all around the square up to T, the twentieth house. We changed our names. In 'A' Restaurant live Mr. A., his wife Mrs. A., their son A-1, and their daughter A-2. In 'B' Restaurant live Mr. B., Mrs. B., B-1, and B-2; it's very simple."

"Is there anything else unusual in your Constitution?"

"We have a different calendar in Krakatoa. It too is a Restaurant Calendar. The months are shorter. There are twenty days to the Krakatoan month, and they are named after the families, 'A' Day, 'B' Day, 'C' Day, and so forth up to 'T' Day. There are eighteen months to the Krakatoan year. Each day of one of our months, we eat at a different restaurant. On 'A' Day, we eat at the A.'s Restaurant, on 'B' Day at the B.'s, and so forth. Each family only has to work on his day of the month."

"That's reasonable," I remarked. "But tell me, how did each restaurant get to be so different? You have told me that all of the families come from San Francisco. From what I can see and hear of them they all seem to be Americans, yet their houses are as varied and international as the pavilions at a World's Fair."

"We are all Americans here. The international restaurants were built simply to give variety to our days. When, in the early stages of our lives here, we found that we could all live happily under the Restaurant Government, we decided to make each restaurant different so that on certain days we could look forward to having a food which was unusual and good to eat. We Americans all have different inherited tastes so we decided that each restaurant should serve the food of a different nation. We arranged this alphabetically also. The A.'s run an American restaurant and serve only real American cooking. You are now eating at the B.'s. This is a British chophouse. The C.'s run a Chinese restaurant. The D.'s run a Dutch restaurant, the E.'s an Egyptian restaurant; you can run through the alphabet up to T. The T.'s run a Turkish coffeehouse."

"And you, Mr. F., run a French restaurant?"

"It's as easy as that," said Mr. F.

"Is there a Krakatoan restaurant?" I asked.

"Naturally. It is run by Mr. K. and specializes in dishes of strictly native foods; odd dishes prepared from the bread of the bread trees, the milk from the trunks of the milk palms; coconuts, bananas and more exotic fruits, and mostly the wonderful fish which are so easily found in the ocean which surrounds us. We couldn't think of what style of architecture to use for a Krakatoan restaurant, so we invented one. It is made out of crystal glass bricks, to suggest the diamond mines which are the island's most guarded treasures; and inside most of these glass bricks we have sealed rare and colorful tropical fish, because for many months they were our main source of food. It looks like a house made of ice cubes and fresh fish and is a very inviting place to eat on 'K' Day of the hot summer months."

"What sort of restaurant do the S.'s run?" I asked.

"A Swedish smorgasbord restaurant."

"And R.?"

"He runs a Russian tearoom."

"What a wonderful place this island is!" I exclaimed. "I am certainly looking forward to 'I' Day, because I love spaghetti."

"Mr. I.'s Italian restaurant serves the best," Mr. F. assured me.

"Have you names for the months of the year?"

"We do in a way, but the names of the months are very seasonal and depend entirely on the stocks of food we have on hand. We now have a surplus of lamb, so we voted to call this the Month of Lamb. Each restaurant has been asked to serve a lamb specialty on its menu. Today is 'B' Day of the Month of Lamb, so we are having British mutton chops. British mutton chops are hard to beat. On 'F' Day, my day, I will serve lamb chops, with béarnaise sauce, or perhaps I will serve a roast of lamb cooked with garlic. On 'T' Day the Turkish coffehouse will specialize in shish kebab, which is lamb cooked on metal skewers. Of course our restaurants serve a choice of meats, but in the Month of Lamb you can always count on one lamb dish in all the menus."

"The more I hear of Krakatoa, the more I like it. There's just one more thing which puzzles me. How do you get your supplies? How did you get all of the materials to build these houses?"

"That was a direct result of the Restaurant form of government. We are all so happy here that none of us has any desire to give away the secrets of Krakatoa's diamond mines. We have given up fighting between ourselves for selfish control of the mines, so we have nothing to keep us from taking frequent trips to foreign countries. We always go to different countries. We cover up our trail by frequently selling our freighter and buying a new one. No boat of ours has ever been seen in two different countries. By simply picking up a handful of diamonds from the floor of our mines we are able to make enough money in foreign countries to fill a new freighter each trip with the best of everything we need. The last of our houses was completed recently. They have taken seven years to build. It has been a long and gradual process on which we have all worked very hard."

"How about me?" I asked. "I have just arrived here. I have no family. Do you want me to change my name? Should I start building myself a restaurant? I hate to think that I am in any way upsetting anything here. Another restaurant would ruin your calendar. What do you want me to do?"

"I am afraid," said Mr. F., "that you will have to be in the peculiar but rather happy position of being a perpetual guest. You may stay in my house as long as you want, or move around if you wish. As for the food situation, you will simply follow our daily calendar and eat with us every day. When a family prepares for eighty people, it isn't at all bothered by an extra guest. As for changing your name, I wouldn't advise it at all. Since you won't have a restaurant there will be no need to name a day after you. Another good reason is that the twenty-first letter in the alphabet is 'U.' You wouldn't want to be called Mr. U. Every time somebody said, 'Hey, you!' you would have to turn around. If someone asked you who you are, you would have to answer, 'I am U.' You would keep overhearing snatches of conversation which would bother you. If someone were to tell a friend, 'I want to see you tonight,' you would wonder what was meant by 'you.' You would keep asking yourself, 'Does "you" in this case mean "you" or "U"? If "you" means "U" and "U" is me, then that lady wants to see me tonight.' And then you would wonder why. I tell you, Professor Sherman, 'U' is a bad name."

I laughed at this and agreed with Mr. F. to leave my name alone.

E. E. CUMMINGS

In Just-

in Just-
spring   when the world is mud-
luscious the little
lame balloonman

whistles   far   and wee

and eddieandbill come
running from marbles and
piracies and it's
spring

when the world is puddle-wonderful

the queer
old balloonman whistles
far   and   wee
and bettyandisbel come dancing

from hop-scotch and jump-rope and

it's
spring
and
     the

          goat-footed

balloonman   whistles
far
and
wee

MEINDERT DEJONG

When Meindert DeJong was eight he left Holland, his native country, for the United States. He and his family settled in Grand Rapids, Michigan, and the first thing he did was look about for the sea by whose shores he had grown up. But there's no ocean near Grand Rapids.

Mr. DeJong has written many books and the setting is usually either Holland or our own Midwestern farm country. The four I like best are *The Tower by the Sea, The Wheel on the School, Journey from Peppermint Street,* and *Along Came a Dog,* from which the selection below is taken.

No human being, no matter how smart we get to be, will ever know what it feels like to be a hawk, a rooster, a little red hen, or a dog. Certain scientists who study animal behavior can tell us a good deal about how and why they act as they do. But to get some notion of how they *feel* we have to depend on writers like Mr. DeJong.

Along Came a Dog is about a little red hen who has had her toes frozen off during the icy winter, and about a big black dog who somehow feels it is his duty to protect her. Whenever I read this chapter the real world seems to turn into a barnyard. Just for a few minutes, of course, but to create those few minutes requires a writer with an extraordinary sympathy for how animals *may* feel.

The Dog and the Rooster

THE BIG DOG crashed against the bottom of the loosened board, and drove it away from the wall. He plunged through the opening.

Down below, at his crashing lunge, everything stopped in the barnyard. But in the week the chickens had become used to the dog plunging down into the wagon box. The next moment in the barnyard everything went on as before.

In the midst of a group of white chickens the little red hen was in a hen fight for some hen reason. The crash of the dog had interrupted the fight, but now the little hen leaped up at her white enemy again. The fight resumed where it had left off.

The fight was mean, unfair, one-sided. While the little red hen was fighting one white hen, other white hens darted in and pecked her. The little hen, blinded with rage, chugging with frustrated rage, leaped up, raked at the puffed white chest before her with her useless, harmless knucklebones. The whole group closed in on her. The little hen went down squawking, buried under white hens. . . .

The rooster heard the squawking, came around the barn on a run. The white hens scattered, and there was only the little hen sprawled in the dust. The rooster charged at her, rapped her viciously—as if beating her for having got herself beaten. The little hen croaked out a wretched squawk. At that sound the dog leaped out of the wagon and ran to the little hen. He ran right over the rooster, knocked him sprawling. The rooster picked himself up, pushed past the dog, and ran up the ramp to sulk in the henhouse.

The big dog, plume tail waving in friendliness and greeting, touched his nose to the little red hen, and she raised her head and looked up at him. He nuzzled her again, but they really had no way of showing their friendship. But here he was now, their day together could begin. The chickens that had scuttled away came back—the normal barnyard life was resumed. . . .

Side by side the big dog and the little hen ranged the barnyard. They roved about the barn and the henhouse, scrounging along the walls for hidden grain kernels and chicken tidbits. The little hen picked up things, tested them for food taste, rejected or gobbled them. The dog tagged on behind. The pickings were lean this hungry morning. . . .

The dog sniffed out a kernel of corn stuck under the curved tooth of a harrow—one kernel for his huge, hungry body. He flopped to his side, rooted like a pig, to force the kernel free. The little hen darted in, greedily pecked up the kernel the dog had freed. The dog got up, looked at her, and accepted it meekly. But the tip of his tail wavered in a wistful question.

The little hen darted away. The dog hopefully poked his nose under the harrow once more, but the little hen squawked and he pulled himself free, hurried to her. It was all that was needed. The white hen pecking the little red hen scuttled away.

The two stood together again. The dog looked longingly across the field at the distant swamp. His tail began waving, brushed the little hen. Then he started forward on a determined lope into the field and whatever it might hold for him by way of food. The little hen ran with him. But she ran only so far from the barnyard, then, frightened by the strangeness, she uttered a single quick cackle, turned, and fluttered back. The dog stood looking at her, tail waving in indecision, but then he trotted after her. He had made himself her unquestioning slave. He stayed with the little red hen. It was his life. He was there to protect her and to put a quick end to her eternal fights. It was his duty. He had made it his duty.

The little hen did not know, could not accept, or could not remember that her new place was at the very bottom of the flock. By some inexorable flock code she had been shoved down to the number one hundred position—the last and the least of all the flock since she had lost her toes. And since she was at the very bottom, all the others had the right to lord it over her, peck and maul and bully her. That the little hen would not, or could not, accept. When they pecked her she fought, and when she fought she lost—toeless she was harmless. But always she fought again.

Only the big rooster was still somewhat impartial. When she fought with another hen, he separated the two impartially with a slashing blow or two with the side of his hard bill. But always he seemed to rap the little hen harder. Always he seemed to knock her down.

The big dog ignored the rooster, and the rooster ignored him, except when the rooster from some rooster instinct stepped in to punish the little hen for fighting. That the big dog would not allow. He did not snap or snarl at the rooster—he simply walked him down. And the rooster nearly always remembered to keep his distance. He seemed to sense that the big dog had little patience with him; he seemed to accept the fact that the dog had made himself a sort of rooster-protector to the little hen.

It was the new life the dog had established for himself. He was the little hen's protector, and he was her slave. He loved it. It gave him a purpose and a duty. He loved it maybe more than he loved the little red hen.

If the little hen did not sense it or accept it, in some dim way the dog seemed to understand that by the code of the flock he and the little hen were really outcasts, and if not quite outcasts—since he was too big and powerful—at least they were outsiders. More and more the big dog tried to lead the little hen away from the flock into the fields beyond the barnyard. More and more the little hen—tired of constant peckings, and of being eternally bullied—tended to follow him away from the flock. But the strangeness, the wideness and emptiness of the stretching fields always scared her back to the barnyard. She would step along beside the dog only up to such a point. Then panic and alarm would overtake her and she would tear back to the busy barnyard, away from the big silence of the field. The dog would patiently trot after her. . . .

There was nothing more to be found in the pecked-over barnyard. There was no food in the henhouse feed hoppers. Hungry and restless, the flock began to stray farther and farther afield. Hunger made them dare to step out under the high, empty sky over the flat, silent field. And the big dog led them. And the little hen walked at his side.

The flock did not follow very far. The chickens spread over the near field, but they stayed in groups and tight little clusters. Like the little hen, they reached a certain point in the big strangeness where they would suddenly lift heads in alarm, eye the high sky, and then in wild, cackling fright race back to the barnyard. When one started for the barn, the others would catch her panic, and chickens would bolt from everywhere. Gradually they would edge into the field again, but the presence of hawks over the swamp, the fear of hawks, kept the hens close to the barnyard.

The little hen had gone too far into the field. Once, in panic, she turned from the dog, and made a short, hurtling flight back. But when her flight ended, and she stumbled down in the grass, she saw that the big barn still looked far away. The dog was near. The dog waited for her. She ran back to the dog, and he led the way to the swamp again.

From the swamp came a whirrring and sawing of thousands of hidden insects. The mysterious swamp stirred, weed tops waved, bushes sighed and bent. A wind swept the tall plumes of high swamp grasses, bent them toward the little hen, and to the little hen it was as if the whole waving reed field flowed toward her like water, and would engulf her. She stood paralyzed, eyes glazed. Then, when the wind passed, she noticed that the dog had trudged on, and to her it seemed as if the dog had gone under in the waves of bowing reeds.

At the edge of the swamp an old willow had fallen, had gone on growing, its leaves and limber branches hanging only inches from the ground. Far behind the little hen, faint over the field, came the rooster's hawk warning—from the top of the ramp the rooster was warning of hawks. At that sound the lone little hen panicked. She flew toward the willow, plunged to the ground and scurried under the tipped-down branches of the fallen willow.

Under the low, leaning trunk of the willow tree, she found a depression in the ground. She squeezed herself down into the cupped hollow. The leaves of the tipped-down branches curtained around her, shut out the sight of the swamp. They even seemed to dim the shrillness of insects. The little hen felt securely hidden. Panic seeped out of her. She began fussing with the cupped hollow to shape it more to her liking. She tugged a few weed stalks and some dead grass around her body, and now it was a nest. A secret, hidden, dark nest! And now she wanted to lay an egg in the most hidden nest. The little hen became quiet. The time had come to lay an egg.

The dog had plunged into the waving, shoulder-high, plumy grass, because there had been a trail and a smell of some small animal. It spelled food. Absorbed in the scent before his nose, he hurried on. But the trail was lost in wateriness that stood at the roots of the reeds and the grasses. The dog still splashed on. Suddenly, beyond the reeds, he plunged into the deeper swamp—a long, twisting sheet of stagnant, still water. Slithery things stirred in the shallow water at the swamp's edge, squirmed, flashed, wriggled.

The dog plunged into the swamp in pursuit of whatever moved there. He bit the water, but always whatever skittered and wriggled in the shallows flashed away into deeper water. The hungry dog became shrewd, splashed no more, but stood still, paws motionless. Something wriggled against a paw—a tiny crayfish. The dog lunged, snapped . . . it was small, it squirmed about his teeth, but the dog gave it a hard bite, a quick taste, and swallowed. Suddenly he looked back to where the big barn must rise behind the fringe of trees and brush. It was as if the small, quick taste reminded him of something. And then the dog knew—the crayfish had faintly tasted like the egg the chicken in the barn had dropped down to him from the high beam.

He immediately left the swamp. He trotted faster and faster. Near the willow he circled a moment, found the spot from which the little red hen had fluttered up, but there her track ended. The dog hurried on to the barn.

The little red hen had heard the dog circling and sniffing, but she stayed silent and secret in the nest under the leaning trunk of the willow. Sure of herself in the great importance of laying an egg, she let the dog rustle away across the field.

In the barnyard the dog ran straight for the open doorway of the basement of the barn. He hurriedly climbed the sagging hay loader, shoved himself up through the trapdoor. The white hen was in the hay on the barn floor. The dog ran to her. The chicken stood paralyzed, eyes glassy with alarm, as the dog stopped expectantly before her. But her eyes flicked to the dog's shaggy, wet coat. She darted her beak at the dog, stripped away a drop of water. At the taste of water she boldly pushed in, pecked up at the dog's dripping chest—too thirsty to be afraid. She pulled hairs. It nipped, it stung. Almost carelessly the dog opened his big mouth and closed it over her back. A hoarse squawk squeezed out of the chicken. At that squawk the dog immediately dropped her. She scuttled away. . . .

The flock had wandered off into the field again. The rooster stood alone on the high ramp, watching, listening—worried and concerned. The barnyard lay empty below the ramp. A single sparrow flew down from the roof of the barn. The rooster ducked, but then he used the sparrow's flight as an excuse to warn his flock of hawks. Once again he whirred out his alarm warnings—hawks overhead. From everywhere in the near field hens rose, thrashed in clumsy flight toward the barnyard.

The rooster stood high and silent and important on the ramp looking down on this scared flock. But having been warned of nonexistent hawks once too often, the flock began to doubt the rooster. They had made too many useless flights back to the barnyard. They cocked eyes to the empty sky, saw nothing threatening. The seeds and insects in the field beckoned. There was food in the field; the flock scattered again.

From the ramp the frustrated rooster whirred a useless alarm call after them—hawks overhead. The flock paid him no attention. On the ramp the rooster wound himself into a hateful rage. But there was no hen near to vent his rage on. Feeling foolish, feeling useless, the rooster stood confused and alone on the high ramp.

In the barn the dog awoke. He ran to the loosened board in the wall and plunged down.

The crash of the dog alarmed the lone rooster on top of the ramp. With a hoarse squawk he flew down from the ramp, and ran toward his scattered flock in the field. Alone in the barnyard, the hungry dog searched for grain kernels. There was nothing to be found. In the henhouse a chicken cackled. The dog trotted to the basement of the hay barn as if the cackling had made him hopeful that the imprisoned white hen might have laid an egg for him.

Under the hay loader in the tuft of hay that had fallen down from the trapdoor a chicken had made a nest. There were three eggs in the partly concealed nest. The dog picked up an egg. His teeth closed on it. The egg crashed and splashed in his mouth, its sweetness oozed over his tongue. The tip of the dog's tail waved gratefully. He reached for the second egg.

In the field the rooster rolled out a hawk warning. The warning shut itself off abruptly as the rooster himself ducked into a clump of weeds. This time the warning was real. The hens in the field sensed it. Now there was no hysteria, no panic, no flight. All over the field the hens became flattened white lumps, frozen into motionlessness under any grass tuft or weed clump. Overhead a hawk flew, flew low, looking down on the field with brazen, bold eyes. Suddenly the hawk chose to fly on, sailed high, flew away in busy swiftness, and was gone from the sky.

The rooster stood up. He called to his hens—threatening, coaxing, commanding. They all ran flat-tailed through the grass toward home and the safety of the barnyard. The rooster drove them on with his warnings and orders.

Behind the rooster—far behind him from the looming brush edge of the swamp—came a shrill cackling. It went on and on. The little hen had laid an egg in the secret, hidden nest under the willow. Now she cackled and cackled shrill triumph beyond the tree.

The rooster wheeled, rolled out his alarm calls to her. He coaxed, he called, he ordered. The little hen did not listen. She ran back and forth cackling the magnificent event of the egg up to the sky. A bluebird flew over the field, reminding the rooster of hawk dangers again.

In the field all the scuttling flock had stopped at the familiar homey sounds of the little hen's cackling. Hawk forgotten, chickens raised their heads and stood listening to the distant shrill song of the little hen. They started back into the field.

The rooster warned direly of the bluebird. No one believed him, no one paid any attention. The rooster went berserk with rage. In hate and frustration he charged toward this farthest-away, most obstinate little hen of all his flock.

The little hen saw him coming, and so that he would not discover her secret nest, she ran to him. But when she reached him, the rooster knocked her down, thrashed her unmercifully. She struggled up and tried to skulk away in the deep grass; he overtook her and beat her down again. Overhead a dot-high hawk, hurrying to the home nest with a mouse in its talons, swept a bold eye down to the scene of the fearful beating. For a moment the hawk circled, hovered, but then decided to fly on with the small prize already in its possession.

Completely unaware of the hawk, the rooster in blood-blinded rage went on thrashing the little hen. She slipped from under him, tried to squeeze away toward the willow. But the rooster came down on her and the little hen squawked.

In the barn the dog heard the distant squawk above the crunching sound of the second egg he was shattering under his teeth. He grabbed the last egg, pulled it into his mouth. Again the little hen squawked. Egg still in his mouth, the dog whirled and ran toward the sound.

The rooster was insanely hammering the little hen. His wings were spread with the effort. His beak gaped in his wheezing. Little tiny fluff feathers clung to the sides of his bill. Still he thrashed her.

Then the big dog was there, silent, ominous. He opened his mouth, let the egg roll, snatched the rooster up and away from the little red hen—held him high, shook him savagely. One wing slipped from the dog's hold, beat wildly in the dog's face, blinded him. The dog dropped the rooster for a new hold. In silent terror the rooster scuttled away, flew up, bolted up toward the faraway safety of the henhouse and barn. But he had to land after his desperate short flight, and when he stumbled down the dog was there. The hapless rooster flew up again, stumbled down, ran in witless, wing-pumping panic before the silent dog. Always the dog was under or behind him. The rooster ran out before him, mouth gaping, his breath coming out of his open beak in hoarse, pained gasps. He somehow forced himself up into a last short flight, but he could hardly raise himself above the weed stalks.

At last the rooster felt the familiar packed ground of the barnyard. He stumbled toward the ramp. The ramp was crowded with chickens. The rooster wobbled away again, staggered up the rise from the deep barnyard to the yard of the house. He managed to squirm around the corner of the house, squatted there, wheezing painfully, eyes closed.

The dog poked his nose around the corner of the house. In the desperate strength of terror, the rooster hurled up, flew into the unseen chicken wire around the little parsnip garden. He caught his neck in an opening of the chicken wire, uttered a deep squawk, thrashed his wings, hung still.

The dog came trotting up. He reared up, leaned against the fencing, and sniffed at the dead rooster. Then to his ears came the first rattle of the old car from far down the road. The dog dropped to the ground, hurried away to hide in the barn.

In the far field the beaten little hen heard the old car come rattling. She raised her head, and saw the white egg the dog had dropped in the grass. Forgetting her hurt, she got up and immediately began fussing with the egg. She hooked her bill behind it, pulled it free of the grass tufts, rolled the egg toward her secret nest under the willow tree. She worked the egg over the rim of the nest until at last, with a faint click, it rolled down beside her own egg. Then the little hen settled herself on the two eggs. She clucked little motherly sounds at the two lovely eggs under her. She was proud of her eggs, and her hurt was forgotten.

PALMER BROWN

Giddy Liddy Gandaway

Giddy Liddy Gandaway
Plotted late and planned away,
Sold her home and land away,
To join the gypsy jugglers
And to drive their crimson van.

Giddy Liddy Gandaway
Tripped the saraband away,
Gave her lily hand away,
To wed a turbaned tinker
With a jeweled frying pan.

Giddy Liddy Gandaway
Danced the gypsy band away,
Tambourined to Mandalay,
To cool the temple monkeys
With a silver gilded fan.

Giddy Liddy Gandaway
Faded while she fanned away,
Flew like chaff or sand away,
To vanish as completely
As the windblown winnowed bran.

Today I Found a Secret

Today I found a secret,
  Clenched it in my fist,
Tied it in a handkerchief,
  Gave each knot a twist.

Took it to my bedroom,
  Stuck it in a box,
Turned the key a dozen times,
  Jammed and plugged the locks.

Pounded flat the hinges,
  Nailed the lid with tacks,
Wrapped the box in silverfoil,
  Sealed the knots with wax.

Folded it in canvas,
  Stitched the seams up tight,
Hid it in the sugar bin,
  Waited until night.

Tiptoed in the garden,
  Dug the safest place,
Buried it beneath the grass,
  Smoothed away each trace.

Scattered leaves above it,
  Said a special spell.
Want to know what's hidden there?
  Think I'd ever tell?

ARTHUR C. CLARKE

The Nine Billion Names of God

"THIS IS a slightly unusual request," said Dr. Wagner, with what he hoped was commendable restraint. "As far as I know, it's the first time anyone's been asked to supply a Tibetan monastery with an automatic sequence computer. I don't wish to be inquisitive, but I should hardly have thought that your—ah—establishment had much use for such a machine. Could you explain just what you intend to do with it?"

"Gladly," replied the lama, readjusting his silk robe and carefully putting away the slide rule he had been using for currency conversions. "Your Mark V computer can carry out any routine mathematical operation involving up to ten digits. However, for our work we are interested in *letters*, not numbers. As we wish you to modify the output circuits, the machine will be printing words, not columns of figures."

"I don't quite understand . . ."

"This is a project on which we have been working for the last three centuries—since the lamasery was founded, in fact. It is somewhat alien to your way of thought, so I hope you will listen with an open mind while I explain it."

"Naturally."

"It is really quite simple. We have been compiling a list which shall contain all the possible names of God."

"I beg your pardon?"

"We have reason to believe," continued the lama imperturbably, "that all such names can be written with not more than nine letters in an alphabet we have devised."

"And you have been doing this for three centuries?"

"Yes. We expected it would take us about fifteen thousand years to complete the task."

"Oh." Dr. Wagner looked a little dazed. "Now I see why you wanted to hire one of our machines. But exactly what is the *purpose* of this project?"

The lama hesitated for a fraction of a second, and Wagner wondered if he had offended him. If so, there was no trace of annoyance in the reply.

"Call it ritual, if you like, but it's a fundamental part of our belief. All the many names of the Supreme Being—God, Jehovah, Allah, and so on—they are only man-made labels. There is a philosophical problem of some difficulty here, which I do not propose to discuss, but somewhere among all the possible combinations of letters which can occur are what one may call the *real* names of God. By systematic permutation of letters, we have been trying to list them all."

"I see. You've been starting at AAAAAAAAA . . . and working up to ZZZZZZZZZ . . ."

"Exactly—though we use a special alphabet of our own. Modifying the electromatic typewriters to deal with this is, of course, trivial. A rather more interesting problem is that of devising suitable circuits to eliminate ridiculous combinations. For example, no letter must occur more than three times in succession."

"Three? Surely you mean two."

"Three is correct. I am afraid it would take too long to explain why, even if you understood our language."

"I'm sure it would," said Wagner hastily. "Go on."

"Luckily it will be a simple matter to adapt your automatic sequence computer for this work, since once it has been programmed properly it will permute each letter in turn and print the result. What would have taken us fifteen thousand years it will be able to do in a hundred days."

Dr. Wagner was scarcely conscious of the faint sounds from the Manhattan streets far below. He was in a different world, a world of natural, not man-made, mountains. High up in their remote aeries these monks had been patiently at work, generation after generation, compiling their lists of meaningless words. Was there any limit to the follies of mankind? Still, he must give no hint of his inner thoughts. The customer was always right . . .

"There's no doubt," replied the doctor, "that we can modify the Mark V to print lists of this nature. I'm much more worried about the problem of installation and maintenance. Getting out to Tibet, in these days, is not going to be easy."

"We can arrange that. The components are small enough to travel by air—that is one reason why we chose your machine. If you can get them to India, we will provide transport from there."

"And you want to hire two of our engineers?"

"Yes, for the three months which the project should occupy."

"I've no doubt that Personnel can manage that." Dr. Wagner scribbled a note on his desk pad. "There are just two other points—"

Before he could finish the sentence the lama had produced a small slip of paper.

"This is my certified credit balance at the Asiatic Bank."

"Thank you. It appears to be—ah—adequate. The second matter is so trivial that I hesitate to mention it—but it's surprising how often the obvious gets overlooked. What source of electrical energy have you?"

"A diesel generator providing fifty kilowatts at one hundred ten volts. It was installed about five years ago and is quite reliable. It's made life at the lamasery much more comfortable, but of course it was really installed to provide power for the motors driving the prayer wheels."

"Of course," echoed Dr. Wagner. "I should have thought of that."

The view from the parapet was vertiginous, but in time one gets used to anything. After three months George Hanley was not impressed by the two-thousand-foot swoop into the abyss or the remote checkerboard of fields in the valley below. He was leaning against the wind-smoothed stones and staring morosely at the distant mountains whose names he had never bothered to discover.

This, thought George, was the craziest thing that had ever happened to him. "Project Shangri-La," some wit at the labs had christened it. For weeks now the Mark V had been churning out acres of sheets covered with gibberish. Patiently, inexorably, the computer had been rearranging letters in all their possible combinations, exhausting each class before going on to the next. As the sheets had emerged from the electromatic typewriters, the monks had carefully cut them up and pasted them into enormous books. In another week, heaven be praised, they would have finished. Just what obscure calculations had convinced the monks that they needn't bother to go on to words of ten, twenty, or a hundred letters, George didn't know. One of his recurring nightmares was that there would be some change of plan and that the High Lama (whom they'd naturally called Sam Jaffe, though he didn't look a bit like him) would suddenly announce that the project would be extended to approximately 2060 A.D. They were quite capable of it.

George heard the heavy wooden door slam in the wind as Chuck came out onto the parapet beside him. As usual, Chuck was smoking one of the cigars that made him so popular with the monks—who, it seemed, were quite willing to embrace all the minor and most of the major pleasures of life. That was one thing in their favor: they might be crazy, but they weren't bluenoses. Those frequent trips they took down to the village, for instance . . .

"Listen, George," said Chuck urgently. "I've learned something that means trouble."

"What's wrong? Isn't the machine behaving?" That was the worst contingency George could imagine. It might delay his return, than which nothing could be more horrible. The way he felt now, even the sight of a TV commercial would seem like manna from heaven. At least it would be some link with home.

"No—it's nothing like that." Chuck settled himself on the parapet, which was unusual, because normally he was scared of the drop. "I've just found what all this is about."

"What d'ya mean—I thought we knew."

"Sure—we know what the monks are trying to do. But we didn't know *why*. It's the craziest thing—"

"Tell me something new," growled George.

"—but old Sam's just come clean with me. You know the way he drops in every afternoon to watch the sheets roll out. Well, this time he seemed rather excited, or at least as near as he'll ever get to it. When I told him that we were on the last cycle he asked me, in that cute English accent of his, if I'd ever wondered what they were trying to do. I said, 'Sure'—and he told me."

"Go on, I'll buy it."

"Well, they believe that when they have listed all His names—and they reckon that there are about nine billion of them—God's purpose will be achieved. The human race will have finished what it was created to do, and there won't be any point in carrying on. Indeed, the very idea is something like blasphemy."

"Then what do they expect us to do? Commit suicide?"

"There's no need for that. When the list's completed, God steps in and simply winds things up . . . bingo!"

"Oh, I get it. When we finish our job, it will be the end of the world."

Chuck gave a nervous little laugh.

"That's just what I said to Sam. And do you know what happened? He looked at me in a very queer way, like I'd been stupid in class, and said, 'It's nothing as trivial as *that*.' "

George thought it over for a moment.

"That's what I call taking the Wide View," he said presently. "But what d'ya suppose we should do about it? I don't see that it makes the slightest difference to us. After all, we already knew that they were crazy."

"Yes—but don't you see what may happen? When the list's complete and the Last Trump doesn't blow—or whatever it is they expect—we may get the blame. It's our machine they've been using. I don't like the situation one little bit."

"I see," said George slowly. "You've got a point there. But this sort of thing's happened before, you know. When I was a kid down in Louisiana we had a crackpot preacher who said the world was going to end next Sunday. Hundreds of people believed him—even sold their homes. Yet nothing happened; they didn't turn nasty as you'd expect. They just decided that he'd made a mistake in his calculations and went right on believing. I guess some of them still do."

"Well, this isn't Louisiana, in case you hadn't noticed. There are just two of us and hundreds of these monks. I like them, and I'll be sorry for old Sam when his lifework backfires on him. But all the same, I wish I was somewhere else."

"I've been wishing that for weeks. But there's nothing we can do until the contract's finished and the transport arrives to fly us out."

"Of course," said Chuck thoughtfully, "we could always try a bit of sabotage."

"Like hell we could! That would make things worse."

"Not the way I meant. Look at it like this. The machine will finish its run four days from now, on the present twenty-hours-a-day basis. The transport calls in a week. OK, then all we need do is to find something that wants replacing during one of the overhaul periods—something that will hold up the works for a couple of day. We'll fix it, of course, but not too quickly. If we time matters properly, we can be down at the airfield when the last name pops out of the register. They won't be able to catch us then."

"I don't like it," said George. "It will be the first time I ever walked out on a job. Besides, it would make them suspicious. No, I'll sit tight and take what comes."

"I *still* don't like it," he said seven days later, as the tough little mountain ponies carried them down the winding road. "And don't you think I'm running away because I'm afraid. I'm just sorry for those poor old guys up there, and I don't want to be around when they find what suckers they've been. Wonder how Sam will take it?"

"It's funny," replied Chuck, "but when I said good-bye I got the idea he knew we were walking out on him—and that he didn't care because he knew the machine was running smoothly and that the job would soon be finished. After that—well, of course, for him there just isn't any After That . . ."

George turned in his saddle and stared back up the mountain road. This was the last place from which one could get a clear view of the lamasery. The squat, angular buildings were silhouetted against the afterglow of the sunset; here and there lights gleamed like portholes in the sides of an ocean liner. Electric lights, of course, sharing the same circuit as the Mark V. How much longer would they share it? wondered George. Would the monks smash up the computer in their rage and disappointment? Or would they just sit down quietly and begin their calculations all over again?

He knew exactly what was happening up on the mountain at this very moment. The High Lama and his assistants would be sitting in their silk robes, inspecting the sheets as the junior monks carried them away from the typewriters and pasted them into the great volumes. No one would be saying anything. The only sound would be the incessant patter, the never-ending rainstorm, of the keys hitting the paper, for the Mark V itself was utterly silent as it flashed through its thousands of calculations a second. Three months of this, thought George, was enough to start anyone climbing up the wall.

"There she is!" called Chuck, pointing down into the valley. "Ain't she beautiful!"

She certainly was, thought George. The battered old DC-3 lay at the end of the runway like a tiny silver cross. In two hours she would be bearing them away to freedom and sanity. It was a thought worth savoring like a fine liqueur. George let it roll around his mind as the pony trudged patiently down the slope.

The swift night of the high Himalayas was now almost upon them. Fortunately the road was very good, as roads went in this region, and they were both carrying torches. There was not the slightest danger, only a certain discomfort from the bitter cold. The sky overhead was perfectly clear and ablaze with the familiar, friendly stars. At least there would be no risk, thought George, of the pilot being unable to take off because of weather conditions. That had been his only remaining worry.

He began to sing but gave it up after a while. This vast arena of mountains, gleaming like whitely hooded ghosts on every side, did not encourage such ebullience. Presently George glanced at his watch.

"Should be there in an hour," he called back over his shoulder to Chuck. Then he added, in an afterthought, "Wonder if the computer's finished its run? It was due about now."

Chuck didn't reply, so George swung round in his saddle. He could just see Chuck's face, a white oval turned toward the sky.

"Look," whispered Chuck, and George lifted his eyes to heaven. (There is always a last time for everything.)

Overhead, without any fuss, the stars were going out.

ROSEMARY AND STEPHEN VINCENT BENÉT

Nancy Hanks

(1784–1818)

If Nancy Hanks
Came back as a ghost,
Seeking news
Of what she loved most,
She'd ask first
"Where's my son?
What's happened to Abe?
What's he done?

"Poor little Abe,
Left all alone
Except for Tom,
Who's a rolling stone;
He was only nine
The year I died.
I remember still
How hard he cried.

"Scraping along
In a little shack,
With hardly a shirt
To cover his back,
And a prairie wind
To blow him down,
Or pinching times
If he went to town.

"You wouldn't know
About my son?
Did he grow tall?
Did he have fun?
Did he learn to read?
Did he get to town?
Do you know his name?
Did he get on?"

Daniel Boone

(1735–1820)

When Daniel Boone goes by, at night,
The phantom deer arise
And all lost, wild America
Is burning in their eyes.

Abigail Adams
(1744–1818)

If you would be
Wise or rare,
Pick your grandmother
With care.

There's no doubt about it,
The Adamses were lucky,
For the one that *they* picked
Was both witty and plucky.

She had all of the virtues
And most of the graces,
And believed that all wives
Should stay right in their places.

Now, John had no tact,
But his Abigail did,
A salient fact
Which she tactfully hid.

Alone and unaided,
She raised sons and daughters,
While John went to Congress
Or over wide waters.

She could lord it in London
Or skimp it at home,
And manage both households
With equal aplomb.

For Abigail's metal
Was strong as fine steel,
And Abigail's manners
Exceeding genteel.

Her pride and her cleverness,
All of her treasure,
Were bequeathed to her sons
In a bountiful measure.

This accounts for the Adamses,
How then could they fail?
But *what* were the forces
That made Abigail?

LEWIS CARROLL

Alice's Adventures in Wonderland and its sequel, *Through the Looking-Glass,* are the world's best-known children's books. The man who wrote them also wrote *A Syllabus of Plane Algebraical Geometry,* which seems odd. He invented the White Rabbit, the disappearing Cheshire Cat, the Red Queen, the White Queen, the Mock Turtle, and dozens of other queer creatures of his imagination. He also invented what we now call Scotch tape, a "Nyctograph" for taking notes in the dark, the modern book jacket, the first self-photographing device, and many unusual card games.

This tall, thin clergyman made a living teaching mathematics at Oxford University in England. He was a fussy, stiff-backed fellow who never married, was a loving friend to little girls, stammered (except when he talked to children), and was so shy that he even hid his hands under a pair of gray-and-black cotton gloves. He was a first-rate photographer during the pioneer period of camera art. His real name was Charles Lutwidge Dodgson, pronounced *Dodson.* (English proper names often have what seems to Americans odd pronunciations—the Cholmondeley family, for instance, calls itself *Chumley.*)

We remember July 4 as Independence Day. The second most famous July 4 in history was July 4, 1862. On that day Lewis Carroll was rowing up the Isis River, on which Oxford stands. In the boat were his friend Canon Duckworth and three little girls named Liddell. One of them, his favorite, was ten-year-old Alice, and she is really the Alice of *Alice in Wonderland.*

As Carroll rowed he began to invent a story to amuse the little girls. As he said later, "I . . . sent my heroine straight down a rabbit hole without the least idea what was to happen afterwards." Alice pestered him to write the story down for her. He did, and much to his surprise it turned out to be the most famous children's story ever written.

Still, not all children like it. Those who believe in always being sensible may find it puzzling or boring.* But if you like nonsense, language, the odd tricks you can play with words, if you can believe, like the White Queen, "as many as six impossible things before breakfast," then *Alice* and its sequel are for you.

*In 1931, I've read, China banned *Alice in Wonderland* because "animals should not use human language."

It all begins with Alice following a White Rabbit and falling down a rabbit hole. She has a series of startling adventures in the subterranean Wonderland. In the course of these adventures she changes size, falls into a Pool of Tears, meets a Duck, a Dodo, a Lory, and an Eaglet, a Caterpillar smoking a hookah, a baby who turns into a pig, and a Cheshire Cat who disappears, except for its grin. The Cat suggests that she visit the house of either the March Hare or the Mad Hatter—it doesn't matter which, as they're both mad. She reaches the March Hare's house and finds herself in the middle of an odd gathering.

A Mad Tea-Party

THERE WAS a table set out under a tree in front of the house, and the March Hare and the Hatter were having tea at it: a Dormouse was sitting between them, fast asleep, and the other two were using it as a cushion, resting their elbows on it, and talking over its head. "Very uncomfortable for the Dormouse," thought Alice; "only as it's asleep, I suppose it doesn't mind."

The table was a large one, but the three were all crowded together at one corner of it. "No room! No room! they cried out when they saw Alice coming. "There's *plenty* of room!" said Alice indignantly, and she sat down in a large armchair at one end of the table.

"Have some wine," the March Hare said in an encouraging tone.

Alice looked all round the table, but there was nothing on it but tea. "I don't see any wine," she remarked.

"There isn't any," said the March Hare.

"Then it wasn't very civil of you to offer it," said Alice angrily.

"It wasn't very civil of you to sit down without being invited," said the March Hare.

"I didn't know it was *your* table," said Alice: "it's laid for a great many more than three."

"Your hair wants cutting," said the Hatter. He had been looking at Alice for some time with great curiosity, and this was his first speech.

"You should learn not to make personal remarks," Alice said with some severity: "It's very rude."

The Hatter opened his eyes very wide on hearing this; but all he *said* was "Why is a raven like a writing desk?"

"Come, we shall have some fun now!" thought Alice. "I'm glad they've begun asking riddles—I believe I can guess that," she added aloud.

"Do you mean that you think you can find out the answer to it?" said the March Hare.

"Exactly so," said Alice.

"Then you should say what you mean," the March Hare went on.

"I do," Alice hastily replied; "at least—at least I mean what I say—that's the same thing, you know."

"Not the same thing a bit!" said the Hatter. "Why, you might just as well say that 'I see what I eat' is the same thing as 'I eat what I see'!"

"You might just as well say," added the March Hare, "that 'I like what I get' is the same thing as 'I get what I like'!"

"You might just as well say," added the Dormouse, which seemed to be talking in its sleep, "that 'I breathe when I sleep' is the same thing as 'I sleep when I breathe'!"

"It *is* the same thing with you," said the Hatter, and here the conversation dropped, and the party sat silent for a minute, while Alice thought over all she could remember about ravens and writing desks, which wasn't much.

The Hatter was the first to break the silence. "What day of the month is it?" he said, turning to Alice: he had taken his watch out of his pocket, and was looking at it uneasily, shaking it every now and then, and holding it to his ear.

Alice considered a little, and then said, "The fourth."

"Two days wrong!" sighed the Hatter. "I told you butter wouldn't suit the works!" he added, looking angrily at the March Hare.

"It was the *best* butter," the March Hare meekly replied.

"Yes, but some crumbs must have got in as well," the Hatter grumbled: "you shouldn't have put it in with the bread knife."

The March Hare took the watch and looked at it gloomily: then he dipped it into his cup of tea, and looked at it again: but he could think of nothing better to say than his first remark, "It was the *best* butter, you know."

Alice had been looking over his shoulder with some curiosity. "What a funny watch!" she remarked. "It tells the day of the month, and doesn't tell what o'clock it is!"

"Why should it?" muttered the Hatter. "Does *your* watch tell you what year it is?"

"Of course not," Alice replied very readily: "but that's because it stays the same year for such a long time together."

"Which is just the case with *mine*," said the Hatter.

Alice felt dreadfully puzzled. The Hatter's remark seemed to her to have no sort of meaning in it, and yet it was certainly English. "I don't quite understand you," she said, as politely as she could.

"The Dormouse is asleep again," said the Hatter, and he poured a little hot tea upon its nose.

The Dormouse shook its head impatiently, and said, without opening its eyes, "Of course, of course: just what I was going to remark myself."

"Have you guessed the riddle yet?" the Hatter said, turning to Alice again.

"No, I give it up," Alice replied. "What's the answer?"

"I haven't the slightest idea," said the Hatter.

"Nor I," said the March Hare.

Alice sighed wearily. "I think you might do something better with the time," she said, "than wasting it in asking riddles that have no answers."

"If you knew Time as well as I do," said the Hatter, "you wouldn't talk about wasting *it*. It's *him*."

"I don't know what you mean," said Alice.

"Of course you don't!" the Hatter said, tossing his head contemptuously. "I daresay you never even spoke to Time!"

"Perhaps not," Alice cautiously replied; "but I know I have to beat time when I learn music."

"Ah! That accounts for it," said the Hatter. "He won't stand beating. Now, if you only kept on good terms with him, he'd do almost anything you liked with the clock. For instance, suppose it were nine o'clock in the morning, just time to begin lessons: you'd only have to whisper a hint to Time, and round goes the clock in a twinkling! Half-past one, time for dinner!"

("I only wish it was," the March Hare said to itself in a whisper.)

"That would be grand, certainly," said Alice thoughtfully; "but then—I shouldn't be hungry for it, you know."

"Not at first, perhaps," said the Hatter: "but you could keep it to half-past one as long as you liked."

"Is that the way *you* manage?" Alice asked.

The Hatter shook his head mournfully. "Not I!" he replied. "We quarreled last March—just before *he* went mad, you know—" (pointing with his teaspoon at the March Hare) "—it was at the great concert given by the Queen of Hearts, and I had to sing

'Twinkle, twinkle, little bat!
How I wonder what you're at!'

You know the song, perhaps?"

"I've heard something like it," said Alice.

"It goes on, you know," the Hatter continued, "in this way:

'Up above the world you fly,
Like a tea-tray in the sky.
Twinkle, twinkle—' "

Here the Dormouse shook itself, and began singing in its sleep, "*Twinkle, twinkle, twinkle, twinkle—*" and went on so long that they had to pinch it to make it stop.

"Well, I'd hardly finished the first verse," said the Hatter, "when the Queen bawled out, 'He's murdering the time! Off with his head!' "

"How dreadfully savage!" exclaimed Alice.

"And ever since that," the Hatter went on in a mournful tone, "he won't do a thing I ask! It's always six o'clock now."

A bright idea came into Alice's head. "Is that the reason so many tea things are put out here?" she asked.

"Yes, that's it," said the Hatter with a sigh: "it's always teatime, and we've no time to wash the things between whiles."

"Then you keep moving round, I suppose?" said Alice.

"Exactly so," said the Hatter: "as the things get used up."

"But what happens when you come to the beginning again?" Alice ventured to ask.

"Suppose we change the subject," the March Hare interrupted, yawning. "I'm getting tired of this. I vote the young lady tells us a story."

"I'm afraid I don't know one," said Alice, rather alarmed at the proposal.

"Then the Dormouse shall!" they both cried. "Wake up, Dormouse!" And they pinched it on both sides at once.

The Dormouse slowly opened its eyes. "I wasn't asleep," it said in a hoarse, feeble voice, "I heard every word you fellows were saying."

"Tell us a story!" said the March Hare.

"Yes, please do!" pleaded Alice.

"And be quick about it," added the Hatter, "or you'll be asleep again before it's done."

"Once upon a time there were three little sisters," the Dormouse began in a great hurry; "and their names were Elsie, Lacie, and Tillie; and they lived at the bottom of a well—"

"What did they live on?" said Alice, who always took a great interest in questions of eating and drinking.

"They lived on treacle," said the Dormouse, after thinking a minute or two.

"They couldn't have done that, you know," Alice gently remarked. "They'd have been ill."

"So they were," said the Dormouse; "*very* ill."

Alice tried a little to fancy to herself what such an extraordinary way of living would be like, but it puzzled her too much: so she went on: "But why did they live at the bottom of a well?"

"Take some more tea," the March Hare said to Alice, very earnestly.

"I've had nothing yet," Alice replied in an offended tone: "so I can't take more."

"You mean you can't take *less*," said the Hatter: "It's very easy to take *more* than nothing."

"Nobody asked *your* opinion," said Alice.

"Who's making personal remarks now?" the Hatter asked triumphantly.

Alice did not quite know what to say to this: so she helped herself to some tea and bread-and-butter, and then turned to the Dormouse, and repeated her question. "Why did they live at the bottom of a well?"

The Dormouse again took a minute or two to think about it, and then said "It was a treacle well."

"There's no such thing!" Alice was beginning very angrily, but the Hatter and the March Hare went "Sh! Sh!" and the Dormouse sulkily remarked, "If you can't be civil, you'd better finish the story for yourself."

"No, please go on!" Alice said very humbly. "I won't interrupt you again. I daresay there may be *one.*"

"One, indeed!" said the Dormouse indignantly. However, he consented to go on. "And so these three little sisters—they were learning to draw, you know—"

"What did they draw?" said Alice, quite forgetting her promise.

"Treacle," said the Dormouse, without considering at all, this time.

"I want a clean cup," interrupted the Hatter: "let's all move one place on."

He moved on as he spoke, and the Dormouse followed him: the

March Hare moved into the Dormouse's place, and Alice rather unwillingly took the place of the March Hare. The Hatter was the only one who got any advantage from the change; and Alice was a good deal worse off than before, as the March Hare had just upset the milk jug into his plate.

Alice did not wish to offend the Dormouse again, so she began very cautiously: "But I don't understand. Where did they draw the treacle from?"

"You can draw water out of a water well," said the Hatter; "so I should think you could draw treacle out of a treacle well—eh, stupid?"

"But they were *in* the well," Alice said to the Dormouse, not choosing to notice this last remark.

"Of course they were," said the Dormouse: "well in."

This answer so confused poor Alice that she let the Dormouse go on for some time without interrupting it.

"They were learning to draw," the Dormouse went on, yawning and rubbing its eyes, for it was getting very sleepy; "and they drew all manner of things—everything that begins with an M—"

"Why with an M?" said Alice.

"Why not?" said the March Hare.

Alice was silent.

The Dormouse had closed its eyes by this time, and was going off into a doze; but, on being pinched by the Hatter, it woke up again with a little shriek, and went on: "—that begins with an M, such as mousetraps, and the moon, and memory, and muchness—you know you say things are 'much of a muchness'—did you ever see such a thing as a drawing of a muchness!"

"Really, now you ask me," said Alice, very much confused, "I don't think—"

"Then you shouldn't talk," said the Hatter.

This piece of rudeness was more than Alice could bear: she got up in great disgust, and walked off: the Dormouse fell asleep instantly, and neither of the others took the least notice of her going, though she looked back once or twice, half hoping that they would call after her: the last time she saw them, they were trying to put the Dormouse into the teapot.

"At any rate I'll never go *there* again!" said Alice, as she picked her way through the wood. "It's the stupidest tea party I ever was at in all my life!"

Just as she said this, she noticed that one of the trees had a door leading right into it. "That's very curious!" she thought. "But everything's curious today. I think I may as well go in at once." And in she went.

Once more she found herself in the long hall, and close to the little glass table. "Now, I'll manage better this time," she said to herself, and began by taking the little golden key, and unlocking the door that led into the garden. Then she set to work nibbling at the mushroom (she had kept a piece of it in her pocket) till she was about a foot high: then she walked down the little passage: and *then*—she found herself at last in the beautiful garden, among the bright flower beds and the cool fountains.

Here are some of the best-loved nonsense verses scattered through the two "Alice" books.

Father William

"You are old, Father William" the young man said,
  "And your hair has become very white;
And yet you incessantly stand on your head—
  Do you think, at your age, it is right?"

"In my youth," Father William replied to his son,
  "I feared it might injure the brain;
But, now that I'm perfectly sure I have none,
  Why, I do it again and again."

"You are old," said the youth, "as I mentioned before.
  And have grown most uncommonly fat;
Yet you turned a back-somersault in at the door—
  Pray, what is the reason of that?"

"In my youth," said the sage, as he shook his gray locks,
  "I kept all my limbs very supple
By the use of this ointment—one shilling the box—
  Allow me to sell you a couple?"

"You are old," said the youth, "and your jaws are too weak
  For anything tougher than suet;
Yet you finished the goose, with the bones and the beak—
  Pray, how did you manage to do it?"

"In my youth," said his father, "I took to the law,
  And argued each case with my wife;
And the muscular strength which it gave to my jaw
  Has lasted the rest of my life."

"You are old," said the youth, "one would hardly suppose
  That your eye was as steady as ever;
Yet you balanced an eel on the end of your nose—
  What made you so awfully clever?"

"I have answered three questions, and that is enough,"
  Said his father. "Don't give yourself airs!
Do you think I can listen all day to such stuff?
  Be off, or I'll kick you downstairs!"

The Crocodile

How doth the little crocodile
  Improve his shining tail,
And pour the waters of the Nile
  On every golden scale!

How cheerfully he seems to grin,
  How neatly spreads his claws,
And welcomes little fishes in,
  With gently smiling jaws!

Beautiful Soup

Beautiful Soup, so rich and green,
Waiting in a hot tureen!
Who for such dainties would not stoop?
Soup of the evening, beautiful Soup!
Soup of the evening, beautiful Soup!
  Beau—ootiful Soo—oop!
  Beau—ootiful Soo—oop!
Soo—oop of the e—e—evening,
  Beautiful, beautiful Soup!

Beautiful Soup! Who cares for fish,
  Game, or any other dish?
Who would not give all else for two p
ennyworth only of beautiful Soup?
Pennyworth only of beautiful Soup?
  Beau—ootiful Soo—oop!
  Beau—ootiful Soo—oop!
Soo—oop of the e—e—evening,
  Beautiful, beauti—FUL SOUP!

Speak Roughly to Your Little Boy

Speak roughly to your little boy,
  And beat him when he sneezes:
He only does it to annoy,
  Because he knows it teases.

WOW! WOW! WOW

I speak severely to my boy,
  I beat him when he sneezes:
For he can thoroughly enjoy
  The pepper when he pleases.

WOW! WOW! WOW!

Jabberwocky

'Twas brillig, and the slithy toves
  Did gyre and gimble in the wabe:
All mimsy were the borogoves,
    And the mome raths outgrabe,

"Beware the Jabberwock, my son!
  The jaws that bite, the claws that catch!
Beware the Jubjub bird, and shun
    The frumious Bandersnatch!"

He took his vorpal sword in hand:
  Long time the manxome foe he sought—
So rested he by the Tumtum tree,
    And stood awhile in thought.

And, as in uffish thought he stood,
  The Jabberwock, with eyes of flame,
Came whiffling through the tulgey wood,
    And burbled as it came!

One, two! One, two! And through and through
  The vorpal blade went snicker-snack!
He left it dead, and with its head
    He went galumphing back.

"And hast thou slain the Jabberwock?
  Come to my arms, my beamish boy!
O frabjous day! Callooh! Callay!"
    He chortled in his joy.

'Twas brillig, and the slithy toves
  Did gyre and gimble in the wabe:
All mimsy were the borogoves,
    And the mome raths outgrabe.

SHEILA BURNFORD

Sheila Burnford is a Canadian writer. She's been a war nurse, an ambulance driver, and she holds a pilot's license. Her best book, *The Incredible Journey,* is based on real animals but the journey itself is imaginary. On a 250-mile trek through the wilderness what would happen to a wheat-colored Siamese cat, an old white English bullterrier, and a young red-gold Labrador retriever? In the episode that follows the cat has been separated from his two companions and encounters, as you'll see, a savage lynx.

The Incredible Journey

FROM CHAPTER EIGHT

THE CAT went on through the early morning mists, still following the trail of the dogs; and here it could not have been very old, for he found a partly chewed rabbit-skin, and several other clues, near some rocks where they had evidently passed a night, and the scent was still quite sharp to his acute sense. They had cut across country at one point, through several miles of deep spruce and cedar swamp, so that the going was, alternately, soft and dry and strewn with needles, then damp and spongy. It was a gloomy place, and the cat appeared uneasy, frequently glancing behind him as if he thought he were being followed. Several times he climbed a tree and crouched on a branch, watching and waiting. But whatever it was he scented or imagined showed equal cunning, and never appeared.

But the cat remained wary and suspicious, and felt with every nerve in his body that something was following—something evil. He increased his pace, then saw with relief that the area of deep, gloomy bush was coming to an end: far ahead of him he could see patches of blue sky which meant more open country. An old fallen tree lay ahead of him on the deer trail he was following. He leaped onto the trunk to cross it, pausing for a brief second, then every hair on his back rose erect, for in that moment he heard quite distinctly and felt rather than saw the presence of the following animal—and it was not very far behind him. Without further delay the cat leaped for the trunk of a birch tree, and clinging with his claws looked back along the path. Into view, moving with a velvet tread that equaled his own, came what appeared to be a large cat. But it was as different from the ordinary domestic cat as the Siamese himself was different.

This one was almost twice as large, chunky and heavy, with a short bobtail and thick furry legs. The coat was a soft gray, overlaid with a few darker spots. The head differed only from an ordinary cat's in that it was framed in a ruff of hair, and the ears rose into tufted points. It was a wild, cruel face that the Siamese saw, and he recognized instinctively a wanton killer—and one that could easily outclass him in strength, ferocity and speed. He scrambled as far up the young birch as he could go, and clung there, the slender trunk swaying under his weight. The lynx stopped in the center of the trail, one heavy paw lifted, gazing up with gleaming malicious eyes; the Siamese flattened his ears and spat venomously, then looked quickly around, measuring his distance for escape. With a light bound the lynx landed on top of the fallen tree trunk, and for another endless moment the two pairs of eyes tried to outstare one another, the Siamese making a low eerie hissing noise, lashing his tail from side to side. The lynx leaped for the birch, straddling it easily with powerful limbs; then, digging in the long claws, he started up the trunk towards the cat, who retreated as far as was possible, and waited, swaying perilously now. As the heavy weight came nearer, the tree bent right over, and it was all that the cat could do to hold on. The lynx reached a paw out to its full length and raked at the cat, tearing a strip of the bark away. The cat struck back, but the tree was waving wildly, and he lost his grip with the movement, and fell. The tree was so far bent over that he had not too far to fall, but even in that short time he twisted in the air and landed on his feet, only to hear a heavier thud a few yards away; the tree, whipping back, had dislodged the lynx almost at the same time, but the heavier animal had fallen with more impetus and less agility; for a split second it remained where it was, slightly winded. The cat took his advantage of that second and was off like a streak, running for his life up the narrow deer trail.

Almost immediately he heard the other animal close behind. It was useless to turn and fight; this was no stupid bear who could be intimidated, but a creature as remorseless and cunning as the cat himself could be, to other smaller animals. Even as he ran he must have known that flight was hopeless too; for he leaped with desperation up the trunk of another tree; but they were all saplings and there was a little length of trunk for him to climb. This time the enemy was more cunning: it followed only halfway up, then deliberately swayed the pliant young tree from side to side, determined to shake the cat off. The situation was desperate and the cat knew it. He waited until he was on the lowest arc of the swing, then, gathering up his muscles under him until he was like a coiled spring, he leaped for the ground. The lynx was almost as quick, but it missed by a hairsbreadth when the cat swerved violently, then doubled on his tracks and shot like a bullet into a rabbit burrow that opened up miraculously in the bank before him. The terrible claws so close behind slashed harmlessly through empty air. The cat forced himself into the burrow as far as he could go, and crouched there, unable to turn and face what might come, for the burrow was very narrow. His pursuer, too, dropped to a crouching position, then pushed an exploratory paw into the burrow. The cat was fortunately out of reach, so the lynx lowered its head and rashly applied one malevolent green eye to the hole, withdrawing it quickly, however, and shaking the tawny ruffed head in baffled fury when a flurry of earth hit it full in the face—the cat's hind legs were working like pistons, hurling the earth back out of the hole.

The lynx drew back, to work out its next approach. Complete silence fell in the clearing, and all seemed peaceful and quiet in contrast to the wildly beating heart of the desperate, trapped cat.

Systematically the lynx began to dig away the earth around the entrance to the burrow with its powerful forepaws, and was so engrossed that it failed to hear, or to scent, the soft downwind approach of a young boy wearing a bright red jacket and cap and carrying a rifle, who had entered the bush from the fields beyond. The boy was walking softly, not because he had seen the lynx, but because he was out after deer: he and his father, half a mile away, were walking in a parallel course, with prearranged signals, and the boy was very excited, for this was the first time his father had considered him responsible enough to accompany him with his own rifle. Suddenly he saw the infuriated animal scrabbling away at the earth, and heard it growling softly as a continuous hail of earth coming from an unseen source covered it. In that same instant the animal looked up and saw the boy. It crouched low, snarling, and no fear showed in its eyes, only pure hatred. In a split-second decision, whether for fight or flight, it sprang; and in the same instant the boy raised his rifle, sighted and fired, all in one quick motion. The lynx somersaulted in the air and fell, its breath expelled in a mournful whistle as it hit the ground; the forelegs jerked once, a last spasm of nerves flickered across the fur, and it lay dead.

The boy was trembling slightly as he approached the dead animal, unable to forget the look of evil, savage fury on the catlike face which now lay before him, lips still curled back over white, perfect fangs. He stood looking down at his unexpected victim, unwilling to touch it, waiting for his father, who presently came, panting and anxious, calling as he ran. He stopped, staring at the tawny body lying on the pine needles, and then at the white face of his son.

He turned the animal over and showed the boy the small neat hole where the bullet had entered.

"Just below the breastbone." He looked up, grinning, and the boy smiled shakily.

The boy reloaded his rifle and tied his red neckerchief on a branch, marking the entrance to the clearing for their return. Then they walked off down the trail together, still talking, and the hidden cat heard their voices receding in the distance.

When all was silent he backed out of his refuge, and emerged into the sun-dappled clearing, his coat covered with sandy dirt. Completely ignoring the dead body even though forced to step around it, he sat down within ten yards of it, coolly washing his fur from the end of his tail to the tip of his nose. Then he stretched himself luxuriously, and with a final gesture of contempt turned his back on the lynx and dug into the earth with his hind claws to send a last shower of dirt over the animal's face. That done, he continued on his way, cool and assured as ever.

Two days later he caught up with the dogs. He came out on the crest of a hill forming one side of a valley, where a small stream meandered between alder-grown banks. Across the valley, clearly discernible among the bare trees on the opposite slope, he saw two familiar and beloved golden and white figures. His tail switched in excitement; he opened his mouth and uttered a plaintive, compelling howl. The two figures on the hill opposite stopped dead in their tracks, listening to the unbelievable sound as it echoed around the quiet valley. The cat leaped onto an overhanging rock, and as the hollow, raucous howl went ringing back and forth again the dogs turned questioningly, their eyes straining to seek the reality of the call. Then the young dog barked frenziedly in recognition and plunged down the hillside and across a stream, closely followed by the old dog. Now the cat began to run too, bounding like a mad thing down the hill, and they met on the banks of the little stream.

The old dog nearly went out of his mind with excitement: he covered the cat with frantic licking; twice he knocked him over with his eager thrusting head; then, carried away with enthusiasm, he started on the same tight intricate circles that he had used on the collie, whirling nearer and nearer until he finally burst free from the circle and rushed at the cat, who ran straight up the trunk of a tree, twisted in his own length, then dropped on the back of the dog below.

All through this performance the young dog stood by, slowly and happily swinging his tail, his brown eyes alight and expressive, until at last his turn came when the old white clown collapsed in an ecstatic panting heap. Then the Labrador walked up to the cat, who rose on his hind legs, placing black forepaws on the neck of the great dog who towered above him, gently questing at the torn ear.

It would have been impossible to find three more contented animals that night. They lay curled closely together in a hollow filled with sweet-scented needles, under an aged, spreading balsam tree, near the banks of the stream. The old dog had his beloved cat, warm and purring between his paws again, and he snored in deep contentment. The young dog, their gentle worried leader, had found his charge again. He could continue with a lighter heart.

JOHN LENNON AND PAUL MCCARTNEY

Eleanor Rigby

Ah, look at all the lonely people.
Ah, look at all the lonely people.
Eleanor Rigby picks up the rice in the church where a wedding has been,
lives in a dream.
Waits at the window, wearing a face that she keeps in a jar by the door,
Who is it for?
All the lonely people, where do they all come from?
All the lonely people, where do they all belong?
Father McKenzie, writing the words of a sermon that no one will hear,
No one comes near
Look at him working, darning his socks in the night when there's nobody there,
What does he care?
All the lonely people, where do they all come from?
All the lonely people, where do they all belong?
Ah, look at all the lonely people.
Ah, look at all the lonely people.

Eleanor Rigby died in the church and was buried
along with her name.
Nobody came.
Father McKenzie, wiping the dirt from his hands as
he walks from the grave.
No one was saved.
All the lonely people, where do they all come from?
All the lonely people, where do they all belong?

The Blanket

Retold by Francelia Butler

ON A SMALL FARM in the south of France lived a man, his wife, and his son. With them lived his old father. This arrangement was not satisfactory to the wife. She was constantly complaining about the old man.

"When he eats, he slurps his soup," she said. "And he lets it drizzle down his beard. It makes me sick at my stomach and I cannot digest my food properly."

Her husband yielded to her demands and asked his father to eat his food in the adjoining room. But her complaints continued.

"Every time I look up from my plate," she said, "he is always staring out in my direction. I can't stand his eyes on me."

Finally, she made an ultimatum: "Either he goes or I do."

The son, sad about the affair, but having no choice but to lose either his wife or his father, chose to send his father away.

"I know it's winter, father," he said, "but my wife simply won't stand your presence here any longer. I must ask you to leave."

The father nodded. "Of course, son, I will go."

Remorseful at sending his father out in the middle of winter, the son asked his little boy to go to the barn and fetch the horse blanket.

"At least, father, the blanket will help to keep you warm."

The little boy left and was gone a long time. Finally, he returned, but he had only half the blanket. He had cut it jaggedly in two.

"What have you done that for?" the father demanded. "You have ruined a perfectly good blanket."

"Father," the little boy replied, "I was saving half of it for you and mother when you get old."

RAY BRADBURY

When Ray Bradbury and I were both much younger I wrote a prefatory note for one of his finest books, *The Martian Chronicles*. Whenever I look around at the world and get scared, I reread his inscription in my copy: "With gratitude from this chronicler who will put in a good word for the Fadimans when the Martians land!"

Ray Bradbury is a famous science-fiction writer. He writes mainly for grown-ups but young people understand him better. Actually, his finest work isn't really science fiction at all but fantasy, often rooted in a childhood that must have been one of the most wildly imaginative ones ever lived. As a small boy, he tells us, he fell in love "with monsters and skeletons and circuses and carnivals and, at last, the red planet Mars. From these primitive bricks I have built a life and a career."

To tell the truth, though he's written wonderful stories about incredible machines, I'm not sure he likes machinery much. He doesn't drive and he doesn't fly, to my knowledge. The chilling story that follows takes a dim view of one of the most marvelous of all machines—the television set around which "the people sat like the dead."

As I say, there's something in his stories that grips young people, teenagers mostly. If you like "The Pedestrian," try his collection, one hundred tales in all, called *The Stories of Ray Bradbury*.

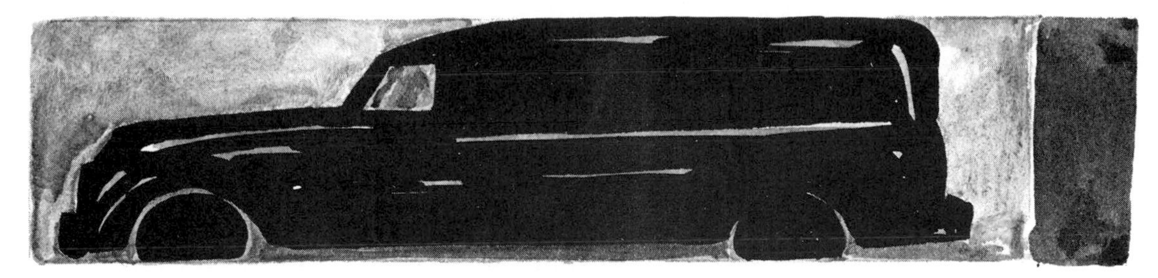

The Pedestrian

TO ENTER out into that silence that was the city at eight o'clock of a misty evening in November, to put your feet upon that buckling concrete walk, to step over grassy seams and make your way, hands in pockets, through the silences, that was what Mr. Leonard Mead most dearly loved to do. He would stand upon the corner of an intersection and peer down long moonlit avenues of sidewalk in four directions, deciding which way to go, but it really made no difference; he was alone in this world of A.D. 2053, or as good as alone, and with a final decision made, a path selected, he would stride off, sending patterns of frosty air before him like the smoke of a cigar.

Sometimes he would walk for hours and miles and return only at midnight to his house. And on his way he would see the cottages and homes with their dark windows, and it was not unequal to walking through a graveyard where only the faintest glimmers of firefly light appeared in flickers behind the windows. Sudden gray phantoms seemed to manifest upon inner room walls where a curtain was still undrawn against the night, or there were whisperings and murmurs where a window in a tomblike building was still open.

Mr. Leonard Mead would pause, cock his head, listen, look, and march on, his feet making no noise on the lumpy walk. For long ago he had wisely changed to sneakers when strolling at night, because the dogs in intermittent squads would parallel his journey with barkings if he wore hard heels, and lights might click on and faces appear and an entire street be startled by the passing of a lone figure, himself, in the early November evening.

On this particular evening he began his journey in a westerly direction, toward the hidden sea. There was a good crystal frost in the air; it cut the nose and made the lungs blaze like a Christmas tree inside; you could feel the cold light going on and off, all the branches filled with invisible snow. He listened to the faint push of his soft shoes through autumn leaves with satisfaction, and whistled a cold quiet whistle between his teeth, occasionally picking up a leaf as he passed, examining its skeletal pattern in the infrequent lamplights as he went on, smelling its rusty smell.

"Hello, in there," he whispered to every house on every side as he moved. "What's up tonight on Channel Four, Channel Seven, Channel Nine? Where are the cowboys rushing, and do I see the United States Cavalry over the next hill to the rescue?"

The street was silent and long and empty, with only his shadow moving like the shadow of a hawk in midcountry. If he closed his eyes and stood very still, frozen, he could imagine himself upon the center of a plain, a wintry, windless Arizona desert with no house in a thousand miles, and only dry riverbeds, the streets, for company.

"What is it now?" he asked the houses, noticing his wristwatch. "Eight-thirty P.M.? Time for a dozen assorted murders? A quiz? A revue? A comedian falling off the stage?"

Was that a murmur of laughter from within a moon-white house? He hesitated, but went on when nothing more happened. He stumbled over a particularly uneven section of sidewalk. The cement was vanishing under flowers and grass. In ten years of walking by night or day, for thousands of miles, he had never met another person walking, not once in all that time.

He came to a cloverleaf intersection which stood silent where two main highways crossed the town. During the day it was a thunderous surge of cars, the gas stations open, a great insect rustling and a ceaseless jockeying for position as the scarab beetles, a faint incense puttering from their exhausts, skimmed homeward to the far directions. But now these highways, too, were like streams in a dry season, all stone and bed and moon radiance.

He turned back on a side street, circling around toward his home. He was within a block of his destination when the lone car turned a corner quite suddenly and flashed a fierce white cone of light upon him. He stood entranced, not unlike a night moth, stunned by the illumination, and then drawn toward it.

A metallic voice called to him:

"Stand still. Stay where you are! Don't move!"

He halted.

"Put up your hands!"

"But—" he said.

"Your hands up! Or we'll shoot!"

The police, of course, but what a rare, incredible thing; in a city of three million, there was only *one* police car left, wasn't that correct? Ever since a year ago, 2052, the election year, the force had been cut down from three cars to one. Crime was ebbing; there was no need now for the police, save for this one lone car wandering and wandering the empty streets.

"Your name?" said the police car in a metallic whisper. He couldn't see the men in it for the bright light in his eyes.

"Leonard Mead," he said.

"Speak up!"

"Leonard Mead!"

"Business or profession?"

"I guess you'd call me a writer."

"No profession," said the police car, as if talking to itself. The light held him fixed, like a museum specimen, needle thrust through chest.

"You might say that," said Mr. Mead. He hadn't written in years. Magazines and books didn't sell anymore. Everything went on in the tomblike houses at night now, he thought, continuing his fancy. The tombs, ill-lit by television light, where the people sat like the dead, the gray or multicolored lights touching their faces, but never really touching *them*.

"No profession," said the phonograph voice, hissing. "What are you doing out?"

"Walking," said Leonard Mead.

"Walking!"

"Just walking," he said simply, but his face felt cold.

"Walking, just walking, walking?"

"Yes, sir."

"Walking where? For what?"

"Walking for air. Walking to see."

"Your address!"

"Eleven South Saint James Street."

"And there is air *in* your house, you have an air *conditioner*, Mr. Mead?"

"Yes."

"And you have a viewing screen in your house to see with?"

"No."

"No?" There was a crackling quiet that in itself was an accusation.

"Are you married, Mr. Mead?"

"No."

"Not married," said the police voice behind the fiery beam. The moon was high and clear among the stars and the houses were gray and silent.

"Nobody wanted me," said Leonard Mead with a smile.

"Don't speak unless you're spoken to!"

Leonard Mead waited in the cold night.

"Just *walking*, Mr. Mead?"

"Yes."

"But you haven't explained for what purpose."

"I explained; for air, and to see, and just to walk."

"Have you done this often?"

"Every night for years."

The police car sat in the center of the street with its radio throat faintly humming.

"Well, Mr. Mead," it said.

"Is that all?" he asked politely.

"Yes," said the voice. "Here." There was a sigh, a pop. The back door of the police car sprang wide. "Get in."

"Wait a minute, I haven't done anything!"

"Get in."

"I protest!"

"Mr. Mead."

He walked like a man suddenly drunk. As he passed the front window of the car he looked in. As he had expected, there was no one in the front seat, no one in the car at all.

"Get in."

He put his hand to the door and peered into the back seat, which was a little cell, a little black jail with bars. It smelled of riveted steel. It smelled of harsh antiseptic; it smelled too clean and hard and metallic. There was nothing soft there.

"Now if you had a wife to give you an alibi," said the iron voice. "But—"

"Where are you taking me?"

The car hesitated, or rather gave a faint whirring click, as if information, somewhere, was dropping card by punch-slotted card under electric eyes. "To the Psychiatric Center for Research on Regressive Tendencies."

He got in. The door shut with a soft thud. The police car rolled through the night avenues, flashing its dim lights ahead.

They passed one house on one street a moment later, one house in an entire city of houses that were dark, but this one particular house had all of its electric lights brightly lit, every window a loud yellow illumination, square and warm in the cool darkness.

"That's *my* house," said Leonard Mead.

No one answered him.

The car moved down the empty riverbed streets and off away, leaving the empty streets with the empty sidewalks, and no sound and no motion all the rest of the chill November night.

BASHŌ

Some of you may have been gently compelled in school to write haiku. If so, you know that haiku is a Japanese verse form of seventeen syllables (in Japanese) arranged in three lines of five, seven, and five syllables each. It tries to say much in little by suggesting rather than stating. The finest haiku evoke, in few words, ideas or feelings that one would not at first think are connected. For example, in the second one below by Bashō the jump of a frog calls up feelings of the peace of nature, the antiquity of time, and perhaps other feelings, too. Usually the haiku has at its center something small, apparently unimportant: a crow, a frog, a fly, a mosquito.

The greatest of haiku poets is Matsuo Bashō, usually called simply Bashō (1644–1694). His real name was Matsuo Munefusa. Something of a hermit, he often retired to a hut made of plantain leaves, which in Japanese is *bashō*. Hence his pen name.

Two Haiku

Translated by Dorothy Britton

On a leafless bough
  In the gathering autumn dusk:
    A solitary crow!

Listen! a frog
  Jumping into the stillness
    Of an ancient pond!

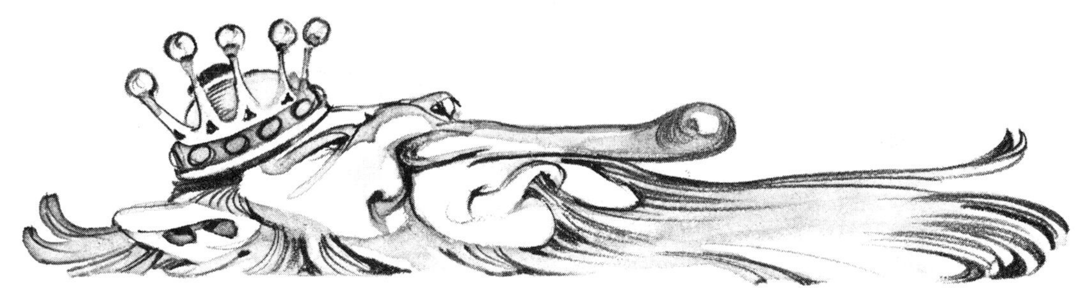

GODFRIED BOMANS

Nothing

Translated by Patricia Crampton

THE KING was walking in his garden. It was the middle of May. The sun was shining, the fountains leaped sparkling into the air, and goldfish the size of dolphins shot through the glittering water. An orchestra was playing in the arbor and seven dancing girls were dancing through the rose gardens. Jugglers were juggling everywhere and a ventriloquist was performing on the center path. The king yawned.

"If only something would happen," he said. "This is quite deadly."

But he could not think of anything that ought to happen, because everything he could think of was already happening. Then he called his Minister of Pleasure and Entertainment and said:

"Please think of something new."

"Fireworks," said the minister.

The fireworks arrived. The rockets, arrows and fireballs shot into the air and finally the whole palace flew into the air with them.

"How boring," said the king, when it was all over. "Can't you think of something *nice?*"

"A circus," said the minister.

The circus arrived. There was a camel which played the flute and six elephants who did something which elephants do not usually do and there was a spotted beast which could say "Thank you." The king sat in the front row, yawning until the tears sprang into his eyes.

"Well, that's over now," he said when it was finished. "Can't you think of anything which made you say: now that is *really* funny?"

"Myself," said the minister. He took off his coat and went and stood on his head in the grass. Then he spun round like a mad thing, humming a song.

"Feeble," said the king, when he had finished. "I want to see something precious. A glass house, with diamond windows. And when it's finished, I shall smash it up with a stick."

A house was built. Everything, tables, chairs, pillows, beds and the coal in the cellar, was made of glass, and the diamond windows sparkled like diamonds. When it was ready the king ran through it, smashing it up with a stick. The splinters flew round his head and his ears were full of them. But when everything was broken and he wanted to think up a new idea the minister said: "There's no money left."

"Then sell the palace," said the king.

"The palace has been blown up."

"The humming top again," said the king, "that was the best thing."

"Get it yourself," said the minister. And he went away.

Then the king realized that he was poor. He picked up his stick again and set out into the world. He met many people and asked them all for work and bread. But the people asked: "What can you do?"

And he replied: "Nothing. Nothing at all."

The people shrugged their shoulders and went on their way.

Now it happened one day that he came, tired and hungry, to a field where a man was lying on his back, gazing at the sky.

"What are you doing there?" asked the king curiously.

"Nothing," said the man, "nothing at all."

"Just so," said the king. "I have been doing that for twenty years."

"I do it for twenty minutes," said the man, "and even then I begin to get thoroughly bored."

He got up and began to reap the corn, and the king reaped with him. When it was evening they lay down among the sheaves and looked at the stars. This went on for several weeks. Then the king returned to his kingdom, his usefulness restored. He looked over the wall at the palace gardens and saw that there were now fourteen dancers dancing through the rose garden. There were spotted animals who not only said "Thank you," but also "Keep to the right" and "See you tomorrow," and the sun stood like a pale balloon between the explosions of the fireworks. A new king sat on his throne, looking on and yawning.

"Listen to me!" cried the former king. "Go and work! Work all day and rest in the evening. Then you will know what it is to do nothing for ten minutes. It is heaven on earth, the paradise of paradises!"

The new king lifted his head and yawned.

"Chase that tramp off," he said. "He bores me too."

JOY ADAMSON

Joy Adamson wrote an extraordinary book about a strange friendship. It's called *Born Free* and tells the story of the rearing of a lion cub. Mrs. Adamson was the wife of a game warden in Kenya, Africa, a paradise of wildlife. Her husband, George, was forced in self-defense to shoot a lioness. Then he found her three tiny cubs in a rock crevice, and not quite knowing what else to do, brought them home. Two of them were disposed of to a zoo, but the tiniest one, Elsa, they decided to rear.

At the time the extract below begins Elsa is several months old and Mrs. Adamson has become a kind of mother to her. Nuru is their native helper and Pati is a tame hyrax, a small mammal that looks a little like a guinea pig.

These few pages from Mrs. Adamson's fine book give us a good picture of Elsa's habits during her growing-up period, and what it must be like to have a lioness for a house pet.

Elsa Meets Other Wild Animals

OFTEN, IT WAS TOUCHING to see her torn between her hunting instinct and her wish to please us. Anything moving seemed to her, as it would to most dogs, just asking to be chased; but, as yet, her instinct to kill had not fully developed. Of course, we had been careful never to show her her goat meat alive. She had plenty of opportunity of seeing wild animals, but as we were usually with her when this happened, she gave chase merely in play and always came back to us after a short time, rubbed her head against our knees, and told us with a low miaow about the game.

We had animals of all kinds around our house. A herd of waterbuck and impala antelope and about sixty reticulated giraffes had been our neighbors for many years. Elsa met them on every walk, and they got to know her very well and even allowed her to stalk them to within a few yards before they quietly turned away, and a family of bat-eared foxes got so used to her that we were able to approach to within a few paces of the burrows of these timid animals while their cubs rolled in the sand in front of the entrance holes, guarded by the parent foxes.

Mongooses also provided Elsa with a lot of fun. These little creatures, no bigger than a weasel, live in abandoned termite hills, which, made as they are of cement-hard soil, constitute ideal fortresses. Standing as high as eight feet and built with many air funnels, they also provide cool shelters during the heat of the day. About teatime the mongoose comedians leave their stronghold and feed on grubs and insects until it becomes dark, when they return home. That was the hour at which our walks often made us pass them. Elsa would sit absolutely still in front of the anthill besieging them, apparently deriving great satisfaction from seeing the little clowns popping their heads out of the air funnels, only to give a sharp whistle of alarm and disappear like shadows.

But if the mongooses were fun to tease, the baboons were infuriating. They lived in a leopard-safe dormitory, on a sheer cliff, near our house. There they would spend the night in safety, clinging to the slightest depression in the rock. Before sunset they always retired to this refuge, and the cliff appeared to be covered with black spots. From their safe position they barked and shrieked at Elsa, who could do nothing in retaliation.

It was an exciting moment when the cub met her first elephant, an anxious one too, for poor Elsa had no mother to warn her against these animals who regard lions as the only enemies of their young and therefore sometimes kill them. One day Nuru, who had taken her out for her morning walk, came back panting to say that Elsa was "playing with an elephant." We took our rifles and he guided us to the scene. There we saw a great old elephant, his head buried in a bush, enjoying his breakfast. Suddenly Elsa, who had crept up from behind, took a playful swipe at one of his hind legs. A scream of shocked surprise and injured dignity followed this piece of impertinence. Then the elephant backed from the bush and charged. Elsa hopped nimbly out of his way and, quite unimpressed, began to stalk him. It was a very funny though an alarming sight, and we could only hope that we should not need to use our guns. Luckily, after a time, both became bored with the game; the old elephant went back to his meal and Elsa lay down, close by, and went to sleep.

During the next few months the cub took every opportunity that came her way to harry elephants, and there were many such occasions for the elephant season was beginning. This meant an annual invasion by herds numbering several hundred animals. The great beasts seemed to be very familiar with the geography of Isiolo and always went to the places where the best maize and brussels sprouts grew. Apart from this and in spite of a dense African population and motor traffic, they behaved very well and gave little trouble. As our home, which is three miles distant from Isiolo, is surrounded by the best browsing, a large number of the invaders come to visit us, and an old rifle range in front of the house has become their favorite playground. At this season, we have therefore to be very careful on our walks for small groups of elephants are always about. Now, having to protect Elsa as well as ourselves made us all the more alert.

One day at noon Nuru and Elsa returned home followed by a large number of elephants; from our dining-room window we could see them in the bush. We tried to divert her attention but she had turned and was determined to meet the advancing herd. Then, suddenly, she sat down and watched them as they turned away and walked in single file across the rifle range. It was a grand parade as one after another emerged from the bush in which Elsa crouched, giving them her scent. She waited until the last of about twenty elephants had crossed, then she followed them slowly, her head held in a straight line with her shoulders, her tail outstretched. Suddenly the big bull in the rear turned and, jerking his massive head at Elsa, screamed with a high-pitched trumpeting sound. This war cry did not intimidate her, and she walked determinedly on; so did the big elephant. We went out and, following cautiously, saw glimpses of Elsa and the elephants mingling together in the undergrowth. There were no screams nor any sound of breaking branches, which would have indicated trouble. All the same, we waited anxiously till eventually the cub reappeared looking rather bored with the whole business.

But not all the elephants which Elsa met were so amiable as these. On another occasion she succeeded in starting a colossal stampede. The first thing we heard was tremendous thundering on the rifle range, and when we reached the scene we saw a herd of elephants racing downhill, with Elsa close behind them. Finally she was charged by a single bull, but she was much too quick for him and in time he gave up the attack and followed his companions.

Giraffes provided her with great fun too. One afternoon, when we were out with her, she took on fifty. Wriggling her body close to the ground and shivering with excitement, she stalked them, advancing step by step. The giraffes took no notice of her, they just stood and watched her nonchalantly. She looked at them and then back at us, as though she wanted to say: "Why do you stand there like candlesticks and spoil my stalking?" Finally she got really cross and, rushing full speed at me, knocked me flat.

Toward sunset, we ran into a herd of elephants. The light was failing rapidly but we could just see the shapes of elephants in all directions.

It has always seemed miraculous to me that these colossal animals can move noiselessly through the bush and are thus able to surround one without warning. This time there was no doubt that we were cut off. Wherever we looked for an opening to slip through, an elephant blocked the way. We tried to hold Elsa's attention, for it was not a moment for her to start one of her games with the giants. But all too soon she spotted them and dashed into their midst, then she was beyond our control. We heard screams and shrill piercing cries; my nerves were on edge, for, however carefully we maneuvered through the dark bush, there stood an elephant confronting us. At last we managed to make our way out and reached home, but, of course, without Elsa. She only returned much later; apparently she had had great fun and certainly did not understand why I was a nervous wreck.

A euphorbia hedge borders our drive; no ordinary animal will break through it because it contains a caustic latex. If the smallest drop of this substance touches the eyes it burns the membrane most painfully and will inflame it for many days. It is therefore given a wide berth by all animals except elephants, who love eating its juicy twigs and after a night's meal leave big open gaps.

Once, when I was feeding Elsa in her enclosure, I heard the unmistakable rumbling of elephants behind this hedge, which borders her wooden house, and there, sure enough, were five of the giants crunching loudly and making a meal of the only barrier which stood between us. Indeed, at the time I am writing about, the hedge was already a poor sight owing to their attentions.

To add to the excitement of Elsa's life there was now a rhino living close to our house. One evening at dark, when we were returning from a walk, the cub suddenly darted behind the servants' quarters. A tremendous commotion ensued. We went to find out what it was about and saw Elsa and the rhino facing each other. After a few moments of indecision, the rhino, snorting angrily, retreated with the cub in hot pursuit.

The following evening I was walking with Elsa and Nuru—we were late and it was getting dark—when suddenly the Somali grabbed my shoulder, thus preventing me from walking straight into the rhino, which stood behind a bush, facing us. I leapt back and ran. Luckily Elsa, who had not seen the rhino, thought I was playing a game and followed me. This was fortunate, for rhinos are unpredictable creatures who are apt to charge anything, including trucks and trains. The next day, however, Elsa had her fun; she chased the animal for two miles across the valley, Nuru loyally panting behind her. After this experience the rhino took itself off to quieter quarters.

By now we had established a routine for Elsa. The mornings were cool; it was then that we often watched the impala antelope leaping gracefully on the rifle range and listened to the chorus of the awakening birds. As soon as it got light Nuru released Elsa and both walked a short distance into the bush. The cub, full of unspent energy, chased everything she could find, including her own tail.

Then, when the sun got warm, she and Nuru settled under a shady tree and Elsa dozed while he read his Koran and sipped tea. Nuru always carried a rifle to protect them both against wild animals but was very good about following our instructions "to shout before shooting." He was genuinely fond of Elsa and handled her very well.

About teatime the two of them returned and we took over. First, Elsa had some milk, then we wandered into the hills or walked in the plain; she climbed trees, appeared to sharpen her claws, followed exciting scents of stalked Grant's gazelle and gerenuk, which sometimes played hide-and-seek with her. Much to our surprise, she was fascinated by tortoises, which she rolled over and over; she loved playing, and never did she miss an opportunity of starting a game with us—we were her "pride" and she shared everything with us.

As darkness fell we returned home and took her to her enclosure, where her evening meal awaited her. It consisted of large quantities of raw meat, mostly sheep and goat; she got her roughage by breaking up the rib bones and the cartilages. As I held her bones for her I would watch the muscles of her forehead moving powerfully. I always had to scratch the marrow out for her; she licked it greedily from my fingers, resting her heavy body upright against my arms. While this went on, Pati sat on the windowsill watching us, content to know that soon her turn would come to spend the night cuddled around my neck and that then she would have me to herself.

Till then, I sat with Elsa, playing with her, sketching her, or reading. These evenings were our most intimate time, and I believe that her love for us was mostly fostered in these hours when, fed and happy, she could doze off with my thumb still in her mouth. It was only on moonlight nights that she became restless; then she padded along the wire, listening intently, her nostrils quivering to catch the faintest scent which might bring a message from the mysterious night outside. When she was nervous her paws became damp and I could often judge her state of mind by holding them in my hands.

ISAAC ASIMOV

The Feeling of Power

JEHAN SHUMAN was used to dealing with the men in authority on long-embattled earth. He was only a civilian but he originated programming patterns that resulted in self-directing war computers of the highest sort. Generals consequently listened to him. Heads of congressional committees too.

There was one of each in the special lounge of New Pentagon. General Weider was space-burned and had a small mouth puckered almost into a cipher. Congressman Brant was smooth-cheeked and clear-eyed. He smoked Denebian tobacco with the air of one whose patriotism was so notorious, he could be allowed such liberties.

Shuman, tall, distinguished, and Programmer-first-class, faced them fearlessly.

He said, "This, gentlemen, is Myron Aub."

"The one with the unusual gift that you discovered quite by accident," said Congressman Brant placidly. "Ah." He inspected the little man with the egg-bald head with amiable curiosity.

The little man, in return, twisted the fingers of his hands anxiously. He had never been near such great men before. He was only an aging low-grade technician who had long ago failed all tests designed to smoke out the gifted ones among mankind and had settled into the rut of unskilled labor. There was just this hobby of his that the great

Programmer had found out about and was now making such a frightening fuss over.

General Weider said, "I find this atmosphere of mystery childish."

"You won't in a moment," said Shuman. "This is not something we can leak to the firstcomer. Aub!" There was something imperative about his manner of biting off that one-syllable name, but then he was a great Programmer speaking to a mere technician. "Aub! How much is nine times seven?"

Aub hesitated a moment. His pale eyes glimmered with a feeble anxiety. "Sixty-three," he said.

Congressman Brant lifted his eyebrows. "Is that right?"

"Check it for yourself, Congressman."

The congressman took out his pocket computer, nudged the milled edges twice, looked at its face as it lay there in the palm of his hand, and put it back. He said, "Is this the gift you brought us here to demonstrate. An illusionist?"

"More than that, sir. Aub has memorized a few operations and with them he computes on paper."

"A paper computer?" said the general. He looked pained.

"No, sir," said Shuman patiently. "Not a paper computer. Simply a sheet of paper. General, would you be so kind as to suggest a number?"

"Seventeen," said the general.

"And you, Congressman?"

"Twenty-three."

"Good! Aub, multiply those numbers, and please show the gentlemen your manner of doing it."

"Yes, Programmer," said Aub, ducking his head. He fished a small pad out of one shirt pocket and an artist's hairline stylus out of the other. His forehead corrugated as he made painstaking marks on the paper.

General Weider interrupted him sharply. "Let's see that."

Aub passed him the paper, and Weider said, "Well, it looks like the figure seventeen."

Congressman Brant nodded and said, "So it does, but I suppose anyone can copy figures off a computer. I think I could make a passable seventeen myself, even without practice."

"If you will let Aub continue, gentlemen," said Shuman without heat.

Aub continued, his hand trembling a little. Finally he said in a low voice, "The answer is three hundred and ninety-one."

Congressman Brant took out his computer a second time and flicked it. "By Godfrey, so it is. How did he guess?"

"No guess, Congressman," said Shuman. "He computed that result. He did it on this sheet of paper."

"Humbug," said the general impatiently. "A computer is one thing and marks on paper are another."

"Explain, Aub," said Shuman.

"Yes, Programmer. Well, gentlemen, I write down seventeen, and just underneath it I write twenty-three. Next I say to myself: seven times three—"

The congressman interrupted smoothly, "Now, Aub, the problem is seventeen times twenty-three."

"Yes, I know," said the little technician earnestly, "but I *start* by saying seven times three because that's the way it works. Now seven times three is twenty-one."

"And how do you know that?" asked the congressman.

"I just remember it. It's always twenty-one on the computer. I've checked it any number of times."

"That doesn't mean it always will be, though, does it?" said the congressman.

"Maybe not," stammered Aub. "I'm not a mathematician. But I always get the right answers, you see."

"Go on."

"Seven times three is twenty-one, so I write down twenty-one. Then one times three is three, so I write down a three under the two of twenty-one."

"Why under the two?" asked Congressman Brant at once.

"Because—" Aub looked helplessly at his superior for support. "It's difficult to explain."

Shuman said, "If you will accept his work for the moment, we can leave the details for the mathematicians."

Brant subsided.

Aub said, "Three plus two makes five, you see, so the twenty-one becomes a fifty-one. Now you let that go for a while and start fresh. You multiply seven and two, that's fourteen, and one and two, that's two. Put them down like this and it adds up to thirty-four. Now if you put the thirty-four under the fifty-one this way and add them, you get three hundred and ninety-one, and that's the answer."

There was an instant's silence and then General Weider said, "I don't believe it. He goes through this rigmarole and makes up numbers and multiplies and adds them this way and that, but I don't believe it. It's too complicated to be anything but hornswoggling."

"Oh no, sir," said Aub in a sweat. "It only *seems* complicated because you're not used to it. Actually the rules are quite simple and will work for any numbers."

"Any numbers, eh?" said the general. "Come, then." He took out his own computer (a severely styled GI model) and struck it at random. "Make a five seven three eight on the paper. That's five thousand seven hundred and thirty-eight."

"Yes, sir," said Aub, taking a new sheet of paper.

"Now"—more punching of his computer—"seven two three nine. Seven thousand two hundred and thirty-nine."

"Yes, sir."

"And now multiply those two."

"It will take some time," quavered Aub.

"Take the time," said the general.

"Go ahead, Aub," said Shuman crisply.

Aub set to work, bending low. He took another sheet of paper and another. The general took out his watch finally and stared at it. "Are you through with your magic-making, Technician?"

"I'm almost done, sir. Here it is, sir. Forty-one million, five hundred and thirty-seven thousand, three hundred and eighty-two." He showed the scrawled figures of the result.

General Weider smiled bitterly. He pushed the multiplication contact on his computer and let the numbers whirl to a halt. And then he started and said in a surprised squeak, "Great Galaxy, the fella's right."

The President of the Terrestrial Federation had grown haggard in office and, in private, he allowed a look of settled melancholy to appear on his sensitive features. The Denebian War, after its early start of vast movement and great popularity, had trickled down into a sordid matter of maneuver and countermaneuver, with discontent rising steadily on earth. Possibly, it was rising on Deneb too.

And now Congressman Brant, head of the important Committee on Military Appropriations, was cheerfully and smoothly spending his half-hour appointment spouting nonsense.

"Computing without a computer," said the president impatiently, "is a contradiction in terms."

"Computing," said the congressman, "is only a system for handling data. A machine might do it, or the human brain might. Let me give you an example." And, using the new skills he had learned, he worked out sums and products until the president, despite himself, grew interested.

"Does this always work?"

"Every time, Mr. President. It is foolproof."

"Is it hard to learn?"

"It took me a week to get the real hang of it. I think you would do better."

"Well, said the president, considering, "it's an interesting parlor game, but what is the use of it?"

"What is the use of a newborn baby, Mr. President? At the moment there is no use, but don't you see that this points the way toward liberation from the machine. Consider, Mr. President"—the congressman rose and his deep voice automatically took on some of the cadences he used in public debate—"that the Denebian War is a war of computer against computer. Their computers forge an impenetrable shield of countermissiles against our missiles, and ours forge one against theirs. If we advance the efficiency of our computers, so do they theirs, and for five years a precarious and profitless balance has existed.

"Now we have in our hands a method for going beyond the computer, leapfrogging it, passing through it. We will combine the mechanics of computation with human thought; we will have the equivalent of intelligent computers, billions of them. I can't predict what the consequences will be in detail, but they will be incalculable. And if Deneb beats us to the punch, they may be unimaginably catastrophic."

The president said, troubled, "What would you have me do?"

"Put the power of the administration behind the establishment of a secret project on human computation. Call it Project Number, if you like. I can vouch for my committee, but I will need the administration behind me."

"But how far can human computation go?"

"There is no limit. According to Programmer Shuman, who first introduced me to this discovery—"

"I've heard of Shuman, of course."

"Yes. Well, Dr. Shuman tells me that in theory there is nothing the computer can do that the human mind cannot do. The computer merely takes a finite amount of data and performs a finite number of operations upon them. The human mind can duplicate the process."

The president considered that. He said, "If Shuman says this, I am inclined to believe him—in theory. But, in practice, how can anyone know how a computer works?"

Brant laughed genially. "Well, Mr. President, I asked the same question. It seems that at one time computers were designed directly by human beings. Those were simple computers, of course, this being before the time of the rational use of computers to design more advanced computers had been established."

'Yes, yes. Go on."

"Technician Aub apparently had, as his hobby, the reconstruction of some of these ancient devices, and in so doing he studied the details of their workings and found he could imitate them. The multiplication I just performed for you is an imitation of the workings of a computer."

"Amazing!"

The congressman coughed gently. "If I may make another point, Mr. President—the further we can develop this thing, the more we can divert our federal effort from computer production and computer maintenance. As the human brain takes over, more of our energy can be directed into peacetime pursuits and the impingement of war on the ordinary man will be less. This will be most advantageous for the party in power, of course."

"Ah," said the president, "I see your point. Well, sit down, Congressman, sit down. I want some time to think about this. But meanwhile, show me that multiplication trick again. Let's see if I can't catch the point of it."

Programmer Shuman did not try to hurry matters. Loesser was conservative, very conservative, and liked to deal with computers as his father and grandfather had. Still, he controlled the West European computer combine, and if he could be persuaded to join Project Number in full enthusiasm, a great deal would be accomplished.

But Loesser was holding back. He said, "I'm not sure I like the idea of relaxing our hold on computers. The human mind is a capricious thing. The computer will give the same answer to the same problem each time. What guarantee have we that the human mind will do the same?"

"The human mind, Computer Loesser, only manipulates facts. It doesn't matter whether the human mind or a machine does it. They are just tools."

"Yes, yes. I've gone over your ingenious demonstration that the mind can duplicate the computer, but it seems to me a little in the air. I'll grant the theory, but what reason have we for thinking that theory can be converted to practice?"

"I think we have reason, sir. After all, computers have not always existed. The cavemen with their triremes, stone axes, and railroads had no computers."

"And possibly they did not compute."

"You know better than that. Even the building of a railroad or a ziggurat called for some computing, and that must have been without computers as we know them."

"Do you suggest they computed in the fashion you demonstrate?"

"Probably not. After all, this method—we call it 'graphitics,' by the way, from the old European word 'grapho,' meaning 'to write'—is developed from the computers themselves, so it cannot have antedated them. Still, the cavemen must have had *some* method, eh?"

"Lost arts! If you're going to talk about lost arts—"

"No, no. I'm not a lost art enthusiast, though I don't say there may not be some. After all, man was eating grain before hydroponics, and if the primitives ate grain, they must have grown it in soil. What else could they have done?"

"I don't know, but I'll believe in soil growing when I see someone grow grain in soil. And I'll believe in making fire by rubbing two pieces of flint together when I see that too."

Shuman grew placative. "Well, let's stick to graphitics. It's just part of the process of etherealization. Transportation by means of bulky contrivances is giving way to direct mass transference. Communications devices become less massive and more efficient constantly. For that matter, compare your pocket computer with massive jobs of a thousand years ago. Why not, then, the last step of doing away with computers altogether? Come, sir, Project Number is a going concern; progress is already headlong. But we want your help. If patriotism doesn't move you, consider the intellectual adventure involved."

Loesser said skeptically, "What progress? What can you do beyond multiplication? Can you integrate a transcendental function?"

"In time, sir. In time. In the last month I have learned to handle division. I can determine, and correctly, integral quotients and decimal quotients."

"Decimal quotients? To how many places?"

Programmer Shuman tried to keep his tone casual. "Any number!"

Loesser's lower jaw dropped. "Without a computer?"

"Set me a problem."

"Divide twenty-seven by thirteen. Take it to six places."

Five minutes later Shuman said, "Two point oh seven six nine two three."

Loesser checked it. "Well, now, that's amazing. Multiplication didn't impress me too much because it involved integers, after all, and I thought trick manipulation might do it. But decimals—"

"And that is not all. There is a new development that is, so far, top secret and which, strictly speaking, I ought not to mention. Still—we may have made a breakthrough on the square root front."

"Square roots?"

"It involves some tricky points and we haven't licked the bugs yet, but Technician Aub, the man who invented the science and who has an amazing intuition in connection with it, maintains he has the problem almost solved. And he is only a technician. A man like yourself, a trained and talented mathematician, ought to have no difficulty."

"Square roots," muttered Loesser, attracted.

"Cube roots, too. Are you with us?"

Loesser's hand thrust out suddenly. "Count me in."

General Weider stumped his way back and forth at the head of the room and addressed his listeners after the fashion of a savage teacher facing a group of recalcitrant students. It made no difference to the general that they were the civilian scientists heading Project Number. The general was the overall head, and he so considered himself at every waking moment.

He said, "Now square roots are all fine. I can't do them myself and I don't understand the methods, but they're fine. Still, the project will not be sidetracked into what some of you call the fundamentals. You can play with graphitics any way you want to after the war is over, but right now we have specific and very practical problems to solve."

In a far corner Technician Aub listened with painful attention. He was no longer a technician, of course, having been relieved of his duties and assigned to the project, with a fine-sounding title and good pay. But, of course, the social distinction remained, and the highly placed scientific leaders could never bring themselves to admit him to their ranks on a footing of equality. Nor, to do Aub justice, did he, himself, wish it. He was as uncomfortable with them as they with him.

The general was saying, "Our goal is a simple one, gentlemen—the replacement of the computer. A ship that can navigate space without a computer on board can be constructed in one-fifth the time and at one-tenth the expense of a computer-laden ship. We could build fleets five times, ten times, as great as Deneb could if we could but eliminate the computer.

"And I see something even beyond this. It may be fantastic now, a mere dream, but in the future I see the manned missile!"

There was an instant murmur from the audience.

The general drove on. "At the present time our chief bottleneck is the fact that missiles are limited in intelligence. The computer controlling them can only be so large, and for that reason they can meet the changing nature of antimissile defenses in an unsatisfactory way. Few missiles, if any, accomplish their goal, and missile warfare is coming to a dead end, for the enemy, fortunately, as well as for ourselves.

"On the other hand, a missile with a man or two within, controlling flight by graphitics, would be lighter, more mobile, more intelligent. It would give us a lead that might well mean the margin of victory. Besides which, gentlemen, the exigencies of war compel us to remember one thing. A man is much more dispensable than a computer. Manned missiles could be launched in numbers and under circumstances that no good general would care to undertake as far as computer-directed missiles are concerned . . ."

He said much more, but Technician Aub did not wait.

Technician Aub, in the privacy of his quarters, labored long over the note he was leaving behind. It read finally as follows:

"When I began the study of what is now called graphitics, it was no more than a hobby. I saw no more in it than an interesting amusement, an exercise of mind.

"When Project Number began, I thought that others were wiser than I, that graphitics might be put to practical use as a benefit to mankind, to aid in the production of really practical mass-transference devices perhaps. But now I see it is to be used only for death and destruction.

"I cannot face the responsibility involved in having invented graphitics."

He then deliberately turned the focus of a protein depolarizer on himself and fell instantly and painlessly dead.

They stood over the grave of the little technician while tribute was paid to the greatness of his discovery.

Programmer Shuman bowed his head along with the rest of them but remained unmoved. The technician had done his share and was no longer needed, after all. He might have started graphitics, but now that it had started, it would carry on by itself overwhelmingly, triumphantly, until manned missiles were possible with who knew what else.

Nine times seven, thought Shuman with deep satisfaction, is sixty-three, and I don't need a computer to tell me so. The computer is in my own head.

And it was amazing the feeling of power that it gave him.

YEVGENY YEVTUSHENKO

Lies

Translated by Robin Milner-Gulland and Peter Levi

Telling lies to the young is wrong.
Proving to them that lies are true is wrong.
Telling them that God's in his heaven
and all's well with the world is wrong.
The young know what you mean. The young are people.
Tell them the difficulties can't be counted,
and let them see not only what will be
but see with clarity these present times.
Say obstacles exist they must encounter,
sorrow happens, hardship happens.
The hell with it. Who never knew
the price of happiness will not be happy.
Forgive no error you recognize,
it will repeat itself, increase,
and afterwards our pupils
will not forgive in us what we forgave.

For Grown-ups Only

Speaking as a Grandfather

The editor of this anthology and writer of some few thousand words contained in it is at this moment nearing his eighty-second year. That is as distant from childhood as one cares to imagine. It might seem an impertinence therefore for him to bring together from twenty-four countries a large sampling of children's literature, chosen with the taste of an admitted ancient.

Yet I think this odd procedure can be defended.

One of the familiar consolations of advanced years is a certain detachment. As two negatives affirm, so may a double or even triple generation gap permit one to contemplate the world of childhood with a nicer understanding than is possible for those closer to it in time. Grandparents and grandchildren, the enders and the beginners, are not rivals but natural friends. Had Oedipus, where the three roads crossed, met the *father* of his father, Sophocles would have had no play.

Childhood is the only period, one hears it said, in which we know that we are eternal, death being for "the others." The young are as convinced of deathlessness as the old are of mortality. But this forms a ground for fellowship rather than estrangement. The old, nearing extinction, can by that very token perhaps be more sensitive to the springing promise of the young than can the self-absorbed middle-aged human creature, racked by competitive urges, caught up in life's powerful flood tide.

Should these speculations sound large and windy, I fall back on familiar experience and point to a well-known trick of the mind: as we age, though we may clean forget what occurred yesterday, we all the more vividly recall our childhood. Perhaps it is because there are fewer options open to us. Our minds are less busy with possibilities. The very lack of clutter affords room for the evocation of one's faraway past, for a roving backward to the era of infinite options. Being put on the shelf has its advantages. From a shelf, parts of the chamber, obscured from other angles, move into visibility.

Is this sentimentality? Possibly. But a useful sentimentality. If it is not mere self-indulgence, it can work to evoke in us that other self, the hidden child, without whose collaboration any discussion of the contents of this *Treasury* stiffens into the bleak and academic.

The Hidden Child

The child, we know, is something more, or less, but in any case other, than an embryonic "civilized" adult. At times—Golding's implacable *Lord of the Flies* makes this clear—he or she gives the impression of a small savage. In their classic *Children's Games in Street and Playground* the Opies cite Bertrand Russell's ". . . it is biologically natural that [children] should, in imagination, live through the life of remote savage ancestors." Sometimes the child ("in imagination") looks like part of a weird non-Darwinian evolutionary process: such enchanting freaks as those disguised children, the Hobbits and the Moomins, represent another order of creation. Or again, the child seems akin to an animal: the most persuasive animal stories have either been written for children (Beatrix Potter; the *Jungle Books*) or appropriated by them (*The Yearling*). And there are even times when the child (though rarely after the age of eight or nine) identifies with inanimate nature itself. Think of those moments of union in which Huck is as much river as boy; and there are similar instances from Book I of Wordsworth's *Prelude*. Freud's related "oceanic feeling" is not unfamiliar to sensitive children. Indeed, parents are often exasperated by the de-individualizing stupor into which the child occasionally seems to fall. He is, we complain, absentminded; that is, he diffuses into a brown study where mind does not matter. (Today's young people who try hallucinogens may be seeking a gateway to the oceanic trance of childhood, preferring it to the apparently unrewarding bustle of adulthood.)

Why is fantasy a favorite genre in children's literature? Surely in part because it is rooted in the notion of transformation. The plasticity of our early years goes very deep. Whitman tell us:

> *There was a child went forth every day,*
> *And the first object he look'd upon, that object he became,*
> *And that object became part of him for the day or a*
> *certain part of the day,*
> *Or for many years or stretching cycles of years.*

As children we are princes in disguise; stones and plants, beasts and winds; jet planes and jet pilots; the toys in a shop, the shop, the shopkeeper; the dancer and the dance. If I question the child, he dutifully reports that he is "playing," returning to me the word I have taught him. But "playing" only roughly describes it, because multiple-being is larger than mere doing, deeper than let's-pretend. Of course the child does not "believe" he is Snoopy. Momentarily, however, he can empty his consciousness of all except Snoopy feelings. " 'Making believe' is the gist of his whole life," says Robert Louis Stevenson, "and he cannot so much as take a walk except in character."

Now this protean, quicksilver being, we all know, must lie couched and call-up-able within the masters of children's literature. We do not really understand how Lewis Carroll can also at will be Alice, or Meindert DeJong be Siebren in *The Journey from Peppermint Street*, or Sanchez-Silva become a little boy who in turn becomes an ant in *Ladis and the Ant*. Even the process by which Shakespeare is at once a sane playwright and a mad king is less mystifying. At least both Shakespeare and Lear are adults, dwelling in the same age-zone. But the author of a first-rate children's book breaks the laws of time, being at the same time old and young, master of his mature, static identity, yet somehow also in phase with the shifting identity-in-formation of the child.

In her twenties Ann Taylor was one of the authors of *Original Poems for Infant Minds* (1804). At eighty she spoke for many writers of children's books and to some degree for all their appreciative adult readers: "The feeling of being a grown woman, to say nothing of an *old* woman, does not come naturally to me." A century after Ann Taylor we find Erich Kästner putting the matter explicitly. The child hidden within the grown-up "stands on a footstool and looks out upon the world through the man's eyes, as if they were windows." Such a man "contemplates the world, stories, dreams, the great and small adventures of life, language itself, with two pairs of eyes. He has a large pair of ears, and a small. Inside his head is another head, a child's head. He laughs, he weeps with two voices. His curiosity, his astonishment are twofold." Again and again we find the masters in agreement on this point. Thus Maurice Sendak: "Reaching the kids is important, but secondary. First, always, I have to reach and keep hold of the child in me."

There is no other branch of literature that requires of the writer quite such a queer bifurcation. His seems a crazy business, almost literally so, for as he writes he must be beside himself. Part of the fascination of children's literature for the grown-up—a fascination lost on the child—lies precisely in this property of doubleness. Those who write it are compounds. Their shingle should read: *Monster at Work.*

Much in the same way the ideal editor of this *Treasury* should be a chimera, half grown-up, half child—or perhaps a superchild. He should properly, not merely conventionally, use the first person plural. He should be able to read with double vision, absorbing two books in one, the book as the child perceives it, the book as the knowledgeable adult perceives it. He should be able concurrently to feel as child and as grown-up; to remember, yet to repress the sensation of remembering; to enjoy without judging, yet to judge without blunting the edge of enjoyment. Mission Impossible? It may be.

Still, we critics and anthologists of children's literature keep trying to square the circle. We do this even though we know that we are not even *reading* what children read. We read "literature," they a book. And yet it is not all frustration. As suggested, even I, a grandfather, can at times dissolve a part of me into my own childhood. Only a part, only at times, for a flashing interval, the mini-life of the glowing coal. Yet, however evanescent the experience, it is necessary. Not sufficient. But necessary.

How is the trick performed, the hidden child called forth? No one quite knows. The masters merely tell us that it happens, and, being creators, not introspective psychologists, they are themselves puzzled by the phenomenon. The critic or anthologist is an even worse case, because in him the hidden child is far less alive than in a Pamela Travers, a Josef Guggenmos, a Marcel Aymé.

We feel, of course, that the evocation of the hidden child is linked to Coleridge's "streamy nature of association, which thinking curbs and rudders." But it is not merely a matter of remembering concrete events of our childhood. All of us can do that. It is re-creating the thick, specific tone, the how-it-felt, of the event and manipulating the child of long ago so that it is *he* or *she,* not *you,* that does the feeling.

Ten minutes before the above lines were written, I received a letter from a friend, a learned art critic and philosopher of esthetics, acknowledging the receipt of a study of children's literature I had done. He writes: ". . . you made me remember what I thought I had forgotten. A hot summer afternoon around 1920, for instance, in Fulton, Illinois. I was barefooted, and picking my way across a freshly oiled dirt street to the public library to return *The Water Babies.*" The streamy associative faculty that can put together Kingsley and the feel of bare feet is required for anyone daring to write about or collect the literature of childhood.

For Proust his madeleine; and for each of us perhaps some other secret charm or mental amulet to draw us back along the path to our beginnings. I do not know why, but if I repeat to myself, "Turn again, Whittington, thrice Lord Mayor of London," or "How many miles to Babylon?" I at once find that I can enter a child's book with a shade more sensibility than if I open it without the aid of the incantation. Yes, this curious business has its serendipities. Backing the basin in the bathroom of a house I once lived in was an oblong looking-glass. By sheer accident I discovered that it was so hinged it could open like a little door; and that, opening it, I suddenly looked out upon the hitherto unsuspected street. Not an earth-shattering discovery? True—yet for me a useful one. I felt, if but for a moment, that vibration of other worlds to which children respond when they poke about in an attic or an abandoned, cluttered lot. It is the magic casement thrill of a thousand children's books, *Alice* being merely the most famous. But note that the looking-glass worked only once. That is, I am old, I get used to things all too quickly. Furthermore, objects, being palpable, have only limited talismanic powers. They generate weaker fields of force than memories.

Permit me one other illustration. Sometimes, in the course of my reading, I find it advisable to feel four years old. This is not easy. I use a certain charm of which all I can say is that it helps a little. When I was four, I slept in the same bed with my nine-year-old brother. It was an ancient four-poster with brass knobs on the posts. My brother would gravely assure me that, if he looked at one of those brass knobs long enough, he could "see the whole world in it." I tried, too, and failed, but nevertheless had an uneasy feeling that, as I knew my brother to be extremely wise, there must be *something* to it. And so, drifting toward sleep, I would keep my eyes fixed on the knob, feeling a bit scared, a bit hopeful of the miracle, a bit many other things that do not lend themselves to words. Whatever I felt, I felt as a four-year-old. But even today, recalling that knob, that bedpost, and that brother, I can sense my remote past thickening somewhere within me. And—though you need not believe this—that makes it easier for me to understand why the authors of *Mother Goose,* for example, are very fine writers indeed. It makes it possible for me to remember how funny Peter the Pumpkin-eater seemed when I first heard about him, and thus refresh my pleasure today in his domestic problem.

I must at once state that the process I have so clumsily described has little to do with nostalgia. I am not in love with my childhood (which, as I know now, though I did not know it then, was not a happy one) nor with the child I was. My talismanic devices include memories that have little to do with wonder or any "romantic" emotion. At six I watched a policeman put a bullet through the head of a horse that had broken its leg on the icy street. At once I became aware that life's underside was crawling with pain and violence. In consequence such tragic books as George MacDonald's *At the Back of the North Wind* (for tragic it is) could be better absorbed by my small self.

No, one need not love one's childhood. Nor, shocking as it may sound, need the writer of or about children's literature love children, except in the most general way. (Obviously one who *dis*likes, or more often *fears*, children cannot write about them.) What he must love, if he is a storyteller, are his child *characters*, which is different from loving children. For example, in reading Professor Tolkien's discussions of fairy tales, one hardly gets the impression that he is in love with children. What counts is that he cares deeply for his Hobbits. Despite the sweetness of her letters to children, there is little evidence that Beatrix Potter really loved them; her stories are often tender, her personality was tough. In his sensitive study Roger Lancelyn Green writes of C. S. Lewis: ". . . the Narnian stories were not told to actual children; nor had he any but the most superficial acquaintance with the species at the time of writing." Some of the best writers of children's books resent being so called. They are not writing love letters to the little ones, but trying to fashion works of art. Love in excess may even harm the writer. What he must be is not in love with children but, even if at a distance, *interested* in them—and unreservedly interested in the child hidden within himself.

Some first-rate writers have been "good with youngsters," as clearly Lewis Carroll was, though his affections were limited to preadolescent girls. Some, equally clearly, have not been "good," with no harmful effect on their work. Jules Verne probably belongs in the latter category.

Nor does being a parent help. Many outstanding living writers of children's literature have chosen to remain unmarried. As for the dead, one could make a long list of members of the Celibates' Club. Among them, to name only a handful, were Edward Lear, Lewis Carroll, Louisa May Alcott, Carlo Collodi, Maria Edgeworth, Lucretia Peabody Hale, Hans Christian Andersen, Selma Lagerlöf, Jean Ingelow, Charles and Mary Lamb, Christina Rossetti, Anna Sewell, Frances Browne, Charlotte Yonge, Kate Greenaway, Elinor Mure (author of the earliest extant written version of *The Three Bears*), Sarah Orne

Jewett, Palmer Cox, Susan Coolidge (*What Katy Did*), Mary Howitt, Catherine Sinclair, Dr. Isaac Watts, Jane Taylor, and Oliver Goldsmith (if indeed he wrote *Goody Two-Shoes*, which is far from established). Jacob Grimm was a bachelor; James Catnach, the nineteenth-century printer of chapbooks for the young, was one also, as was the Swedish anthologist Henrik Reuterdahl. Anne Carroll Moore, among the greats in the field of children's librarianship, remained single. Finally, the reader may draw any conclusion he cares to from the circumstance that at least three famous names associated with children's stories apparently had little, if any, sexual vitality: Carroll, Ruskin, Barrie.

A great many writers, of course, did love children and wrote with a specific favorite child, or favorite children, in mind. The classic examples are Lear and Carroll, as well as Milne, Hugh Lofting, and Jean de Brunhoff. Even forbidding (and childless) Mrs. Barbauld wrote most of her stories for her adopted nephew Charles, just as the (also childless) Maria Edgeworth read her first tales to her little brothers and sisters. And it was to the little convalescent Edith Story that the "great benevolent giant" Thackeray read, chapter by chapter, *The Rose and the Ring*. Despite these instances the heart of the matter seems to lie less in the writer's relationship to the live children about him than to the live child within him.

This familiar but basic proposition emerges as soon as we pass in rapid chronological review the whole procession of children's literature. One feature stands out immediately: the historic shift from a body of ephemeral work produced by unalloyed adults to one of higher quality produced by adults alloyed in varying degrees by their childhood. It is hard to determine when the shift began—in England perhaps with Catherine Sinclair, perhaps with Edward Lear. But it is fair to say that from about 1920 we see clearly the emergence of a numerous class of writers who are conservators of their childhood, as were in an earlier generation such rare specimens as Alcott, Mark Twain, and a few others. They represent a true mutation, almost inconceivable in the days of Thomas Day, Arnaud Berquin, and Joachim Heinrich Campe. Crass theories of the marketplace or those based on the mere expansion of the field do not explain the mutation. It has to do with a nebulous but profound sociopsychic movement, involving the "discovery" of the child. It is as though the tribe of children's writers suddenly began to rid themselves of repressions that for long had hindered their imaginative freedom.

One thinks at once, of course, of Freud. The fact is that his emphasis on the importance of infancy and early childhood has had only a modest effect on the literature itself. Children's literature constantly lags behind grown-up literature in its sensitivity to intellectual revolutions. But Freud, or rather the whole Freudian ambiance of our day, may well have stimulated the children's writer to retrospective self-analysis and so to the evocation of the child hidden within himself.

The Hidden Child and the Mainstream

This anthology restricts itself to what is admittedly only a tributary literature. But the relationship between mainstream and tributary is not quite exhausted when we identify it as one of ancestor and descendant. If, as we know, children's literature is directly associated with memories of childhood, and if it can be shown that mainstream literature is to any significant extent indirectly so associated, then the link between the two becomes more interesting.

We think at once of Freud's preoccupation with the child's repressed traumas and their later expression or sublimation in neurosis and art. But it is best not to make too much of this, best to refrain from a glib application of the jargon, beginning with the Oedipus complex. Freud himself warns us: "Whence the artist derives his creative capacities is not a question for psychology." We males may resent our fathers to the point of potential patricide; but most of us, unable to profit from the resentment, turn out to be not Dostoevsky but mere bookkeepers, salesmen, and anthologists.

Nevertheless, one or two of Freud's insights bear on our theme. He speaks, for example, of the "foster child" fantasy, the feeling a child often has that he is really the scion of mysterious, other, perhaps even royal parents. The fantasy, Freud correctly points out, lies at the root of much mainstream literature. This is even more markedly the case with children's literature. In "The Creative Writer and Daydreaming" (1908) Freud speculates on whether certain writers may not be triggered by an experience linked to a forgotten childhood memory. In this essay he also discusses children's play, connecting it with daydreaming, which in turn he connects with the writer's activity. The bond between literature, especially poetry, and play has been remarked by many others, especially Huizinga and Sewell. "In any true man," says Nietzsche, "hides a child who wants to play." Is not the dancing, singing

Zarathustra something of a great child? Speaking of the British General Strike of 1926, Richard Hughes writes:

> This was no nation grimly enduring a crisis, but one unexpectedly let out of school and enjoying a lovely romp—which just went to show what a crass mistake it is to suppose that the grown-up has any less need of play than the child! He probably needs even more; and the fact that he mostly gets less is the likeliest reason he's often so much more badly behaved.

How far may we venture in tracing these links? If children's literature is the overt expression of the child, is mainstream literature his covert expression? Common sense tells us the answer is no: where is the child in *Père Goriot, Measure for Measure, Le Misanthrope?* Yet the suspicion persists that just as there is an easily detected child in Hugh Lofting, there may be one almost impossible to detect in T. S. Eliot. If this were totally untrue, it would be hard to explain why through the centuries literally scores of highly intelligent creators have stressed the connection between the child and the mature poet or novelist. The linkage is suggested in its most cautious form by Doudan: "There is a certain *enfantillage* [child's play, childishness] of the imagination that we must retain all our lives."

With Wordsworth's more insistent feeling on this point we are familiar, as with the somewhat similar view of De Quincey, who was influenced by him. Carried to excess, it is the heart of Novalis's cry: "All poetry must be fairy tale-ish [*märchenhaft*]." Says Baudelaire: "Genius is childhood rediscovered," and again: ". . . genius is nothing but childhood distinctly formulated, but now endowed, in order to express itself, with virile and powerful organs. Still, I do not claim to offer this idea to physiology as anything better than a pure conjecture." The Franco-American novelist Julian Green says, "The child dictates, the man writes it down." Says Rainer Maria Rilke: "Never believe fate's more than the condensation of childhood." (Rilke here has in mind his own, the poet's "fate.") It was Jean Cocteau who divided people into two kinds: poets and grown-ups. And there is Picasso's frequently quoted remark, uttered as he examined some children's drawings: "When I was their age I could draw like Raphael; but it has taken me my whole life to learn to draw like them."

The reader may demur on the ground that these are mere enthusiastic proclamations, some of them by romantics—in Baudelaire's phrase, "pure conjecture." I do not claim they are "the truth." But, to be fair, I draw attention to a close and systematic formulation, by a reputable scholar, of the idea we have been considering.

The scholar is Jean-Paul Weber, a leading French critic and aesthetician. His "esthétique des profondeurs" turns on a basic proposition that he applies not only to literature. The proposition is: "Art is the remembrance of childhood." In his instructive introduction to Weber's *Psychology of Art*, Robert Emmet Jones summarizes the complex Weberian thesis thus: ". . . the entire work of an author is the result of a memory or a situation largely forgotten since childhood." Weber does not reject the Freudian approach, but his notion of the dominating "themes" or obsessions in the artist's work appears to go beyond Freud. "Let me say only that every writer, every dramatist seems to me to write only to symbolize, modulate, unconsciously, a childhood theme, sometimes two, rarely three; and that every work—including the existence of the artist—is a modulation, more or less clear, more or less firmly structured, of one or another aspect of this theme, or of this counterpoint of themes." His book concludes with a detailed analysis of "the Nose," which Weber claims as one of the dominant themes in all of Gogol's work and which "appears in this author in such a way that it would be impossible to find its source other than in the childhood of the author. . . ."

I find the thesis "Art is the remembrance of childhood," though brilliantly argued, far too sweeping. Yet one cannot read Weber, or reflect on the long line of creative men who have expressed similar ideas, without wondering if there is not at least some truth in the notion. Certain writers to whom it clearly applies at once spring to mind: Mark Twain; Proust, of course; Dickens, as Edmund Wilson classically demonstrated in "Dickens: The Two Scrooges"; Nabokov, who, speaking of the stimuli back of his Russian poems, refers to his "never-resolved childhood." The reader will think almost effortlessly of other instances.

If children's literature and mainstream literature are linked by the child concealed, in different ways, in both, the study of either should cast light on the other. Children's literature is no back eddy, but part of the broad current of moving language on which civilization, that of the child and that of the man or woman who is also partly a child, floats.

Surveying this broad current, we normally accord children's literature only tributary status. Fair enough: the Ohio, assured of being a river in its own right, does not complain that it is not the Mississippi.

But there is a restricted sense in which children's literature—more narrowly, a part of it—may be said to be Mississippian rather than Ohioan. This is the case whenever a grown-up reads a child's book without feeling that it is one. As statistics cannot report what is really crucial (what goes on inside the human mind), there are no hard facts and fancy graph-curves to back my impression that the number of such grown-ups is growing. These readers are of a breed quite different from the coy adults who can descend into children's books like so many slumming Lady Bountifuls. No, they simply find themselves enjoying on an "adult level" such writers as Henri Bosco, William Mayne, Paula Fox, or Vadim Frolov. These writers are not Stendhals, Henry Jameses, or Solzhenitsyns. But they are masters of an art sufficiently intricate to engage the adult without rousing in him a feeling that he is reading what is "meant for children."

If we attend to those who admittedly have an emotional investment in our field, we hear again and again the opinion that a good child's book is also a good adult's book. Thus C. S. Lewis: ". . . no book is really worth reading at the age of ten which is not equally (and often far more) worth reading at the age of fifty"; and again: "I am almost inclined to set it up as a canon that a children's story which is enjoyed only by children is a bad children's story." Thus Florence Barry: "There never was a good children's book that a grown-up person could not enjoy." Thus Mark Twain slyly: "I conceive that the right way to write a story for boys is to write so that it will not only interest boys but strongly interest any man *who has ever been a boy*. That immensely *enlarges the audience*."

One should not carry this cheerful doctrine too far. There are formidably intelligent readers who, once born, skipped childhood, or so it would seem. It is hard to imagine the critic F. R. Leavis chuckling over *The Peterkin Papers*. (Indeed, the very vision of a chuckling Leavis can brighten one's entire day.) But to the degree that (some) adults can read (some) children's literature quite as they read any other, such literature may be classed as mainstream, to be enjoyed and judged by mainstream standards.

Among adult readers of this nature we should include the cultist. From time to time the cultist upgrades a children's writer, making him the object of close, not to say solemn, critical scrutiny. Cultism is often valuable, for it may perceive deep layers of meaning that the child may be incapable of recognizing. For example, there is more in Edward Lear's longer poems—which are tragic as well as comic—than meets the child's eye. The classic example of cultism is Lewis Carroll, virtually an Established Church. He in fact does merit continual reanalysis. Then there is the small but faithful sect of Oz communicants. Over the years, too, the boys' books of Jules Verne have drawn profundities from French critics. During the sixties the Verne cult, mainly in consequence of the curious works of Marcel Moré, received a new infusion of energy. Thus sophisticated iconolatry helps to unite a certain portion of children's literature with the mainstream and swells its double audience.

Though it is only tangentially related to the care and feeding of the literary mainstream, we should note also the development of a double audience for children's films based on children's books. This double audience is fused; that is to say, children and adults seem to receive from children's films roughly the same kind of pleasure. This has not always been the case. In Victorian days you "took" the children to the pantomime, as in 1904 you "took" them to *Peter Pan*. Doubtless both young and old enjoyed these performances. But it would appear that in those days the old were conscious of patronizing an entertainment designed for children. Their appreciation was heavily tinctured with an indulgent tenderness toward the little ones. Indeed, as the adult watched the stage, he luxuriated in the extra pleasure of feeling himself to be an actor, too—benevolent uncle, playful father, humorously understanding mother. Barrie, as cunning a psychologist as playwright, understood this perfectly. He must have felt, on opening night, that he could rely on the strong-palmed adults to clap their hands first, cry out that they believed in fairies, and so save Tinker Bell's life. They cooperated. The children, however, went beyond cooperation. They believed. Thus the audience remained dual.

It is hard to pinpoint the moment when the fusion process started. I suggest 1933, when Disney was still an artist, not a culture-pollutant. We grown-ups, enjoying the sensational triumph of *The Three Little Pigs*, suddenly felt that this brilliant animation of a nursery tale was sized and shaped for us all. We did not feel separate from the children. The bars were down. From that time on we no longer "took" the children to the movie house to see a kiddie film. Instead, we all went to see a—film. The film or television show might be as vulgar and cretinous as *Doctor Dolittle;* as flat-footed as *Emil and the Detectives;* as charming a distortion of the original as *Mary Poppins;* or as exquisitely close to the author's spirit as the Royal Ballet's delightful *Tales of Beatrix Potter*, or the fine English version of E. Nesbit's *Railway Children*. In all cases the film was viewed, not as children's fare, but simply as art, good, mediocre, or bad. Thus, with its classics translated into other forms, children's literature, appealing to all ages, surfaces, though in a different guise, as part of the Mississippi mainstream.

Children's Literature as Preservative

One measure of the development of children's literature is found in the degree of its advance beyond the mere rehandling of folk materials. Much more important, however, is the fact that these ancient roots are never cut. Current children's writing, for instance, despite its sharp skew toward the experimental, continues to be nourished by them. The literature's normal habit, like that of its readers, is conservative. It inclines to repetition, refrain, ritual, even routine; to modulation rather than to mutation. And this attachment to its cloudy origins in oral tradition, tales and incantations of the street, handed-down stereotypes of nursery and fireside, can work to the advantage of grown-up literature.

We can distinguish at least three ways in which children's literature furnishes aid and comfort to its elder brother. The first involves the simple matter of story-telling. We are all aware that one school of dissectors of the contemporary novel believes that story itself, linear narrative with a beginning, a middle, and an end, stands in need of formal burial. Some of my grown-up readers may side with these mortuary sophisticates, while others remain persuaded that we are so made as to forever turn with pleasure to the tale-teller and the tale. Nevertheless, it is true that plain serial narrative is today exposed to heavy fire. Few serious novelists think any longer of using the straight-line design of *David Copperfield*, even assuming their ability to do so. Should we therefore conclude that story is dead, or relegated to non-elite media—television serial, suspense yarn, comic strip? Is it not safer to hedge the bet? Even if every good living novelist should suddenly awake to find himself writing like Natalie Sarraute or Samuel Beckett, why not retain, if only in cold storage, those hoary tale-telling devices Homer inherited? You never can tell. The whirligig of time brings in its revenges, and we may rediscover the archaic pleasures a plain story has to offer.

And it is precisely here that children's literature makes a small but useful contribution. The young will never desert their Mr. Micawber, the tale that holdeth children from play and old men from the chimney corner. Their literature keeps the idea of narrative alive and fresh, whether it be as simple as *Old Mother Hubbard* or as subtle as Russell Hoban's *Mouse and His Child.* In Jean de Brunhoff, *Goldilocks and the Three Bears*, Perrault, and Sendak, one scholar, Peter Brooks, finds "narratives of a simplicity and strength which it is difficult to duplicate without going back to Greek tragedy." While a bit strong, the statement encloses a kernel of truth. The child approves the "simplicity and strength" of a tale clearly told. And this partiality is likely to endure in the grown-up, so that he may in the end resist the blandishments of *chosisme* and *anti-roman*. In any case, the very idea of narrative is kept alive. It is this narrative-preserving power of the books children love that was surely in the mind of the distinguished critic George Steiner when he wrote: "Above all, the art of the story demands a listener. . . . Today the only listeners are the children, and that is why so much of the real gold of literature, from Aesop to Dickens, is in their keeping."

Children's literature, then, helps preserve the art of plain narrative. It also, by specializing in and developing certain ancient genres, keeps these fresh for use by the mainstream. In prose these genres include myth, fantasy, fairy tale, beast fable. In verse they include lullaby, nonsense rhyme, folk rhyme. If we wipe out these and many other related genres, adult literature, which makes frequent use of them, would be so much the poorer. It is true that mythology and folklore are also kept alive by scholarship, but only as areas of inquiry. As myths and folktales, as pathways of experience, they are kept alive mainly by children's books. Very few grown-ups read Homer. But many of us remain vaguely familiar, from our childhood memories, with Circe and the Cyclops and Penelope. It is this saving remnant of association that helps the quite unchildlike Joyce to deepen our appreciation of his *Ulysses*. John Updike's *Centaur* is but one of hundreds of complex modern fictions that craftily exploit myths absorbed unconsciously in our childhood. Vanguard writers —Anne Sexton, Donald Barthelme—use fairy tales such as *Snow White* and *Rumpelstiltskin* for eerie adult purposes of their own. Major poets—Lorca, Brecht—draw on folk materials kept fresh by the conservative dynamic of children's books.

We touch, third and finally, on a matter more elusive and controversial: the question of the existence of racial archetypes and, assuming their existence, their connection with the preservative powers of children's literature. Jung's theory of the collective unconscious was perhaps more fashionable in the forties than it is today. Genetics has not yet confirmed the reality of those images he defines as "the formulated resultants of countless typical experiences of our ancestors." The theory, however, sound or unsound, seems to have persuaded many thoughtful critics that the content, or subcontent, of much elite and indeed of much popular literature often reflects deeply recessed racial memories.

For the purposes of our discussion we need merely point to what is apparent. Whether or not a "collective unconscious" exists, certain motives, themes, and images are found in adult literature, often in complex disguises, from the archaic period right up to our own day. Whether we call them archetypes or something else matters little. The word is but a helpful metaphor. What interests us is that any tabulation of these archetypes at once reveals that they are constantly used, and so kept in general circulation, by both the modern and the traditional literature of childhood. Its conservatism lies behind the reappearance of archetypes in such contemporary classics as the Narnia series.

The notion of the miniature man, for example, seems to be deeply hidden in our racial fantasy life. It occurs in dozens of folktales. (These tales were not, of course, originally designed for children but in practical fact are part of their literature.) The archetypical Tom Thumb is transformed by genius into the story of Lilliput, a part of adult literature—though significantly it also soon becomes part of children's literature. The Quest, another archetypical symbol, permeates children's literature, is thus kept alive in the imagination of the race, and reappears in forms as complex as *Ulysses* or even parts of *Lolita*.

A tributary pays tribute. The tribute made available by the preservative powers of children's literature has helped to swell the mainsteam.

The Case for a Children's Literature

But if a children's literature is to exist as "an intelligible field of study," in Arnold Toynbee's phrase, it must justify that existence on grounds beyond its contribution to mainstream literature. It must assert some qualified claim as a sovereign state, however small. Even if a cultural sirocco were instantaneously to dry up the mainstream, a children's literature would still have to show that it is identifiable as an entity.

On the surface the literature seems to need no defense. If it is but a by-product, what is the meaning of the avalanche of children's books that annually descends upon the bookstores? What shall we say of the thousands of children's book editors, authors, artists, anthologists, librarians, professors—even critics? Is there not a gigantic, nearly worldwide industry, working away to satisfy the child's demand for something to read—or at any rate the parents' demand for something to give the child to read? Can we not, like Samuel Johnson kicking the stone to refute Bishop Berkeley's theory of the nonexistence of matter, merely point to the solid reality and say, "I refute it thus!"?

No, we must do a little better than that, just as Johnson should have known that kicks and phrases, however forcible, do not really dispose of idealism in episcopal gaiters. Let us therefore first glance briefly at the case *against* a children's literature.

The man in the street puts it in simple terms: children's literature cannot amount to much because "it's kid stuff." The assumption here is that by nature the child is "inferior" to or less than the adult. His literature must be correspondingly inferior or less. Give the kid his comic, while I read grown-up books. But does not this amiable condescension shelter a certain insecurity? As racism is the opium of the inferior mind, as sexual chauvinism is the opium of the defective male, so child-patronage may be the opium of the immature adult. In certain ways the child is patently inferior, but I would maintain that as an imaginative being—the being who does the reading—he is neither inferior nor superior to the adult. He must be viewed as the structural anthropologist views the "primitive"—with the same unsentimental respect, the same keen desire to penetrate his legitimate, complex symbol-system and idea-world.

There is, however, a more sophisticated case against a children's literature. Scholars have expressed it both negatively and positively.

Negatively the thing is done by omission. Literary historians omit children's literature, as they might omit the "literature" of Pidgin English. The English novelist Geoffrey Trease offers a key example. He refers to "Legouis and Cazamian's *History of English Literature*, in which no space is found, in 1378 pages, for any discussion of children's books and the only Thomas Hughes mentioned is not the immortal author of *Tom Brown's Schooldays,* but an obscure Elizabethan tragedian." Further examples are legion. Marc Slonim's authoritative *Modern Russian Literature from Chekhov to the Present* (1953) has no mention of Kornei Chukovsky as children's author. Hester R. Hoffman's *Reader's Adviser* (1964) finds space in its 1300 pages for a bibliography of Lithuanian literature, but not for Louisa May Alcott. C. Hugh Holman's *Handbook to Literature* (1972) is alert to inform us about weighty literary matters from *abecedarius* to *zeugma*, but not about children's literature. That phenomenal compendium *Die Literaturen der Welt in ihrer mündlichen und schriftlichen Überlieferung*, edited by Wolfgang v. Einsiedel (1964), covers 130 assorted literatures, including the Malagasy, but from its 1400 pages you would never suspect that some writers have written for children. In volume two of David Daiches's standard *Critical History of English Literature* we find an otherwise excellent account of Kipling, but one from which we would never guess that he wrote masterpieces for children. While it is only fair to say that there do exist literary histories and reference manuals, notably those of recent years, that acknowledge children's books, the normal (and influential) stance of scholarship has been one of unconscious put-down by omission.

A few critics are more explicitly skeptical. In 1905 Benedetto Croce wrote: "The art of writing for children will never be a true art." And again: "The splendid sun of pure art cannot be tolerated by the as yet feeble eye of the young." He argued also that the writer's ever-present consciousness of his child public inhibited his freedom and spontaneity.

In our time, too, there have been some thoughtful students to echo Croce's negative judgment. They claim that they cannot trace a sufficiently long tradition or identify an adequate number of masterworks. Robert Coles, for instance, who has himself done much to increase our understanding of the current juvenile literary scene, cannot find in the literature "style, sensibility, vision."

As long ago as 1896, the German educationist Heinrich Wolgast aroused a storm of controversy, echoes of which are still heard, merely by his statement that "creative children's literature must be a work of art." In 1969 the French scholar Isabelle Jan felt it necessary to begin her book with the question: "Does a children's literature exist?" Three years later, in a thoughtful article, "The Classics of French Children's Literature from 1860 to 1950," she gave a cautious answer to her question, confining the issue to her own country: "French children's literature . . . does not constitute a *literature* in the strict sense. Quite unlike English children's literature it has neither continuity nor tradition."

It is apparent that the esteem in which any vocation is held affects its development. If children's literature is not generally felt to be an identifiable art, important in its own right, potentially creative minds will not be drawn to it, and it will languish or become a mere article of commerce. It is, then, worthwhile to attempt a brief outline of our case.

Apologists must at once concede that the children themselves couldn't care less. For them, books are to be read, not analyzed; enjoyed, not defended. They are only mildly curious as to who writes them, except insofar as a Richard Scarry, a Joan Walsh Anglund, or a Maurice Sendak operates, like Wheaties, as a brand name. They do, of course, vigorously favor one book over another, but hardly on the basis of any rationale of values. Nor do they, unlike adults, show much interest in being up-to-date in their reading. The annual juvenile best-seller lists are loaded with titles first published a score of years ago. Children are proof against literary fads, literary gossip, and especially literary critics. For them, books are no more literature than street play is physical exercise. The defense of their literary kingdom they cheerfully leave to their elders.

This elder rests that defense on the following not entirely distinguishable grounds.

First comes the slippery concept we call tradition. A literature without a traceable history is hardly worthy of the name. If we relax our definition to the point of zero tension, children's literature may claim a foggy origin in Saint Anselm's eleventh-century *Elucidarium*, possibly the first book of general information for young students. That would take our "tradition" back about nine hundred years. But common sense tells us that the good saint is no true source. He no more begat Lewis Carroll than the eleventh-century author of the *Ostromir Gospel* (often cited as the beginning of Russian literature) begat Dostoevsky.

Moving ahead a few hundred years we encounter an unidentifiable German who, between 1478 and 1483, issued *Der Seele Trost* ("The Soul's Consolation"), a religious tract explicitly addressed to children. Though valueless as literature, it may claim a little more legitimacy than the *Elucidarium*. One can view it as the *Urvater* of that long succession of moral tales that by this time should have turned children into paragons of virtue. If we reject *Der Seele Trost* we might accept as a point of origin *Der jungen Knaben Spiegel* ("The Boy's Mirror") of Jörg Wickram, perhaps the first "realistic" novel aimed at youth. Appearing in 1555, it would make children's literature date back over four hundred years. And so we could proceed, making more and more plausible claims as we approach modern times, until we come to "T.W." 's

Little Book for Little Children. The authority Percy Muir, dating it around 1712, considers it one of the fist books designed for the entertainment of little ones. Push on a few years. In 1744 we meet John Newbery's publication *A Little Pretty Pocket Book*, from which English children's literature is conventionally dated. But at once we recall that Perrault's fairy tales appeared almost half a century prior to this; and from the head of Perrault French children's literature may be said to spring.

Perhaps it is fair to say, then, that children's literature, strictly defined, is nearly three hundred years old; less strictly, perhaps five hundred years old. How many mainstream literatures can claim an equally venerable tradition?

Second comes the matter of masterpieces. Here we must admit that unfortunately one word must serve two somewhat different meanings. *Oedipus Rex* is a masterpiece. But so is *Mother Goose*. Both are true to human nature. Beyond that they have little in common. Instead of defining—a lengthy task—what makes a masterpiece of children's literature, I will take the lazy man's way out. I will assert dogmatically that in its three-hundred-plus years of history the literature has produced first-order works of art in sufficient number, perhaps fifty, to support our case. Some are already classics in the simple sense that, enduring over the decades or centuries, they are still enjoyed by large numbers of children. Indeed, are they not more *naturally* "classical" than many mainstream classics? It takes the whole educational machinery of the French Republic to sell its boys and girls on Corneille. But Perrault, Jules Verne, even Madame de Ségur seem to survive by their own vitality.

To the nuclear core of individual high-quality works we should add the total oeuvre of another fifty outstanding writers whose product as a whole is impressive but of whose works we cannot so confidently assert that any single book stands out. Here are a few such writers: Lucy Boston, Colette Vivier, E. Nesbit, Arthur Ransome, William Mayne, Eleanor Farjeon, René Guillot, Paul Berna, Tove Jansson, Gianni Rodari, Joan Aiken, Hans Baumann, José Maria Sanchez-Silva, Rosemary Sutcliff, David McCord, William Pène du Bois, James Krüss, John Masefield, I. B. Singer, E. L. Konigsburg, Ruth Krauss, Kornei Chukovsky, Henri Bosco, Madame de Ségur, Ivan Southall.

In our view any literature worthy of the name also gains in health and variety through the nourishment supplied by writers of the second or third class, even by writers commonly scorned as purveyors of mass reading. Children's literature is rich in writers of ephemeral appeal and even richer in manufacturers of unabashed trade goods. But in a way this circumstance strengthens rather than weakens our case. The ladder theory of reading must not be swallowed whole. Yet it is true that children often normally work up from Enid Blyton or *Nancy Drew* to more challenging literature, whereas a *kitsch*-happy adult tends to stay *kitsch*-happy.

Third, our case rests also on the fact that, like science fiction, children's literature is a medium nicely adapted to the development of certain genres and themes to which mainstream media are less well suited. In "On Three Ways of Writing for Children" C. S. Lewis remarks that the only method he himself can use "consists in writing a children's story because a children's story is the best art form for something you have to say: just as a composer might write a Dead March not because there was a public funeral in view but because certain musical ideas that had occurred to him went best into that form." In the same essay, referring to E. Nesbit's Bastable trilogy, he speaks of the entire work as "a character study of Oswald, an unconsciously satiric self-portrait, which every intelligent child can fully appreciate"; and goes on to remark that "no child would sit down to read a character study *in any other form*" (italics supplied).

The major genre (perhaps nonsense verse is just as major) whose development is largely the work of children's literature is fantasy. Adult fantasies of a high order of course exist. But the form seems peculiarly suited to children; and children seem peculiarly suited to the form. Consequently we can trace a long line of fantasies, growing constantly in expressiveness and intricacy. MacDonald, Carroll, Collodi, Baum, de la Mare, Barrie, Lagerlöf, Grahame, Aymé, Annie Schmidt, C. S. Lewis, Tolkien, Saint-Exupéry, Rodari, Juster, Hoban—these are a few of the many writers who have found children's fantasy well fitted to statements about human life that are conveyable in no other way. While a fairy tale for grown-ups sounds spurious, the fairy tale for children still has successful practitioners. This *Treasury* contains many examples.

There are certain experiences we have all had that, though also handleable in adult fiction, seem to take on a higher authenticity in juvenile fiction. For example, moving. For the child, moving from one neighborhood to another may be as emotionally involving as a passionate love affair is to the adult. For the adult a new neighborhood is a problem in practical adjustment; for the child, who must find a fresh peer-group to sustain him, it can be another planet.

But it is not only minor themes, such as moving, or major genres, such as fantasy, to which children's literature throws open its portrals. It also offers a natural home for certain symbols frequently held to be part of our unconscious, and universally present in myth.

Take the Cave. The Cave has an eerie, backward-transporting effect on us all, a sacral mix of awe, terror, and fascination. Whether this is linked to racial recollection, to persistent memory of the womb, or to some still undiscovered kink in the psyche, we may never know. But we have all observed that the unnameable Cave-feeling is peculiarly marked in the child. With no real cave available, he will, out of a chair or a huddle of blankets, construct a reasonable facsimile. It is therefore not surprising to find in his literature a body of work ringing the changes on this archetypal symbol. It is no accident that Alice starts her dream life by falling through a hole in the ground; or that the most recallable episode in *Tom Sawyer* occurs in a cave. Richard Church's *Five Boys in a Cave*—an excellent suspense story—stands as the perfect type of a whole school of speleological literature, mainly for boys. France, a great land for caves, offers many examples. We can go back as far as 1864 to Jules Verne's *Journey to the Center of the Earth*, which is really about a vast cavern. Indeed, his masterpiece, *Twenty Thousand Leagues under the Sea* (1870), may be read as a vision of a watery cave. Exactly a century later Norbert Casteret's *Dans la nuit des cavernes*, extremely popular with the young, continued to exploit the theme. One of the works of nonfiction that retains its appeal is Hans Baumann's *Caves of the Great Hunters* (German publication 1961). This deals with caves and other prehistoric sites actually discovered by boys and girls—and in one case by a dog, an animal that long ago became a first-class citizen of the republic of childhood. There is, too, Sonnleitner's vast, curious *Höhlenkinder*, whose first part was published as long ago as 1918 and which, despite its almost archaic tone, refuses to die. Over 300,000 copies have been sold in the German edition and only a few years ago it was translated into English.

The Cave is but one of a group of themes, freighted with symbolic content, that find powerful development in children's literature. Related to its magical appeal is the child's affinity for the nonartificial, or for places man has abandoned to nature. A vast apparatus is needed to condition the human being to the fabricated, technological surround to which he now seems fated. But, until so conditioned, the child normally relates himself to a nontechnological world, or its nearest approximation. "The literature of childhood," remark the Opies, "abounds with evidence that the peaks of a child's experience are not visits to a cinema, or even family outings to the sea, but occasions when he escapes into places that are disused and overgrown and silent." Dozens of children's writers know and feel this, foremost among them William Mayne. Only Samuel Beckett has made grown-up literature out of a dump. But in children's stories (Clive King's *Stig of the Dump*, for example) it is a familiar background, and it must be in part because such abandoned environments represent a symbolic triumph over the forces of "progress," forces the child must be *taught* to respect. As Huck says, "I been there before."

Traversing the literature of childhood we shall come upon other symbolic motifs that, though part of the stuff of general literature, receive special stress in children's books: the Foundling, the Quest (especially the Quest for the Father), the Imaginary Companion, the Secret, the Dream, the Golden Age, Little People, and (simplest, deepest of all) Food.

In short, any public defender of a children's literature will rest part of his case on the medium's high aesthetic capacity to embody certain specific themes and symbolic structures, often more imaginatively than does the mainstream.

But the advocate must go beyond this. A body of writing ambitious to be called a literature may point to a tradition. It may claim to include a fair number of masterworks. It may make certain statements with marked effectiveness. But it must also demonstrate that it has both scope and the power to broaden that scope. A specialized, nonadaptive literature risks the fate of the dinosaur.

First, as to scope. Obviously children's literature cannot boast the range, amplitude, inclusiveness of general literature. General literature records human experience; and human experience, though not absolutely, is by and large a function of the flow of time. The child's book, though not limited to the reflection of his actual experience, is limited by what he can understand, however dimly; and understanding tends to enlarge with experience.

But we must not be too quick to pass from the dimensions of length and breadth to that of depth, and say that children's books can never be as "deep." The child's world is smaller than the grown-up's; but are we so sure that it is shallower? Measured by whose plumb line? Is it not safer to say that, until the child begins to merge into the adolescent, his mental world, though of course in many respects akin to that of his elders, in many others obeys its own private laws of motion? And if this is so, it might be juster to use one plumb line to measure the depth of his literature, and a somewhat different one for that of his elders. No one will deny the depth of Dostoevsky's Grand Inquisitor episode. But who is to say that, to a sensitive child reader, William Mayne's *Game of Dark* does not convey an equally profound intimation of the forces of evil? Here are six lines of a "song" called "*Firefly*," by Elizabeth Madox Roberts. A seven-year-old genius might have written it; and any seven-year-old child can read it with pleasure.

A little light is going by,
Is going up to see the sky,
A little light with wings.

I never could have thought of it,
To have a little bug all lit
And made to go on wings.

The child who feels all that these six lines convey (especially the fourth) is caught up in profound reflection on the very nature of creation. The aesthetic experience is for the child no less rich than would be for the adult a reading of Eliot's *Four Quartets*. The scale differs, the "thickness" does not.

To return to the matter of scope: it is clear that traditionally the child's literature has been closed (nowadays there are narrow apertures) to certain broad areas of human experience: mature sexual relationships; economic warfare in its broadest aspects; and in general the whole problematic psychic universe that turns on the axletree of religion and philosophical speculation. That vast library generated by Unamuno's tragic sense of life is one that —though there are certain exceptions—is not micro-reflected in the child's books. Though again one must qualify, his is a literature of hope, of solutions, of open ends. To say that is to acknowledge the limits of its scope.

But if we turn to form rather than content, the judgment becomes a little less clear-cut. Children's literature contains no epic poems, not only because it developed long after the age of the epic but because its audience is ill-suited to the epic length. As for its lyric poetry, it includes several forms—nonsense verse, nursery rhymes, street rhymes, lullabies—in which the adult lyric tradition is comparatively defective. But in general its verse forms are simple and restricted as against the variety and complexity of mainstream verse. The literature contains little drama, whether in prose or verse, worth serious attention. It has so far evolved nothing closely resembling the traditional essay, although in an acute comment Jean Karl points to its remarkable powers of mutation: "Who would have dreamed that the familiar essay, no longer popular with adults, would suddenly be found in children's books, presenting all sorts of abstract ideas in picture-book form?" The reference here is to what are often called "concept books." A first-rate example is James Krüss's *3 x 3*, pictures by Eva Johanna Rubin, which is essentially a graphic expository essay on the abstract idea of threeness.

But almost all the other major genres, whether of fact or fiction, are represented. Some, like the ABC book and the picture book, are virtually (as would naturally be the case), unique to the literature. So, in the same way, are children's books written by children themselves: Daisy Ashford's *Young Visiters* (1919), surely one of the dozen funniest books in English, or *The Far-Distant Oxus* by Katharine Hull and Pamela Whitlock, written when the authors were fourteen and fifteen respectively. Children's fiction can be so experimental as to be reactionary: Gillian Avery has written Victorian novels that are not parodies or pastiches, but interesting in themselves.

Most fictional forms one can think of are represented on the children's shelves. Some, such as the fairy tale, the fantasy, the fable, the animal story, and the adventure yarn, can be found there in rich and highly developed profusion. The historical novel, especially in England, flourishes to a degree that makes it possible to hail Rosemary Sutcliff *tout court* as one of the best historical novelists using the language. Even the minor genre of the detective story is presented, long before Poe, in *The Trail* by Mrs. Barbauld (mid-1790s).

There are dozens of subgenres and sub-subgenres that are by nature given special prominence in children's literature: certain kinds of jokes and riddles; stories of toys and dolls, stuffed animals, animated objects; "bad boy" and "bad girl" stories; "career novels"; a whole school of chimney-sweep stories; children's puppet plays; "waif" novels; the school story; the vacation novel; and many others. We do not dispose of the matter when we say that these forms are simply a response to the child's natural interests, any more than we dispose of Proust when we say that his work is a response to the adult's interest in depth psychology. In both cases literature is enriched by the evolution of fresh vehicles for the imagination.

While no absolutely first-rate history or biography has been written for children, I would claim that the field has produced at least one masterly autobiography, on its own level as worthy of study as the *Confessions* of

Rousseau or Saint Augustine: Laura Ingalls Wilder's *Little House* series, a selection from which appears in this *Treasury*.

It is fair to say, then, that the scope of our literature, though it has its lacunae, is astonishingly broad. But it is not only broad. It has the capacity to broaden further, to invent or assimilate new forms, themes, and attitudes, to devise original techniques of exposition and narration. The texts of Maurice Sendak are as "new" in their way as Joyce's *Ulysses* once was. So is the picture book itself, really a product of modern times, with its power to tell a story simultaneously in two mediums: Elsa Holmelund Minarik's *Little Bear* series illustrates this well. The all-picture book has evolved even more ingenious modulations: Mitsumasa Anno's dreamlike series of gravity-defying, non-Euclidean *jeux de construction* is only one startling example. The trick three-dimensional book (pop-ups, for example), though hardly part of literature, is nonetheless ingenious, satisfying, and a specific response to the child's desire to manipulate, change, construct.

Finally, contemporary children's literature has in the last decade or two found it possible to handle, even if not always successfully, a whole constellation of themes it was formerly denied: everything from drug addiction to homosexuality.

The contemporary "teenage" or "young adult" novel has still to prove itself as art. Yet it bears witness to the flexibility of children's literature, its power to enlarge its range, to experiment with new forms and themes. Without such power its claim to be a "literature" would be vitiated. Indeed, its receptivity is now of so high an order as to blur its boundaries. "Less is more," says Browning's Andrea del Sarto, a phrase Mies van der Rohe applied perhaps too rigorously. Yet it holds profound truth. Lately the human race has become aware of the fatality lying at the heart of unchecked growth. It is possible to argue that a similar fatality inheres in the unchecked growth of any art form. We may—the returns are far from all in—be witnessing such a wild cancerous proliferation in the body of children's literature.

To complete our case I offer two last considerations, one turning on the matter of scholarship, the other on the matter of institutions. Both may be debater's points. All they do is point to the probability of the literature's existence. In themselves they do not constitute firm evidence of its high quality or organic integrity.

A literature is the sum of its *original* communications, especially its better ones, more especially its best. Still, it is hard for us to meditate upon a literature as an intelligible field of study until the nonoriginal communicator, the theorist and historian, has worked upon it. Had Aristotle never lived, classical Greek literature would still rank supreme. Nonetheless, the *Art of Poetry* helps us to perceive its topography and distinguish its boundaries. The specific identity of any art becomes more firmly established as it develops self-consciousness. Of that self-consciousness critics, scholars, and historians are the expression.

It would seem that you cannot produce a theory without something to theorize about, nor a history without something to chronicle. Or is this always true? A. Merget's *Geschichte der deutschen Jugend-literatur* ("History of German Juvenile Literature") appeared in 1867, before the existence of any literature worthy of the name. But this striking example of German thoroughness does not completely undermine the feeling we have, when we see a signpost, that it is probably pointing to some place that is actually there.

Many years ago, when I started this project, I thought all I had to do was read a few thousand original communications called children's books, think about them, and make my selections. I knew, of course, that there were several standard histories that should probably be read, too. But soon I became aware that there were almost (well, not quite) as many books *about* children's literature as there were books *of* children's literature, and that anyone who wished to handle the literature wisely would have to become familiar with a learned corpus of astonishing proportions.

In one of his few transparent lines of verse Mallarmé complains, "*La chair est triste, hélas! et j'ai lu tous les livres* [The flesh is sad, alas, and all the books are read]." I can subscribe to neither half of the hexameter. Even after many years' sampling of the scholarly literature, my flesh remains moderately cheerful; and it is a dead certainty that I have not read all the books. No one could. Few disciplines of such modest dimensions have evoked so much commentary as that associated with children's books and reading. The children themselves would be dumbfounded, perhaps explode into hilarious laughter, could they realize what alps of research and theory have been reared since Perrault, his eye on both young and old, first set down the tale of Little Red Riding-Hood.

I intend no mockery. The body of criticism and history is not only formidable; it is valuable. It points up the importance of what at first might seem a minor field of investigation. Though some of it, inevitably, is but dusty poking into the deservedly dead, and much of it duplicative, yet as a whole it reflects a solid tradition, of acute importance in the shaping of the minds and hearts of children.

There are few "developed" countries that have not produced a scholarly literature. It is vast in the cases of the United States, Britain, most of Europe, the Soviet Union, and Japan. While I have not yet met with such material from Liberia, I have pored over Paul Noesen's *Geschichte der Luxemburger Jugendliteratur*, keeping in mind that the population of Luxembourg, counting every child, is 374,000.

True, the burden of our case rests on the original communications rather than on the commentaries. But it is only fair to set against such doubting Thomases as Coles and Croce the counterweight of a host of creative writers and thoughtful scholars for whom a children's literature is as much *there* as his mountain was for Mallory. Among the creators of that literature who have defended its integrity are James Krüss, Eleanor Cameron, Maurice Sendak, I. B. Singer, J. R. R. Tolkien, C. S. Lewis, Kornei Chukovsky. Among the scholars who have analyzed its properties, staked out its limits, and celebrated its charms are the Frenchman Paul Hazard, the Italian Enzo Petrini, the Swiss Hans Cornioley, the Englishman Brian Alderson, the Canadian Sheila Egoff, the Swede Eva von Zweigbergk, the Iberian Carmen Bravo-Villasante, the Netherlander J. Riemens-Reurslag, the Luxembourger Paul von Noesen, the Argentinian Dora Pastoriza de Etchebarna, the Mexican Blanca Lydia Trajo, the New Zealander Dorothy White, the Israeli Uriel Ofek, the Norwegian Jo Tenfjord . . . the catalogue, though not endless, is impressive.

The mere existence of institutions is, of course, no argument for the values they incorporate: the Mafia, one supposes, is as intricate and efficient an institution as one could well desire. Yet the complex world network of children's libraries, book and record clubs, research centers, publishers, scholarly magazines, academies, book councils, "book weeks," prizes and awards, summer schools, writers' associations, radio and television programs (but switch on a red light here), illustration exhibits, book fairs—all this, while alloyed with commercialism, bureaucratization, cliquishness, and a certain inappropriate solemnity, nevertheless demonstrates the existence of a large and lively world of children's literature.

This *Treasury* tries to explore a fair part of that world.

Index of Titles

Index of Contributors

Index of First Lines